Chicana/o and Latina/o Fiction

Chicana/o and Latina/o Fiction

The New Memory of Latinidad

YLCE IRIZARRY

UNIVERSITY OF ILLINOIS PRESS

Urbana, Chicago, and Springfield

First Illinois paperback, 2019
© 2016 by the Board of Trustees
of the University of Illinois
All rights reserved
1 2 3 4 5 C P 5 4 3 2 1
∞ This book is printed on acid-free paper.

Library of Congress Control Number: 2016931699
ISBN 978-0-252-03991-1 (hardcover)
ISBN 978-0-252-08428-7 (paperback)
ISBN 978-0-252-09807-9 (e-book)

This book is dedicated to those
who share their stories.

Contents

Acknowledgments

Reading, writing, and revising is the academic's story. Nonacademics will tell you that the story never ends; however, it does have chapter breaks. During the many semesters of my academic life, family and friends supported my career moves, even when that meant visiting me in frighteningly cold places with no ethnic restaurants. Long before graduate school, my sisters, Nicole, Simone, and Bernadette, spent many hours at the dining room table helping me study. I would not have a place at the table with my students without my sisters' teaching and encouragement. To our great sadness, Simone left us on April 14, 2011. Fabulously creative, she nurtured my love for words and the story traditions of our parents. Growing up in a bicultural family—Puerto Rican and Dominican—meant inheriting two cultural narratives. Thank you, Daddy, for knowing what stories I needed to hear and when. Mommy, I finally understand why you could not tell us some of your stories. *Bendición.*

I owe a tremendous thank you to my intellectual *madrinas*, the godmothers who helped me dream. To Julie Olin-Ammentorp: you introduced to me multiethnic literature and the possibilities of an academic life. To Kathryn Hume: you were my most rigorous professor; you continue to provide intellectual stimulation and excellent professional advice. To Marta Caminero-Santangelo: when I thought I had missed the scholar's boat, you helped me reenter academia, and you remain an inspiring humanist. For Dawn Durante, my editor at University of Illinois Press, *thank you* seems insufficient for your interest, guidance, and collegiality.

My desk has not been a lonely place. Thank you, Leni Marshall, for embodying determination and grace. Nancy Cardona, the day you sent me home with a stack of Chicana studies books was the day I committed to *la causa*. Elena Machado Sáez, Marion C. Rohrleitner, David J. Vázquez: my work is far richer because of your influence. Denise Galarza Sepúlveda, Suzanne Begnoche, Liza Ann Acosta, Janis Sloka III, Mark Bringman, Diane Dutka, Ernie Marshall: thank you for being reminders of life outside academia. To my students: you have no idea how much I feel the love, people.

Thank you to the colleagues, office staff, librarians, student workers, and grant committees who supported my work—those named here and those unnamed. My department chair at the University of South Florida, Hunt Hawkins, facilitated the conditions to make this book its best iteration. Gary Lemons, thank you for pushing me to do the work we are called to do and for keeping me in Spirit. Many thanks go to my research assistant, Megan Mandell, who bravely and efficiently helped in copyediting this manuscript in her first few weeks of working with me. Thank you to my former East Carolina University colleagues and friends, who shared research, teaching, writing, and tenure-earning secrets: Rod Roberts, Mikko Tuhkanen, Lisa Beth Robinson, and the Trivia Crew, Absent-Minded. The amazing skills of my research assistant Olivia Everett at East Carolina University helped me begin the project.

My ability to conceive of writing a book started with the generous financial support and professional development the Committee on Institutional Cooperation Pre-Doctoral Fellowship (CIC) provided by during my graduate study. The skills I needed to perform the writing and research were honed in the English Department of The Pennsylvania State University. The Florida Education Fund supported the completion of this manuscript with a McKnight Junior Faculty Development Fellowship (2010–2011). The Humanities Institute at the University of South Florida extended that writing time with a summer grant (2011).

Last but never least, thank you, my beloved Pompie—foot warmer, snack accomplice, and expert in the complex work of napping.

Chicana/o and
Latina/o Fiction

Neocolonialism's Bounty

From Arrival *to New Memory*

The two friends will glance at the horizon, breathe in the
warm air, deeply. And through the lens of their dreams,
Gina will finally see a brand new memory.
—Elías Miguel Muñoz, *Brand New Memory*

"*La Migra* never comes at harvest time." Mexican immigrants taught me this expression in the early 1990s. The phrase reveals a profound truth: raids by immigration agencies, popularly called *la migra*, rarely occur at harvest. So what happens after the work is finished? Farm owners and government agencies must return foreign workers to their nations of origin or integrate them into local socioeconomic structures. The use of foreign nationals for agricultural and industrial labor in the United States has created the need to incorporate African, Asian, European, and Indigenous peoples, their languages, and their cultural practices. In comparison to the months'-long steamship travel late-nineteenth-century immigrants faced, contemporary immigrants, particularly those of Hispanic descent, can migrate between the United States and their homelands in a few days or weeks.[1]

Technology has made it ever cheaper for migrants to contact and travel home to maintain national and cultural allegiances.[2] The retention of such allegiances by guest workers and demands for social equity by the descendants of African slaves, Native Americans, and Asian indentured servants fomented the twentieth-century assimilation phenomenon known as *multiculturalism*. In *Multiculturalism: A Critical Reader*, David Theo Goldberg dates the formalization of multiculturalism to social justice movements: "the civil rights and countercultural movements of the 1960s signaled a shift from the prevailing assimilative standard to the new one of *integration*" (6). Goldberg argues that the sociopolitical arm of multiculturalism "has stressed more or less genuine attempts to define and service improvements in conditions for those who continue to be identified as 'minorities,' all the while serving up good subjects for the monocultural model" (6). Goldberg explains that "broadly conceived, multiculturalism is critical of and resistant to the necessarily reductive imperatives of monocultural assimilation" (7). The volume presents extended arguments concerning multiculturalism's variants, including, but not limited to, conservative, left-liberal, critical, pre-Modern, and modernist multiculturalism(s).

The variant most relevant to Chicanas/os and Latinas/os is left-liberal.[3] In "White Terror and Oppositional Agency: Towards a Critical Multiculturalism," Peter McLaren asserts, "Liberal multiculturalism argues that a natural equality exists among whites, African Americans, Latinos, Asians, and other racial populations. . . . Unlike their critical counterparts, they believe that existing cultural, social, and economic constraints can be modified or 'reformed' in order for relative equality to be realized" (51). This conception of multiculturalism, when used as a method of facilitating equity, invites ethnic groups to recall cultural losses—such as losses of language, ethnic uniqueness, and political power—caused by US neocolonialism.[4] The United States engages in neocolonialism through its veneer of recognizing and respecting the sovereignty of Cuba, the Dominican Republic, Mexico, and Puerto Rico, among other nations. For the purposes of this study, the broad definition of *neocolonialism* stated in the *Oxford English Dictionary* is applicable: "the acquisition or retention of influence over other countries, especially one's former colonies, often by economic or political measures." US multicultural literatures—texts about African, Asian, Hispanic, and Native Americans in particular—have frequently addressed neocolonialism through portrayals of cultural losses and resignation to some form of integration.[5]

The violence and genocide wrought by the Spanish Conquest has emplaced a critical *aporia* of information on pre-Columbian Caribbean history. The dearth of anthropological material to connect Hispanic Caribbean people to their ancestral Arawak, Carib, and Taino cultures explains the scant literature foregrounding pre-Columbian Caribbean culture.[6] A few narratives, including Antonio Benítez-Rojo's *Mar de las Lentejas* (1979), Alejandro Morales' *The Rag Doll Plagues* (1991), and Alicia Gaspar de Alba's *Calligraphy of the Witch* (2007), fictionalize Iberian colonialism from the perspective of the *criollo*, the first settlers of Iberian and Indigenous origin. More commonly, Latina/o literature uses allusions to religions such as *Santería*, oral poetic and storytelling traditions, and foodways to connect African and Caribbean cultural origins lost through US neocolonialism and migration.[7] The invocation of the mythic *Aztlán* in Chicana/o literatures is another example of contemporary literature addressing cultural loss. Native American and African American writers have attempted to reconstruct Indigenous and African collective memory, respectively. One need consider only the most successful contemporary US American multicultural fiction to see how it thematizes cultural losses and challenges to integration.

Immediately following the civil rights era, an ethnic writer's renaissance began with the publication of texts including but not limited to Piri Thomas' *Down These Mean Streets* (1967), Ernesto Galarza's *Barrio Boy* (1971), Ishmael Reed's *Mumbo Jumbo* (1972), Tomás Rivera's . . . *And the Earth Did Not Devour Him* (1973), Maxine Hong Kingston's *The Woman Warrior: Memoirs of a Girlhood Among Ghosts* (1976), and Leslie Marmon Silko's *Ceremony* (1977). In the 1980s, the following books continued the dissemination of contemporary ethnic writing in the United States: Alice Walker's *The Color Purple* (1982), Oscar Hijuelos' *Our House in the Last World* (1982) and *The Mambo Kings Play Songs of Love* (1989), Louise Erdrich's *Love Medicine* (1984), Sandra Cisneros' *The House on Mango Street* (1984), Esmeralda Santiago's *When I Was Puerto Rican* (1986), Toni Morrison's *Beloved* (1988), Amy Tan's *The Joy Luck Club* (1989), and Bharati Mukherjee's *Jasmine* (1989). Even more diverse writing about cultural loss and the problems of integration into the Euro-American mainstream have appeared in the last two decades: Charles Johnson's *Middle Passage* (1991), Julia Alvarez's *How the García Girls Lost Their Accents* (1992), Cristina García's *Dreaming in Cuban* (1993), Sherman Alexie's *Reservation Blues* (1995), Gloria Naylor's *Mama Day* (1997), Jhumpa Lahiri's *Interpreter of Maladies* (1999), Ernesto Quiñonez's *Bodega Dreams* (2000), and Khaled Hosseini's *The Kite Runner* (2003), among others.[8]

Left-liberal multiculturalism and critical race theory have contributed to the increased publication of multiethnic literatures. Scholars including Derrick Bell, Richard Delgado, Jean Stefancic, and Patricia J. Williams developed critical race theory based on structural analyses of the US legal system. They suggested the impossibility of left-liberal reform by citing what Cornel West called "the historical centrality and complicity of law in upholding white supremacy (and concomitant hierarchies of gender, class, and sexual orientation)" as the obstacle to structural change (xi). According to Delgado and Stefancic, critical race theorists "represent ways of thinking about and assessing social systems and groups that incorporate recognition that race is a central structure of social systems; that racism is institutionalized; that everyone within the systems can reproduce the symptoms of the system; and that racial and ethnic identities are not fixed" (xvii).[9] Those revelations, unfortunately, have had little effect on juridical, educational, and other institutions plagued by inequity. Some critical race theorists argue that the multicultural discourse used by these institutions has been collapsed into dangerous rhetoric: "The notion of 'color-blindness' is now more likely to be advanced by political groups seeking to dismantle policies, such as Affirmative Action, initially designed to mitigate racial inequality. Calls to get 'beyond race' are popularly expressed, and any hint of race consciousness is viewed as racism" (Omi, "The Changing Meaning of Race" 245). Nonetheless, in the United States, efforts to ameliorate those disruptions through proposed social policy and curricular revision continue.[10]

Multiculturalism and its variants have made sociopolitical gains; however, response to difference remains at the heart of today's foreign terrorism and domestic violent crime. In 2014, one could not avoid media reports and images of radical Islamic terrorists beheading non-Muslims in the Middle East and on US soil. As a Florida resident, I witnessed the sites where US social and legal systems remain utterly inequitable during the trial of George Zimmerman for the murder of Trayvon Martin. Upon Martin's death, the African American community was at odds with the Latina/o community. The initial media depiction of George Zimmerman as white, and the later assertions that he could not be racist against blacks because he was Latino, could not obscure the racial profiling Zimmerman committed. While various ethnic, religious, and social groups demanded "Justice for Trayvon," Zimmerman's acquittal of second-degree murder left many people feeling that nothing had changed for young black men since the civil rights era. In Ferguson, Missouri, the refusal of the Grand Jury to charge Officer Darren Wilson of any crime related to his murder of another young black man, Michael Brown, left that city's residents vulnerable to more riots, looting, and violent crime. Shortly after that Grand Jury's failure to indict Officer Wilson, a New York Grand Jury also failed to indict police officers in the choke-hold death of Eric Garner, an African American man alleged to have been the target of NYPD harassment for routinely selling illegal cigarettes. As the Black Lives Matter movement suggests, police brutality against African Americans knows no gender, class, or criminal status limits. On July 13, 2015, Sandra Bland died in police custody after having been arrested three days earlier on a traffic violation in Waller County, Texas. She was returning from a job interview at her college alma mater, Texas A&M University–Prairie View. The FBI has opened an investigation on her arrest and death; her family has filed a wrongful death lawsuit.

Following the civil rights era, universities radically altered general education curricula, particularly shifting what they defined as "literature." Continuing through the radicalism of the 1970s and political correctness of the 1980s, the recovery and increasing publication of multicultural literature facilitated the development of "area" studies: Africana, ethnic, women's, and queer, among others. As Goldberg illustrates, however, pluralist strains of liberal multiculturalism "enabled the institutionalization of the sorts of ethnic and women's studies programs sought more radically in the name of resistance and transformation, thereby appropriating the ideas by undercutting the practice" (8). Within this veritable genesis and immediate backlash against multiculturalism, I entered higher education. In my final year of college, the first book I ever read by an ethnic American writer was, not surprisingly, Sandra Cisneros' *The House on Mango Street* (1989). She, Joseph Geha, Maxine Hong Kingston, Gloria Naylor, James Welch, and other multiethnic authors became my heroines and heroes; I was, though, deeply troubled by the fact that I was encountering them at the end of my education.

When I began my graduate studies in 1993, the culture wars were raging. That same year, in the essay "Opposition and the Education of Chicana/os," Laura Elisa Pérez summarized my future experiences as a "minority" intellectual: "In the minority experiences at the university, it becomes a commonplace that one is guilty of some kind of intellectual inadequacy or incompetence until one proves otherwise, or until one successfully deploys a politics of assuagement; that is, until one's politics—conservative or progressive— are approved" (Pérez 272).[11] Stuart Hall's theorization of cultural studies, in particular, was challenging the institutionalization of academic disciplines. His 1990 essay "The Emergence of Cultural Studies and the Crisis of the Humanities" was simultaneously retrospective and prophetic. Though I would not read this essay until 1996, the heart of what I took away from it remains with me: "cultural studies is not one thing; it never has been one thing" (11).

During my graduate education, seminars and conferences were boxing rings where the titles at stake were the recognition not only of the value of the literatures I loved but also of my value as an intellectual practicing cultural studies. Born in the United States, I am an English-dominant Puerto Rican/ Dominican who grew up on suburban Long Island: my presence in academia was contested often, by Anglos, Chicanos, and Latinos alike.[12] My experiences of extra- and intra-ethnic discrimination compelled me to examine the gross disparities in the cultural rhetorics I faced daily. Cultural studies gave me the tools to engage those disparities, and Hall, the words to understand my intellectual odyssey: "[Cultural studies] was always in a critical relation to the very theoretical paradigms out of which it grew and to the concrete studies and practices it was attempting to transform" (Hall 11). The culture wars are not over, though they are generally referred to in the past tense.[13]

The inception and deconstruction of multiculturalism and the development of cultural studies play a fundamental role in the epistemological concerns I explore in this study.

The final type of multiculturalism McLaren outlines, "Critical and Resistance Multiculturalism," informs my research and teaching. The following assertion epitomizes the most difficult experiences of discrimination people of color routinely experience and witness: "Differences occur *between* and *among* groups and must be understood in terms of the specificity of their production" (McLaren 53). Growing up *mita y mita*, a Spanish expression appropriated to "measure" ethnic composition—being half Puerto Rican and half Dominican—I was painfully aware of the differences between my parents' national allegiances. It would not be until I entered higher education that I would understand how the desire to measure and claim supposedly better ways of being Latina/o was inherently problematic. These perspectives have led me to identify the relationships between difference and discrimination. The primary goal of this study is to help readers see these patterns within ethnic communities—not between Anglo and Latina/o communities.

My interest and engagement of multicultural heterogeneity is, as Goldberg finely describes, "concerned with contesting oppressive power, marginality, and exclusion in local contexts" (33). The local contexts of my critical heterogeneity include my commitment to teaching books my students describe as those "no one else teaches" and in challenging these students to explore topics where "there is no research available!" Those local contexts often surprise students because they *expect* Chicana/o and Latina/o literature to lament *only* the differences between these worlds and the Anglo-American world. High school students' perceptions have been shaped by certain discourses of multiculturalism when they enter college classrooms. By the time they leave, though, many of them also seek "to transform the academy—the knowledge authorized in the academy's name and the institutions of which it is comprised and that do its bidding—to incorporative ends" in their own work, internships, student groups, and other communities (Goldberg 33).

Left-liberal multiculturalism tends to ignore a myriad of social differences and the discourse about them within ethnic communities. As a result, diverse groups of writers have been united by their "difference" from the Anglo-American mainstream.[14] The result is that their heterogeneity—differences from one another—has been elided.[15] Further complicating this critical problem is the tendency for the issues examined by multiethnic authors in their later books to receive less attention than those explored in their first.[16] Established Chicana/o and Latina/o authors such as Julia Alvarez, Cristina

García, Sandra Cisneros, Rolando Hinojosa-Smith, Lucha Corpi, and Esmeralda Santiago illustrate the movement away from the ethnic *bildungsroman*. These authors and others tend to draw on experience clearly outside their own lives in their later books by rewriting national histories and experimenting with various forms of genre fiction, such as the detective novel, science fiction, and gothic/horror.[17]

Ethnic literature canons *within* the "American" literature canon do exist. Scholars and anthology publishers of Chicana/o and Latina/o literature have established the "Latina/o" canon by collapsing the two identities and privileging the autoethnography[18] of certain writers—Julia Alvarez, Rudolfo Anaya, Gloria Anzaldúa, Sandra Cisneros, Junot Díaz, Cristina García, Oscar Hijuelos, Rolando Hinojosa-Smith, and Gregory Nava, among others.[19] In the essay "So Much Depends," Julia Alvarez reflects on how multiculturalism has shaped the reception of her writing (163–170). She laments the shortcomings of criticism foregrounding ethnic authenticity: "I hear the cage of a definition close around me with its 'Chicano and Latino subject matter,' 'Chicano and Latino style,' 'Chicano and Latino concerns'" (Alvarez 169). Alvarez contends that she and other ethnic authors desire to be part of the broader American literary tradition, not to be "a mere flash in the literary pan" (169). If readers consider her novels, *In the Time of the Butterflies* (1994) and *In the Name of Salomé* (2000), both historical fictions about the Dominican Republic, Alvarez's movement away from the problems of integration is unquestionable.

Chicana/o and Latina/o Fiction is my contribution to critical, resistant, and transformative multiculturalism(s). This book shows how authors respond to left-liberal multiculturalism's failures and denaturalize its illusory promises of ethnic integration.[20] These failures are visible as the narratives examine disruptions of cultural practice (*loss*), the homogenization of difference (*reclamation*), resistance to gender, race, and class hierarchy (*fracture*), and conceptualizations of empowering cultural imaginaries (*new memory*). The four narratives explore the conscious engagement of cultural memory central to Chicana/o and Latina/o literature: the narrative of loss, the narrative of reclamation, the narrative of fracture, and the narrative of new memory.

This book extends the scope of contemporary literary scholarship by offering readers chances to hear the stories Chicanas/os and Latinas/os remember about themselves, not the stories of those subjugating them.[21] *Chicana/o and Latina/o Fiction* distinguishes itself from other analyses by focusing on the problems and possibilities of empowerment *within* ethnic communities because it is within these narrative spaces that authors tell stories that have little, if anything, to do with integration to the Anglo-American world. For example, in his study *The Latino Body: Crisis Identities in American Literary and Cultural Memory* (2007), Lázaro Lima provides a wonderful analysis of "the conditions under which it becomes necessary to create a specific Latino subject of American cultural and literary history" (6). *Chicana/o and Latina/o Fiction*, in contrast, is interested in the process of the creation of *latinidades*—modes of ethnic identification within Chicana/o and Latina/o America, not Anglo-America.[22]

Narrative as Knowing: Fictions of the Self

The field of multiethnic literary studies has vacillated between historical and narrative modes of analysis. In some instances, historical analysis is more effective in textual interpretation; for example, one would be remiss in not applying historical criticism to fictions portraying real eras and zeitgeists, such as García's *The Agüero Sisters* (1997). In other instances, examining genre-focused texts such as Hinojosa-Smith's procedural detective novel, *Ask a Policeman* (1998), or a work of fantasy, such as Daniel José Older's collection *Salsa Nocturna: Stories* (2012), narratological analysis is equally, if not more, effective in illustrating a text's potential meanings. The readings of the narratives presented in the study make use of a variety of critical approaches in conversation with historical and narratological discourses. Some discussions reflect anticolonial perspectives and woman of color feminism. Other discussions apply Marxist and New Historicist concepts to texts. In some chapters, cultural and queer studies are foregrounded. All of the approaches intersect, though, in narratology.

Eminent narratologist Frank Kermode argued that "fictions are for finding things out, and they change as the needs of sense-making change. Myths are agents of stability, fiction the agents of change" (39). Because of the consistent displacement inherent in Chicana/o and Latina/o experience, fiction is a discursive space within which individuals can explore—but not necessarily affirm—their ethnic cultures' practices. The narratives delineated in *Chicana/o and Latina/o Fiction* explore whether those practices should be maintained. Reading these literatures through a neocolonial framework undermines the discourses of authenticity some publishers and scholars use to promote Chicana/o and Latina/o literature within the parameter of "ethnic authenticity."[23] Early in the multicultural literature boom, Werner Sollors published the germinal study *Beyond Ethnicity: Consent and Descent in American Literature* (1986).[24] In "Ethnicity and Literary Form," he asserts, "Readers are most curious about the *content* of ethnic writing and often look for the survival of cultural baggage. Influenced by older approaches to ethnic survivals, they search for supposedly 'authentic' literature and are less concerned with formal aspects, let alone syncretisms and stylistic innovations" ("Ethnicity and Form" 237; emphasis in original). Traceable to the past, visible in the present, and welcoming the future, the narratives of *loss, reclamation, fracture,* and *new memory* are the cultural repositories for communities finding things out about themselves both through and outside the rhetoric of US neocolonialism.

This book approaches Chicana/o and Latina/o narrative from a rhetorical perspective. It assumes that narrative is, above all, a communication between the author(s) and implied but not necessarily identified audience(s). The communication can be true or false (loosely defined as nonfiction or fiction) but is best understood to be a process, as Rimmon-Kenan has argued: "In the empirical world, the author is the agent responsible for the production of the narrative and for its communication" (3). Another premise of this study is that the narratives defined here are best understood when combining understanding of reality or its representation (history) and the creative force of the imagination (narratology).[25] Rimmon-Kenan's comparison of formalist and postformalist theories is useful here: "Whereas in mimetic theories (i.e., theories which consider literature as, in some sense, an imitation of reality) characters are equated with people, in semiotic theories they dissolve into textuality" (33). My project is not to integrate Chicana/o and Latina/o literature in the evolution of narrative itself; such a project would be interminable, because as David Herman illustrates, "we have witnessed a small but unmistakable explosion of activity in narrative studies" (1). The dialectical categories Herman discusses, such as "Classic Narratology" and "Postclassical Narratology," have strengths and weaknesses, as all taxonomies do.[26]

The goal of this project is to outline these specific—certainly not the only—narratives recurrent in Chicana/o and Latina/o literatures. *Chicana/o and Latina/o Fiction* is not a variation of formalist literary theories espoused in Cleanth Brooks' *The Well Wrought Urn* (1947) or Northrop Frye's *The Anatomy of Criticism* (1957). The four narratives are not archetypes; however, it would be remiss to not acknowledge the usefulness of formalist and poststructuralist taxonomy. The terms Scholes and Kellogg coin, *didactic, historical, mimetic,* and *romantic,* are just as useful as Bakhtin's terms, *discourse, heteroglossia,* and *polyphonic.* The concept of the narratives developing in Chicana/o and Latina/o literature reflects an ongoing negotiation of form and meaning. That the narratives are told with varying elements, techniques, and genres should indicate their narrative dynamism, not a mutual inclusivity to either historical or mimetic representation. This book identifies overall narrative patterns but situates them as conversations occurring in explicit historic and cultural discourses.

Chicana/o and Latina/o literature particularly demonstrate the increasing focus on empowerment—economic, political, and sexual—within Chicana/o and Latina/o America—not within Anglo-America. Using historical and narratological approaches, this study unites narrative most readers find unlikely companions; however, it remains attuned to racial, linguistic, economic, religious, and other differences among the ethnic communities portrayed. The later novels of successful multiethnic authors explore larger cultural discourses, transnational migrations, and shifting literary aesthetics. The differences in scope and style between Dominican American Junot Díaz's first story collection, *Drown* (1996), and his second book, the novel *The Brief Wondrous Life of Oscar Wao* (2007), provide a good example of this authorial development. Similar differences can be marked between the first and fourth books of African American novelist Toni Morrison, *The Bluest Eye* (1970) and *Beloved* (1987), as well as the first and third of Esmeralda Santiago's novels, *When I Was Puerto Rican* (1986) and *América's Dream* (1997).

The very broad applicability of the four narratives is evident within other ethnic literary traditions, including in experimental and genre-specific forms of literature. Within African American literature, for example, historical novels comprise a genre Bernard Bell has called the neo-slave narrative.[27] Novels such as David Bradley's *The Chaneysville Incident* (1977), Ishmael Reed's *Flight to Canada* (1976), Toni Morrison's *Beloved* (1988) and *A Mercy* (2008), and Charles Johnson's *Middle Passage* (1991) are narratives of loss foregrounding lost ancestors, forgotten languages, and tribal decimation. Native American texts foregrounding mergers of a spiritual past and sterile present are similar narratives of loss: N. Scott Momaday's *House Made of Dawn* (1966), James Welch's *Fools Crow* (1984), Leslie Marmon Silko's *Ceremony* (1989), Sherman Alexie's *Indian Killer* (1996), and Louise Erdrich's *The Last Report of the Miracles at Little No Horse* (2009).

Asian American literatures offer narratives of loss as well; for example, Maxine Hong Kingston's *Woman Warrior: Memoirs of a Girlhood among Ghosts* (1975) and Peter Bocho's story collection *Dark Blue Suit* (1997) portray lost connections to China and the Philippines, respectively. Within the larger body of Asian American literature, though, authors foreground the stories of transnational ethnic communities. Sesshu Foster's novel, *Atomik Aztex*, provides a useful example of the limits of reading work through ethnic identity or strict historical context. Sesshu Foster is Asian and Anglo-American: how can readers analyze his work through the framework of the four narratives? *Atomik Aztex* is speculative fiction; it is part revisionist history, part social commentary, and part fantasy narrative about Mexican America. This text is a narrative of loss; it does not offer the reader a vision of escape from colonial or neocolonial subjectivity.[28] Karen Tei Yamashita's *Tropic of Orange* (1997) does not fit perfectly into ethnic or historical analytical frameworks either. Yamashita is a Japanese American author whose work is transcultural. *Tropic of Orange* focuses on a United States–Mexico context; another of her novels, *Circle of Cycles* (2001), is about Japanese laborers in Brazil. Though each varies from the others in narrative style, all five of these Asian American texts mentioned tell a familiar tale, the narrative of loss.

In its approach to contemporary ethnic literatures, *Chicana/o and Latina/o Fiction* departs from what Ramon Saldívar has been calling *postrace aesthetics*. Using the paradigm he calls "historical fantasy," Saldívar argues that "in the twenty-first century, the relationship between race and social justice, race and identity, and indeed, race and history requires these writers to invent a new 'imaginary' for thinking about the nature of a just society and the role of race in its construction" ("Historical Fantasy, Speculative Realism, and Postrace Aesthetics" 574). Saldívar's project is similar to Lima's; they both maintain a focus on the relationships between Anglo-America and Chicana/o and Latina/o Americas. Yet Saldívar raises an important issue: novelty. What is the importance of the recurrences of the story or its newness, of any work of contemporary fiction? Such a question returns us to genre. Wallace Martin offers a very useful way of interpreting newness in *Recent Theories of Narrative*. Martin notes, "the originality of recent fiction and narrative theory has drawn attention away from scholarly and historical studies that convey their insights in traditional terminology. As the example of John Barth shows, what appears to be new may simply be something that has been forgotten" (*Recent Theories* 28). Recognizing the old in the new does not diminish the value of the work. Rather, such intertextuality augments the value of older works and places newer works in a conversation that might be forestalled if texts are read in isolation. This conversation is precisely what broke "THE" canon.

The co-authored novel *Lunar Braceros 2125–2148* (Rosaura Sánchez and Beatriz Pita 2009) offers a good example of Chicana/o fiction that cannot be easily characterized as one of the four narratives. As a work of historical fantasy or science fiction, *Lunar Braceros 2125–2148* does not tell a typical science fiction story, set in a postapocalyptic dystopia with an emphasis on the dangers of manipulating technology. The novel imagines a world that cannot be explained solely by a historical analysis of specific factual events or through an analysis of its generic devices. From 2125 to 2148, all races of people have been segregated by class and by state-determined social value. An attention to solely race simplifies the novel's crisis. Rather, the specific exploitation of literally expendable laborers motivates a panethnic, transnational revolution replicating the "agit-prop" strategies of social justice movements of the 1920s and 1960s. By moving in the past, present, and future simultaneously, the novel invites readers to question the value of socially constructed discourses: education, gender, history, parenthood, and science. The novel is better situated through a frame of interpretation as defined by Amy J. Elias: the *metahistorical romance*. In *Sublime Desire: History and Post-1960s Fiction* (2001), Elias outlines the relationship between historiography and narrative, arguing that "metahistorical consciousness models itself as post-traumatic consciousness, akin to the state of mind of war survivors, and that as such it finds traditional models for Western history inadequate to deal with the late-twentieth-century realities it faces" (Elias xii). A focus on trauma is especially apt for certain science fiction and fantasy texts within multiethnic literatures.[29]

Rather than setting the novel in an undefined future time and space, the authors of *Lunar Braceros 2125–2148* incorporate extant historical events, political movements, and national legislation, offering the reader an understanding of the current reality as a repetition of the past, not an imagination of a better future. The novel uses varying typography, illustrations, and other visuals to construct a polyphonic discourse on the coming revolution; these devices are representative of perhaps forgotten or insufficiently studied literature, particularly Mexican American women's literature of the nineteenth century. Elias' definition of the metahistorical romance is applicable to *Lunar Braceros 2125–2148* and other texts, including *The Rag Doll Plagues* (1992) and *Salsa Nocturna: Stories* (2012). Her assertion is apt for describing the texts just mentioned: "Caught between its post-traumatic turn toward the historical sublime and its obsessions with social realities, the metahistorical romance is led to a compulsive, repetitive turning toward the past that is a ceaselessly deferred resolution to the questions of historical agency it poses" (Elias xii). The increasing publication of ethnic science fiction, fantasy, and ghost noir exemplifies this turning to the past without a projection of a more just or ethnically diverse utopian future. Recently, the first historical anthology of multiethnic science fiction was published. The editors of *Long Hidden: Speculative Fictions from the Margins of History* (2014) describe their project thus: "There is a long and honorable legacy of literary resistance to erasure. This anthology partakes of that legacy. It will feature stories from the margins of speculative history, each taking place between 1400 and the early 1900s and putting a speculative twist—an element of science fiction, fantasy, horror, or the unclassifiably strange—on real past events" (Crossed Genres).

The genre of life writing—including memoir, autoethnography, and creative nonfiction—offers another understanding of the problem of ethnicity being simplified too often in literary criticism.[30] Judith Ortiz Cofer, for example, articulates a complex racial identity in her life writing, especially in her creative nonfiction work "The Story of My Body": "I was born a white girl in Puerto Rico but became a brown girl when I came to live in the United States" (*The Latin Deli* 135). This intersection of ethnicity and geography has been present in Chicana/o and Latina/o literature; however, because scholars have analyzed ethnicity in relation to Anglo-American culture, Chicana/o and Latina/o literatures' treatments of multiple races, ethnicities, classes, sexual orientations, and geographic origins have been underexplored. Racial difference is just one of several differences these writers explore within their books.

This study's focus on internal difference is particularly visible in the contemporary era in narratives of fracture and narratives of new memory. Examples of these narrative types include but are not limited to the following: John Rechy's *City of Night* (1965), Rolando Hinojosa-Smith's *Estampillas del valle* (1973), Dolores Prida's *Beautiful Señoritas* (1977), Cherríe Moraga's *Loving in the War Years: lo que nunca pasó por sus labios* (1983), Cisneros' *The House on Mango Street* (1984), Gloria Anzaldúa's *Borderlands/La Frontera: The New Mestiza* (1987), Lucha Corpi's *Eulogy for a Brown Angel* (1991), Arturo Islas's *The Rain God* (1991), Judith Ortiz Cofer's *The Latin Deli* (1993), Ana Castillo's *So Far from God* (1993), Demetria Martínez's *Mother Tongue* (1993), Julia Alvarez's *In the Time of the Butterflies* (1994), Virgil Suárez's *Going Under* (1996), Junot Díaz's *Drown* (1996), Loida Maritza Pérez's *Geographies of Home* (1998), Cristina García's *The Agüero Sisters* (1997) and *Monkey Hunting* (2003), Margarita Cota-Cárdenas' *Puppet* (2000), Ernesto Quiñonez's *Bodega Dreams* (2000) and *Chango's Fire* (2004), Angie Cruz's *Soledad* (2002), and Jennine Capó Crucet's *How to Leave Hialeah* (2009). Not all of the texts above are fiction; included are multigenre memoir, drama, and autoethnography. Even though Chicana/o and Latina/o literature do not always perfectly converge in themes and style, they do converge frequently in their emphasis on internal problems and possibilities for empowerment.

The preceding discussions of the wealth of multiethnic literature might seem to suggest the variants of multiculturalism were successful. Recent political actions and legislations, unfortunately, suggest the losses of its few gains. In an organized, national movement challenging institutionalized racism, students and parents across the country protested state-legislated obstacles to the proposed federal legislation the Dream Act. The state of Arizona, for example, illustrates that we are not "one nation" in efforts to empower immigrants.[31] Moreover, as I revised this in Florida, the 2014 gubernatorial election campaigns revealed significant confusion about the Dream Act: both candidates reversed their positions, and state legislation allowing undocumented students to pay in-state tuition was stalled for months. Perhaps this should not be a surprise. When US senators drafting the Immigration Act in 2013 embraced the moniker "Gang of Eight" and used the term *surge* to describe border control,[32] they reinscribed the view of the undocumented as criminals to be rounded up—yet again—into cattle cars in the name of national security, rather than representing the undocumented as people deserving equal access to education.

Arrival: A Tall Tale

"We have arrived": this phrase is cliché. Popular conceptions about *arrival*— that individuals or ethnic groups attain social mobility through the assimilation of three generations of immigrants—simplify the possibilities for *arrival* in the contemporary era.[33] For early twentieth-century Western European immigrant groups such as the Irish or Italians, arrival meant economic success and a public recognition of it.[34] This notion of arrival, a variation of assimilation, was predicated on the desire to shed ethnic or national identity, enter the *Crèvecoeurian* melting pot, and emerge an *American*.[35] For mid- through late-twentieth-century Hispanic-descended immigrants, arrival functions differently: arrival means success *without* losing cultural specificity. It means being recognized not only as American but also as Chicana/o or Latina/o.[36]

What new understandings might readers gain about the relationships among Chicanas/o and Latinas/os as represented in contemporary literature? American studies, border theory, critical race theory, cultural studies, ethnic studies, postcolonial studies, sociology, and women's studies all contributed to the development of the Chicana/o and Latina/o literary studies. If one traces literary criticism since the 1970s, it is clear that the problematic nature of acculturation evolved as the literatures' central trope and then as scholars' focus. This focus, though, has obscured depictions of another consistent exploration: the mediation of identity *within* Chicana/o and Latina/o America. Chicana/o and Latina/o narratives are actively challenging the rhetoric of arrival and its failure to accurately reflect the experiences of the communities the literatures portray. *Chicana/o and Latina/o Fiction* begins by asking what happens to communities when arrival loses its centrality as a narrative trope.

The concept of arrival is perhaps nowhere more dramatically engaged than in Tomás Rivera's novella . . . *y no se lo tragó la tierra / And the Earth Did Not Devour Him* (1971).[37] Set in the 1950s, the book depicts a year in the life of migrant workers in the southwestern United States. In the chapter "When We Arrive," disembodied subjunctive voices trail in and out, echoing one another in plans and hopes. The workers' plans range from buying a car "so we don't have to travel this way, like cattle" to "getting a good bed for my vieja" (Rivera 143–145). Their hopes reveal the instability of migrant life. Basic comforts become luxuries: "How I wish we were there already so we could lie down, even if it's on a hard floor," and exploitation undermines hard-earned progress: "And then when we return, I have to pay him back double. Four hundred dollars. . . . Some people have told me to report him because that's way too much interest but now he's even got the deed to the house" (Rivera 144).

Toward the end of the year that has been lost to him, the young, unnamed protagonist has become disillusioned of his own hopes in America's empty promises: "When we arrive, when we arrive, the real truth is that I'm tired of arriving. Arriving and leaving, it's the same thing because we no sooner arrive and . . . the real truth of the matter . . . I'm tired of arriving" (Rivera 145).[38] Even as the desire for arrival is articulated, it is problematized; with despair and disbelief, the narrator concludes: "I really should say when we don't arrive because that is the real truth. We never arrive" (Rivera 145). Rivera's text suggests that arrival has never truly been possible for Chicanas/os and Latinas/os as a whole, despite its potent and enduring appeal. Dark-skinned, working-class, or working-poor individuals who have recently entered the country, or who embrace their ethnonational origins, face significant barriers to such a form of acculturation.

Racial discrimination and disparity in access to public education contribute to the impossibility of arrival. A significant challenge to arrival, however, emerges from within Chicana/o and Latina/o communities themselves: cyclical immigration. Unlike most European and Asian immigrants of the late nineteenth and early twentieth centuries, undocumented and documented Chicanas/os and Latina/os have continually walked, swam, driven, or flown between their nations of origin and the United States. The relatively easier travel between nations results in the maintenance of economic, linguistic, familial, and political allegiances to their homelands. Allegiance is often measured by immigrants' practice of remittance: sending money to one's nation of origin and participating in social and political activity relative to conditions in that nation. To describe these practices, anthropologist Peggy Levitt coined the term "social remittances" in *The Transnational Villagers* (2001). Caminero-Santangelo noted that these economic practices often distinguish experiences of transnationalism among Latino groups (*On Latinidad* 17).

Juan Flores developed Levitt's concept further in *The Diaspora Strikes Back: Caribeño Tales of Learning and Turning* (2010), proposing that the "cultural remittance" is a process in which far more than capital and labor exchange occurs through transnational migration.[39] Flores suggests, "to understand the potential deeper significance of all 'transfers' emanating from diasporas, our notion of culture needs to embrace collective, ideological, as well as artistic meanings of the term" (*Diaspora Strikes Back* 9). For Chicanas/os or Latinas/os born in the United States or naturalized, remittance persists because citizenship does not guarantee these groups equitable access to economic opportunity, political representation, or education.[40] This is especially true for Puerto Ricans, who have been citizens since imposition of the Jones Act in 1917.[41]

Within literature depicting Chicana/o and Latina/o communities, the negotiation of identity is often depicted as characters feeling forced to choose one side of the "hyphen": to give up their cultural identity or to fail to arrive.[42] If arrival is exhausted, what scholarly contribution does this study offer? *New memory*. Juxtaposed, these words seem an obvious paradox; however, in the context of Chicana/o and Latina/o fiction, they are mutually inclusive concepts. Elías Miguel Muñoz's novel *Brand New Memory* (1998) inspires the title and scope of this study.[43] One of his several English-language novels, *Brand New Memory* draws on the stories central to Chicana/o and Latina/o literature and culminates in the *narrative of new memory*. Benito and Elisa Domingo left Cuba in 1966. As their only daughter, Gina, approaches her *quinceañera*, she reflects upon a common theme of Cuban American literature: the *narrative of loss* of Cuba.

The novel illustrates Gina's brief *narrative of reclamation*—her attempt to create her ethnic identity through video documentary. Narrated in third-person omniscient voice as well as via first-person streams-of-consciousness, *Brand New Memory* replicates film structure. A textual symbol (~~~~) separates every few scenes, functioning as individual cells do in a filmstrip. These breaks advance the novel rapidly, dizzying Gina and the reader. The novel's extended use of the cinematic performs a *narrative of fracture* about history and memory. It plays on recurring visual tropes in ethnic literatures in general: photographs as incomplete and static memory, and windows and mirrors as reflection and containment.[44]

If reading the novel through Muñoz's ethnicity or historically, through his or his characters' migration experience, readers might falsely assume that the novel is about communism in Cuba. The novel's filmic suture of moments and scenes into a polyphonic story distinguishes it from most Cuban exilic literature. The extensive references to photographs illustrate Walter Benjamin's discussion of photos as archive: "The photograph, fine child of the age of mechanical production, is only the peremptory of a huge modern accumulation of documentary evidence (birth certificate, diaries, report cards, letters, medical records, and the like), which simultaneously records certain apparent continuity and emphasizes its loss from memory" (204). Every book in this study employs photos as part of its storytelling; in *Brand New Memory*, there are few documents available to assemble Gina's documentary. While the crisis of *Brand New Memory* is rooted in the Domingo family's loss of Cuba, an understanding of the rise of communism is insufficient to understand this loss or the novel's central story, the narrative of new memory. Thus, Benjamin's point is a succinct illustration of how ekphrasis functions in identity narratives: "Out of this estrangement comes a conception of personhood, identity . . . which because it can not be 'remembered,' must be narrated" (Benjamin 204).

Gina's parents have never actually told their daughter why they left: "The truth that looms over their home is that Gina's parents went through hell in Cuba. But what does that mean?" (Muñoz 3). Gina's struggle to remember Cuba echoes the struggle of Pilar, the slightly older protagonist of Cristina García's novel *Dreaming in Cuban* (1993): "And there's only my imagination where our history should be" (138). Because the novel relies on third-person narration, the use of the cinematic, ekphrastic, and allegorical, Muñoz spends little narrative time rewriting communist Cuba. This significant departure from Cuban American novels such as *Dreaming in Cuban* and Oscar Hijuelos' *Our House in the Last World* is key to understanding Muñoz's authorial project.[45] Because he was not a Havana exile, Muñoz ultimately tells a different story, a new memory of Cuba. This narrative of new memory is as it suggests: *brand new*. Published in 1998, the year of the hundredth anniversary of the Cuban-Spanish-American War and on the eve of the new millennium, Muñoz tells us a story that moves beyond exilic nostalgia, condemnation of Castro, and indictment of US neocolonialism.[46]

Muñoz's narrative of new memory frames Cuba in the present, splicing it from a single frame black and white unmoving camera still into a technicolor video. In depicting a new memory of Cuba, Muñoz deconstructs accepted "truths" about the first wave of Cuban exiles. As Ruth Behar notes in the introduction to the literary anthology *Bridges to Cuba/Puentes a Cuba* (1995), "Cuba since the revolution has been imagined as either a utopia or a backward police state" (2). Muñoz rejects this binary by revealing that Gina's parents come from two distinct classes; their romance was unsanctioned by Cuba's social hierarchy, and communism had little, if anything, to do with their immigration.[47] Behar explains that the impetus for the anthology "grew out of the conviction that there is another map of Cuba" (3). *Brand New Memory* embodies this impetus, and Muñoz is "mapping a country that's not on the map," just as Dominican American author Julia Alvarez expressed the goal of her writing (*Something to Declare* 173).

The island travels to Gina in this narrative of new memory.[48] She discovers the box full of letters her mother had hidden; her grandmother, Abuela Estela, has been writing to Gina for years. In a distinct contrast to the exile story in *Dreaming in Cuban*, where the granddaughter has access to memory and thus longs for reunion with her grandmother, Gina does not feel anything for her abuela: "The Cuban woman was a bunch of words on paper, unskilled writing, hard-to-read-Spanish sentences. You don't start loving a person in the blink of an eye, even if that person happens to be your father's mother" (Muñoz 64). Once Abuela Estela visits, Gina begins to realize how insular her world is and how tenuous her connection to Cuba. The narrator's description of the next phase of Gina's journey foreshadows a rocky displacement from the *Cuba de ayer*.[49] Muñoz writes, "She's contaminated by nostalgia for a land she never saw. The pain of exile is hers too. (A pain her parents have repressed.) Her grandma's lot, a lifetime of struggles, Gina claims it all. . . . Her inescapable fate: soon to become one of the aliens" (Muñoz 150). Passages such as this reveal a critical aspect of Muñoz's narrative of new memory: Americans become Cuban rather than Cubans becoming American.

The vague sentiments Gina's parents express do not do justice to Cuban cultural memory, nor do Gina's naïve attempts to *be* Cuban. What are readers supposed to understand about Cuba in reading this novel or any text characterized as a narrative of new memory? As the novel moves toward its close, the omniscient narrator intrudes: "Gina Domingo has been thrown into a situation for which no one has prepared her (not even her grandmother), into a living text (whose language she hasn't yet learned how to read)" (Muñoz 217). Here, Muñoz fully realizes his authorial project. The living text Gina does not know is the last of the four stories examined in this book: the narrative of new memory. Gina will learn Cuban customs and meet family she has never known. Her friendships with her grandmother and her cousins develop new memories because they were always family, but now they can actually create memories of each other rather than relying on faded photographs, old letters, and secondhand stories. Gina's trip also functions as a new memory for Abuela Estela; she will be part of Gina's connection to Cuba. Published in 1998 and perhaps inspired by the restrictions in travel to Cuba and the third wave of Cuban immigration via the Freedom Flotilla in 1994, the text's hope toward this new memory has been somewhat realized. Muñoz was prophesying a near future where Cubans and Cuban Americans will have an entirely new understanding of one another—one crafted by their communication and physical interaction. In 2014, President Barack H. Obama began to reestablish normal diplomatic relations with Cuba; on May 29, 2015, he formally removed Cuba from the list state sponsors of terror, facilitating additional easing of travel and commercial exchange with Cuba.

The epigraph at the beginning of the introduction comes from the final words of *Brand New Memory*; to comprehend Gina's narrative of new memory, readers must understand the three narratives that precede it. Gina's efforts to create a documentary of her origins evoke the relationship between identity and story. Stuart Hall's theorizations of ethnicity are particularly instructive. His argument that "identity is a narrative of the self; it's the story we tell about the self in order to know who we are" succinctly describes the relationship between story and self, which is the larger project of the books discussed in this study ("Ethnicity: Identity and Difference" 16). But how do authors tell the story of the self?

Chicana/o and Latina/o Fiction illustrates some of Hall's larger arguments about identity, particularly his conception of why and how we tell stories: "We tell ourselves the stories of the parts of our roots in order to come into contact, creatively, with it. So this new kind of ethnicity—the emergent ethnicities—has a relationship to the past, but it is a relationship that is partly through memory, partly through narrative, one that has to be recovered. It is an act of cultural recovery" ("Ethnicity: Identity and Difference" 19). Chicana/o and Latina/o literature are neither simply treatments of social inequity nor concerned only with acculturation to the Anglo-American mainstream. Both are literary responses to US neocolonialism and its legacies: multiculturalism and arrival.

Rewriting Neocolonialism's Story

Loss, reclamation, fracture, and *new memory* are all types of response; they are ways of telling stories about oneself and one's community. As a literary response to US neocolonialism, each narrative is representative. The narratives follow a general chronological pattern and often function in pairs. The narratives of loss and reclamation coincide with the Manifest Destiny and neocolonialism of the nineteenth century; such texts explore issues of acculturation in relation to Anglo-America because, at this time, Mexican and Caribbean peoples experienced the initial stages of US neocolonialism. The narratives of loss and reclamation are often visible in first-generation immigrant narratives, regardless of the period of publication; this is because those immigrants' experiences of neocolonialism have just begun. The latter two narratives, fracture and new memory, coincide with the rise and decline of civil rights movements such as *El Movimiento*, the Brown Berets, the Young Lords' Movement, and MECHA.[50]

Texts written at the middle or end of the twentieth century, and now in the twenty-first century, are more usefully situated as narratives of fracture and new memory because they, too, reflect the evolving literary response to the historical and continuing realities of US neocolonialism. Narratives of fracture and new memory are more often told by the "1.5," or second-generation immigrant characters, because they lack the memory of loss and have no desire to reclaim the cultural artifacts of their parents or ancestors.[51] Though the books may reference the tropes of other narratives—they tend to in critical metafictional moments—each book illustrates a single narrative most consistently. In differentiating these stories about Chicana/o and Latina/o America, *Chicana/o and Latina/o Fiction* delineates a broad framework for the literatures. As illustrated earlier, the framework presented here is not applicable to all Chicana/o, Latina/o, or other ethnic American fiction: no framework is unilaterally appropriate or useful. Rather, this analysis offers readers a general frame for situating the literatures in relation to one another historically and narratologically.

Chicana/o and Latina/o Fiction develops a broader parameter for discussing contemporary fiction about distinct Hispanic-descended groups in the United States than has been offered to date; it is also a relevant framework for other forms of creative writing. Various genres, especially narrative poetry and drama, tell stories, so this framework is useful in reading such works. Nuyorican protest poetry of the 1960s and 1970s offers especially good examples of narratives of loss told in verse. Pedro Pietri's collection, *Puerto Rican Obituary* (1973), and Tato Laviera's volume, *La Carreta Made a U-Turn* (1979), clearly depict life in hostile urban New York, where Puerto Ricans struggle with external oppression.[52] Each of these works is a narrative of loss, illustrating cultural, linguistic, and economic losses. In some of the Nuyorican poetry of the late 1970s and 1980s, those losses culminate in Puerto Ricans turning against one another. The stories evolve into narratives of fracture as the Nuyorican identity defines itself in opposition to a Boricua identity, and female poets such as Sandra María Esteves and Nina Serrano develop feminist poetics reclaiming African American and indigenous epistemologies.[53]

In the same decade, Dolores Prida's play *Beautiful Señoritas* (1977) began to link issues of neocolonialism across Caribbean communities.[54] Prida's work has enjoyed less critical success; this can be explained partially by the politics of *cubanidad*. In 1986, Prida was subject to protest of her work when it was scheduled for presentation at the inaugural Festival of Hispanic Theater in Miami. According to scholar María Cristina García, Prida was "a vocal supporter of the revolution" (196), and she was considered "persona non grata in the émigré community" (197). Prida's less-well-known but important two-act drama is particularly interesting because the four characters, initially beauty contestants and later nameless "Women 1–4," clearly represent nations subject to US neocolonialism: "Miss Little Havana" (Cuba); "Miss Commonwealth" (Puerto Rico); "Miss Chile Tamale" (Mexico); and "Miss Chiquita Banana" (Guatemala or Central America in general). The play depicts each of the characters' lack of unique cultural identity. The play's characters fracture the perception that the ethnic identity "Latina" has one signification. As the women compete for the beauty crown, they realize how the contest's ideology has constructed them as abstract ethnic women, ignoring the specificity of their cultures and individual experiences. Woman 3, formerly "Miss Chiquita Banana," articulates this best: "I look for myself and I can't find me. I only find someone else's idea of me" (Prida Act 2). Ultimately, the Women 1–4 sabotage the contest by withdrawing from it. They also begin a process of deprogramming a young girl who is aspiring to the only model of femininity before her: a one-dimensional, racialized, heterosexual sex object. Thus, *Beautiful Señoritas* (1977) is a powerful dramaturgical example of the narrative of fracture.

Neocolonialized communities have never been racially or politically homogenous.[55] This fact may seem obvious, especially in some Chicana/o literature's attempts to recuperate indigenous ancestries, in some Latina/o literature's attempts to recuperate African ancestries, and both literatures' efforts to reconcile those with European ancestries. Much literary criticism, however, has focused on the competing of static ethnonational identities wherein authors often depict individuals trying to reconcile cultural ideologies with very old roots in Iberian culture with newer branches in contemporary culture. Such ideologies were transplanted by colonialism and exacerbated by US neocolonialism. Cristina García's highly successful text *Dreaming in Cuban* (1993) is an example of ethnic literature often read as a narrative about hyphenated (Cuban-American) identity that can be read quite differently as a narrative of fracture.

Throughout the novel, the protagonist, Pilar, attempts to understand her place in Cuba's political spectrum. Her grandmother Celia represents a pro-Castro, radical communism, and her mother, Lourdes, represents an anti-Castro, conservative capitalism. Given Pilar's assertion that she belongs in New York "not instead of [Cuba] but more than [Cuba]," it is easy to see why critics have focused on the novel's issues of acculturation to the Anglo-American mainstream (236). Reading the text as a narrative of fracture, however, illuminates how Pilar's grandmother's life was shaped by the colonialism of Spain and the neocolonialism of the United States, which both contributed directly to the communist revolution. Celia mourns a lover who returns to Spain, since Cuba is a lesser place—a remnant of the Spanish empire—now ambiguously connected to the United States. Celia's voice emerges through the epistolary: letters to her former lover expose Cuba's pre-Castro polemics. When she marries Jorge del Pino, his mother and sister torment her; they are mulattos who lighten their skin and fear identification as black Cubans. Reading the novel as a narrative of fracture could focus on the racial and class differences that prompted the communist revolution in Cuba.

The books explored here reveal an inward gaze that seeks to address how individuals position themselves within Chicana/o and Latina/o America. The historical and narratological approach of *Chicana/o and Latina/o Fiction* parallels a different aspect of Hall's theorization of cultural identity. Hall argues that cultural identity is "always constructed through memory, fantasy, narrative and myth. Cultural identities are the points of identification, the unstable points of identification or suture, which are made within the discourses of history and culture. Not an essence but a *positioning*" ("Cultural Identity and Diaspora" 11). *Chicana/o and Latina/o Fiction* emphasizes the problems and possibilities for empowerment within specific ethnic and geographic communities; thus, Hall's assertion is particularly apt: "there is always a politics of identity, a politics of position, which has no absolute guarantee in an unproblematic, transcendental 'law of origin'" ("Cultural Identity and Diaspora" 113). Hall's view of identity as a continuum informs my thesis: "We have to now reconceptualize identity as a *process of identification,* and that is a different matter. It is something that happens over time, that is never absolutely stable, that is subject to the play of history and the play of difference" ("Ethnicity: Identity and Difference" 15). *Chicana/o and Latina/o Fiction* illustrates the literatures' progression away from a preoccupation with difference from Anglo-America toward a preoccupation with difference within Chicana/o and/or Latina/o America.

The terms *imperialism, colonialism, decolonialism, internal colonialism, postcolonialism,* and *neocolonialism* have all been used to describe foreign and domestic policies between dominant and subordinate nations.[56] The term *neocolonialism*[57] was first used in 1961 in reference to the United States' relationship with the Hispanic Caribbean. US neocolonialism has been hemispheric, if not global: it has engaged this process not only in the Hispanic Caribbean but also more generally in the Caribbean Basin (Guatemala, El Salvador, Nicaragua, Haiti, Panama) and nations of South America (Chile and Argentina).[58] Neocolonialism is the most apt characterization of US foreign policy beginning at the end of the nineteenth century.

US neocolonialism has varied within each nation where it has been operative. The people of some nations did not enact the same mass migration to the United States as did populations from Mexico and the Hispanic Caribbean. Greater distance from the United States, brutal civil wars, and the United States' refusal to provide sanctuary for refugees partially explain variations in migration patterns.[59] Neocolonialism is best suited to describe the relationships between the United States and Hispanic Caribbean and Central American nations; it is a hybrid of imperialism and colonialism. To call these nations neocolonial, however, does not imply that they have no agency or that the United States physically forced mass numbers of people to migrate to its continental territory. Calling Chicanas/os and Latinas/os neocolonial subjects acknowledges the subtle economic and political conditions created by US foreign policy resulting in the need for immigration to the United States.

In *Neo-colonialism: The Last Stage of Imperialism* (1965), Kwame Nkrumah argued that neocolonialism would develop as a form of imperialism following the decolonization of Africa. His differentiation between colonialism and neocolonialism informs this study: "In place of colonialism as the main instrument of Imperialism we have today neo-colonialism. The essence of neo-colonialism is that the State, which is subject to it, is in theory, independent and has all the outward trappings of international sovereignty. In reality, its economic system and thus its political policy is directed from outside" (ix). The United States engages in neocolonialism specifically through its veneer of recognizing and respecting the sovereignty of Cuba, the Dominican Republic, Mexico, and Puerto Rico.[60] For the purposes of this study, the broad definition of *neocolonialism* stated in the *Oxford English Dictionary* is applicable: "the acquisition or retention of influence over other countries, especially one's former colonies, often by economic or political measures."

US neocolonialism is distinct from seventeenth- through nineteenth-century African, European, and Asian models of colonialism. The primary difference is that in its neocolonialism, the United States deliberately moves resources, especially human resources, into its own borders. This differs from European and Asian colonial models characterized by settlement of the colonizing subjects, exploitation of the colonized as labor, and the exportation of natural resources and material goods produced for the domestic and foreign markets of the colonizing nation. Colonialism and neocolonialism differ significantly in this manner as well: the governing structures within colonialism simply do not exist in neocolonialism, as Nkrumah suggests. Rather, the dominant nation places local military or governing authorities under its influence, if not control.

Lora Romero also differentiated US from European colonialism: "Just as the British and French practice of indirect rule maintained an elite native class, Spanish deployment of mestizo descendants of colonizers to govern New World territories created a class of colonial subjects for which U.S. history offers no exact equivalent" (798). Neocolonialism differs from internal colonialism as well; historian Mario Barrera explains the latter as a situation in which "the dominant and subordinate populations are intermingled, so there is no geographically distinct metropolis separate from the colony" (qtd. in Muñoz, *Youth, Identity, Power* 153). Whether migrants come from a former US colony, protectorate, or commonwealth is moot; they come from nations tremendously influenced by the United States' economic, military, political, and cultural power.[61]

Because US intervention and influence does not end in formal decolonization, *postcolonialism* is not always the best descriptor for the United States' foreign policy. As a term to describe Chicana/o and Latina/o literatures, *postcolonialism* has been the subject of considerable debate. Mary Pat Brady's comments on terminology are useful: "*Post* is always a temporal term, even though it also has a spatial valence (consider its homonym *post*). This preference for its temporal dimension over its spatial in contemporary usage hints as to why *border* has come to appeal so thoroughly to many critics: it is from the vantage point of a (universal) border that theorists of the temporal 'post' may wish to operate" ("The Fungability of Borders" 174). In this way, postcolonial theory can unintentionally replicate the very structures it seeks to critique. Brady further argues that "border fungability" is a problem because "the dialectic of space and time encourages a linear narrative of national development: nations emerge along a linear, temporal scale that begins with feudalism and ends with cosmopolitan modernity" (Brady 178). Postcolonialism reinscribes this spatial temporal fiction. Postcolonialism tells the *story* of transition from the feudal to the modern and from the occupied to the sovereign: "national borders utilize the fantasy that on one side of the border a nation exists in one phase of temporal development while the nation on the other side functions in a different stage of temporality" (Brady, "The Fungability of Borders" 178). This story, or fantasy as Brady calls it, constantly reifies itself and perpetuates the belief that when someone "crosses a border that person transmogrifies, as it were, into someone who is either more or less advanced, or more or less modern, or more or less sophisticated" ("The Fungability of Borders" 178). Postcolonialism alone, in its binary epistemology, is less useful for the interpretation of Chicana/o and Latina/o cultural production. Ramón Saldívar's claim that the *post* of *postrace* "is not like the post of poststructuralism; it is more like the post of postcolonial, that is, a term designating not a chronological but a conceptual frame, one that refers to the logic of something having been 'shaped as a consequence of' imperialism and racism,'" still evokes a past connotation, especially in its use of "shaped" and "consequence of" ("Historical Fantasy, Speculative Fiction, and Postrace Aesthetics" 575). The *post* of *postcolonialism* evokes what Lora Romero so deftly argued: "Postcolonialism would seem to imply that the fight is over and that the oppressed won" (798).[62]

The United States has drawn on the labor resources of its "good neighbors" to meet its periodic needs for low-cost labor and to spur economic development. Initiated by Franklin Roosevelt in 1933 and later termed the "Good Neighbor Policy" by Herbert Hoover, this policy was purported to be an end to US intervention in Latin American politics. In the short term, it did end US occupations of Nicaragua (1933) and Haiti (1934). In the long term, economic and political manipulation of foreign rulers and covert financing and training of foreign militaries have replaced direct military interventions. The redistribution of foreign populations as sources of cheap labor, however, remains the hallmark of US neocolonialism. From the 1930s through the 1980s, US legislation mandated the sterilization of poor and dark-skinned Puerto Rican women, facilitating their employment in Puerto Rican factories or their immigration to New York City to work in the garment district, the service industry, and as domestics.[63] Similarly, the United States operated the Bracero Program for over twenty years (1942–1964) to fulfill short-term labor needs. Starting during World War II, the United States transported Mexicans across the border to provide agricultural labor. Once the war ended, US corporations continued to utilize Mexican labor in industry, particularly along the United States–Mexican border.[64] *Neocolonialism* is the best descriptor for the United States' actions and the literatures that respond to those actions and their long-term effects.[65]

In a literary period where we can assess the gains and failures of left-liberal multiculturalism, the claims of Alvarez and other writers merit serious consideration. Even though such writers resist the ethnic terms describing their writing, I retain them because they do in fact write about Chicana/o and Latina/o communities in most of their texts. The use of such terms does not degrade into a narrow reading of the literature; rather, these terms serve as a general context for readers less familiar with the cultural origins and differences among the writers and subjects in their books. Several factors contribute to the privileging of autoethnography, or what I call the *arrival text*. First, marketing and publishing issues affect which texts are disseminated widely; in the 1980s and 1990s, in particular, ethnic literature enjoyed a viable presence made possible by small presses such as Arte Público, Aunt Lute, Kitchen Table, South End, and Third Woman. Large publishers including Norton, Penguin, and Vintage then routinely purchased copyrights and published later editions of some of these works.

The implementation of multiculturalism and affirmative action policies then introduced the study of ethnic literature in public education. As Sollors argued, scholars, who do shape what and how people read, less often study "the innovative aspects of ethnic writing, the invention of ethnic traditions, the syncretism and modernism that characterizes so many of the forms of ethnic culture in America" (*Beyond Ethnicity* 240). José F. Aranda presents a similar concern when he notes that "ethnic scholars have generally proceeded by a more separatist critical philosophy, arguing for the need to develop literary histories that are more focused on, and sensitive to, minority issues," and that such critical knowledge "has come at the expense of producing histories for ethnic communities that falsely separate them from the mainstream populace, reproducing in fact the very same asymmetrical power relations that are routinely denounced in calls to reform the American literary canon" (xi). The use of ethnicity as a promotional tool creates a nexus of scholarly problems we have yet to solve in an ever more transnational country.[66]

Metaphor and Methodology

Chicana/o and Latina/o Fiction illustrates that readers have much to gain by studying US Cuban, Dominican, Mexican, and Puerto Rican texts comparatively. In the context of neocolonialism and its progeny, left-liberal multiculturalism, the problems of uncritical multiculturalism become visible in curricular reform. Established narrative modes and genres have long been visible within Chicana/o and Latina/o literature: autobiography, bildungsroman, *testimonio,* the detective novel, and more recently, graphic novels, science fiction, fantasy, horror, ghost noir, and speculative fiction. Problematically, though, scholars tend to read and teach books through biographic criticism, not through the genres they cultivate.[67] If one considers the development of ethnic writers, the arrival text functions as a first stage of writing about immigrant experience as well as the first stage in a writer's public identity.[68] Even for writers who are from communities historically present longest in North America and subsequently the United States—Native, Mexican, and African Americans—this metaphor functions because each of these groups has been subject to a form of internal colonialism, as Barrera and others have argued.[69]

To varying degrees, monographs about these communities have problematized static notions of identity; however, scholars have actively engaged constructions of class, race, gender, and sexuality perpetuated from *outside* the ethnic community. Marta Caminero-Santangelo makes a critical assertion about pan-Latino scholarship in her study *On Latinidad*: "Interactions between characters from the author's own ethnic group and other 'Latino' groups have been represented infrequently or not at all" (9). This book studies the convergences and divergences of each of these groups as related to cultural membership *within* ethnic communities, aiming to contribute to the growing corpus of comparative Latina/o literary studies.

The project of uniting various Hispanic-descended peoples in academic contexts is fraught: Caminero-Santangelo usefully observes that it is "difficult indeed to pinpoint what exactly might link people of Chicana/o, Puerto Rican, Cuban, Dominican, and Central/South American descent into a singular, collective ethnicity labeled Latino or 'Hispanic'" (*On Latinidad* 6). The unison of these groups has been problematic since multiculturalism promoted their study. In an edited volume published at the cusp of the multiethnic boom, *The Invention of Ethnicity* (1989), Sollors reviews the critical assumptions about ethnic literature and concludes, "the studies that result from such premises typically lead to an isolationist, group-by-group approach that emphasizes authenticity and cultural heritage within the individual, somewhat idealized group—at the expense of more widely shared conditions and cultural features, of dynamic interaction and syncretism" ("Introduction" xiv). Nearly two decades later, Caminero-Santangelo confirms, "Literary critics have generally followed suit by dealing with the separate ethnicities separately, even in critical texts that wrap them together under the broader umbrella term 'Hispanic'" (*On Latinidad* 9). A growing but still conspicuously small number of comparative monographs evidence this difficulty.

Chicana/o and Latina/o Fiction offers readers a wide survey of texts, one not limited by an author's gender or ethnic origin but united by the literary motif, memory, and the strategies these authors have used to depict the phenomenology of Chicana/o or Latina/o America. This study deliberately explores some now-canonical writers, including Ana Castillo, Judith Ortiz Cofer, Junot Díaz, and Tómas Rivera, in conjunction with less critically popular but equally prolific writers, including Angie Cruz, Demetria Martínez, Elías Miguel Muñoz, and Ernesto Quiñonez, to expand critical and popular conceptions of both literatures. The study discusses the books to which I return, again and again, as a reader and a teacher.

The methodology of this book is to read these literatures acknowledging the specific ethnic and historical contexts present in the books and engaging the narratives through shared generic recurring patterns. My earlier disclaimer bears repeating: no single theory or study can encompass the full range of production in Chicana/o and Latina/o literature. No critical theory emerges from the ether: *Chicana/o and Latina/o Fiction* is an interdisciplinary study that draws on developments in American, Chicana/o, and Latina/o studies. As Raphael Dalleo and Elena Machado Sáez illustrate in *The Latina/o Canon and the Emergence of Post-sixties Literature* (2007), "reviewers reading through the lens of multiculturalism focus on the politics of cultural translation, often speaking of building bridges and of the author as a translator" (4). The first theoretical text of women of color feminism, *This Bridge Called My Back: Writings by Women of Color* (1981), was compiled and edited by Chicana feminist theorists Gloria Anzaldúa and Cherríe Moraga. The anthology contains writing by a range of women of color and uses multiple innovative forms. The metaphor of the bridge was embraced and widely deployed in Chicana/o and Latina/o literature, as well as in other disciplines, while much of the volume's generic experimentation was elided.[70] Twenty years later, Gloria Anzaldúa and Ana Louise Keating compiled extensive and important reflections on women of color feminism in *This Bridge We Call Home: Radical Visions for Transformation* (2002). So powerfully employed by Anzaldúa and Moraga's anthology, the bridge metaphor begs reflection in light of urban renewal peaking in the 1990s. Urban bridges and local highways linking interstates to other highways have more often functioned to contain—to separate rather than unite—mainstream and multicultural Americas.

Focusing on narrative developments catalyzed by US neocolonialism across and within Chicana/o and Latina/o literatures would be impossible without Anzaldúa's terrifically important work *Borderlands/La Frontera: The New Mestiza*. Anzaldúa's work was a call to cross and recross all borders constraining identity; however, this is not always how the work has been engaged. Cultural studies scholars have drawn attention to this issue since the 1990s through the years following Anzaldúa's premature death in 2004. Yvonne Yarbro-Bejarano's 1998 article, "Gloria Anzaldúa's *Borderlands/La Frontera*: Cultural Studies, 'Difference', and the Non-Unitary Subject," deftly illustrates both the widely varying and decontextualized use of "the border" as a metaphor and the critiques made of the text's "essentialism." She argues that these uses have undermined Anzaldúa's original project: "two potentially problematic areas in the reception of *Borderlands* are the isolation of this text from its conceptual community and the pitfalls in universalizing the theory of *mestiza* or border consciousness, which the text painstakingly grounds in specific historical and cultural experiences" (Yarbro-Bejarano, "Gloria Anzaldúa's *Borderlands/La Frontera*" 7). My uses of Hall's theories of identity are similar to Yarbro-Bejarano's; we both emphasize the constructedness of identity. She reminds scholars that Anzaldúa insists that "mestiza consciousness is not a given but must be produced, or 'built' ('lumber', 'bricks and mortar', 'architecture'). It is spatialized ('a piece of ground to stand on'), racialized (mestiza), and presented as a new mythology, a new culture, a nondualistic perception and practice" (Yarbro-Bejarano, "Gloria Anzaldúa's *Borderlands/La Frontera*" 13).

Mary Pat Brady challenges popular usage of the border as metaphor: "the concept of borders has similarly gained a currency that enables it to perform a variety of theoretical labors; it functions, for example, as a term to describe a personality disorder ('borderline'), the effects of navigating multiple subjectivities, the liminal space between binary categories, or the potential complexities of relationships where difference is central to the narrative of those relationships" ("Fungability of Borders" 172). Claire Fox has argued that in cultural studies, the border "is rarely site-specific. Rather, it is invoked as a marker of hybrid or liminal subjectivities, such as those that would be experienced by persons who negotiate among multiple cultural, linguistic, racial, or sexual systems throughout their lives. When the border *is* spatialized in these theories, the space is almost always universal" (Fox, "The Portable Border" 61). The lack of specificity—within its particular Chicana/o cultural context—is the result of what José David Saldívar suggests is a consistent erasure of Mexican America.[71]

Anzaldúa's conversation with the Caribbean has not been without its challenges. Frances Negrón-Muntaner's 2006 insightful essay "Bridging Islands: Gloria Anzaldúa and the Caribbean" discusses the potential and problems of Anzaldúa's work being spatialized in Cuban and Puerto Rican theories of identity. Negrón-Muntaner notes, "The reception of Anzaldúa's work then reproduces the very cleavages that her border thinking, rooted in the multiple and irreducible subjections of the body, proposes to undo. In this regard, border thinking remains largely ingrained in paradigms organized according to a hierarchy of oppressions where colonial, class, and racial subject positions are comfortably ungendered at the top" ("Bridging Islands" 277). Citing Juan Flores' early acknowledgment and variation of Anzaldúa's theories and Walter Mignolo's later "generous appropriation" of them, Negrón-Muntaner illustrates how the use of border can be useful but reproduce the same oppositional thinking Anzaldúa sought to undo ("Bridging Islands" 277). Negrón-Muntaner asserts, "Mignolo, who prominently factors the Caribbean in his work and has generously appropriated Anzaldúa's writings in defense of alternative epistemologies, unceremoniously dismisses the 'question of gender' as a concern to be 'bypassed' in the interest of discussing such presumably gender-neutral matters as 'language, ethnicity, and the geopolitics of the insular Carib'" (Mignolo qtd. in Negrón-Muntaner, "Bridging Islands" 276). The centrality of the border as a framework can be an obstacle to the comparison of Chicana/o and Latina/o writing if all aspects of border experience, especially gender, are not taken fully into account. My engagement of the border in this study seeks consistency with Anzaldúa's discourse on the phenomenology of living in an explicitly physical location between Mexico and the United States. Anzaldúa's original conceptualization of the border in relation to external oppressions, however, is less relevant to my comparative methodology.[72]

More research on the internal complexities of ethnic communities is needed. The literary rejection of arrival and the theorization of narratives of loss, reclamation, fracture, and new memory owe much to the instructive scholarship of José F. Aranda. His study *When We Arrive: A New Literary History of Mexican America* (2003) dared to read Chicana/o literature in parallel relation to Puritan literature. Aranda chooses to reframe the Mexican American literary tradition through "the rise of Chicana/o literature within a larger institutional history, produced during the 1930s, 1940s, and 1950s, that conflates a Puritan myth of origins with a literary history in which American literature is heralded as the product and producer of social dissent" (xvii). As a comparative analysis of Chicana/o and Latina/o literature, this book endeavors to meet Aranda's call for a new Chicano/a studies "revealing the history of this community on its own complicated internal terms, not simply terms that suggest an oppositional relationship to Anglo America" (5). *Chicana/o and Latina/o Fiction* offers one of few "more historical and contemporary studies that look at the patterns of interaction between, and among, a multiplicity of groups" (Omi, "The Changing Meaning of Race" 251).

Scholars in the fields of Chicana/o and Latina/o literary studies have been exploring some of the same literatures considered in this study, though to different ends.[73] This project continues the critical trajectory of germinal comparative studies, including Ellen McCracken's *New Latina Narrative* (1996), Raphael Dalleo and Elena Machado Sáez's work in *The Latino/a Canon and the Emergence of Post-sixties Literature* (2007), and David J. Vázquez's *Triangulations: Narrative Strategies for Navigating Latino Identity* (2011). McCracken's comparative study examined Latina writing, framing the literatures as agents of postmodern ethnicity. Dalleo and Machado Sáez merge literary criticism with an examination of market aesthetics. Vázquez's study considers life writing to illustrate how Latina/o identity is differently constituted than Anglo-American discourses of the self.

Chicana/o and Latina/o Fiction performs critical work in the growing field of comparative Latina/o literary studies. Marta Caminero-Santangelo's monograph *On Latinidad: U.S. Latino Literature and the Construction of Ethnicity* (2007) has been instrumental in modeling literary criticism that is both attentive to ethnonational difference and able to present broader arguments relevant to the field. Her study achieves an important evaluation of how the field of Latina/o literary studies has developed and what questions remain underexplored. Lyn Di Iorio Sandín's monograph, *Killing Spanish: Literary Essays on Ambivalent U.S. Latino/a Identity* (2004), studies the work of several groups, though it applies the reading of the literatures as "ambivalent" to a single Chicana novel, Yxta Maya Murray's *Locas*. Juan Flores' *The Diaspora Strikes Back: Caribeño Tales of Learning and Turning* (2010) compares Puerto Rican, Cuban, and Dominican cultural production to illustrate the circularity of art and social practice among diasporic Latinos. David J. Vázquez's *Triangulations: Narrative Strategies for Navigating Latino Identity* (2011) compares Chicano and Puerto Rican male writers and Puerto Rican and Dominican female writers.

Comparative analyses of literature written by authors separated by geographical distance but linked by geopolitical or geocultural similarity also inform my approach. *Hispanic Caribbean Literature of Migration: Narratives of Displacement*, within which I published an early version of chapter 1 of this book, is an example of hemispheric American literary history. The volume performs critical projects akin to earlier monographs, such as Silvia Spitta's *Between Two Waters: The Literary Transculturation of Latin America* (1995) and volumes such as Frances R. Aparicio's and Susana Chávez-Silverman's *Tropicalizations: Transcultural Representations of Latinidad* (1996). Karen Christian's study, *Show and Tell: Identity as Performance in U.S. Latina/o Fiction* (1997), analyzes fiction from both literatures; however, as McCracken does, Christian collapses self-identified Chicana/o authors under the term "Latina/o" and reads texts through a single critical trope, "performativity." Both William Luis' *Dancing between Two Cultures: Latino Caribbean Literature Written in the United States* (1997) and Juan Flores' *From Bomba to Hip Hop: Puerto Rican Culture and Identity* (2000) called for a renewed critical unison of Latina/o and Latin American literatures.

By considering which cultural memories function to keep characters in stasis and which function to move characters forward, this books shows that Chicana/o and Latina/o literature have been moving toward new memory since the civil rights era. As suggested earlier, this literary movement is, however, shaped by a much older story: the story of US neocolonialism. For Chicanas/os and Latina/os, the possibilities for arrival have been fundamentally different from those of other ethnic groups in the United States. Two centuries of US neocolonialism have conditioned these possibilities. More so than internal economic or political strife, the United States' economic investments in, military occupation of, political reorganization of, and military departures from Caribbean and Central American nations have continually spurred most of the Hispanic-descended immigration into its borders.[74]

The Four-Storied Study: Chapter Overviews

I draw on José Luis González's germinal work on Puerto Rican identity, *El País de Cuatro Pisos y Otros Ensayos / The Four-Storeyed Country and Other Essays* (1980), to evoke the structure of this book's chapters as building upon one another, simultaneously revealing both the foundations and the futures of Chicana/o and Latina/o literature. Thus, chapter 1, "Narratives of Loss: Tracing Migrations," begins with an overview of US neocolonialism and its role in the development of nineteenth-century Chicana/o literature. Outlining the thematic development of Chicana/o and Latina/o literature, the chapter illustrates that despite the critical success of the arrival text, writers engaged issues within Chicana/o and Latina/o America well before the multicultural literature boom of the 1980s. Chapter 1 discusses a germinal Chicano novel exemplifying the narrative of loss: Tomás Rivera's . . . *And the Earth Did Not Devour Him* (1971). To set up a discussion of Dominican American short stories in *Drown* (1996) by Junot Díaz, the chapter then outlines the very similar development of US neocolonialism in the Hispanophone Caribbean. Rivera's novella is set in rural Texas migrant communities; Díaz's text follows the movements of a single family in urban New Jersey. Together, Rivera's and

Díaz's books illustrate how the narrative of loss permeates both Chicana/o and Latina/o literature, even when the losses depicted occur within distinct temporal, geographic, and cultural spaces.

"Narratives of Reclamation: Embodying Ritual and Allegory," chapter 2, opens with a review of the proliferation of Chicana literature following El Movimiento. The review frames the discussion of the narrative of reclamation in the Chicana novel *So Far from God* (1993) by Ana Castillo. To illustrate the recurring but varying pattern of this narrative, the chapter analyzes the Dominican American novel *Soledad* by Angie Cruz (2001). Both of these novels portray characters finding out whether ritual is effective in reclaiming their identity. This chapter unites fiction about two communities with distinct geographic and cultural contexts and illustrates how the narrative of reclamation permeates both Chicana and Dominicana phenomenology. By paying special attention to the novels' constructions of femininity, depictions of the abuse of the female body, and reconfigurations of communal and domestic spaces from patriarchal to matriarchal, the chapter delineates the convergences of a text set in the rural Southwest, *So Far from God*, with a text set in the urban Northeast, *Soledad*.

Chapter 3, "Narratives of Fracture: Definining *Latinidades*," illustrates how one's cultural identity is defined just as much, if not more, by geographic location, gender, class, and political ideology than by perceived race or ethnic self-identification. The chapter analyzes two texts by Puerto Rican authors to show how individuals challenge rigid notions of ethnonationalism: Judith Ortiz Cofer's *The Latin Deli: Telling the Lives of Barrio Women* (1993) and Ernesto Quiñonez's *Bodega Dreams* (2000).[75] Set in the proximate urban Northeastern cities—Paterson, New Jersey, and New York City, respectively—with large populations of Puerto Ricans, other kinds of Latinas/os, and other underrepresented ethnic populations, the books challenge persistent definitions of *puertorriqueñidad*. Methodologically, this chapter departs from the first two in that the books are set in similar urban spaces and ethnic communities. Chapter 3 is attentive to the narrative differences in gender dynamics, educational access, and zeitgeists of political ideology depicted by Ortiz Cofer and Quiñonez. Ortiz Cofer portrays the confinement women experience due to patriarchal Puerto Rican family values; Quiñonez portrays the confinement Puerto Rican men experience due to their ethnonational loyalties.

"Narratives of New Memory: Ending the Neocolonial Story," chapter 4, examines how authors Demetria Martínez and Elías Miguel Muñoz have crafted exemplars of the narrative of new memory. The first half of the chapter discusses how Martínez's novel *Mother Tongue* (1993) illustrates new memory constructed transnationally, as self-conception by Chicanas/os and Latinas/os changes through contact with refugees of Central American civil wars: exiles with different experiences of internal political oppression and external US neocolonialism. The second half of the chapter illustrates how Muñoz's novel *The Greatest Performance* (1991) creates a new memory of Cuban exile, defined neither by exilic nostalgia for Cuba nor by assimilationist desire to arrive in America. Its narrators select values and practices that define them, particularly those defining their sexual identity and political ideology. Both novels are hybrid texts, meshing formal literary genres with informal modes of writing. Ekphrastic, the novels' ruminations on their reproductions of song lyrics, journals, video recordings, photographs, newspaper clippings, action bulletins, and poetry become sites for the narrative of new memory. Chapter 4 analyzes novels with the same central portrayal: the changing experience of exile in the United States. *Mother Tongue* portrays the experiences of Central American refugees of the 1980s; *The Greatest Performance* portrays two Cubans' ethnonational and sexual exile.

"Belonging in Chicana/o and Latina/o Fiction" concludes the study by exploring how the narrative of new memory is a locus for empowerment. Because all of the works discussed originate in transnational contexts, the conclusion invites additional thinking about the relationships among Chicana/o, Latina/o, and Latin American cultural memory and ideological solidarity. Chicanas/os and Latinas/os are increasingly born within the United States. Contemporary writers portraying them do not necessarily share the linguistic, cultural, spiritual, or political practices of their predecessors. Because of the generational and cultural variations between their literatures, the critical models we have for understanding US multiethnic literatures need revision.

1

Narratives of Loss
Tracing Migrations

That year was lost to him. At times he tried to remember
and, just about when he thought everything was clearing
up some, he would be at a loss for words.
—Tomás Rivera, *. . . And the Earth Did Not Devour Him*

Our money is always welcome in Santo Domingo, but
not our intellectual or cultural ideas. . . . I don't want to
say this, but sometimes you have to get recognized from
outsiders before your own culture values what you are.
—Junot Díaz, "Diaspora and Redemption"

The opening chapter of Tomás Rivera's *. . . And the Earth Did Not Devour Him*, "The Lost Year," establishes the novella's dominant theme: loss. Arte Público published a bilingual version of the text, originally written in Spanish, in 1987. The novella's structure and content emphasize loss as an unidentified narrator recounts the experiences of frequently nameless characters, moving through unnamed towns, seeking work. The young narrator and the voices in conversation with him describe tangible losses of family, health, possessions, rights, and opportunities. Accompanying these are the narrator's intangible but visceral losses of self-esteem, religious faith, and economic aspiration.

The novella's events occur within the narrator's extended dream state. Sleep, or the disassociation of one's body from one's mind, is a way to survive events outside one's control.[1] Rivera uses sleep to explain the narrator's inability to articulate the losses he witnesses and experiences. As the epigraph illustrates, the boy describes a circular process in which he cannot orient himself to time or place. He cannot distinguish between calling himself and someone calling his name; he cannot grasp temporal or physical reality: "It almost always began with a dream in which he would suddenly awaken and then realize he was really asleep. Then he wouldn't know whether what he was thinking had happened or not" (Rivera 83). The dream state parallels the novella's events, which are unbelievable in that the narrator cannot fully articulate the exploitation, racism, brutality, and illness migrant workers endure. "The Lost Year" culminates in the loss of the narrator's epistemological and ontological certainty.

"The Lost Year" becomes a nightmare reality, one for which the author tries to prepare the reader: "But before falling asleep he saw and heard many things" (Rivera 83). In his essay "Contemporary Mexican American Literature: 1960s–Present," Raymund A. Paredes asserts an optimistic interpretation of the novella. He contrasts Rivera's 1973 novella with José Antonio Villareal's 1959 novel, *Pocho*, arguing, "whereas an earlier Mexican-American writer, José Antonio Villarreal, had depicted a Mexican-American family that was all but blown apart by assimilationist pressures, Rivera's work proclaims a people's vitality despite almost unspeakable hardships" ("Contemporary Mexican American Literature" 1105). When communities immigrate en masse because their lives are drastically altered by war, political oppression, or economic chaos, they see and hear many things—most prevalent among them, loss.[2]

Even when their vitality facilitates their survival, their losses are no less felt and remembered. Because loss is a principal motif in literature foregrounding colonization and migration, it makes sense to frame the origins of Chicana/o and Latina/o literary histories as narratives of loss. The narrative of loss delineates territorial dispossession, changes in geographic location, disruptions in families, and the unequal syncretism of cultures wrought by US neocolonialism. This chapter begins with an overview of neocolonialism and Chicana/o literature and then discusses . . . *And the Earth Did Not Devour Him* (1987), a germinal text that exemplifies the narrative of loss. The chapter then examines the very similar development of US neocolonialism in the Caribbean to set up a discussion of the short story collection *Drown* (1996) by Dominican American Junot Díaz.

Neocolonialism as We Have Known It: Chicana/o America

US foreign policy in regard to the Caribbean, Central America, and Latin America in general is one of intervention. The United States has a neocolonial relationship with Mexico. The United States developed this policy as Spain's colonial power declined in the nineteenth century. In the years following

Mexico's independence, the United States engaged in several interrelated legislative, financial, and military actions that helped it gain control of the territory now known as the US Southwest. In August 1821, Congress passed the Missouri Compromise; this legislation had great importance for the southwestern territories bordering the midwestern region of land acquired through the Louisiana Purchase (1803). The Missouri Compromise determined how new territories would enter the Union: as slave or nonslave states.

In December 1821, shortly after this legislation passed, Stephen F. Austin began the first settlement of Americans in Mexican territory. Two years later, President James Monroe issued the Monroe Doctrine (1823) as an Executive Declaration. The doctrine had two purposes; first, it was intended to reject any European interference in North and South American affairs, especially any efforts by Spain to regain its former territories. It simultaneously asserted the United States' right to intervene in Central and South American affairs: "In the war between those new Governments and Spain we declared our neutrality at the time of their recognition, and to this we have adhered, and shall continue to adhere, provided no change shall occur which, in the judgment of the competent authorities of this Government, shall make a corresponding change on the part of the United States indispensable to their security."[3] Thus, the Monroe Doctrine sanctioned US intervention whenever national security or territorial control was perceived to be at risk.

Approximately ten years after Texas declared its independence from Mexico (1836), the United States annexed it (1845), reopening the "slave-state" question addressed by the Missouri Compromise (1821). Since Texas had been under Mexican control at the time of the Compromise, the new territory's statehood—slave or nonslave—had to be determined before it could join the Union. On December 29, 1845, when Texas entered the Union, it had the option for its citizens to own slaves, because it lay south of the 36°30′N Missouri state boundary. The next year, continuing land disputes between Texans and Mexicans erupted in the Mexican-American War (1846–1848). The Treaty of Guadalupe Hidalgo (1848) ended the war, creating the United States–Mexico border. Mexico ceded extensive territories comprising present-day Arizona, California, Nevada, New Mexico, Utah, and half of Colorado.[4]

The Treaty of Guadalupe Hidalgo had many provisions; the principal geographic one has directly shaped the United States' past and current relationship with Mexico. The United States promised to honor the land grants distributed to Mexicans by the Spanish monarchy beginning in the sixteenth century. Differences in conceptions of landownership and the United States' failure to honor those grants in Texas and New Mexico have had lasting effects. What had been free-range cattle land used by Mexican *Tejanos* be-came fenced-in cultivated farmland used by Anglo-Texans. The agricultural production by *Nuevo Mexicanos* also changed when their lands when the government did not stop squatters from seizing lands from the local owners.[5] In both states, people known as *reclamantes*, descendants of those compelled to give up their land, continue to petition for the return of their ancestral lands. Popular literature addressed these issues immediately, and this part of the treaty remains a source of legal battles.

The treaty marks the formal beginning of the United States' neocolonial relationship with Mexico; it radically changed the geographic, economic, and cultural landscapes of both nations. A large population of Mexicans was subsumed within the US populace by the treaty. In his groundbreak-ing study of Chicana/o literature, *When We Arrive: A New Literary History of Mexican America* (2003), José F. Aranda explores "the interrelationships between Chicana/o and literature and mainstream literary discourses" (x). His foreword reviews Chicana/o literary history, and his succinct assertion supports my claim: "Chicano/a studies has been in the business of recovering the ruptured, alienated culture and history of people of Mexican descent since the Treaty of Guadalupe Hidalgo in 1848" (Aranda xiii–xiv). This "move-ment" of thousands of Mexicans into US territory—not US settlers moving into another nation's territory—set the United States on a new path, the path of neocolonialism. The United States' neocolonial web is intricate and the impetus for much of Chicana/o and Latina/o literature.

Scholars have consistently addressed the significance of the Mexican-American War to Chicana/o literature. Similarly, especially in the years im-mediately before and after the centennial of the Cuban-Spanish-American War, scholars revisited literary engagement of the war. In 2000, José David Saldívar called for a more nuanced consideration of it in "Looking Awry at 1898: Roosevelt, Montejo, Paredes, and Mariscal."[6] A year later, Manuel Mar-tín-Rodríguez examined dates significant to Chicano literary history—1598, 1848, 1898, and 1998—in the essay "'A Net Made of Holes': Toward a Cultural History of Chicano Literature" (2001). He describes the relationship between 1898 and 1998 as creating "a sense of conclusion" because "1898 signaled the end of the Spanish empire in the Americas" (Martín-Rodríguez 12). For Chicana/o and Latina/o literatures, 1898 more significantly marks a shift in the physical direction of the United States' neocolonial path. To understand Chicana/o literature, one must recognize the losses the Treaty of Guada-lupe Hidalgo catalyzed—geographic, economic, and cultural. To understand Latina/o literature, one must consider how the Cuban-Spanish-American War compounded the losses initiated by the Mexican-American War.[7]

Until the mid-1990s, most literature scholars dated Mexican American literature to *El Movimiento*. Some scholarship dates the literature back to the nineteenth century; most recently, others have argued for a colonial origin, dating the literature's origins to the Spanish Conquest.[8] In my view, the origins of Chicana/o literature are best located in the eighteenth century, at the first appearance of literary accounts of contact and conflict with Anglo-American settlers from the United States, written from the perspective of those born in the New World. Paredes explains, "Although a distinctive Mexican-American literary sensibility was not to emerge for several generations, the signing of [the Treaty of] Guadalupe Hidalgo, more than any other event, required that the southwestern Mexicans begin to rethink their relationships to the old country and to the United States" ("Early Mexican American Literature" 1081).[9] Chicana/o narratives of loss illustrate continued navigations of these relationships through the twentieth century and into the twenty-first.

Since 1993, the Recovering the US Hispanic Literary Heritage Recovery Project has been instrumental in identifying and publishing texts explicitly depicting the losses catalyzed by the Treaty of Guadalupe Hidalgo. María Amparo Ruiz de Burton's novel *The Squatter and the Don* (1885) and *The Collected Stories of María Cristina Mena* (written from 1913 to 1931; published in 1997) complete our understanding of social problems developing from the new relationship between Mexico and the United States: class conflict, intermarriage, social mobility, and the racist subordination of dark-skinned or Native American southwestern populations.[10] Nineteenth-century texts span the narrative of loss: from decrying geographical losses to portraying cultural losses. Mid-twentieth-century narratives of loss focus on fading cultural identity, as in Fabiola Cabeza de Baca's *We Fed Them Cactus* (1954) and José Antonio Villareal's *Pocho* (1959). Both novels portray devastating social losses such as communal and familial disintegration.[11]

Until the recovery projects began, scholars often located the origins of Chicana/o writing with Rudolfo "Corky" Gonzales' poetic, epic biography of Mexican America, *Yo Soy Joaquín* (1967). Literary production of the 1960s and 1970s reflected the direct political response to US neocolonialism: Mexican American nationalism. Nationalism simultaneously constructed and affirmed the ethnopolitical subjectivity of the Chicana/o during El Movimiento. Whereas periodical nonfiction and serialized fiction dominated nineteenth-century literary response, the production of drama and performance poetry characterized the literature of El Movimiento. Luis Valdez's *Teatro Campesino*, founded in 1965, helped support the development of the United Farm Workers and university-student-led protests in California, linking the two movements.[12] The early 1970s saw a waning of the politics of El

Movimiento in the literary production of this decade, but the narrative of loss still predominates. Texts such as Rivera's . . . *And the Earth Did Not Devour Him* (1971) and Rudolfo Anaya's *Bless Me, Ultima* (1974) reflect severe economic and sociological problems within Texas and New Mexico, respectively.[13]

Part of the legacy of various specific civil rights movements—the Black Power movement, the American Indian Movement, El Movimiento, and the Young Lords' movement—is the dissemination and validation of these communities' aesthetic productions. After the decline of El Movimiento, scholars might not have been able to imagine the success of ethnic American literatures. Indeed, some critics argue that multicultural literatures remain at the margins of the US literary canon. Over the last thirty years, however, ethnic writers have garnered the most prestigious literary awards available: the Pulitzer Prize (N. Scott Momaday, 1969; Oscar Hijuelos, 1990; and Junot Díaz, 2008); the American Book Award (Charles Johnson, 1990, and Denise Chávez, 1994); the National Book Critic's Circle Award (Maxine Hong Kingston, 1981, and Louise Erdrich, 1984); MacArthur Awards (Leslie Marmon Silko, 1983; Sandra Cisneros, 1995; and Junot Díaz, 2011); and of course, the Nobel Prize for Literature (Toni Morrison, 1993). These awards signal consistent evolution in what is perceived as important American literature.

Critical and popular interest in Chicana/o and Latina/o literature is also evident in major publishers' nearly concurrent releases of literary anthologies within the last decade: *The Prentice Hall Anthology of Latino Literature* (2001), *Herencia: The Anthology of Hispanic Literature of the United States* (2002), *US Latino Literature Today* (Pearson 2005), *Latino Boom: An Anthology of US Latino Literature* (Pearson 2006), and *The Norton Anthology of Latino Literature* (2011).[14] Following the anthologies, *The Routledge Companion to Latino/a Literature* (2013) offers a wide range of historical, ethnonational, and topical discussions relevant to the study of the literatures.

For over four hundred years, African, Asian, Native, and Hispanic peoples have been writing within the "New World"; however, the last four decades represent the most critically and popularly significant period of their production. An ethnic writers' canon—a cadre of writers from underrepresented ethnic groups—is visible within the broader US American literature canon. Some scholars have chosen to call the proliferation of this writing from underrepresented ethnic communities a "boom."[15] Others have rejected this idea, citing historical, economic, and political factors in the suppression of writing by various ethnic minorities since the Spanish Conquest.[16] The ethnic literatures discussed above share narrative concerns and qualities with

Chicana/o and Latina/o literatures, but the latter literatures tell the first of the four stories, the narrative of loss, in distinct ways from the other ethnic literatures.

"When We Arrive": Remembering Loss in . . . *And the Earth Did Not Devour Him*

Displaced by the loss of Spanish feudal lands, nineteenth-century peasant farmers sought agricultural work on American farms and in domestic service. The US Border Patrol, now technologically advanced and heavily armed, did not exist until 1925. Because there was no system of identification for US citizens until the creation of the Social Security Act in 1935, Mexicans and Mexican Americans freely crossed and recrossed the border for nearly a century after the Mexican-American War. In the twenty-first century, the economic and political changes caused by the passage of North American Free Trade Agreement (NAFTA) still compel Mexicans to cross the border, despite the dangers.

As Lázaro Lima asserts, "Mexicans living in the newly consolidated United States found themselves classed as foreigners in places they had inhabited even from Mexico's Independence from Spain" (22). The 1994 passage of NAFTA encouraged the industrialization of the border. NAFTA has had some positive effects on job creation but it has created more effects that are negative by worsening environmental pollution, facilitating drug and human trafficking, and proliferating violent crime. NAFTA has not succeeded in creating employment opportunities or educational access in Mexico rivaling those in the United States. The kinds of jobs created—mechanical assembly, pharmaceutical production, and garment piecework—pay low wages and often use the labor of women and children. This type of labor, if it has not yet been outsourced to nations with even less environmental regulation and less protection of workers' rights (such as China or India), often requires long, isolated travel for young women, which has been linked to the brutal rapes and murders of women in border towns, particularly Ciudad Júarez.[17] The border remains a site of violent loss for men and women seeking a living wage.[18]

At the start of this chapter, I briefly sketched how the narrative of loss is engaged in Rivera's important text . . . *And the Earth Did Not Devour Him*. Rivera structures the novel through dateless vignettes told by unnamed narrators, with a central narrator of a young but unstated age. It is tempting to consider the text as postmodern in nature—it lacks linearity, changes abruptly from third-person narration to stream-of-consciousness to dialogue, and has very loosely connected chapters, suggesting that there is not a single story or that the story cannot be completely told. Lázaro Lima suggests that the novella does not fall squarely into the categories imposed on it to date: novel or novella. Rather, Lima argues that reading the work "requires the suspension of generic formulae so that we can attend to the Chicano reality to which it alludes as testimonial evidence of a body of people who have stood outside historic representation" (78). Yet testimonio, as the extensive literary, anthropological, and linguistic scholarship on it illustrates, is a genre unto itself, characterized by the assertion of nonfiction or factual representation of race-, class-, or gender-based oppression. Oral cultural forms can become textual genres, so it is helpful to consider . . . *And the Earth Did Not Devour Him* within the traditions of the *estampa*, a literary sketch, and the *acto*, a one-act play as developed in *Teatro Campesino*. Unlike a postmodern aesthetic,[19] the vignettes are mimetic and didactic rather than historical or romantic.[20] The narratives are neither metafictional nor self-reflexive. Rather, similar to *actos*, each short chapter depicts a major experience by workers as they migrate.[21] The experiences teach the workers, particularly the children, about the harsh realities of migrant life.

The book's chapters do not provide an explicit time setting; however, references to World War II and the Korean War suggest that the book's events occur in the early 1950s. This lack of temporal specificity is deliberate: because the workers travel as they work to harvest various crops, the seasonal labor demands of bosses who hire them define their sense of time. Most of the characters are unnamed; they perform a modernist synecdoche. The workers exist as part of vast labor machine, having lost their individuality. Similar to Charlie Chaplin's character in the film *Modern Times*, the migrants are cogs in what will eventually become Big Agra in the 1970s: ever-larger farms using migrants as expendable labor.[22]

In "Time as a Structural Device in Tomás Rivera's . . . *y no se lo tragó la tierra*," Alfonso Rodríguez examines Rivera's use of temporal cycles toward the construction of meaning in the text. He argues, "In the attempt at creating a modern art form, Rivera elaborates a complex of aesthetic elements; one of these elements is time, which appears simultaneously as a major theme and a structural device" (Rodríguez 135). Paredes also suggests that the novella is structured temporally, through "twelve sketches (representing the months of the narrator's lost year), each introduced by a brief anecdote, and an introduction and closing" ("Contemporary Mexican American Literature" 1106). He argues, "The narrative device of anonymity enhances the representational quality of the work; Rivera, for the most part, is not depicting distinct individuals but an assortment of poor people bound in a common experience" (Paredes, "Contemporary Mexican American Literature" 1106). The lack of identification—temporal, spatial, and personal—begins the narrative of loss and illustrates a major theme in Chicana/o literature, one elucidated by Gloria Anzaldúa's *Borderlands/La Frontera: The New Mestiza*.

Anzaldúa's theorization illustrated that Mexican and Mexican American migrant workers exist at labor's borders: between nations and between sites of production and distribution. Nationally, Chicanas/os belong neither to Mexico nor to the United States, regardless of their citizenship. Ironically, the lack of belonging simultaneously reifies them as a threat to US nationalism: "The danger borders pose to North American critical theory is that through theory's use of borders as natural, inert, and transparent, the work the border actually does within discourse goes unnoticed. But *border* is no benign term sitting flatly, descriptively, within the economy of an argument. If that were the case, the border would not be so crucial to the still-under-negotiation concept of US national citizenship" (Brady, "The Fungibility of Borders" 186). In . . . *And the Earth Did Not Devour Him*, half of the novella's sections illustrate these themes most explicitly: "The Lost Year," "Why Do Y'all Go to School So Much?," "Hand in His Pocket," "A Silvery Night," " . . . And the Earth Did Not Devour Him," and "When We Arrive."

The untitled section that follows "The Lost Year" begins with the question, "Why do y'all go to school so much?" illustrating how young children understand class reality (Rivera 97).[23] One child asks another, presumably the principal narrator, why they should study because they have nothing to gain from it. The child who asks the question uses a southern expression—*y'all*—and may be one of the Anglo-American migrant workers appearing in other vignettes. Her perspective sheds light on the reality of laboring classes: poor whites, as well as poor Mexican Americans, have little hope of social mobility. The child summarizes the economic structure of the world deftly: "The ones who have to be on their toes are the ones who are higher up. They've got something to lose. They can end up where we're at. But for us what does it matter?" (Rivera 97). Many parents who are immigrants hope to put their children in a better economic position than their own, and thus, they encourage their children's education. In a cruel irony, this desire for economic improvement has terrible consequences for the narrator.

"Hand in His Pocket" is one of the longer vignettes exploring another narrative of loss: the disintegration of the family unit. Precisely as the nuclear family is being encouraged in Anglo-America, in Mexican America, both nuclear and extended families are being separated. For the narrator's parents, sending their child to relatives for access to education means the child has a chance to escape the parents' migrant fate. The narrator loses not only the protection of family but also the security in the *idea* of family, itself. His parents send him to stay with Don Laíto and Doña Bone, paying the couple board with the expectation that their son will be able to finish school, which will help him get a job where he does not have to migrate. Soon the narrator realizes that "everything that people used to say about them behind their backs was true" (Rivera 98). The couple steals and increasingly puts the narrator to work, and the wife engages in unconcealed prostitution.

In the most horrific turn of events, the couple kill a Mexican migrant worker whom the narrator calls a "wetback," presumably because the narrator was born in the United States and had been there longer than the victim or because the narrator was a guest worker with documentation.[24] The term *wetback* is an American English colloquialism; it differs from *mojado*,[25] the literal Spanish translation of the adjective *wet*. As Marta E. Sánchez explains, the two terms have been conflated through acts of authorship and translation, though each term has distinct and multiple connotations. Sánchez notes of the literary *mojado*, "To some Mexicans, he may represent a trickster figure, wily enough to pass undetected" (8). Moreover, "unlike 'wetback,' the semantic resonance does not extend into illegality or criminality" (Sánchez 8). Unlike the narrator's caretakers, the migrant worker they kill emphasizes their criminality—not his or the narrator's.

The belief that Don Laíto and Doña Bone would take care of the boy unravels brutally. They leave the bloody, dead migrant in the child's bed and make him dig the man's grave. In an even more disturbing use of power, the couple gives the boy a haunting gift a few months after he has left their care: "They had a present for me. A ring. They made me put it on and I remembered that it was the one the wetback had on that day. As soon as they left I tried to throw it away but I don't know why I couldn't" (Rivera 101). The boy now equates being away from home with danger, shame, and guilt; he feels that there is "Not even anyone to worry about him," as Doña Bone describes the murdered man. His belief leaves him vulnerable to the loss of familial and ethnonational kinship (Rivera 100). The narrator explains, "And the worst was that for a long time, as soon as I would see a stranger, I'd slip my hand into my pocket. That habit stayed with me for a long time" (Rivera 101).

"Hand in His Pocket" can also be interpreted through Castronovo's theory of *necro citizenship*, which describes the relationship between biological (individual) death and social (collective) death. The more poignant loss Rivera's text suggests in the context of necro citizenship is that the Mexican body can be denied social integration *within* Mexican America. Several times the narrator expresses disbelief that the couple could do this because his father had paid them. What he realizes is that even though Don Laíto and Doña Bone are not the "higher ups" his friend refers to, they are "higher up" on the social scale within Mexican America and thus have something to lose. Retaining their status drives them to obtain as much material comfort as possible, even if that means stealing from their own relatives, friends, and countrymen.

A vignette that illustrates how the narrator experiences another loss is "A Silvery Night." Testing the beliefs of his parents, the narrator speculates that if there is no Devil, then there is no God, though he cannot utter those words: "But if there's no devil neither is there . . . No I better not say it" (Rivera 106). The boy comes to understand atheism though a series of logical conclusions: "Now he understood everything. Those who summoned the devil went crazy, not because the devil appeared, but just the opposite, because he didn't appear" (Rivera 107). Extending this discourse from "A Silvery Night," the narrator continues to describe his loss of faith in social institutions and in God in ". . . And the Earth Did Not Devour Him." The death of family members due to illness devastates him. Tuberculosis removes extended family members, his aunt and uncle, from his life: "They had caught tuberculosis and had been sent to different sanitariums. So, between the brothers and sisters, they had split up the children as best they could" (Rivera 108). The couple dies, separated, and the narrator feels, for the first time, "hate and anger," which only increases when his father and brother suffer sunstroke (Rivera 108).

As the narrator carries his brother home in the titular story, ". . . And the Earth Did Not Devour Him," he questions the purpose of life itself. He tries to understand his physical relationship to the land. The boy asks his mother, "How come we're like this, like we're buried alive? Either the germs eat us alive or the sun burns us up" (Rivera 109). The narrator questions God's relationship to them, asking, "Why us, burrowed in dirt like animals with no hope for anything?" (Rivera 109). Religious studies scholar Hector Avalos likens this questioning to biblical meditations on suffering, especially in the rhetoric of Ecclesiastes.[26] He asserts that the author "questions the purpose of any human activity" (Avalos 160). The boy's questions lead to the experience of his greatest fear: "And without even realizing it, he said what he been wanting to say for a long time. He cursed God. Upon doing this, he felt that fear instilled in him by the years and his parents. For a second he saw the earth opening up to devour him" (Rivera 111). The story closes with one of the few first-person narrations of resistance in the text: "Not yet, you can't swallow me up yet. Someday yes. But I'll never know it" (Rivera 112). The questioning of God is another biblical parallel; however, as Avalos notes, while Job laments his suffering, he does not curse God, as the narrator does (161). When the earth does not devour the young narrator, he feels at peace.[27]

Toward the book's end, the unnamed youth concludes: "We never arrive" (Rivera 145). In the chapter titled "When We Arrive," the narrator's voice intermingles with other workers' as they migrate. Separated by a single line break in the text, the free and direct speech positions the reader as if he or she is on the truck with the workers. The multiple first-person narrations assert rage, hope, and resignation: "This is the last fuckin' year I come out here. As soon as we get to the farm, I'm getting the hell out" (Rivera 143). Some speakers are positive, but their optimism is quickly undercut by the reality and memory of their experiences: "If things go well this year, maybe we'll buy us a car so we won't have to travel this way, like cattle" (Rivera 144). As he listens to those around him, the narrator bitterly concludes: "Arriving and leaving, it's the same thing because we no sooner arrive and . . . the real truth of the matter . . . I'm tired of arriving. I really should say when we don't arrive because that's the real truth" (Rivera 145). The chapter ends with an emphasis on the psychological movement typical to migrant life: a constant vacillation between hope and disillusion. Even as the desire to arrive is articulated, it is problematized: the narrator utters what has become the community's mantra, "When we arrive, when we arrive. . . ," with despair and disbelief (Rivera 145).

Neocolonialism as We Have Known It: Latina/o America

Issues of cultural membership and political sovereignty developed nearly concurrently for Mexicans and Hispanic-descended populations of the Caribbean. These issues recall the prophetic and germinal essay "Nuestra América," written by José Martí in 1891.[28] Martí prophesied US Imperialism at the same time that Cuba, Puerto Rico, and the Philippines were nearing the end of Iberian colonialism. Martí had reason to believe that US expansion in North America would continue in the only direction it could: south. To prevent US dominance, Martí argued, Latin Americans needed to elide their racial and class differences to unite.[29] This conception of pan-Latino solidarity was hemispheric; the nineteenth century saw most of Spain's former colonies gain their independence, but these gains had the potential to leave Latin America fragmented and vulnerable to imperialism. Philosophy scholar Linda Martín Alcoff observes, "The concept of a pan-Latino identity is not new in Latin America: Simón Bolívar called for it nearly two hundred years ago as a strategy of anticolonialism but also because it provided a new name for the 'new peoples' that had emerged from the conquest. And influential leaders including Jose Martí and Che Guevara followed Bolívar in promoting a broad Latin American solidarity" ("Latinos and Categories of Race" 232). US neocolonialism within the Caribbean Basin occurred more than a century ago; why, then, does it have such resonance today?

The movement of colonized people into its own borders defines US neocolonialism. The United States has enabled this movement not only by facilitating poor economic conditions at home for the colonized people, drawing them here for work, but also by legislating the movement of populations to meet the United States' labor needs. The neocolonial practices of the United States in Mexico and the Hispanic Caribbean are very similar. While the specific events facilitating neocolonialism in Cuba and the Dominican Republic vary from those in Mexico and Puerto Rico, all four nations have experienced some form of US neocolonialism and thus converge in their literary responses to it.

Military occupations are part of the broad neocolonial process deemed necessary to protect US economic interests. The same patterns of economic manipulation, military intervention, and political reorganization of Mexico characterize the US occupations of Cuba, the Dominican Republic, the Philippines, and Puerto Rico. In 1917, the Jones Act made Puerto Ricans US citizens, making Puerto Rican men eligible for the draft during World War I. A generation later, while Anglo-American women became "Rosie the Riveter" working in industrial factories, Puerto Rican women on the island and the mainland completed the garment and millinery work Rosie left behind. The Bracero Program (1942–1964) legislated the employment of thousands of Mexicans in the United States, filling the places of Anglo-American men who had been drafted for World War II. Once the immediate labor need had ended, the United States had to accommodate a surplus population. Some workers returned to Mexico; others remained, working in manufacturing industries or as migrant workers performing seasonal harvests, as do the characters in . . . *And the Earth Did Not Devour Him*. Not all of the workers who arrived or remained during this period were *braceros*; some were immigrants derisively called wetbacks because they swam across the Rio Grande or entered via some other way undetected, as noted above.

Unlike immigrants who fled devastating agricultural conditions, such as the Irish during the potato famines (1847–1855) or the Europeans who fled depression following World War I (1920–1921), for the most part, immigrants from the Caribbean have not come to the United States to begin a new life and forget their homelands. As Juan Flores has persuasively argued, comparative analyses with European immigration patterns are ineffective: "Puerto Ricans came here as foreign nationals, a fact that American citizenship and accommodationist ideology tend to obscure; but they also arrived as a subject people" ("Puerto Rican Literature" 213). Cuba and the Dominican Republic might not seem to fit the neocolonial model I have been defining because they are not US territories. US neocolonialism, however, actually functions best for the colonizer when one nation influences another without direct annexation, as in the cases of Cuba and the Dominican Republic. Such relationships allow the colonizer to profit through the development of new markets for goods, access to natural resources, and a supply of low-cost labor without the permanent military, socioeconomic, or political responsibilities of governing and maintaining a national infrastructure. US neocolonialism is responsible for the two major catalysts of Cuban and Dominican migration: the rise of Fidel Castro and the fall of Rafael Leónidas Trujillo. It is important to consider how the United States' early twentieth-century occupations of Cuba (1898–1902, 1906–1909, 1912–1913) and the Dominican Republic (1916–1924, 1964–1965) led to these events.

In the months preceding the close of the Cuban-Spanish-American War (1896–1898), the US Senate vigorously debated what the role of the nation should be in the Hispanic Caribbean once the war ended. Cuba and Puerto Rico were fighting for independence from Spain's colonialism, just as North American colonies had fought Great Britain for their independence during the American Revolutionary War. The Philippines were also fighting for independence from Spain—what relationship would the United States cultivate with this archipelago? In shaping the postwar development of the islands, would the United States be repeating the colonialism of European nations? The importance of the Hispanic Caribbean increased after the economic crash and recession that began in 1893. Political stability in the region was necessary for the continued production of goods and the opening of new markets. At the very least, US investments in the sugar industry had to be protected; beyond that, unregulated trade opportunities, access to natural resources, and strategic military launch points were compelling incentives to aid the Spanish colonies.[30] The crux of Congress's debates was not *if* the United States should deploy its increasing political power but *how* it should deploy that power. Any relationship the United States developed with these islands had to be planned carefully; for example, Senator George Vest of Missouri argued, "Every schoolboy knows that the Revolutionary War was fought against the colonial system of Europe."[31] It would be hypocritical for the United States to engage in colonialism, since the nation was founded on the principle of self-governance. The debates continued through February 1899, after which the Treaty of Paris was finally ratified.

Not long after the Cuban-Spanish-American War, the United States assisted the Panamanians in the Thousand Days' War against the French. When Panama achieved independence in 1903, the United States took over the construction of the Panama Canal, completing it in 1914. The canal remained under American control until 1999, giving the United States strategic military and economic control of the Caribbean Basin for nearly a century. The significance of such control ought not to be underestimated. The United States' political activities in the Caribbean Basin, in Central America, and later in nations in the Pacific clearly reflect the United States' hemispheric, not continental, expansionism.[32]

The United States used two principal strategies to reorganize Cuba and Puerto Rico. First, US-appointed administrators governed the islands so the islands' agricultural systems could be replaced by industrial production. Low-cost labor and freedom from taxation inspired American companies and local governments to first consolidate agricultural production. Small farms called *fincas* were seized and converted to larger farms. When the sugar industry began to decline and the Great Depression worsened in the 1930s, the United States industrialized the islands. Though both the mainland and the local populations reaped the benefits of industrialization, the negative consequences for the environment and living conditions on the islands remain significant. Extensive farmlands in Puerto Rico became the sites for pharmaceutical and garment factories. These economic changes displaced many Puerto Rican agricultural workers; they had to migrate to urban areas or to the United States for work. Urban slums, such as *La Perla* of San Juan, developed as people relocated to the city in search of work but were unable to buy property or build permanent homes. While President Barack Obama's intent to close tax loopholes would help nations such as Mexico and the Dominican Republic, Puerto Rico, as a US territory, remains vulnerable to continued neocolonialism. Cuba, now under the control of Raúl Castro, is becoming capitalist; Cubans may now purchase and sell homes, vehicles, and other property. While the United States has not completely lifted its embargo, family relief visits have increased, and Raúl Castro has indicated that he will open Cuba to foreign investment, especially tourist industries.[33]

The second form of reorganization occurred solely in Puerto Rico. Beginning in 1937, through the help of local government officials, the US government legislated and carried out the sterilization of thousands of dark-skinned, illiterate, and poor women to solve the "overpopulation" problem. The campaign united neocolonial labor discourse with that of eugenics. This massive sterilization campaign relied on the deception that *la operación* was temporary birth control.[34] The campaign encouraged single, childless young women to enter the workforce and help support their younger siblings. Such specific legislated redistribution of populations into US continental borders defines neocolonialism in opposition to colonialism. The process of neocolonialism in the Caribbean has been rapid and quite visible: first, economic interests require political stability; military intervention or political manipulation creates stability; and finally, political reorganization maintains political and economic stability. Neocolonialism has been more successful in some aspects than in others. Despite the United States' economic and legislative control of Puerto Rico, the island suffers economically; a large percentage of the population is dependent on US social programs, and the commonwealth's bond rating was downgraded due to escalating debt.[35]

The migration patterns of other Caribbean peoples reveal a significant difference in their acculturation. The "first wave" of Cuban immigrants, who chose exile rather than life under Fidel Castro, popularly believed that the United States was a temporary home, not a new homeland. The "second wave" of Cubans, over 125,000 refugees, entered the United States via the Mariel Boatlift in 1980.[36] Dominicans have also emigrated in two major waves: (1) an initial exile wave escaping the dictatorship of Trujillo or the political instability immediately following his assassination in 1961 and (2) a second wave, following an economic crisis in the 1980s, of approximately 225,000 refugees. Evident in Cuban texts such as *Our House in the Last World* and *Dreaming in Cuban* and Dominican novels such as *How the García Girls Lost Their Accents* and *Soledad*, both of these waves of immigrants believed that their migration to the United States would be temporary.

The rise of communism in Cuba and the political instability in the Dominican Republic have been responses to the United States' persistent interference. When Fidel Castro assumed power in 1959, he effectively removed American influence over Cuba, which President Fulgencio Batista facilitated. Similarly, Rafael Leónidas Trujillo rose to power after the United States had occupied the Dominican Republic for nearly a decade and then left him in charge of the Guardia Nacional. Trujillo's coup d'état and lengthy dictatorship greatly reduced American influence in the nation's affairs, particularly its economic development and agricultural production. Trujillo reduced the national debt, including paying off the country's loans from the US government and banks.[37] The consistently US-backed leadership of Joaquín Balaguer (1960–1962, 1966–1978, 1986–1996) following the deposition of Trujillo's elected successor, Juan Bosch (February 27, 1963–September 25, 1963), suggests that the United States' intervention lies at the core of these political shifts and subsequent large migrations.

If we explore Chicana/o and Latina/o literature from their shared project of representing neocolonial experience, it becomes evident that the tropes of the literatures converge more often than they diverge. Until the early twenty-first century, many scholars in English literary studies studied Cuban, Dominican, Mexican, and Puerto Rican American literatures in isolation from one another, tending to represent the groups as culturally and politically homogeneous.[38] The colonial uses of internal race and class markers remains somewhat neglected in contemporary literary criticism; knowing the origins and uses of the markers is critical in understanding the heterogeneity of the groups. Race hierarchy, in particular, is an aspect of that heterogeneity; it is perpetuated through *colorism*.[39] Colorism is a system of preference for lighter skin shades within ethnic communities. These hierarchies are a recurring part of the narrative of loss and central to the stories of *Drown*; they illustrate Alice Walker's early warning about the dangers of oppressive intersectionality: "For colorism, like colonialism, sexism, and racism, impedes us" (291).

A consistent project in the analysis of Chicana/o and Latina/o literature is the development of an appropriate theoretical vocabulary that does more than apply concepts that do not fit the historical conditions shaping the literatures.[40] In the article "Ethnicity, Ethics, and Latino Aesthetics," a precursor to his book *Mestizaje: Critical Uses of Race in Chicano Culture* (2006), Rafael Pérez-Torres raises important questions regarding the terms scholars have relied on within Chicana/o and Latina/o studies, including *Chicana/o*, *Latina/o*, *latinidad*, and *mestizaje*.[41] None of these terms is encompassing, and each of them is potentially problematic, including mestizaje. Because *mestizaje* calls to mind a false binary between mestizos—"mixed" people—and presumably "unmixed" people, it is less useful to this analysis. Scholarship on the construction of whiteness challenges the idea that anyone, perhaps excepting aboriginal peoples, can remain physiologically "unmixed."[42]

Spain's efforts to distinguish Christian bloodlines from Islamic and Judaic ancestries originated the use of terms to differentiate ethnic groups. Church and local administrative officials transported the practice to New World *colonias* to record different racial categories at the birth, marriage, and death of the Spanish settlers and the indigenous, as well as their offspring, *criollos.* Ramón A. Gutiérrez offers this stunning fact about the categories: "Mexico's eighteenth-century legal dictionaries contained as many as fifty different racial mixtures codified as the *Regimen de Castas* (Society of Castes). The Regimen was a code of legal color distinctions most of which were impossible to distinguish visually" ("Hispanic Diaspora and Chicano Identity in the United States" 205). Terms such as *Hispano* and *Indio* were used to differentiate Mexican Americans in New Mexico and Arizona from those in California, who referred to themselves as *Californios*, even though the racial compositions of these people were very similar.

In relation to mestizaje, Pérez-Torres affirms postcolonialism as a theory capable of articulating the performative and enunciative aspects of Chicana/o and Latina/o literature.[43] He argues, "The comparative work that has most sought to understand the particularities of that evasive term 'Chicano and Latino identity' has been the most grounded. Only in specific localities do the contradictions of that term make themselves evident and play themselves out. That is, Latino studies as a form of postcolonial thought makes itself anti-ideological and highlights the enunciative" ("Ethnicity, Ethics, and Latino Aesthetics," Pérez-Torres 545). While we both draw on Homi Bhabha's sense of identity as a product of construction, of *becoming*, Pérez-Torres' position on postcolonialism seems intrinsically concerned with the relationship between dominant and subaltern groups from distinct nations or between majority and minority communities as that relationship is negotiated within the subaltern nation, not the metropolis.

Pérez-Torres discusses the shift in the term's meaning within Chicana/o, Latina/o and Latin American contexts in his more recent contribution to the *Routledge Companion to Latina/o Literature* on the topic of mestizaje. His further nuanced discussion of mestizaje could be especially useful if applied specifically to US neocolonialism: "Since the term arises from a history of invasion and, often, sexual violation, the word also highlights the dissonance between identities that allow unequal access to power, social standing, and privilege. Mestizaje, however, does not necessarily link the patterns of Chicana/o and Latina/o histories beyond a general acknowledgement of the experience of colonial oppression. Frances Aparicio has usefully suggested that "the term 'Latinidades' can be deployed to document the processes by which diverse Latino/as interact with each other, subordinate, and transculturate each other" ("Mestizaje," Pérez-Torres 625). The notion that "culture as a form of becoming emphasizes the dynamic and fluid over the static and the formalized" is striking when applied to relationships within ethnonational groups ("Ethnicity, Ethics, and Latino Aesthetics," Pérez-Torres 544). Such interactions are the focus of the majority of texts examined here. Certainly, this model might be fruitful in discussions of literature published immediately following Cuban-Spanish-American War. Postcolonialism is not as consistently useful, though, in analyzing contemporary literature because the United States has moved, and continues to move, neocolonial subjects into its own borders.

After the mid-twentieth century, in addition to regional self-identifications, the use of politicized terms such as *Chicana/o* by Mexican Americans and *Nuyorican* by Puerto Ricans reflected the increasing political diversity of these communities. The most significant aspect of any of these terms is that whom they name changes over time. Self-identification becomes more complex as the discourse of authenticity moves from rhetoric outside neocolonial communities to rhetoric within them. As Martín Alcoff suggests, "Latin America itself is undoubtedly the most diverse continent in the world, which in turn creates extreme racial and ethnic diversity *within* Latino communities" (234, emphasis in original). Though problematic, the critical separation of Latina/o identities has reaped some benefit; we have learned about specific historical events conditioning each group's acculturation. By not looking at these literatures comparatively, though, scholars have missed opportunities to understand the groups' shared cultural nuances. Examining the processes and effects of US neocolonialism expands a narrow focus on assimilation politics into a broad focus on neocolonial communities' attempts to define their relationships among one another.

Differences in the immigration patterns and the degrees of acculturation among Cubans, Dominicans, and Puerto Ricans are attributable to the United States' distinct relationships with each nation. Puerto Rico's status as a "free associated state" for example, results in continuous migration between the United States and the island. Cubans have the benefit of immediate political asylum.[44] Dominicans, unlike both groups, have no special entrance to the United States; their visa process is long and compounded by their civil laws, making it very difficult to emigrate. Cubans and Dominicans have not enjoyed the relative ease of travel back and forth to their homelands, as have Puerto Ricans and documented Mexicans; most perform very dangerous sea travel in an attempt to reach the US mainland. Since the 1990s, Dominicans have been migrating and working in Puerto Rico, where they have better access to employment and medical care. Puerto Rico has become a stepping-stone to the United States. The complexity of initial migration and the socioeconomic disparities among Puerto Rican, Cuban, and Dominican immigrants is an important theme in the stories of *Drown*.

The authors examined in this chapter defy the notion that their work is primarily concerned with relationships between racial minority and majority communities in the United States. Chicana/o and Latina/o writers are carefully representing how diverse political ideologies, sexual orientations, regional identities, and racial compositions of people determine an individual's status within his or her ethnic community.[45] Readers see Chicanas/os existing in worlds clearly outside the mainstream. In . . . *And the Earth Did Not Devour Him*, Anglos rarely speak, though they are referenced. In *Drown*, the only mentions of Anglo-Americans occur in work or school contexts; most of the narrative action occurs in *el barrio*, where its blocks and its residents are contained by the projects, elevated trains, bridges, and highways.

"This is How You Lose It": Navigating *Dominicanidad* in *Drown*

One of the epigraphs starting this chapter is emblematic of the cultural ocean Junot Díaz navigates as a Dominican American writer. Díaz has noted his lack of recognition from Dominican *literati*, despite his international visibility. Early in his career, Díaz asserted, "I had to leave Santo Domingo to even have a chance to be acknowledged by elites. These are not people who would sit down at my grandfather's house in Villa Juana to have dinner with me" (qtd. in Diógenes Céspedes, Silvio Torres-Saillant, and Junot Díaz 893). Not all Dominican American writers have experienced such exclusion. The work of Julia Alvarez, whose affluent parents fled Trujillo's rule as political exiles, has not only been well received but also catalyzed state-sponsored revision of public memorials of the Trujillo era.[46] Díaz's parents, in contrast, were poor and fled post-Trujillo instability as economic immigrants; his work has not met with the critical success Alvarez's has in their home nation. When discussing the success of *The Brief Wondrous Life of Oscar Wao*, Díaz returns to his indictment of Dominican classism. This disparity in reception is critical in reading Díaz's fiction; he is always concerned with how difference is used to maintain hierarchies.

The differences internal to Dominicans—differences of class, race, and sexuality—structure Díaz's fictive world. The stories in *Drown* defy the perception that Dominican American literature is mainly concerned with assimilation to the Anglo-American mainstream. Rather, these stories explore how class status, sexual orientation, and racial appearance determine one's *dominicanidad.*[47] Winner of the 2008 Pulitzer Prize in Fiction, *The Brief Wondrous Life of Oscar Wao* explores the cyclical migrations of the Cabral family, problematizing the Dominican exile community's loss of personal history and social status. The novel, though, follows the broader analysis of migration first depicted in Díaz's short story collection *Drown* (1996). Both texts depict characters that migrate cyclically, rejecting oppositional conceptions of acculturation and negotiating racial constructs present in both the Dominican Republic and the United States. Because most of the characters in *Drown* are first- or "1.5"- generation Dominican Americans, they have much in common with the characters in Rivera's . . . *And the Earth Did Not Devour Him.*

Díaz's stories are distinct not only from modern European immigrant narratives that privilege acculturation but also from contemporary Hispanophone exile narratives that privilege nostalgia. Díaz's work engages various immigrant literature tropes but ultimately privileges the rejection of most of them, especially the trope associated with acculturation in a Latina/o context, arrival. Early reviews of Díaz's second collection of stories, *This Is How You Lose Her* (2012), focus on his language use and character development, suggesting that Díaz returns to the thematic and stylistic project of *Drown* but narrows his focus to loss in sexual and emotional relationships.[48] The stories of *Drown* represent the author's first efforts to narrativize Dominican migration and the migrant's experiences of disillusion and poverty in Latina/o America.[49] This final section of chapter 1 discusses how the Dominican immigration stories presented in *Drown* are narratives of loss.

The introduction argued that for early twentieth-century European immigrant groups such as the Irish, Italians, or Germans, *arrival* meant social mobility, whereas for Spanish Caribbean immigrants, *arrival* means socioeconomic empowerment without loss of cultural specificity. *Arrival,* thus defined, has never been possible for Hispanophone Caribbean people. People who are dark-skinned, working-class, or recent migrants, or who retain their original linguistic and cultural practices, face barriers to such acculturation. Sociologic research illustrates that Dominicans face discrimination wherever they migrate. In "Reconstructing Racial Identity: Ethnicity, Color, and Class among Dominicans in the United States and Puerto Rico," sociologist Jorge Duany explains how Dominicans experience discrimination in both the United States and Puerto Rico: "In both receiving countries, Dominicans face the intense stigmatization, stereotyping, prejudice, and discrimination to which all people of African origin are subjected" (148). Narratives about the nonexilic immigrations of Dominicans and Cubans in the 1980s expose this rejection.

Portrayals of Dominicans highlight characters that do not leave their country for temporary political refuge or an illusory economic windfall. Rather, they migrate to the United States so they can earn enough money to return and survive in their nation of origin. As narratives of loss, Díaz's stories undermine early twentieth-century depictions of immigrant experience such as the notion that acculturation is desirable and possible. Dominicans are rapidly becoming the largest Hispanic immigrant population in cities such as New York, Miami, Paterson, and San Juan.[50] Unlike Puerto Ricans and Cubans, Dominicans have not significantly benefited from US neocolonialism, especially the second wave of immigrants, which was economic. Literary scholar Marisel Moreno makes this critical distinction about the nature of immigration in the literature of the best-known Dominican American authors, Julia Alvarez and Junot Díaz: "They each represent a distinct type of Dominican exile, political, and economic, respectively" (104). As economic immigrants, Díaz's characters face a literal immigration problem: their unending physical migration either within their nations of origin or between that homeland and the United States.[51] These narratives also function within the discourse community of Latina/o America, not within the broader discourse community of Anglo America. *Drown* shares a lack of temporality with the novella . . . *And the Earth Did Not Devour Him*. *Drown* also utilizes shorter prose and shifts in voice, crafting the stories in a fragmented rhythm that actively resists and contrasts early twentieth-century European immigrant and twentieth-century Chicana/o and Latina/o narratives patterned on the arc of Aristotelian dramaturgy: rising action, crisis, dénouement, and resolution.

The analysis of *Drown* offered here begins with the premise that Dominican identity is as much a social navigation premigration as it is postmigration. In a 2008 interview conducted by Katherine Miranda, Díaz complains about his lack of recognition at home. When asked about the success of his novel and his receipt of the Pulitzer Prize, Díaz noted the reverse process of recognition in the Dominican diaspora: "I don't want to say this, but sometimes you have to get recognized from outsiders before your own culture values what you are" ("Diaspora and Redemption," Díaz 27). The author's experience is visible in his construction of diasporic characters that exist in a cultural stasis, in a third, always becoming cultural space, where they never fully become "American."[52] Díaz's comments reveal a key trope in his narratives: Dominican immigrants are often perceived as not truly Dominican either, because they did not grow into adulthood on the island, did not rise to elite social status on it, or have somehow lost their innate dominicanidad.[53] Even though forty years, or two generations in novel time, separate the publication of the two books, the characters in Díaz's stories are strikingly similar to those of Tomás Rivera. They all experience continual physical migration that transforms into psycho-cultural migration as they reassess their place within their respective cultural diasporas.

In the introduction to *Location of Culture*, Homi Bhabha argues, "What is theoretically innovative, and politically crucial, is the need to think beyond narratives of originary and initial subjectivities and to focus on these moments or processes that are produced in the articulation of cultural difference" (1). This chapter has foregrounded analyses of the cyclical migration of Rivera's and Díaz's characters because the migrations position the characters as always in a process of cultural navigation. Bhabha's often-cited use of the term *in-between* describes the kind of ethnic identity negotiation recurring in the contemporary fiction works in this study, especially the stories of *Drown*. Thus, the *in-between*, *becoming*, or the *beyond* is an intermediate cultural space between a past and a future cultural space. The fact that Bhabha draws on the performance art of Chicano Guillermo Gomez-Peña and Puerto Rican visual artist Pepón Osorio to establish his concept of *beyond* is telling: it suggests that the experience of Chicanas/os and Latinas/os have much in common despite their distinct ethnonational histories.

Defining his conceptualization, Bhabha notes, "The borderline work of culture demands an encounter with 'newness' that is not part of the continuum of the past and present. It creates a sense of the new as an insurgent act of cultural translation" (7). Bhabha's theorization of *beyond* is a complex and interesting space because individuals consistently make choices to define themselves against a past or articulate a not yet accessible future. Postcolonialism, in this way, is useful in interpreting certain stories, especially the narrative of loss. He asserts, "These in-between spaces provide the terrain for elaborating strategies of selfhood-singular or communal—that initiate new signs of identity, and innovative sites of collaboration, and contestation, in the act of defining the idea of society itself" (Bhabha 7). Bhabha, however, focuses more on the relationship between the individual and the new nation—in this case, the United States—as the contested space for the construction of home. In "The Postcolonial and the Postmodern," Bhabha returns to dialectical questions of nation: "The postcolonial prerogative seeks to affirm and extend a new collaborative dimension, both within the margins of the nation-space and across boundaries between nations and peoples" (175). The reading of *Drown* presented here problematizes the relationship with the old home—the Dominican Republic—to illuminate the compounding of losses associated with US neocolonialism.

Stuart Hall's work is especially useful in understanding the relationship between the old home and the new one. Hall asserts that identity is "always constructed through memory, fantasy, narrative and myth. Cultural identities are the points of identification, the unstable points of identification or suture, which are made within the discourses of history and culture. They are not an essence but a positioning. Hence there is always a politics of identity, a politics of position, which has no absolute guarantee in an unproblematic, transcendental 'law of origin'" ("Cultural Identity and Diaspora" 113). Díaz's characters are, as Hall describes, diasporic people; they "are without the illusion of any actual 'return' to the past. Either they will never, in any literal sense, return or the places to which they return will have been transformed out of recognition by the remorseless processes of modern transformation. In that sense, there is no going 'home' again" ("Culture, Community, Nation" 363). The characters do not look at immigration as a path to empowerment; it is a temporary solution to dire poverty.

In *Drown*, the new nation-centered dreams associated with arrival—material successes, freedom of movement, cultural retention—have already been abandoned. Characters have declared arrival inaccessible, and they find themselves drowning in the wake of its impossibility. The primary function of Díaz's stories, as narratives of loss, is to expose the ideologies about immigration created within the diaspora or projected onto Hispanic Caribbean migrants.[54] Díaz challenges readers to question persistent beliefs about the American dream, the homogeny of Hispanophone people, and the interaction within minority communities. Hall's view of identity as a process occurring along a continuum is also key to understanding Díaz's authorial project: "We have to now reconceptualize identity as a process of identification, and that is a different matter. It is something that happens over time, that is never absolutely stable, that is subject to the play of history and the play of difference" ("Ethnicity, Identity and Difference" 15). In the stories of *Drown*, the "play" of these differences becomes evident in the author's critique of both US neocolonialism and Dominican hegemonic discourses on race, class, and sexuality. Díaz uses the narrative of loss to structure the challenges of self-positioning within the Dominican diaspora.

The principal arguments made about *Drown* include discussions of its deconstruction of Dominican masculinity (Méndez 2013), its function as ethnic and sexual bildungsroman, its engagement of sexual citizenship (Stringer

2013; Heredia 2010), and its role as "ghetto fiction" (Di Iorio Sandín 2009). For example, in "Passing and the State in Junot Díaz's *Drown*," Dorothy Stringer argues for the primacy of national identity: "Díaz's fiction could easily be identified with the still-conventional, middlebrow immigrant narrative arching cleaning from individual *Bildung* to national inclusion" (113). The pairing of nation and sexual citizenship elides Díaz's larger and most consistent point: diasporic Dominicans are stigmatized first by nondiasporic Dominicans in terms of cultural belonging, next by Anglo-America in terms of race, and last but not least by Cubans, Mexicans, and Puerto Ricans in terms of class.[55]

Danny Méndez focuses on Díaz's critiques of the intersections of internalized racism and homophobia originating within Dominican culture. His reading of *Drown* complements my own: "Identity processes begun in the Dominican Republic prefigure Dominican identities as the communities in the diaspora. Once within the continental United States Dominicans may experience the additional limits of citizenship but these limits do not originate in migration to the United States; they begin on the island. Thus, it is a mistake to conflate hybridization as such with migration to the United States; rather, it references long-standing Hispanic Caribbean cultural pattern to which members of the diaspora gravitate as they (re)create it in their respective diaspora communities" (5).

Díaz's use of the narrative of loss structures the problems of the Dominican diaspora. He creates a nexus of relationships between the author, narrator, characters, and readers to illustrate the losses that the desire for belonging in Latina/o America creates. Once arrival loses its appeal, how might one narrate Dominican migration experience? The title of *Drown* is the dominant metaphor for the struggle of the characters. They drown—economically and culturally—and are well aware of their failure to arrive. Most characters remain itinerant and emotionally resigned. While they are not agricultural migrant workers as are the characters in . . . *And the Earth Did Not Devour Him*, they are no less nomadic. Yunior and his family must learn how to survive and access power in each urban locale because they have no permanent physical home: "In Díaz's *Drown*, the emotions Mohanty and Martin denote as contrastive within the 'being home' and the 'not being home' paradigms occur in both the Dominican Republic and the United States" (Méndez 126).[56] The characters within *Drown* are challenged to choose how home is, before and after migration.

Because Díaz rejects arrival and foregrounds the narrative of loss, his immigration narrative differs significantly from those projected through the popular Anglo-American rhetoric of immigration. Though the dominant metaphor of the collection is aquatic, most of the narrative action in *Drown* occurs in landed, specifically Dominican, Latino, or Afro-Latino but not Anglo, spaces. The collection begins in *el campo*, the Dominican Republic's premigration rural spaces where poverty is the norm, violence is unpunished, and sexual predation is concealed. The stories are alternatively set in *el barrio*, the United States' postimmigration urban ethnic space enclosed by projects, elevated trains, and highways. The liminality of emigration leaves Díaz's characters always on the threshold of the immigrant wave: sometimes floating, sometimes treading, and sometimes drowning in the spaces between el campo and el barrio.

The stories "Ysrael," "Aguantando," "Drown," and "How to Date a Browngirl, Blackgirl, Whitegirl, or Halfie" reveal how Dominican immigration creates a diaspora that begins with an ever-growing class distance on the island. The stories "Ysrael" and "Aguantando" feature protagonists reconciling abandonment and expectation. "Drown" delineates the fruitless struggle for characters to become American *and* Dominican. Finally, "How to Date a Browngirl, Blackgirl, Whitegirl, or Halfie" depicts how first-generation immigrants negotiate racial and gender constructs in ethnic America. Díaz's characters are immigrants whom I consider to be 1.5ers.[57] They immigrated with their parents as teenagers or young adults; they were not born in the United States. The combination of their newness to the country and their youth makes them concerned with daily survival, not future accomplishment. From an economic standpoint, these characters live day to day, witnessing what they perceive to be other immigrant groups climbing to success while they remain underpaid, on government assistance, or resorting to crime because of barriers to employment such as racial discrimination or their use of Spanish as a dominant language.[58]

"Ysrael" depicts an intranational pattern of migration between two arenas of Dominican life: urban poverty and rural poverty. Nowhere are descriptions of an island paradise: even for the older generations, matter-of-fact assessments of a sustained but not luxurious past replaces nostalgia. The narrator, Yunior, recalls his grandfather bemoaning a time when "a man could still make a living from his *finca*, when the United States wasn't something folks planned on" (Díaz 73). The United States is a source of temporary employment, allowing the rural poor to relocate to the capital or to retire in less severe poverty.[59] The story portrays two brothers' contrasting experiences of this internal migration. For Yunior's brother Rafa, rural Ocoa is a nightmare: "In the campo there was nothing to do, no one to see. You didn't get television or electricity, and Rafa, who was older and expected more, woke up every morning pissy and dissatisfied" (Díaz 4). While Yunior has to be forced onto the bus to Ocoa every summer, he grows reaccustomed to the conditions and boredoms of rural poverty. He asserts, "I didn't mind these summers, wouldn't forget them the way Rafa would" (Díaz 5). Their spatialized relationship as brothers explains their different responses to Ocoa.

Rural Ocoa offers Yunior a sense of importance as a city boy and as his brother's pal that Rafa denies him in Santo Domingo: "In the capital Rafa and I fought so much that our neighbors took to smashing broomsticks over us to break it up, but in the campo it wasn't like that. In the campo we were friends" (Díaz 5). At home, Rafa asserts his dominance by using slurs that expose Dominican racism against Haitians: "Back in the capital, he rarely said anything to me except Shut up, pendejo. Unless, of course, he was mad, and then he had about 500 routines he liked to lay on me. Most of them had to do with my complexion, my hair, the size of my lips. It's the Haitian, he'd say to his buddies" (Díaz 6). These taunts combine typical childlike behavior with a state-sanctioned racism intended to distinguish Dominicans from Haitians. They powerfully reinscribe attitudes about "the proper place" of Haitians—at work for, but not at home in, the country—encouraged by Trujillo. This *antihaitianismo* was perpetuated most recently with a 2013 court ruling stripping Haitian-born Dominicans of their citizenship; as of 2015, Dominicans of Haitian descent are routinely being deported if they cannot provide documentation of their birth in Dominican territory.[60] Díaz was a highly visible critic of the legislation. Subsequently, he became the object of derisive comments about his dominicanidad.[61]

Yunior gives the reader a sense of the disparities and disillusionment the image the United States—generally referred to as *North America* or *Nueva York*—conjures in the minds of the boys long before they immigrate. Perhaps because so few Dominicans had "made it" in the United States by the 1970s, Yunior and those around him are very suspicious of anything connected to America. Nueva York becomes a taunting imaginary: the children simultaneously long for what it offers and loathe the offering. Objects from Nueva York mark those who possess them as traitorous. Ysrael, the mutilated child in Ocoa, is doubly marked. His face is horrifically disfigured; because he is a friendless victim of bullying, his father buys him clothes and toys from New York, marking him as an outsider in his own community. These gifts provide Yunior a reason to hate, not just taunt, the boy: "Ysrael's sandals were of stiff leather and his clothes were North American. I looked over at Rafa, but my brother seemed unperturbed" (Díaz 15).

Ysrael's material possessions, such as his kite and stiff leather sandals, do not bother Rafa; the younger boy's idolization of America does, because it reminds Rafa of his own disjointed relationship to the country: "'Where did you get that?' I asked. 'Nueva York,' he said. 'From my father.' 'No shit! Our father's there too!' I shouted. I looked at Rafa, who for an instant, frowned. Our father only sent us letters and an occasional shirt or pair of jeans at Christmas" (Díaz 16). Rafa and Yunior's father's has been away for years, but his occasional letters and gifts revive their expectations and subsequent feelings of resignation about Nueva York. When Ysrael asserts that the American doctors are going to help him, Rafa attempts to dash the younger boy's hopes: "They're lying to you. They probably just felt sorry" (Díaz 17). Nueva York offers familial and material comfort to very few. Rafa's unwillingness to believe in Nueva York is not merely a thinly veiled hatred for his father. Rather, Nueva York is a riptide of lost family members and hopes.

The story "Ysrael" is one of Díaz's earliest and most significant uses of the narrative of loss. He challenges the desirability of migration to the United States. The perception of the United States by the wave of Dominicans immigrating in the years following Trujillo's 1961 assassination were very different from those of Puerto Ricans and Cubans immigrating during the same era.[62] Díaz engages the readers' and the characters' (Yunior's and Ysrael's) beliefs about migration. Even though Dominicans immigrate, they do not articulate the sense of hope about the United States that Puerto Ricans often do, nor the exilic nostalgia for the old country the first wave of Cubans often express. Dominicans' expectation is to immigrate several times for the explicit purpose of surviving financially on the island.

Aguantando means bearing or standing, in the sense of "putting up with" a situation. The narrator Yunior juxtaposes several kinds of aguantando: what his mother had to bear with a husband absent for five years; what Yunior had to bear as a child waiting endlessly for his father's return; and what they all had to bear as an impoverished family in urban New Jersey. The word is a nice aural resonance on the collection's title: non–Spanish speakers might recognize the word *agua* and suppose it has something to do with water and/or drowning. Moreover, it evokes the principal mode of Dominican immigration: travel by boat and swimming, which often leads to the shark attack or drowning deaths of migrants.[63]

The story offers a radically different migration discourse than that of arrival: rather than drowning in cultural difference, characters drown in expectations of escaping poverty and reuniting as nuclear families. As Yunior asserts, their poverty is so comprehensive that few are worse off: "We lived south of the *Cementerio Nacional* in a wood-frame house with three rooms. We were poor.

The only way we could have been poorer was to live in the *campo* or to have been Haitian immigrants, and Mami regularly offered these to us as brutal consolation" (Díaz 70). This story focuses on the boys' repeated disappointment in their Papi's failure to send for them or to return from Nueva York in a grand style. Yunior notes, "The year Papi came for us, the year I was nine, we expected nothing. There were no signs to speak of" (Díaz 77). Rafa cautions him that though they receive a letter, Papi might not come at all: "It ain't the first time he's made that promise" (Díaz 82). As the adult narrator, Yunior is as bitter as the teenage Rafa. He recognizes the distance between himself and his father, even though Yunior is named after him: "He was pieces of my friends' fathers, of the domino players on the corner, pieces of Mami and Abuelo. I didn't know him at all. I didn't know that he'd abandoned us. That this waiting for him was all a sham" (Díaz 70). Yunior decries Papi's deferred literal arrival due to his failed metaphorical arrival.

The boy's father, Ramón de Las Casas, looms large in these stories, but readers do not learn what actually happened to him until the final story, "Negocios." In that story, Yunior has become aware of his father's extramarital affair with a Puerto Rican woman, as well as his bigamous marriage to a Cuban woman. The ethnicity of these women is suggestive—Díaz is likely criticizing Dominican immigrants' desire to move higher up on the Caribbean social ladder, especially when abandoning your national identity facilitates such movement. In a realistic manner, it reflects Dominican immigration to Puerto Rico beginning in the 1990s; rather than undergoing the expensive and lengthy process of obtaining a visa, Dominicans have gone to Puerto Rico as a first step to marry and gain citizenship.[64] By the time Yunior enters high school, his father has abandoned both of his families, only to begin his own cycle of migration between the two households: he shows up every few months asking both of his wives for money.[65]

The only selection in which Yunior's father is referenced but conspicuously absent is in the titular story, "Drown." The story depicts Yunior's life after his immigration to the United States. In patches of neighborhoods and relationships, he narrates his cultural migration within the United States. Yunior and his family experienced repeat migration related to economics within the Dominican Republic; in New Jersey, their migration reflects not only economic but also emotional resignations. One of these resignations introduces an element that appears one other time in the collection: homosexuality. Yunior describes his friendship with Beto, another young man who, like Ysrael, is doubly marked: he is gay, and he leaves el barrio for college. The story combines the present-day return with Yunior's flashbacks to two years prior, when Beto first leaves.

The Repeating Ebb: Yunior as Storyteller

Danny Méndez reads the stories of *Drown* as explicit illustrations of how one "becomes . . . a Dominican diasporic subject" (117–18). His analysis of the collection frames the narrator's struggles through the metaphor of return, as varying moments of Freudian uncanniness.[66] In the story "Drown," return threatens Yunior's resistance to Dominican compulsory masculinity. The return of Rafa's and Yunior's father threatens the reinscription of a premigration dominicanidad, one created and modeled by Trujillo. Méndez explains "*un tíguere* refers to the kind of cunning working-class urban male who, through his wits and *cojones* (testicles), understands the art of social mobility. This was the image of Trujillo that was projected by his propagandists, who in this way made even his vices—his corruption, his brutality, his lechery, and sexism—into virtues" (127). A former soldier of Trujillo, Ramon de Las Casas fails to be *un tíguere* on the island but is somewhat more successful in using women in New York to climb the immigrant ladder.

Beto's friendship with Yunior reveals a second aspect of Dominican masculinity Yunior resists: homosexuality. Méndez observes, "If, on one side, Yunior deals with (homo)sexuality in his New Jersey community through the signs produced within his own family, on the other side, the topic touches on latent emotional currents abroad in the diasporic experience that are unconsciously but collectively defined, as well as individually felt" (128). Readers observe this consciousness in the first story of the collection, "Ysrael." On the way to La Barbacoa with his older brother to torment the disfigured boy, Ysrael, a man molests Yunior. He resists victimization immediately, calling the man *pato* (Díaz 12).[67] He continues his verbal counter assault, saying, "You low-down pinga-sucking pato," but the muscular pedophile threatens him in a manner clearly invoking Trujillo's punishment for criticizing him: "'You should watch your mouth,' he said" (Díaz 12). Not only has Yunior learned a homophobic discourse in the Dominican Republic at a young age, premigration, but he has also learned to be silent about sexual violence.

As evidenced by the stories "Ysrael" and "Drown," as well as suggested by the entirety of Díaz's novel *The Brief Wondrous Life of Oscar Wao*, it is Dominican communal—not US institutional—homophobia that catalyzes Yunior's struggles with Dominican masculinity. Stringer argues that Yunior's homophobia is part of the "more general protocols of sexual repression and its capacity to destroy or depoliticize friendship" (119). While institutions and the state can teach or validate repressions, Díaz's portrayal of Beto is consistent with *Dominican*, *Latino*, and *Latin American* discourse on homosexuality. The collection's numerous moments of hypermasculinity expressed or enacted by Yunior's father, brother, and friends elucidate this cultural discourse. When Papi is present, for example, he is often berating Yunior for being weak or crying. Moreover, Rafa is the metonym for the boys' father long before they migrate. In "Ysrael," when Yunior exits the bus crying because the pedophile molested and threatened him, Rafa asks him what happened but Yunior remains silent. When Rafa says, "If you can't stop crying, I'll leave you," he becomes their father, using emasculation to justify abandonment or the threat of it, which is to justify the loss of family protection and security (Díaz 13).

This scene is a provocative example of what Méndez describes as the portrayal of family in the later story "Drown": "Punishment, repression, and orality are the surface elements that characterize Yunior's family in this story" (130). The trope of emasculation and crying is one Díaz repeats. Elena Machado Sáez makes a compelling argument about Díaz's similar construction of masculinity and homosexuality in the novel *The Brief Wondrous Life of Oscar Wao*. She presents a stunning reading of the character Yunior as a closeted, homophobic gay man; because Oscar is a nerd[68] whose prowess is literary, not sexual, Oscar queers and destabilizes Dominican masculinity. Machado Sáez argues, "In light of the fact that this act (like the novel as a whole) is a fiction constructed by Yunior as narrator, the motivation for 'resolving' Oscar's queerness is tied to the threat which that identity represents to Yunior's own sexuality" ("Dictating Desires" 548). She concludes, "the beauty that Iris embodies and that gives purpose to Yunior's continued role as narrator is a beauty that reconciles Yunior's queer desires with those that Dominican masculinity dictates he should have" (Machado Sáez, "Dictating Desires" 550).

Even if one chooses not to read either Yunior—the one in *Oscar Wao* or the one in *Drown*—as a closeted homosexual, the materialist conception of "queer" described by David William Foster forecloses a "straight" reading of the short story "Drown." He explains that the word *queer* "has come to signify the critique of the heterosexist paradigm" (7). Asserting that "all forms of subjective identity are, in the view of most queer theorists, inextricably intertwined," Foster concludes that "queer studies, therefore, have become a site for not only bringing race, class, and ethnicity into a discussion of homoeroticism, but for showing that it is imperative to construct a calculus of all elements of subjective identity" (8). As a queer Dominican, Beto would not belong in his own neighborhood and he would not be welcome in Yunior's house. Yunior's introduction of Beto shows they once shared familial belonging: "He's a pato now, but two years ago we were friends and he would walk into the apartment without knocking, his heavy voice rousing my mother from the Spanish of her room and drawing me up from the basement, a voice that cracked and made you think of uncles or grandfathers" (Díaz 91). Since Yunior's father has been so absent, Yunior associates Beto with the only male figures he has known. The absence of Yunior's father is painful but sanctioned—Ramon de Las Casas must be el tíguere and create more opportunities for his family. Díaz implies that this absence makes Yunior vulnerable to homosexuality. His father's über-heterosexual masculinity would have been a cultural barrier to Yunior's socialization with Beto.

Readers begin to question the two boys' closeness. Yunior describes his nights alone or with other friends because "Beto would usually be at home or down by the swings, or wouldn't be around at all. Out visiting other neighborhoods" (Díaz 102). Beto is trying to escape the confinement of his community. Yunior recalls Beto saying, "You need to learn how to walk the world. . . . There's a lot out there" (Díaz 102). These excursions likely involved homosexual relationships or socialization; Beto would not be safe in his own neighborhood if he were "out." This is clear when Yunior describes harassing gays when out with other friends (Díaz 102). When Beto was around, the two would skip school and shoplift or go to their favorite spot, the community pool. The pool is the metaphor for his dialectical relationship with Beto, simultaneously empowering and threatening.

Yunior's memories of the pool trigger his confessional about his sexual memory of Beto: "Twice. That's it" (Díaz 92). The community pool is the one space youth of different ethnicities occupy without overt racism or violence. The space also differentiates people such as Beto, the ones who get out of the neighborhood, from people such as Yunior, those who do not seem to try to leave. While Beto comes and goes, Yunior visits the pool for so long kids his own age do not go there anymore: "Many of the kids here are the younger brothers of the people I used to go to school with. Two of them swim past, black and Latino, and they pause when they see me, recognizing the guy who sells them their shitty dope" (Díaz 92). The water, emblematic of their friendship, is an imperfect oasis: "While everything above is loud and bright, everything below is whispers. And always the risk of coming up to find the cops stabbing their searchlights out across the water" (Díaz 93).

The diction used quickly undermines any positive imagery with which the scene opens. The word *stabbing* suggests the violence of police brutality, evokes sexual penetration, and foreshadows the broken friendship. The friends swim together, but their conversation reveals the loss of equality between them. When Yunior knows what the word *expectorating* means, Beto taunts Yunior and asserts his physical strength: "He was wearing a cross and cutoff jeans. He was stronger than me and held me down until water flooded my nose and throat. Even then I didn't tell him; he thought I didn't read. Not even dictionaries" (Díaz 94). This scene unites Yunior's anxieties about his literacy and his masculinity. Despite the fact that Beto is literally drowning him, Yunior does not meet Beto's demand to tell what he knows. Díaz employs this aspect of Beto's character to contrast widely accepted stereotypes about homosexuals within Euro-American culture, such as the notion that gay men are passive victims, incapable of violence. Díaz also suggests that Beto is a hypocrite; since he is wearing a cross, his Christianity should prevent him from enacting such violence. More importantly, it should also prevent him from acting on homoerotic desire. Many Dominicans are Catholic or Pentecostal; in both religions' doctrines, homosexuality remains an abomination.[69]

After they return to Yunior's house to watch a pornographic film, Beto starts to masturbate Yunior. Yunior does not resist but gets up to leave right after he ejaculates. He fears that he "would end up abnormal, a fucking pato" (Díaz 104). Yunior's fear is rooted not just in the notion that having sex with a man makes you gay but in the more specific discourse on homosexuality within Latino and Latin American culture that asserts the receiver of homosexual penetration is gay, not the giver.[70] To be *pasivo*, the recipient of any form of penetration, makes a man a *pato*.[71] Beto's performance of the sex act is not the source of his estrangement; to call pato an "ordinary obscenity" elides its intense negativity and suggestion of contagion in homophobic discourse (Stringer 120). Yunior is not afraid of patos; he is afraid of "*becoming a pato*" (Díaz 95). Yunior's distinction of Beto changing *from* a friend *to* a pato reinforces this sociolinguistic context. To become a *pato* is *Drown's* recurring narrative of loss: the loss of a specifically *tíguere dominicanidad*.

Yunior returns to the pool the next day, cognizant that Beto could initiate another sexual encounter. Beto offers Yunior two coded escapes. First, Beto puts his hand on Yunior's shoulder, and Yunior describes his response thus: "my pulse a code under his palm" (Díaz 95). Reading that code, Beto says, "'Let's go,' . . . 'Unless of course you're not feeling good'" (Díaz 96). Yunior provides Beto sexual consent when he says, "I'm feeling fine" (Díaz 96). His anticipation and consent to their sexual activity negates the idea that Beto's performance of the sex act is the source of the friends' estrangement. Once they enter the apartment, Beto assumes the role of pasivo; by performing oral sex on Yunior, he makes himself the receiver of a penetrative sex act. Yunior assesses his sense of self and, at least temporarily, no longer seems to fear becoming what he perceives Beto to be, a pato. His active self-construction indicates that he is *activo*: "After I was done, he laid his head in my lap. I wasn't asleep or awake, but caught somewhere in between, rocked slowly back and forth the way the surf holds junk against the shore, rolling it over and over" (Díaz 105). The ocean/holding junk/drowning metaphor performs two functions.

Beto represents another aspect of Yunior's life that he cannot control, one that leaves him feeling caught, like the "junk," between his sexual pleasure derived from men and women. Moreover, though he might not fully understand the performance of sex roles, Yunior no longer sees them in a simplistic binary. Yunior is caught between choosing his narrative of loss. He must sacrifice his love for his friend or he will lose the love of his family and protection of his homophobic barrio friends. Readers feel the tenuous line of emotion Yunior experiences; even though he is "terrified that I would end up abnormal, a fucking pato," he completes the sentence by asserting that "he was my best friend and back then that mattered to me more than anything" (Díaz 104). After their second encounter, Yunior does not use the term *pato* again in the story.

Beto's return is a catalyst to Yunior's realization of his failed *tígueraje* and socioeconomic drowning. Méndez illustrates this deftly: "When Beto leaves for college, Yunior processes these experiences into terms he can deal with by regressing towards old patterns of *tíguere* masculinity, which require on their side an overtness and excess of masculine toughness in the streets" (Méndez 143). Though his mother can usually pay the rent and he can pay for utilities by selling pot, Yunior becomes painfully aware that he "wasn't like [Beto]. I had another year to go in high school, no promises elsewhere" (Díaz 92). Beto's going to college leaves Yunior, literally, without a partner in crime; in their shoplifting, Beto was the one who remained calm and boldly dealt with security guards while in possession of stolen goods. Their last encounter ended with Yunior crying, and he recalls "Beto's hand squeezing mine, the bones in our fingers pressing together" (Díaz 118). Stringer suggests that Yunior's sexual experience confines him to el barrio, drawing on Díaz's comments during an early interview with Céspedes and Torres-Saillant: "Sexual shame and homophobia, particularly the immediate unremarkable homophobia of quotidian homosociality, institutionalize 'self-hate and self-doubt' often in the specific form of passing-for-straight. They thereby help to perpetuate the racial ghetto" (119). Yunior clearly develops self-hate because of his sexual self-doubt; however, neither Beto nor the state ought to be blamed for Yunior's choice to remain in el barrio. This is a point Díaz makes painfully clear in most of the stories of the collection.

Both young men have equal access to education because they attended the same school, but Yunior does not use the resources Beto has accessed. Earlier in the story, Yunior acknowledges two ways out of el barrio: education or military service, both of which he rejects. As Stringer observes, "Beto, whom readers meet only in flashback, always represents possibilities that the narrator perversely refuses" (120). Beto's gift of a book is another element in this narrative of loss. Díaz suggests that Yunior chooses the loss: he throws away not only a friendship but also a potential guide out of el barrio. Yunior recalls, "You can't be anywhere forever, was what Beto used to say, what he said to me the day I went to see him off" (Díaz 107). Because the story ends precisely where it began—with Yunior watching TV with his mother—readers can only conclude Yunior will stay in el barrio forever. Díaz implies Yunior has realized Beto is more of a tíguere than he will ever be; this is a significantly more damaging betrayal than any sex act Beto has performed. Yunior has betrayed himself.[72]

If Beto "betrays" Yunior in any way, it is in the consequence of the movement: his abandonment of Yunior, not el barrio.[73] His return to the neighborhood is precisely the catalyst for Yunior's rejection of him. Beto's leaving for college feels like the abandonment he experienced by his father and then by his brother, who dies from leukemia earlier in the narrative time of the collection's stories. Beto's return is a threat because it is a reminder of each and every abandonment Yunior has experienced. Through Beto's fluid movements—his ability to pass in the neighborhood and outside of it—Díaz criticizes individuals who are offered potential sources of empowerment but reject them without considering the consequences of the rejection. As Lyn Di Iorio Sandín observes, "To be Beto's lover would entail both sexual self-awareness, and participation in the world Beto has entered; college, the world of the 'book' that the narrator throws away, a universe of mobility, learning, change, growth" (121). Díaz addressed his concern about self-defeating actions early in his career, in the same interview Stringer cites: "There's no state in the world that can facilitate all the ambitions of its underclass. So it throws up obstacles—plenty of intoxications, bad schools, aggressive cops, no jobs—and depends on us to do the rest. You don't know how many times I saw a person escape institutional discrimination only to knock themselves down with self-hate and self-doubt ("Fiction Is the Poor Man's Cinema" 893). Díaz distinguishes Yunior's experiences from those common in exile narratives, where adolescents are victims of institutional discrimination. By depicting characters that fail to choose or fail to act, the author challenges modernist and contemporary depictions of immigrants as victims of an unjust industrial age or a hostile urban environment.[74]

"Drown" moves the collection toward Yunior's ruminations about Dominicans' inability to arrive. In "Negocios," he meets his father's other wife, Nilda, hoping to learn exactly how his father could have been a man with two homes and two families. Realizing, however, that he is never going to know exactly what happened in the years his father was gone, he accepts that his father simply was not a great man whom Nueva York defeated. The plot concerning his father goes beyond established tropes of familial separation in immigrant fiction. Díaz revises the reunion of parents and children into an antinarrative about paternalism, nationalism, and internalized racism. Yunior's obsession with his father is a subtle political narrative about patriarchy in the Dominican Republic. Toward the end of Trujillo's reign, citizens who initially supported him realized he had become a brutal tyrant whose economic policies were ineffectual. Trujillo's self-aggrandizement was so extensive that he required that his picture appear in every citizen's home.[75]

Drown refers to the United States' 1965 invasion of the nation, especially the smell of the tear gas used to subdue resisters. The *yanquis* were not welcome; they enacted their own brutality in the forms of these gas attacks, water-hosing, and sexual assaults. Their presence, however, underscored Trujillo's failings prior to his assassination. While Díaz was born in the Dominican Republic after Trujillo's death, the memories and legacies of his brutal reign persisted. Readers know that the only image Yunior has of his father is when he is dressed as a member of Trujillo's Guardia Nacional. As a writer from a nation that does not care to discuss Trujillo with outsiders, Díaz breaks a profound silence on the failure of patriarchy as governance when he parallels the failures of the personal father with those of the national patriarch.[76]

The final story from *Drown* discussed here is "How to Date a Browngirl, Blackgirl, Whitegirl, or Halfie." At first, this story appears to be a technical manual on interracial dating. The narrator has worked out a bitter, self-effacing, and misogynistic system for addressing the internalized racism he experiences. Díaz's attention to racism among people of color, despite their shared experiences of discrimination and second-class American citizenship, is critical. Of course, racism has been prevalent between Anglo-Americans and ethnic minorities; however, it has also been prevalent among Hispanic-descended people.[77] Institutionalized racism against darker-skinned Hispanics originated in medieval Spain, was legislated in the New World, and became commonplace in the Caribbean and the United States following the Cuban-Spanish-American War (1896–1898).[78]

In "The Tribulations of Blackness: Stages in Dominican Racial Identity," Dominican studies scholar Silvio Torres-Saillant traces the development of Dominican racial identity and argues, "A large part of the problem of racial identity among Dominicans stems from the fact that from its inception their country had to negotiate the racial paradigms of their North American and European overseers" (127). Torres-Saillant also links Dominicans' nineteenth-century occupations by Haiti and the United States to shifts in their racial self-conception. His contextualiztion of racism and US neocolonialism is especially apt: "One should look to the vigorous imperial expansion of the United States in the wake of the Spanish-American War of 1898 for the historical context in which the notion of a single Ibero-American race gained currency" (Torres-Saillant, "The Tribulations of Blackness" 137). Rather than reading the overt racism and class distinctions within "How to Date a Browngirl, Blackgirl, Whitegirl, or Halfie" as matter-of-fact descriptions of interracial relationships, one should consider how effectively Díaz illustrates the losses colorism creates: the erasure of nationality and the abortion of self-respect.[79]

"How to Date a Browngirl, Blackgirl, Whitegirl, or Halfie" is the collection's exemplar of the problem of belonging in Latina/o America. Contrasting the collection's other narrative voices, Yunior addresses the reader directly, using a familiar second-person voice and assuming a shared class background: urban Latina/o poor. Make no mistake; this group has its own hierarchy. Yunior offers advice on how to deal with girls from specific neighborhoods, especially on hiding signs of poverty, such as the "government cheese": "If the girl's from the Terrace stack the boxes behind the milk. If she's from the Park or Society Hill hide the cheese in the cabinet above the oven . . . Take down any embarrassing photos of your family in the campo, especially the one with the half-naked kids dragging a goat on a rope leash" (Díaz 145). These instructions delineate the socioeconomic stratification among people of color; though many families in Yunior's city might be on welfare, the importance of hiding the government cheese varies by the girl's neighborhood. Yunior undermines the idea of a monolithic economic background of Dominicans by emphasizing one's origins as urban or from el campo; displaying a picture of yourself in the country would immediately signify your class as rural poor in the Dominican Republic.[80] Méndez notes, "Photographs throughout the collection figure as artifacts imbued with an aura of recollection, spatializing lost or forgotten lived experiences" (136). For Yunior, there is no Puritanical self-reinvention, no Chicano or Nuyorican political self-construction, and no privilege of being a temporary, exotic Cuban exile. Photos spatialize experiences Yunior wants, urgently, not to remember.[81]

Yunior attempts to hide linguistic poverty as well. Having immigrated as a preadolescent, Yunior could retain or lose his Spanish, become English dominant, or become fluently bilingual. In "Drown," readers learned that when he left Santo Domingo at age nine, Yunior could not write his own name. Thus, speaking in Spanish is just as much a class marker for him as is the government cheese. His illiteracy in Spanish directly affects whom he can and cannot impress and for whom he will make the most economic and cultural effort. He notes, "If the girl's from around the way, take her to El Cibao for dinner. Order everything in your busted-up Spanish. Let her correct you if she's Latina and amaze her if she's black. If she's not from around the way, Wendy's will do" (Díaz 145). Redefining the linguistic retentions and losses often assumed about first-generation immigrants is especially important. Under a modern European- or Asian-immigration model, first-generation immigrants would have difficulty acquiring English and would have used their native language dominantly. Yunior's poor education in the Dominican Republic complicates this model, leaving him illiterate in Spanish and not quite fluent in English, the language of neocolonialism. This linguistic distance from other Spanish speakers has significant consequences: Yunior cannot "rap" to women from his own nation or other parts of Latina/o America, or to Spanish speakers from Central or South America.

Yunior's instructions provide the reader with an increasingly unflattering portrait of his racialized sexual hierarchy. He asserts, "If she's a white girl you know you'll at least get a hand job" (Díaz 144) and "a local girl may have hips and a thick ass but she won't be quick about letting you touch" (Díaz 147). The object is to get as close as possible to having sex on the date and this—ironically—becomes more difficult the closer the girl is to Yunior racially. The narrator sets up rules for date conversation based on a strategy of nonconfrontation and emotional distance: "A halfie will tell you that her parents met in the Movement, will say back then people thought it a radical thing to do. . . . She will appreciate your interest. . . . Black people, she will say, treat me real bad. That's why I don't like them. You'll wonder how she feels about Dominicans. Don't ask" (Díaz 146–47). By defining the distances between racially mixed people and those who identify as black, Díaz illustrates the profound effect of black-on-black racism: Yunior assumes that the girl will not like him if she thinks he is more black than Dominican.

Yunior's physiological characteristics prevent him from passing as "white Spanish," superseding his nationality and marking him as black.[82] Sociologist Jorge Duany explains the Dominican Republic's anti-Haitian sentiment and its effect on Dominican self-conception: "It is this sense of national pride and rejection of their own negritude that many Dominican migrants bring with them and must reevaluate when they confront the US model of racial stratification" ("Reconstructing Racial Identity" 152). Yunior's internalized racism is painfully clear when he notes, "Tell her that you love her hair, that you love her skin, her lips, because in truth, you love them more than you love your own" (Díaz 147). The qualities he loves are synonymous with more whiteness. Close to the end of the story, this is perhaps Díaz's most explicit narrative of loss; it challenges the reader, especially a Latina/o reader, to think about why Yunior is aware of, yet persists in, loss of self-esteem. By illustrating an explicit connection between racial preferences and self-hate, Díaz is criticizing multiethnic communities for perpetuating internalized racism.

Beyond Arrival: Toward Narratives of Reclamation

Díaz's stories are striking examples of contemporary immigrant literature defining the need to create an intermediary space where characters can negotiate aspects of each culture into a third cultural membership. This need is so clear because neither culture—Dominican or ethnic American—is an adequate or consistently empowering place to incorporate all of Yunior's experiences as a diasporic Dominican. *Drown*'s attentions to internalized racism, intraethnic racism, and classicism make it highly effective as a narrative of loss. This chapter began with a discussion of tangible losses depicted in Tomás Rivera's . . . *And the Earth Did Not Devour Him*: losses of time, land, and physical health. The literary response Rivera provides to those losses highlights the intangible but perhaps more viscerally felt losses his unidentified protagonist experiences: loss of religious faith, psychological certainty, and hope.

Similar to Chicana/o narratives of loss such as Rivera's . . . *And the Earth Did Not Devour Him*, Díaz's text illustrates the immediate, measurable losses associated with migration: loss of a physical home, loss of memory, loss of language. Díaz's principal narrator, Yunior, also illustrates the ontological losses intrinsic to people who immigrated at an older age: loss of cultural identity, self-esteem, and family stability. These losses are not exclusive to male protagonists. Compounding the economic and cultural losses intrinsic to migration, women often experience losses particular to the consumption and possession of their bodies as sexual objects.

The texts discussed in the next chapter, Ana Castillo's novel *So Far from God* and Angie Cruz's novel *Soledad*, tell readers the story of losses experienced by women through the *narrative of reclamation*. What distinguishes characters in these narratives of reclamation from narratives of loss is that in the former, characters recognize their cultural stasis and begin to seek ways out of it, rather than drowning in the riptides of compulsory heterosexism, chauvinism, misogyny, and tradition.

2

Narratives of Reclamation

Embodying Ritual and Allegory

> Unlike their abuelos and vis-abuelos who thought that
> although life was hard in the "Land of Enchantment" it
> had its rewards, the reality was that everyone was now
> caught in what had become: The Land of Entrapment.
>
> —Ana Castillo, *So Far from God*

> When Trujillo died, the whole country went mad. You
> never seen madness until you see people about to lose
> everything they got.
>
> —Angie Cruz, *Soledad*

While some 1980s Chicana/o and Latina/o fiction emphasizes discrimination by Anglo-Americans and the realities of second-class citizenship, fewer examples of such texts exist within Latina/o literature than in Chicana/o literature. One reason for this difference is that many Mexican Americans have never felt that they needed to physically arrive: they were always here. The figurative sense of arrival described in this study—that individuals or ethnic groups attain social mobility through the assimilation of three generations of immigrants—is complicated for Chicanas/os for at least two reasons. First, many are descended from the indigenous populations living in the New World before the Spanish Conquest and integration; the relocation of Native Americans into geographic areas foreign to them complicates their ancestors' dispossession. Second, the United States' settlement of the previously Spanish territories introduced another racial and cultural mixing, with the Anglo-Americans, which dispossessed them from their lands anew.

Herencia: The Anthology of Hispanic Literature in the United States (2001) outlines three perspectives of Hispanic American literature: Native, Immigrant, and Exile. In discussing Hispanic colonial subjectivity, Nicolás Kanellos argues, "Hispanics were subsequently conquered and/or incorporated into the United States through territorial purchase and then treated as colonial subjects—as were the Mexicans of the Southwest, the Hispanics in Florida and Louisiana, the Panamanians in the Canal Zone and in Panama itself, and the Puerto Ricans in the Caribbean" (Kanellos 5). He gestures to the premise of *Chicana/o and Latina/o Fiction*: "I could also make a case that in many ways Cubans and Dominicans also developed as peoples under US colonial rule during the early twentieth century" (Kanellos 5). This chapter makes and extends the case by analyzing how US neocolonialism inspires the second of the four stories: the *narrative of reclamation*. It analyzes texts about ethnic communities—Chicana and Dominican—not ordinarily analyzed together. Ana Castillo's *So Far from God* and Angie Cruz's *Soledad* show that the narrative of reclamation is pervasive; in reading novels published about different communities and in different time periods, this chapter tells a story about the lives of women of color in the United States. The novels explore whether preserving certain cultural practices helps or hinders them in reclaiming their cultural identity and belonging in their ethnic communities. Read alone, but even more powerfully if read together, the novels *So Far from God* and *Soledad* illustrate how Chicanas and Dominicanas engage in cultural preservation.

The narrative of reclamation is the secondary response to neocolonialism. It directly addresses the physical and cultural losses caused by US neocolonization of the southeastern and southwestern territories previously held by Spain. In the case of Chicana/o literature, the urgent and intimate connection *reclamantes* have to the land is about cultural survival, for both strains of their ancestry: the indigenous and the Iberian. Scholars have used variations of the concept of reclamation as a fundamental trope in Chicana/o literature. Consider these brief examples of the trajectory of critical analysis of *So Far from God*. In *Show and Tell: Identity as Performance in U.S. Latina/o Fiction* (1997), Karen Christian argues, "*So Far from God* can be read as an anti-essentialist project, even though the Chicana narrator's primary concern is to rescue her community's cultural tradition" (23). Analyses presenting decolonial or postcolonial readings of the novel include Naomi H. Quiñonez's 2002 essay, "Re(Riting) the Chicana Postcolonial: From Traitor to 21st Century Interpreter," which asserts reclamation as fundamental to Chicana writing: "For a people who have suffered the loss of language through colonization, this clearly becomes a political act of reclamation" (143). Of Chicana literature in general, Norma Alarcón describes "the need to 'repossess' the land, especially in cultural national narratives, through scenarios of 'origins' that emerge in the selfsame territory, be it at the literary, legendary, historical, ideological, critical, or theoretical level—producing in material and imaginary terms 'authentic' and 'inauthethentic,' 'legal' and 'illegal' subjects" ("Anzaldúa's *Frontera*" 46).

This chapter unites texts from two distinct geographic and cultural origins, with significantly different narrative structures. Castillo's *So Far from God* is set in the rural southwestern United States, in a period ranging from the 1960s through the early 1980s. The novel ends in the 1980s, but it flashes back and engages the radical Mexican American nationalist politics of the 1960s and 1970s. The novel tells its story through an unnamed, not-so-omniscient third-person narrator and the first-person stream-of-consciousness narration of several characters. *Soledad* is set in urban New York, approximately a generation later, from the 1980s to the early years of the twenty-first century. Cruz also uses flashbacks to depict the 1960s, especially the years immediately following the assassination of the Dominican dictator, Trujillo.[1] The latter novel is more traditional in form, using a first-person narration by Soledad, punctuated by first-person stream-of-consciousness narrations by her mother, Olivia. Soledad and her mother, too, seek to reclaim something very important: their dominicanidad. This chapter illustrates how *So Far from God* and *Soledad* are narratives of reclamation by paying special attention to the ways they address the abuses of the female body; how they reconfigure domestic spaces from patriarchal to matriarchal; and how both novels engage woman of color feminism.

From *Aztlán* to *La Frontera*:
The Rise of the Chicana Writer

Following the conclusion of the Mexican-American War (1846–1848), thousands of Mexicans became US citizens. Internal politics, civil war, natural disasters, and most recently the violence associated with Mexican and Salvadoran drug cartels and human trafficking account for most continuing migrations.[2] Kanellos' arguments are important to consider in the development of the Mexican American, and later Chicana/o, literary tradition. Early Mexican American literatures are narratives of loss. As such, they espouse what Kanellos has called a "Native" position that expresses "an attitude of entitlement to civil, political, and cultural rights" (5).[3] It would not be until the literary production of the late 1970s that the split between Mexican Americans who define their cultural identity through Spanish ancestry and

Mexican Americans who define their identity as neither exclusively Spanish descended nor indigenous descended became clear.

Literature produced during El Movimiento, the civil rights movement of Mexican Americans, invoked the mythic land of *Aztlán* to articulate an ethnonational identity for Mexican Americans.[4] The 1969 *El Plan Espiritual del Aztlán* reflects their shift in self-conception: "It openly rejected the government's official classification of Mexican Americans as 'white' in favor of the students' new self-identification as members of La Raza" (Oboler 66). By "breaking with the insistence on the traditional adherence to a 'European only' legacy by previous Mexican-American generation," the activists of El Movimiento embraced their multicultural origins and began to evoke the images of the Chicano as an indigenous warrior—the Aztec (Oboler 66). Several groups organized protests and actions to change the living conditions, educational opportunities, and political representation of Mexican Americans.[5] Part of the political rhetoric of El Movimiento was the belief that while the Treaty of Guadalupe Hidalgo created the border between the United States and Mexico, it was, after all, the gringos who arrived in the Chicanos' homeland, *Aztlán*. The contents of *Aztlán: An Anthology of Mexican American Literature* (1972) reflects the Aztlánists' embrace of nativism and their explicit rejection of the construction of arrival as a romanticized myth about immigration through Ellis Island: "No Statue of Liberty ever greeted our *arrival* in this country. . . . We did not, in fact, come to the United States at all. The United States came to us" (Valdez xxxiii). This statement, which appears in the introduction of the anthology, shows how clearly the literature of Mexican Americans was linked to political life.[6]

Similar to a standard literary anthology, *Aztlán* includes poetry, prose, and drama. The anthology, however, has more in common with hybrid texts of the nineteenth century. The majority of the selections are excerpts from colonial records, congressional reports, articles from the Treaty of Guadalupe Hidalgo, political statements, and action plans. Moreover, the inclusion of noncreative, political documents is a clear statement that literary genres are insufficient to represent Chicana/o experience. *Aztlán* defines the relationship between literature and El Movimiento as mutually inclusive: literature by Mexican Americans could not be divorced from the goals of El Movimiento. This explicit political agenda for Mexican American literature is best illustrated by a portion of the anthology's closing selection, *El Plan Espiritual del Aztlán*: Chicano Youth Liberation Conference. Section Six of "*Punto Segundo*: Organizational Goals," asserts, "We must insure that our writers, poets, musicians, and artists produce literature and art that is appealing to our people and relates to our revolutionary culture" (Valdez 405). The demand for explicit political discourse within Chicana/o cultural production has shaped Mexican American literature since El Movimiento.

The publication of *Aztlán* marks a critical moment in Chicana/o literary history: the shift from the narrative of loss toward the narrative of reclamation. Part of this shift is the result of the dismemberment of Chicano patriarchy in the movement. The second section of *El Plan Espiritual del Aztlán* ends with a clear exclusion of the Chicana in the movement's goals: "Our cultural values of life, family, and home serve as a powerful weapon to defeat the *gringo* dollar value system and encourage the process of love and brotherhood" (Valdez 405). The statement provides insight into the problems contributing to the movement's decline, especially the schism between the movement's male and female participants. Scholars from varying disciplines have discussed the movement's patriarchy. Ramón Gutiérrez notes, "the 'imagined' community of Aztlán in effect excluded women" ("Community, Patriarchy, and Individualism" 47). Literature scholar Juan Bruce-Novoa made a similar assertion that "the monological goals of that literary tradition are subverted when Chicanas reveal the fissures in the interior circle" ("Dialogical Strategies, Monological Goals" 242).

Another section of the anthology engages this issue directly, illustrating that the sexism of the movement was criticized during the movement, not only in hindsight. The section titled "La Causa: la mujer" contains poems and a prose essay, "The Women of *la Raza*," which critiques the movement's machismo. The author, Enriqueta Longauez y Vasquez, articulates sexism as a fundamental problem that continued to erupt in literary challenges: "When the man can look upon 'his' woman as HUMAN and with the love of brotherhood and EQUALITY, then and only then, can he feel the true meaning of liberation and equality himself" (278). Some scholars have suggested that the split in the movement is not reflected in literary productions until the publication of Gloria Anzaldúa's *Borderlands/La Frontera*. The inclusion of feminist writing—especially by Enriqueta Longauez y Vasquez—suggests that the literary articulations of fractured identity started earlier.[7] Certainly, *Yo Soy Joaquín*, Gonzales' epic poem, which embraces multiple ethnicities and religious systems, male and female genders, illustrated such a fractured sense of identity in 1967 almost two decades before Gloria Anzaldúa published *Borderlands/La Frontera*.

The sexism of the Aztlánists was not unique. Chauvinism occurred within other social justice movements: "Indeed, like the men in the Young Lords' party early in its history, Chicanos actively discriminated against [women] throughout the history of their movement" (Oboler 66). Moreover, "Women were denied leadership roles and were asked to perform only the most traditional stereotypic roles—cleaning up, making coffee, executing the orders men gave, and servicing their needs. Women who did manage to assume leadership positions were ridiculed as unfeminine, sexually perverse, promiscuous, and all too often, taunted as lesbians" (Gutiérrez 47). Patriarchal dominance within Chicana/o America fragmented la raza; it lead to the reclamation of femininity evidenced in the poetry of writers including Ana Castillo and Lorna Dee Cervantes in the early 1970s.[8] Aranda's reading of the splits in the movement cites Lucha Corpi's novel *Eulogy for a Brown Angel* (1992) as a portrayal of the schism: "Corpi's revisionist story of the Chicano/a movement is important for the differences it shows existing within the Mexican American community back then, differences that widen because of class and race issues affecting the nation during the 1980s, and finally differences that become the crux of the social alienation faced by legal and illegal Mexican people in the 1990s" (Aranda 4).

Longauez y Vasquez's calls for a discussion of the gender trouble within the Chicana/o community *before* dealing with Anglo-America are clear: "When we talk of inequality in the Mexican American movement we better be talking about total equality, beginning right where it all starts, AT HOME" (278). The ideological split between men and women that began within El Movimiento became one of the major facilitators of contemporary Chicana literature.[9] One of the principal themes of Chicana literature is the challenge to fight sexism within their own communities as well as racial and sexual oppression within Anglo-America. Longauez y Vasquez's call for equality at home is especially important to consider because it demonstrates that at the height of Chicana/o self-distinction from Anglo-America, the distinctions within Chicana/o America were becoming visible.[10]

Not all Mexican Americans embraced the nationalist paradigm. One text best known for its implication that Mexican Americans should desire and work toward arrival in Anglo-America is Richard Rodriguez's *Hunger of Memory: The Education of Richard Rodriguez* (1982). Rodriguez's autoethnography is an example of the political and class diversity among Mexican Americans. His memoir draws on the definition of arrival associated with the migrations of Europeans in the nineteenth and twentieth centuries, which have made it the subject of some criticism, including critiques of the memoir's employment of the rhetoric of exceptionalism.[11] For Rodriguez, what distinguishes undocumented or documented but monolingual Spanish-speaking Mexican Americans from him is public persona.[12] These two groups, unlike

an arrived Rodriguez, "lack a public identity" (Rodriguez 182). Tomás Rivera
focuses on how the semantic differences between Spanish and English shape
Rodriguez's writing. Rivera sees a sense of inferiority in Rodriguez: "Richard
Rodriguez apparently decolonizes himself by seeking to free himself from a
personal voice, but in so trying he will likely enter another colony of despair"
(*"Hunger of Memory* as Humanistic Antithesis" 115).

In his review of El Movimiento and literary politics, Aranda cites Rodriguez's *Hunger of Memory* (1982) and Cherríe Moraga's *Loving in the War
Years: lo que nunca pasó por sus labios* (1983) as works by writers who did
not fit into the Chicano nationalist paradigm. He makes a keen point about
these radically different autobiographies, stating that they "are ironically more
responsible than anything else for the eventual displacement of the myth of
Aztlán in Chicano/a studies" (Aranda 24). He asserts, "For Chicano/a studies,
the success of *Hunger of Memory* is a constant reminder that the American
myth of immigration is alive and well. It is also a cautionary tale about the
limits faced by alternative nationalist discourses when the desires of community include mainstream acceptance, and when calls for ethnic solidarity
run up against equally compelling individual and communal desires for self-
expression" (Aranda 27). Chapter 1 illustrated Rivera's . . . *And the Earth Did
Not Devour Him* as a pivotal example of authors beginning to problematize
the concept of arrival. By the end of the 1980s, however, arrival texts such
as *Hunger of Memory* were displaced within the literary scene. Chicana/o
authors moved away from the narrative of loss and began telling the second
story, the narrative of reclamation.

In addition to the engagement of gender issues in the literature, postmovement Chicana/o texts reclaim local histories. Rolando Hinojosa-Smith (*Klail
City y sus alrededores* [Klail City and its surroundings], 1976) and Denise
Chávez (*Last of the Menu Girls*, 1986; *The Face of an Angel*, 1995) narrate the
experiences of Texans and New Mexicans, respectively.[13] Hinojosa-Smith's
work is especially important in this regard because the novels he writes
about the fictional Belken County are marked by renewed genre manipulation. The novels include many forms of established genres, are polyphonic,
and represent local history through public documents such as legal plead-
ings and newspaper accounts.[14] Even though his novels, especially *Ask a
Policeman*, are procedural detective novels, they consistently foreground
regional identities as they distinguish characters as having "old family"
(native) or "new family" (immigrant) perspectives. To an even greater extent, Chávez's second novel, *The Face of an Angel*, functions as a narrative
of reclamation; it textualizes oral histories as narrated by a character named

Oralia Milcantos—the singer of a thousand songs. The novel also textualizes college writing assignments and an entire book—a waitressing manual. Chávez embeds them as paratexts within the novel's main structure. Both Hinojosa-Smith and Chávez are drawing on the influence of Mexican texts published in the nineteenth century to represent the phenomenology of Chicana/o life in the twentieth century.[15]

The 1980s also witnessed the ideological split of Anglo-American feminists and woman of color feminists.[16] Following the publication of *This Bridge Called My Back: Writings by Radical Women of Color* (1981), the dissemination of African, Asian, Chicana, Latina, and Native American women's literature increased significantly. Two women who would become Chicana feminism's most prominent scholars edited the volume: Cherríe Moraga and Gloria Anzaldúa. In their own poems, autobiographical narratives, and creative nonfiction similar to the pieces in *This Bridge Called My Back*, Moraga and Anzaldúa explicitly address questions of identity formation *within* the Chicana/o community. Critically important, single-authored texts including Moraga's *Loving in the War Years: lo que nunca pasó por sus labios* (1983), Anzaldúa's *Borderlands/La Frontera: The New Mestiza* (1987), and Carla Trujillo's *Chicana Lesbians: The Girls Our Mothers Warned Us About* (1991) are direct treatments of Chicana lesbian experience.[17]

Chicana feminist literary production that emerged in the 1980s remains a multifaceted response to US neocolonialism. Many of the texts produced by Chicanas in this period have been called "mixed" or "hybrid" because they employ multiple genres, visual media, and cultural practices; these forms are related to the evolution of the mixed texts discussed above, established in the nineteenth century, rather than "new" forms of literature.[18] Rebolledo and Rivero assert that women's writing in particular is characterized by "the blending or blurring of various forms: the oral with the written, history with creative autobiography, recipes and narrative, family history and romance" (18). These forms draw on the oral storytelling tradition; more importantly, "the mixing of genre (recipes with fiction, autobiography within romance) was seen by these writers as acceptable because it was a *recuerdo*, a remembering, and because all the narration was underscored by the *cuento* storytelling tradition" (Rebolledo and Rivero 18). The process of genre mixing in the nineteenth century is reengaged in highly visible ways in late twentieth-century Chicana fiction. This is true of writers including Margarita Cota-Cárdenas (*Puppet*, 1985), Ana Castillo (*Mixquiahuala Letters*, 1986; *So Far from God*, 1994), Norma E. Cantú (*Canicula: Snapshots of a Girlhood en La Frontera*, 1995), and Pat Mora (*House of Houses*, 1997), among others. Chicana cultural theorists such as Tey Diana

Rebolledo, Eliana Rivero, Yvonne Yarbro-Bejarano, and Angie Chabram Dern-ersesian have illustrated that the omnipresence of these forms in autobiographical texts functions as a response to Chicano nationalist narratives excluding women's voices.[19]

Borderlands/La Frontera: The New Mestiza (1987) was radical in its depiction of the ambiguity and complexity of Mexican American identity. By uniting myth and fact, mixing first-person narrative and footnote, Anzaldúa exposes the constructedness of history, undermining its normalizing discourse. Anzaldúa's work was the object of criticism, particularly around its engagement of pre-Columbian deities and post-Columbian Mexican history.[20] Anzaldúa's text complicates the theorization of Chicana/o identity through its response to neocolonizing thought that is reinscribed in texts such as Rodriguez's *Hunger of Memory* and Linda Chávez's later memoir, *Out of the Barrio: Toward a New Politics of Hispanic Assimilation* (1991). As a foundational text in Chicana/o, feminist, and queer theories, *Borderlands/La Frontera* has become the subject of much scholarship, including anthologies of responses to and reengagement of its questions.[21] My own education about Chicana/o literature and history is greatly indebted to the theorization of cultural identity in *Borderlands/La Frontera*. The following discussion, however, is not meant to analyze the text in isolation—rather, it will illustrate its early and influential role in discussions of the need to address problems within Chicana/o, not only Anglo, America.

A cursory read of Anzaldúa's *Borderlands* might conclude that the text is focused on the majority, Anglo-Americans. The text does not promote anti-assimilation; rather, it questions the actual possibility of arrival without the mutual acculturation of Anglo-Americans. Anzaldúa writes, for example, "Gringo, accept the *doppelganger* in your psyche. By taking back your collective shadow the intracultural split will heal. And finally, tell us what you need from us" (86). Anzaldúa shows how US neocolonialism generated the narrative of loss within Chicana/o America: the disintegration of families living near the border, the disappearance of Mexican and indigenous cultural practices, and the emasculation of the Chicano. Anzaldúa's main concern, though, is opening discussions about the difficulties of trying to be a Chicana lesbian, a gay Chicano, an academic Chicana/o, and so forth within this *already oppressed* community. The motif of loss of cultural knowledge was visible in nineteenth-century literature. In the late twentieth and early twenty-first centuries, authors respond to this loss in several ways. Two such narrative strategies are the use of allegory and the use of ritual. This chapter now turns to telling the narrative of reclamation in *So Far from God* and *Soledad*.

Living in "The Land of Entrapment": Cultural Dystopia in *So Far from God*

It is unlikely much Chicana fiction would have been published if Anzaldúa's theorization of the border had not had the impact it did. As Aranda notes, "While Gloria Anzaldúa's autobiographical quest for the 'New Mestiza' might get lost in its adaptations by non-Chicano/a scholars, what is not lost, I am sure, is how her text helped redefine Chicano/a studies" (33).[22] *So Far from God* is a fictional manifestation of the critical issues *Borderlands* raises.[23] Castillo titles the novel and opens it with a quote by Porfirio Díaz, dictator of Mexico during the Mexican Civil War: "So far from God—so near the United States." This quote problematizes historic and contemporary portrayals of the United States as a political and religious promised land. The literary tropes of utopia and dystopia are key to understanding how Ana Castillo tells the narrative of reclamation. In Greek etymology, *utopia* combines the meanings of a "good place" and "no place"; in literature, utopias are considered places too good to be true, impossible to exist. *Dystopia*, which is etymologically not precisely the opposite of utopia, means "bad place." To reclaim all that is lost at the border, Castillo tries to imagine a space outside of dystopia. The politics of Chicano America from the 1960s to the 1980s, however, complicate her project. The novel emphasizes the third spaces Chicanas inhabit: the spaces between Mexico and the United States, between nondominant indigenous and dominant institutionalized religious practice, between US citizenship and systematic oppression.[24]

Criticism of *So Far from God* has examined its fantastic elements, aligning Castillo with magical realist writers of Latin America.[25] In the essay "'The Pleas of the Desperate': Collective Agency versus Magical Realism in Ana Castillo's *So Far from God*," Marta Caminero-Santangelo reviews much of this criticism, making a compelling argument that the novel's use of magical realism is ironic.[26] Caminero-Santangelo asserts that "unlike what occurs in other magical realist texts, the magical and the real are not seamlessly interwoven in Castillo's novel; rather, increasingly, they come to stand in stark contrast to each other" ("'The Pleas of the Desperate'" 95). Considering the novel as a whole, not just its moments of seeming magical realism, it can be situated as a work of postmodern fiction revising US neocolonialism's story of Mexican America. Castillo reproduces oral storytelling, complete with digressions, explanations, and speculations of an admitted nonomniscient narrator. This highly self-conscious, metafictional engagement of political history conflicts with the creation of an alternate, magically real world. In a useful discussion of magical realism, archetypes, and allegory, Lyn Di Iorio Sandín foregrounds a view of allegory as posited by Walter Benjamin and Paul de Man. This view suggests that "the ruptures [allegory] represents are more accurate delineations of the fractured modern condition than the totalizing idealizations of the symbol" (6). Moreover, Di Iorio Sandín asserts, "Allegory, like mimicry, is about repetition with a difference" (6).

That difference, especially present in *So Far from God* and *Soledad*, illustrates that the "magic is represented as a contradictory practice: on the one hand, a way of gaining access to the original homeland, on the other a tie to the past that is of questionable use for the new American reality" (Di Iorio Sandín 7). Indeed, Castillo's and Cruz's use of "magic" in these texts is explicitly about reclaiming and reshaping. It is not about accepting, wholesale, a nostalgic version of a cultural past that was somehow more empowering than it is in the present. I follow Di Iorio Sandín's lead in noting that certain US Latina/o writers "choose to reinscribe the notion of the origin as well as to constantly question and subvert the possibility of ever grasping hold of it" (8). As Caminero-Santangelo further argues, "A more discriminating approach to the magical elements in the novel leads us not to García Márquez but to a distinctly different relationship between the magical and the political history with something important to say about the threat of apathy and passivity to forms of collective activism" ("'The Pleas of the Desperate'" 95). Allegories and rituals—when merged with explicit political consciousness—are transformed into practices of collective agency that enact the narrative of reclamation.

Border *Brujas*

Set in the fictional town of Tome, New Mexico, *So Far from God* explores the lives of a mother, Sofi (Wisdom), and her four daughters, each of whom functions symbolically in an extensive allegory of what can be lost and potentially reclaimed at the border: Esperanza [Hope], Caridad [Charity], Fe [Faith], and La Loca [the Crazy One, whose Christian name is forgotten].[27] Porfirio Díaz's conception of Mexico's ambiguous political condition foreshadows the self-conception of Chicana/o life noted in the epigraph at the start of the chapter: "Unlike their *abuelos* and *vis-abuelos* who thought that although life was hard in the 'Land of Enchantment' it had its rewards, the reality was that everyone was now caught in what had become: The Land of Entrapment" (Castillo 172). Castillo's language play resonates the economic and legal battles Mexican Americans wage as a people dispossessed of their ancestral lands. As a narrative of reclamation, the novel explores how the characters attempt to redress physically measurable losses of land, gendered losses of female bodies, and immeasurable, but no less tangible, losses of language, spirituality, and cultural tradition.

The most encompassing response to cultural dispossession is the novel's use of multiple genres, some of which reclaim cultural practice by their inclusion alone. *So Far from God* is an amalgamation of novel kinds and modes, including the history, the romance, the tragedy, the satire, and the picaresque.[28] The text merges twentieth-century *telenovelas* and sixteenth-century picaresques.[29] The picaresque is evinced through the episodic plot development and its emphasis on the lower economic class of the protagonists. Descriptive chapter titles provide synoptic details of events, as well as ideological commentary on them. Pausing at cliff-hanger moments as would a telenovela, the narration is gossipy and high speed. The variation of the established genres amplifies the notion that there is no single way to tell a story, offering a direct challenge to hegemonic narrative theories privileging linear stories told by an omniscient narrator.[30] Multiple genres are used, just as they are in Chicana theory, which draws on multiple modes to bring the realities of border life into sharp relief.[31] *So Far from God* departs significantly, however, from the picaresque and earlier novel forms such as the romance because of its focus on women. The explicit development of Chicana feminism in Sofi is the principal example of this subversion.

So Far from God is a novel in its focus on a central subject: how Chicanas navigate the reclamation of losses at the border, beginning with the loss of a voice to question neocolonialism's master narrative. The text engages the questions and literary practices developing in Chicana literature in the 1980s and early 1990s. Castillo uses code-switching and genre pastiche to highlight textual and cultural practice, both depicting and enacting Chicana feminism.[32] In the essay collection *Massacre of the Dreamers: Essays on Xicanisma* (1994), Castillo renames her conception of Chicana feminism *Xicanisma* to evoke indigenous memory and establish the roots and development of feminism in the pre-Columbian era. Castillo began to formulate this feminism within the specific context of the chauvinism exhibited in El Movimiento: "By the beginning of the new decade, however, many Chicana/ Latina activists, disenchanted, if not simply worn down, by male dominated Chicano/Latino politics, began to develop our own theories of oppression. Compounding our social dilemmas relation to class and race were gender and sexuality" (10). In "*Un Tapiz: The Poetics of Conscientización*," Castillo establishes her poetics as recuperative and revisionary: "We are looking at what has been handed down to us by previous generations of poets, and, in effect, rejecting, reshaping, restructuring, reconstructing that legacy and making language and structure ours, suitable to our moment in history" (*Massacre of the Dreamers* 165). The narrator of *So Far from God* embodies these poetics: she positions herself within an indigenous oral literary tradition but also self-consciously gestures to the Western textual literary tradition.

With tongue-in-cheek humor, the narrator critiques her own storytelling ability in medias res: "But a lot can happen even in between the middle of things, not the least trying the patience of a good ear, and since 'brevity is the noble soul of wit' like *ese* Hamlet said, I will do my best from here on to keep this story to the telling of the events of that day" (Castillo, *So Far from God* 124). The digression is not gratuitous: it responds to arguments that 1990s criticism of Chicana literature and theory lacked grounding in literary history.[33] Moreover, this revision—not just allusion—to Hamlet's lengthy soliloquy is a textual embodiment of Audre Lorde's point that "you cannot dismantle the Master's house with the Master's tools" (Lorde 99). Repeating the style and structure of the Western European literary tradition is not going to dismantle the discourses of racism and sexism those literatures helped to create.

Such narrative strategy is not to be confused with authorial intrusion or postmodern, highbrow intertextuality alone; rather it is representative of Castillo's "struggle to appropriate the 'I' of literary discourse [which] relates to [her] struggle for empowerment in the economic, social, and political spheres" (Yarbro-Bejarano, "Chicana Literature" 139). The narrator's gestures merge oral and written tradition, debunking the literary traditions that accord primacy to written texts. Yvonne Yarbro-Bejarano explains this succinctly: "In other words, the power, the permission, the authority to tell stories about herself and other Chicanas comes from her cultural, racial/ethnic and linguistic community. This authority includes the historical experience of oppression as well as literary tradition" ("Chicana Literature" 141). The narrator is a didactic taleteller that models the merger of political agency with literary production. Self-styled as "highly opinionated," the narrator guides readers through the tale of four sisters forsaken and reclaimed by their community. *So Far from God* tells the stories of the sisters' acts and how their lives are inextricably intertwined with the lives of other Chicanas/os, in a contemporary, feminist version of *Fathers, Martyrs, and Other Saints* (Butler 1866).

Returning to the discussion of left-liberal multiculturalism in the introduction, it is important to note how early in the novel the narrator comments upon the history of Chicano studies programs (Castillo, *So Far from God* 25). Her critique is negative, but more importantly, as Marcus Heide argues of the novel, it "ask[s] to what extent Chicano Studies may empower the community" (173).[34] The sexism Chicanas faced before splitting from their political brothers (Castillo 25), El Movimiento (Castillo 37), and the inefficacy of early Chicano studies programs (Castillo 239) are recurring tropes in the novel.[35] The narrator also delineates contemporary economic and legal practices restricting the physical movement of Chicanas/os, such as the intersections of class and gender ideologies that facilitate adultery, and the compounding of race and class in the rape and mutilation of Chicanas.[36] Castillo crosses and recrosses the political, cultural, religious, and sexual borders constructed by her own culture to voice Chicana self-representation and subjectivity previously largely absent from contemporary American fiction.[37]

The novel contains multiple references to spiritual and cultural practices; however, three significant parts function as ritual ("Doña Felicia's Remedies" and "La Loca's Recipes") or allegory ("The Way of the Cross Good Friday Procession"). The presentations of the rituals appear first in the novel and are linked to individual characters. The allegorization of Christian suffering is also developed throughout the novel but culminates in the polyphonic Good Friday Procession. The insertions of "Doña Felicia's Remedies" and "La Loca's Recipes" illustrate how cultural practices have been passed on through the individuals who use and teach *curanderismo*. The remedies and rituals assume a critical role in the construction of a narrative of reclamation.

Remedios as Ritual

Doña Felicia's remedies are the first cultural practice readers encounter, and they function to illustrate how few Chicanas/os use or remember the healing practices. To reclaim and to preserve them, Castillo incorporates them in the text directly. They are presented in the context of Esperanza's disappearance and Doña Felicia's attempts to divine her whereabouts. The narrator's point of view commands the reader's attention and constructs the text as conversation that includes storytelling, where a disembodied listener asks questions and makes suppositions as the story continues. Doña Felicia, Caridad's landlady, is the local *curandera* who becomes a dear family friend. She is Chicana history itself: born in Mexico, she fought alongside male soldiers in the Mexican Civil

War (1858–1861) and later migrated to the United States (Castillo 44); she is repatriated during the Great Depression (Castillo 61) but returns to America, working as a *bracera* during World War II to avoid redeportation (Castillo 61). Castillo educates a reader unfamiliar with Chicana/o history and reminds more familiar readers with facts from Doña Felicia's life: "Then they lost everything when they were deported back to Mexico in cattle cars along with the rest of the Mexicans who had been brought in as laborers during the days of prosperity" (Castillo 61). As someone who has crossed and recrossed the border, Doña Felicia represents the multilingualism and multiculturalism of Chicanas/os.

Castillo merges postmodern metafiction and formalist techniques in a matter-of-fact omniscient narration to establish the reader's acceptance of these rituals as both pragmatic and spiritual. Just before the remedies appear, the narrator describes the effects of ritual on Caridad, who is learning traditional *curanderismo* from Doña Felicia: "Ritual, in addition to its potent symbolic meanings, was a calming force. Tuesdays and Fridays she prepared a *baño* for herself. Sundays she cleaned her altar, dusting the statues and pictures of saints she prayed to and the framed photographs of her loved ones—with special care to the one of Esperanza who by then, it was known, was a famous prisoner of war" (Castillo 63). Doña Felicia represents a form of biculturalism—the syncretism of religions along the border—by combining indigenous and Catholic ideology and ritual (Castillo 65–71).[38]

Doña Felicia notes the possible causes of the illness necessitating the remedy and the method by which to employ it. She then answers questions about other methods of employment: "You reveal the stomach area, not forgetting to commend yourself to Dios and to repeat the Creed at least three times while you are concentrating, you move the egg on the patient's belly in the sign of the cross, then you break it. Yes, the person may put her hands up so that it doesn't spill off, but where the yolk breaks on her stomach is where the obstruction is" (Castillo, *So Far from God* 65). The remedies themselves are analogous to women's subjectivity: they are part of a matriarchal tradition, but they are not static. They change with each individual who makes use of them. Doña Felicia explains, "To be truthful I don't trust this method as much as my own feeling and my fingers, but I have a lot of practice, so maybe it comes easier to me to just know these things than it will for you right now" (Castillo 66). Her individualization of the remedies provides another example of the failure of institutionalized or established religious and medical practices to work unilaterally. As Delgadillo argues, "By privileging indigenous culture and history, and indigenous women's healing practices, the novelist reclaims an aspect of the ancestral past . . . to create agency and subjectivity for her mestiza and native characters" (906). Doña Felicia is a vital part of the community's memory; the fact that she speaks so infrequently reinforces the overall potential of traditions being lost if they are not actively reclaimed by the current generation of healers. Doña Felicia is Xicanisma.

Theresa Delgadillo, in "Forms of Chicana Feminist Resistance: Hybrid Spirituality in Ana Castillo's *So Far from God*," analyzes the relationship between the spiritual and the political, arguing, "the radical nature of this hybrid spirituality's challenge to the status quo arises not from a reinterpretation of Christianity, but from its embrace of both indigenous and Christian elements" (889). She also suggests, "Although the novel offers examples of religious syncretism, which are inevitable where hybrid spirituality is possible, it does not take a syncretic view of spirituality. That is, it does not attempt to fuse divergent spiritual and religious practices into a unified whole" (Delgadillo 889). Castillo does not unify the religions; rather, the characters' various praise and blame of Catholic saints and indigenous healers suggests that neither alone nor together do various forms of faith solve extant problems. Castillo's inclusion of various "miracles" and "saints," when examined closely, reveals distrust of spiritual practice that is passive in nature.[39]

La Loca, the youngest of the sisters, speaks infrequently. The miraculous elements of her life—her three deaths, resurrection, sainthood, and communion with La Llorona—are more often the focus of analysis on her than her cultural identity is. The presentation of her recipes, representative of a culture of ritual and matrilineal tradition, forms a critical part of the novel as a narrative of reclamation. Her recipes distinguish her from her sisters and other characters in the text. The recipes follow a section of the novel discussing La Loca's relationship with La Llorona and how religious and patriarchal structures co-opted the figure of La Llorona to control women (Castillo 161). La Llorona is first described as "a woman whom everyone knows, who has existed under many names, who has cried over the loss of thousands but who was finally relegated to a kind of 'boogy-woman,' to scare children into behaving themselves, into not straying too far from their mother's watchful eyes" (Castillo 161). La Llorona is tied to pre-Columbian culture, feminizing the mythic Aztlán: "The land was old and the stories were older. Just like a country changed its name, so did the names of their legends change. Once, La Llorona may have been Matlaciuatl, the goddess or the Mexica who was said to prey upon men like a vampire" (Castillo 161). The narrator insists that La Loca was never told the story of La Llorona, so it becomes yet another uncanny aspect of La Loca's ability to communicate with the dead or otherworldly. These metafictional reflections undermine reading La Loca as an element of magical realism.

La Loca's recipes are separated from the novel's frame with their own subheading: "Three of La Loca's Favorite Recipes Just to Whet Your Appetite" (Castillo 165). Similar to the narrative structure preceding Doña Felicia's remedies, La Loca's recipes are preceded by descriptions of her everyday life. These descriptions alert the reader to the fact that even though La Loca learns how to do a lot of things as mundane as playing the fiddle and as complex as performing abortions on Caridad, there is a difference between things one learns alone and things one learns collectively, through the narrative of reclamation: "Above all, Loca knew how to cook. She was, in fact, a better cook than her own mom, even though she learned most of what she knew from Sofi, who had learned what she knew from her own mother, and so on" (Castillo 165). The recipes are introduced through a recollection of La Loca teaching her sister Fe how to cook. La Loca's recipes help maintain cultural practice and help "lost" individuals, such as her sister Fe, reclaim their places in Chicana America.

The narrator modifies instructions on how to make Loca's *adovada*, *posole*, and in the quote below, Loca's *biscochitos*. "In any case, they are made from rich pie pastry dough, to which you add baking powder, sugar to sweeten, and here's the trick, there's always a trick, you know, Fe—a bit of clean aniz seed. Next, you roll it out on the board to about a third of an inch thick (Loca would not say a third of an inch of course, but for our purposes here, I am adding specific measurements myself)" (Castillo 167). The recipes close with the return of the narrator's voice pointing out how the process of cooking brings the women closer together as they tell stories as if "they were old comadres and laughed at the flour that got stuck on their noses" (Castillo 168). Fe has left home physically and culturally. The narrator mentions Fe's desire for material comfort appearing in the form of household appliances, "which she had bought herself with her own hard-earned money from all the bonuses she earned at her new job" (Castillo 171).

La Loca's teaching of Fe is particularly important to the narrative of reclamation. Fe, who has had a strained relationship with her mother and La Loca, reclaims her role in the family and her cultural heritage through the ritualization of foodways. It is in these moments that readers hope Fe will recognize that material comforts and the pride she has in accomplishing things as an individual are a danger to her and her community. Fe's selfish desire to do anything better than her sisters reveals the novel's critique; cultural practice cannot be reclaimed through a passive or an individualistic process. It must be active and it must be communal. The chapter ends foreshadowing Fe's untimely and horrific demise.

Revelation without Restoration

The climactic and most revealing cultural practice, the Way of the Cross procession on Good Friday, brings the novel's events to a dystopic close. These pages, though, exemplify collective activism as the only way for the people of Tome to reclaim their losses. The narrator makes those "Few Random Remarks from the Highly Opinionated Narrator" against the backdrop of a ritual reenactment of Jesus Christ's crucifixion on Good Friday. Echoing themes of Revelation, the narrator decries how Chicanas/os are exploited and eliminated from the planet. The outcries of the participants move to reclaim their physical, environmental, spiritual, and economic health. Clearly implying that Tome has become the sacrificial lamb, the section merges Jesus Christ's crucifixion with the Apocalypse, which begins with environmental destruction: "When Jesus was condemned to death the spokesperson for the committee working to protest dumping radioactive waste in the sewer addressed the crowd . . ." (Castillo 242).[40] The narrator merges Christian and Marxist ideology: "Jesus bore His cross and a man declared that most of the Native and hispano families throughout the land were living below poverty level, one out of six families collected food stamps . . ." (242). Though quite condensed, these quotations illustrate the extent to which the text characterizes reclamation as a collective political and cultural act.

This scene is a fictionalized representation of what Castillo argues for in the final chapter of *Massacre of the Dreamers*: "Xicanisma, therefore, includes an ongoing awareness of our responsibility to ourselves, with those in our personal lives, to those we make alliances with, and to the environment (with all that the word implies)" (224). The description of the procession repeats the three political concerns—environmental destruction, unemployment, and the loss of ancestral lands—echoing the rhythm and numerology of the three-part performance of the Liturgy of the Eucharist, which includes the preparation, consecration, and consumption of the "body and blood of Christ."[41] The narrator states: "Jesus was helped by Simon and the number of those without jobs increased each day. . . . Jesus fell for the second time. . . . Jesus fell a third time. . . . Nuclear plants sat like gargantuan landmines among the people, near their ranches and ancestral homes. . . . Jesus was nailed to the cross . . ." (Castillo, *So Far from God* 242). In this heightened mix of apocalypse and realism, the external realities of Mexican and Native Americans are represented.[42] The spiritual hybridity developed in the novel is based on a specific geographic and historic location that emphasizes racial composition is not synonymous with ethnic identity, spiritual belief, or political ideology.[43]

At each of the twelve Stations of the Cross, individuals speak about the living conditions of Chicanas/os, martyring the community as a whole. Sofi has come to a political awareness about this oppression and has led the community to do the same. The activism reflects a distinguishing feature of Chicana cultural theory: "By delving into this deep core, the Chicana writer finds that the self she seeks to define and love is not merely an individual self, but a collective one" (Yarbro-Bejarano, "Chicana Literature" 141). The final description of Jesus Christ's death repeats all three issues: "Deadly pesticides were sprayed directly and from helicopters above on the vegetables and fruits and on the people who picked them for large ranchers at subsistence wages and their babies died in their bellies from poisoning. . . ! Ayyy! Jesus died on the cross" (Castillo 243).

Sofi and several unidentified speakers name the exploitation they suffer. There is no resurrection in this allegory, but there is reclamation. Individual and communal crisis are yoked in the apocalypse Tome suffers: "In the blend of Catholicism, native belief, self-respect, political action, and reflection, the procession epitomizes the power of a hybrid resistance" (Delgadillo 912).[44] By the novel's close, each of the sisters has been abused by humanity; their lives demonstrate how the acts of individuals and communities are mutually consequential. Caridad was raped, mutilated, and left to die: "No one was even ever detained as a suspect. And as the months went by, little by little, the scandal and shock of Caridad's assault were forgotten, by the news media, the police, the neighbors, and the church people" (Castillo, *So Far from God* 33). Despite this, Caridad is charitable to her community through her curanderismo when she becomes a healer; she has to leave again when a homophobic, obsessive Catholic Penitent literally stalks her to death.[45] Caminero-Santangelo observes that "Caridad might be elevated to the level of myth by her connectedness with nature, but it is highly questionable how such a connection in and of itself helps her, much less the larger community. In the arena of religion, as we have seen, a helpless 'faith' in miracles and magic is ultimately deflated as a route to agency in favor of a liberation theology that combines religious rites with political protest" ("'The Pleas of the Desperate'" 91).

Similar possibilities are visible in the fates of Esperanza and Fe. When Esperanza leaves Tome to report on the political oppression and crisis in the Gulf War, her cultural and geographic community's welfare remains unguarded and its oppressions unprotested: "By then, aside from it being a great career break, it was pretty clear to her that there was no need of her on the home front. Her sisters had recovered" (Castillo 47). Esperanza is murdered;

her physical body is lost, and thus her family can never reclaim it. Her spirit, however, visits La Loca, suggesting that Hope must be manifested in new or different ways outside an individual heroine, healer, or saint (Castillo 158–59). After being betrayed by her first love, Reuben, her El Movimiento compatriot who sleeps with an Anglo woman, Fe screams for days and literally renders herself dumb. She is no longer able to speak in complete sentences (Castillo 154–156). Fe, too, looks for restoration and ways to escape Tome and enjoys the rapid promotions she receives at Acme Corporation.

Once employed at Acme, Fe compounds her own voicelessness by exhibiting "blind Faith;" she fails to persist in asking questions that could save Tome's environment as well as her own life: "Because after Fe died, she did not resurrect as La Loca did at age three. She also did not return ectoplasmically like her tenacious earth-bound sister Esperanza. Very shortly after that first prognosis, Fe just died" (Castillo 186). Rather than exposing and criminalizing Acme's environmental contamination, the FBI blames Fe for the pollution, compounding the painful and debilitating cancer and chemotherapy she undergoes (Castillo 184–89). Caminero-Santangelo reads Castillo's depiction of Fe cynically as well: "Fe's death calls on us to stop suspending our disbelief and to consider the difference between magical solutions (which provide no agency at all since they occur randomly) and real problems" ("'The Pleas of the Desperate'" 85). Caridad's rumination on the losses of her sisters Fe and Esperanza reifies the distance between the magic and the real: "But Fe, who had stroked Caridad's brow so tenderly on that night of restoration when she had returned to the living after her encounter with the *malogra*, was really dead. And you couldn't bring back something that was dead no matter how much you sat on your ankles before your candles and incense and prayed for a word, a sign, no matter what you did" (Castillo 205). When La Loca, isolated from nearly all human interaction, contracts AIDS, she breaks any link between the magic and the real in the novel.

Castillo uses La Loca to reflect 1980s medical discourse on AIDS. Castillo presents her as an innocent: an undeserving, presumed nonrisk victim of AIDS. La Loca represents intravenous drug users and homosexual men, who were rhetorically constructed as high-risk populations by medical practitioners and government health officials. The narrator decries, "It was the Murder of the Innocents all over again, he said, and again, there was lamentation, and weeping and great mourning, not just in Rama as in the Gospels, but this time all over the world. Jesus was stripped of his garments" (Castillo 243). Even if one chooses to read La Loca's contraction of HIV and subsequent development of AIDS as a magical realist moment, Castillo again separates the magic from the real by questioning people's worship of La Loca. The narrator's language is subtle but her critique is pointed: "She was not particularly noted for answering the pleas of the desperate and the hopeless, neither, like el Saint Jude, for example, who is the patron saint of los desesperados. In other words, people never really could figure out who La Loca protected and oversaw as a rule, or what she was good to pray to about" (Castillo 248). Cumulatively, the abuses in the sisters' lives amount to a perhaps irrevocable loss: the loss of religious certainty. *So Far from God* shares this sense of loss with Rivera's . . . *And the Earth Did Not Devour Him*. Castillo's novel suggests that neither Catholic nor Mexican indigenous religious structures help the community reclaim its land, culture, or health. The title of the novel, *So Far from God*, powerfully articulates the physical, linguistic, and spiritual distances between Mexican and Native American cultures defining Chicana experience.

Despite the devastating losses Tome suffers, *So Far from God* does offer readers a narrative of reclamation, visible in its illustrations of how culture and identity can be reclaimed. Chicana experience can change, as seen in a concrete manifestation of Xicanisma: Sofi's public service.[46] Earlier in life, Sofi has been more of an observer than an activist; however, through the abuses of her daughters, she realizes no one can be empowered without collective action. The narrator describes a grassroots movement that begins with Sofi and her *comadre*: "So the two earnest women started their campaign by going around for months talking to neighbors, to fellow parishioners, people at the schools, at the local Y, and other such places to get ideas and help" (Castillo 146). Sofi does not use her own voice in her family until she becomes mayor. The narrator asserts, "She had never raised her voice like that to any of her daughters, but since becoming la Mayor of the Village Council, even if it wasn't official (nor was the village council for that matter since Tome was not incorporated) there was no stopping Fe's mom from ever speaking her mind no more" (Castillo 157). Sofi then uses her voice over and over.

Sofi's voice facilitates tangible reclamations for the community. Residents start a wool cooperative, and Sofi arranges for educational credits based on life experience to be awarded by the local community college. She inspires her neighbors to farm organically and reclaim their community from transborder ills, such as drug trafficking and related violence, through an informal SWAT team (Castillo 146). Her progression from the door-to-door campaign to the founding of the international organization M.O.M.A.S. is a perfect example of what Marcus Heide argues about educational spaces as being "firstly, framed as spaces for negotiating individual and collective identity, and secondly, as intersections of local micropolitics and broader, national or global politics" (173). The narrator describes when Sofi becomes the "founder and la first presidenta of what would become known worldwide and very prestigious, 'Mothers of Martyrs and Saints'" and returns to the lighter, gossipy tone the novel used before the Good Friday Procession. Ironically, the closing of the novel suggests that Tome's problems may return: M.O.M.A.S. becomes commodified (Castillo, *So Far from God* 247) and rumors about its elitism begin (Castillo 247).[47] While Sofi cannot transform Tome into a utopia, she is able to model Xicanisma. The concept of *voice*—of claiming one's voice, of coming to voice, of using one's voice— permeates contemporary literature. A lack of voice, as we have seen in *So Far from God*, is an extremely dangerous lack. That danger is also portrayed in the novel *Soledad*.

Voice as Ritual: Silent Screaming in *Soledad*

Most readers of contemporary fiction, especially high school and college students, developed knowledge about the Dominican Republic through the prolific fiction of Julia Alvarez. Her germinal autoethnography, *How the García Girls Lost Their Accents* (1992), remains on high school and college syllabi even though she has written several other novels, including *In the Time of the Butterflies*, which has been the basis for two Hollywood productions about the era of Trujillo. The national rhetoric of silence characterizing the Trujillato has been persistent until recently. Following the publication of *In the Time of the Butterflies*, Dominicans have contested international perception of themselves through active revisions of public space, particularly spaces that serve to rewrite Trujillo's script of his patriarchal supremacy.[48] The national narrative constructed around the artifacts, images, and museums has moved from recounting the Mirabal sisters' personal violation to a reclamation of collective memory in a traceable sequence of public interventions.[49]

The success of Junot Díaz's novel *The Brief Wondrous Life of Oscar Wao* has exposed an even larger audience to the history and culture of Dominicans. Yet other Caribbean writers made earlier and important fictional contributions to understanding US neocolonialism and interethnic racism. Because of the success of Alvarez's novel and the public memorials that followed it, novels such as Haitian American Edwidge Danticat's *The Farming of Bones* (1999) have garnered critical attention and popular success for their engagement of international silences about the era. Three less renowned but no less important novels, Angie Cruz's *Soledad* (2001) and *Let It Rain Coffee* (2006) and Nelly Rosario's *Song of the Water Saints* (2002), link a single aspect of

Dominican history—the era of Trujillo—to other moments of Dominican history: independence from Spain, occupation by Haiti, the Haitian genocide, and the assassination of Trujillo. This linkage suggests that personal and public memory cannot be separated. Each of these novels portrays their mutual inclusion in distinct ways.[50]

Nelly Rosario and Angie Cruz are Dominican American writers whose novels particularly help readers understand Dominican women's experiences in the decades before and after Trujillo's 1961 assassination. Nelly Rosario's *Song of the Water Saints* reveals not only how the United States' 1916 invasion limited Dominican women's movement on the island but also how economic obstacles to their international migration remained long after the yanquis and Trujillo were removed. *Song of the Water Saints* follows several generations of women but focuses most of the narrative action on the women who grew up in the Dominican Republic. Angie Cruz's *Soledad* reverses that narrative focus by exploring the lives of young Dominican American women haunted by memories of post-Trujillato neocolonialism. *Soledad* examines relationships between gender and movement, the abuse of the female body, and the disjuncture between Dominican women's hopes for and actual possibilities for permanent return to the island.[51] The novel explores how women reclaim their national identity and the control over their bodies through collaborative memory.

Before 1970, only 10 percent of Dominicans living in the United States were foreign born; by 2000, 68 percent were foreign born and immigrated to the United States as children or young adults (Ramirez).[52] In 2003, Dominican studies scholar Daisy Cocco De Filippis urged her colleagues to define a theory of Dominican experience that incorporates both island and US perspectives. De Fillipis advocated that scholars create "scholarship in the field that will move from the inclusion of voices to a new understanding of the Dominican experience" (20). Both of Cruz's novels, *Soledad* and *Let It Rain Coffee*, do just that because they define Dominican women's experiences through the depiction of multiple migrations. These novels differ from US Latina/o narratives that depict a single Puerto Rican migration or Cuban exile or that focus on the desire for arrival. Rather, these novels define a critical aspect of poor Dominican life: intranational migrations precede international migrations. *Let It Rain Coffee* explores this issue as well; to provide opportunity for her family, one of the central protagonists immigrates to Puerto Rico, and then to New York. Such migration, as already noted, is troubled with a constant desire to return home. In *Soledad*, this desire to return manifests itself in a specific narrative of reclamation. The novel tells the story of two women's attempts to reclaim their dominicanidad: Soledad, a college student, and Olivia, her mother.

This section of *Chicana/o and Latina/o Fiction* begins the project of connecting lesser-known texts to better-known texts to open the discourse on representations of Chicana/o and Latina/o life. Little scholarship exists on *Soledad*. The two primary readings about it include its analysis as part of an urban literature/ghetto bildungsroman (Dalleo and Machado Sáez 2007) and as an exploration of the economic and psychological effects of sex tourism on the sex worker (Francis 2011). Dalleo and Machado Sáez read the novel "as a response to the problematic outlined by Junot Díaz's *Drown* and the conflicting writerly agendas of oppositional politics versus nostalgic recuperation" (90). Their reading focuses on the "limits of the ghetto itself as a locale for the representation of the authentic Latina/o subject" (90). Donette Francis explores the relationships between shame and silence in "Novel Insights: Sex Work, Secrets, and Depression in Angie Crúz's *Soledad*." Francis' assertion that "[Olivia's] story is not a model of diaspora that valorizes the homeland, nor does it proffer an idealized version of the American dream or diasporic romance" is a succinct statement about the protagonists' challenges in reclaiming their dominicanidad (59). In reading the novel as a narrative of reclamation, the rest of this chapter considers the losses Olivia experienced first in the Dominican Republic and then in Washington Heights. It then discusses why those losses haunt not only Olivia but also her daughter. The chapter illustrates how, together, the women reclaim their identities.

Bodies Not at Rest

The story begins as Soledad, the primary narrator, has started college and has moved out of her mother's home into an apartment with a friend. She unwillingly returns home when her mother succumbs to depression. In a manner similar to the narrator of . . . *And the Earth Did Not Devour Him*, Olivia moves between sleep and silent wakefulness, remaining catatonic for weeks. She becomes an embodiment of Dominican experience: she has been silent about her life in the Dominican Republic. Her silence should not be interpreted as cultural amnesia or a desire to arrive. Her life in both nations has been so traumatic it literally silences and paralyzes her. Silence is a major trope in the novel, the catalyst not only for its crisis but also for its resolution. Olivia remains conscious but silent and bedridden for most of the novel. Her stream-of-consciousness memories are interspersed between Soledad's narrations, illustrating how the two generations deal with memory, what each perceives as the loss of their dominicanidad, and their consequential sense of nonbelonging to the Dominican diaspora.

Soledad takes place during approximately the same time period as the stories of *Drown*. As the novel flashes back and forth between the 1960s and the 1980s, it focuses more on international migration and the relationship between immigrants and their US-born children than on the internal migrations foregrounded in Díaz's *Drown*. Global economic conditions deteriorated and widespread poverty took over in the Dominican Republic, especially by the 1970s. The tourist industry provided jobs primarily for women, but those low-paying jobs were sufficient motivation to go to the United States, where work was perceived to be abundant and higher paying. Gorda, Olivia's older sister, leaves to secure work to help the family obtain visas. Olivia, as were other young Dominicanas, is lured into the tourist-sex industry that arises when Trujillo is killed and the nation is overrun by foreign investors. The exploitation of sex workers is particularly important in this novel. Olivia's diary of clients reveals the diversity of travelers who are the island's sex-tourists: Greeks, Swiss, French, Chinese, Cuban, Argentinean, American, Spanish, Italian, and German. Francis categorizes the novel as an antiromance in its exposure of the sex tourism industry and its failure to offer positive resolution for the characters: "it astutely brings together timely questions of sexuality and transnational citizenship and thereby challenges an emerging diasporic romance of better fortunes and sexual freedoms abroad" (55).

Through Olivia's first flashback, we learn that at fifteen, Olivia became aware of her body as a burden, because her "father was just waiting until she was old enough to marry her off" (Cruz 47). Olivia desires economic stability and defines freedom as having "a house with a roof that wouldn't tear off every time a hurricane came through. That was all she wanted, to be on her own" (Cruz 47). Francis initially argues, "[T]his scene is perhaps the first instance in which Olivia becomes aware of her sexuality, and it is where she begins to understand that her sexed body can be bartered for financial and material resources. In other words, she learns that she can trade sex for the visa, and importantly, this lesson is taught by her father" (60). Olivia wants freedom; she wants to be "on her own," not married. Moreover, Olivia seeks opportunity to be properly compensated for work; she is lured into the sex tourism industry through blatant deceit.[53] Francis asserts, "Cruz also shifts our gaze from the usual focus on castigation of foreign men consuming and exploiting Dominican females to offer a more internal critique of Dominican men exploiting Dominican women" (58). Olivia is not well paid for her sexual labor, especially when she meets Manolo, the man she would eventually marry: "Manolo had paid the Swedish man in advance so he could have her all to himself" (Cruz 50).

While the other clients repulse Olivia because of their age or physicality, none of them tries to exert the ownership over her body and mind in the way Manolo does. He dominates her when she is a sex worker, telling her how to dress, how to walk, and what to eat. Manolo "didn't let her speak in public" (Cruz 50). Thus, even before they went to New York, Manolo has imposed silence upon Olivia. She agrees to go with Manolo because she believes he can provide a home for her and her child. Her initial observations and reaction to New York's largess and seeming riches mirror early-twentieth-century immigrant novels. Quickly, however, the desire to arrive via the respectability being married can bring her is shattered by the realities of Manolo's abuse and confinement of her. He continues his physical possession of Olivia in New York; it ends when he dies, but it is then that his psychological possession takes over.

The Importance of Whiteness

The perception of race pervades the novel and clarifies why Manolo treats Olivia the way he does.[54] Using a diminutive that marks both race and class to describe him, Olivia recalls: "She immediately assumed he was part of the help. Why else would the *morenito* speak Spanish to her?" (Cruz 48). Race, as Jorge Duany illustrates, is interpreted and classified very differently in the Caribbean, even where people have similar cultural and racial origins. He notes, for example, that the "fluid gradation of phenotypes makes it difficult to discriminate against intermediate groups exclusively on the basis of color and other physical attributes" ("Reconstructing Racial Identity" 162). Olivia's use of the diminutive form of the term *moreno—morenito—*immediately reinforces her sense of class, suggesting that she perceives herself as having, or at least coming from, a higher social position than Manolo.[55] Olivia notes that his skin is the "color of caramelized sugar" and he has "full lips that filled his face," suggesting that he is not a light-skinned Dominican but one with more African physiognomy (Cruz 49).[56]

Similarly to Yunior's comments in the story "How to Date a Browngirl, Blackgirl, Whitegirl, or Halfie," the characters of *Soledad* constantly perform colorism. They make references to skin shade, hair quality, facial features, Haitian blood, and Spanish blood. At the time Manolo had immigrated to the United States, the Dominican population had not yet shifted immigration to Puerto Rico as a stepping-stone. Duany makes an important observation about Dominican racial identity based on his case study of residents in Barrio Gandul: "it is segregated primarily along class lines rather than in terms of skin color or national origin" ("Reconstructing Racial Identity" 162). His observations support reading Olivia's perception of Manolo's class and race as mutually constitutive. Such colorism should not be surprising given the comments Olivia's family makes. Soledad describes how both her grandmother and aunt view her appearance: "And with lots of cariño she runs her hands through my hair which reaffirms to her that there is truly some Spanish blood left in her bloodline. But Gorda has always blamed my straight hair and light skin on the mailman or the airplane pilot" (Cruz 126). Later in the novel, her grandmother returns to the topic of race and tells Soledad, "It was rare to have a man like your [grand]father pick a woman like me as a wife. We were the kind that had a few too many feet in a Haitian kitchen," implying that while Olivia's side of the family might be lighter skinned, that was due to the process of *blanqueamiento*—"whitening" through marriage (Cruz 186). Despite the racial gradations in their ancestry, Olivia's family has a sense that it married up on the social scale before Manolo. The point Olivia makes about Manolo liking her light skin suggests that, ironically, he believes he is the one marrying "up."[57]

The crisis of the novel begins decades before within this racialized context. Pregnant, Olivia cannot return home unless she is married. Even though she is unsure who the baby's father is, she convinces Manolo it is his, and he brings her to New York. After migration, Olivia and her sister experience similar fates: their marriages are strained by the struggle with urban poverty. Gorda's husband abandons her and her daughter, Flaca, and Manolo beats Olivia, blaming her for trapping him in a marriage. He looks for himself in Soledad but cannot bond to her because, ironically, she becomes what he sought in Olivia: "Since the day she was born, he watched her, waited to find a trace of himself in her and the paler she became, her nose, the shape of her eyes, her fine straight hair, neither Olivia's or his, Manolo lost faith in her" (Cruz 140). Even though he wanted to marry up, Manolo's patrimonial pride supersedes his desire for deracination.[58]

Soledad always struggled with her mother, particularly in not understanding Olivia's silence about Manolo and her life in the Dominican Republic. Soledad says, "I imagine her to be more like me, with a desire to see the world, to try new things" (Cruz 6). Soledad was precisely like Olivia; Gorda notes that Soledad was "born with la pata caliente, feet burning to be anywhere but here" (Cruz 1). Soledad longs to escape the neighborhood and resists dating a young man in it because "he's not my type, he's from the hood. I want something better for myself" (Cruz 76). Soledad disdains everything about her home in Washington Heights; her neighborhood and family become a primary site of cultural rejection and the inability to arrive: "It's always like that: just when I think I don't give a shit about what my family thinks, they find a way to drag me back home" (Cruz 1).

The novel is pervaded by Soledad's references to her nonbelonging in Latina/o America. When she first returns to home she notes, "the last thing I want is to look lost or confused about where I'm going" (Cruz 3). In her first encounter with the young man who becomes her cultural antagonist, Richie, she confesses that she gets "anxious over purchasing an avocado that's too ripe or not ready to eat, or *plátanos* that are past their time and will soak up their oil, or dried yucca, or soft potatoes, or moldy peppers" (Cruz 52). In *So Far from God* and *Soledad*, foodways are gendered feminine. In *Soledad*, the ability to select and prepare food is gendered female to the extent that its lack is emblematic not only of a lack of cultural knowledge but also of a failure of feminine sexual maturation: "Worst of all, when I'm going through the vegetables, I feel as if I'm being watched and laughed at, that a woman my age still hasn't figured it out. I can almost hear the other women in the store thinking to themselves, How is she ever getting married, she still doesn't know how to pick fruit" (Cruz 52). These sentiments are echoed in her grandmother's efforts to teach Soledad how to "cook" mofongo, which obviously represents a heterosexual Dominican woman's sexual power: "'Don't let him peek in your pots. You're feeding him and you control your kitchen'" (Cruz 64). Soledad realizes, "That's probably where I go wrong. I let guys peek in my pots too soon" (Cruz 64). These cultural mistakes culminate in a desperate yearning to link her memories of the country with her sense of belonging to its culture: "I haven't been there in a while. But I remember it though" (Cruz 127).

After describing Olivia's physical arrival in New York, Cruz plays on the metaphorical sense of arrival used in this study. Soledad muses, "When I'm sitting on one of those tall bar stools facing the window, watching people walk by, sipping my foamy milk, sprinkled with cinnamon, among other university students, I feel like I've *arrived*" (Cruz 67; emphasis added). Eventually, her friend Caramel shows Soledad that thinking she has arrived in Anglo-America is a false perception masking her self-exclusion from Latina/o America. Caramel teaches Soledad that her individual arrival means nothing unless it benefits her family and her community. Soledad believes she is most comfortable outside the neighborhood, where her poor background is invisible, but ultimately, through her friendship with Caramel and her return home, she realizes she has not been any more comfortable outside Washington Heights than she has been inside it. As Dalleo and Machado Sáez persuasively argue, "Soledad envies Caramel's ability to courageously embody a politics of opposition and critique, one that invokes the Civil Rights and feminist movements" (92). Even when Soledad starts to think about how she feels more at home in the art gallery, Caramel quickly undermines this comfort by asking her a provocative question: "When was the last time you saw a Latina artist in a gallery"? (Cruz 56). Soledad responds, "I never thought about it like that" (Cruz 56).

Caramel's politicization of art makes Soledad cognizant of how she has not arrived: "These places are traps. Don't you see there is no place for us to go from here? Soledad, we need to start our own thing, make our own rules, where the sky is the limit. A place where our mamis can come and visit and not feel like they don't belong" (Cruz 57). It takes more prodding for Soledad to see Caramel's point of view; when Soledad asserts that the gallery people can't be that bad because they hired her, Caramel retorts, "They hired you because you're not brown like me and you have Cooper Union as your passport" (Cruz 58). This comment reveals Caramel's Xicanisma: she is attuned to colorism and institutional racism. Echoing Ana Castillo's critiques about higher education, Caramel acknowledges the racial and class differences members of the Anglo-American mainstream mark between themselves and Chicanas/os or Latinas/os. Caramel's attention to race is not without its own problems; colorism permeates the young women's sexual conversations and friendship as well.

The younger characters of *Soledad* highlight sexual attractions or preference for lighter-skinned individuals as a way to make one another feel as if they are betraying their culture just as the characters in *Drown* and *Bodega Dreams* do.[59] Despite her efforts to get Soledad to recognize the intersectionality of race and class, Caramel simultaneously confines Soledad to a place where she feels Soledad belongs: in sexual relationships with brown men or women. When Caramel says, "I just think your thing for white boys is weird," Soledad protests, "You date white girls. Do I ever say anything about that? I like cute guys, that's all" (Cruz 67). Caramel's sexuality is another challenge for Soledad, one she seems to handle better than the protagonist, Yunior, does in *Drown*. Soledad notes, "After two years of living with Caramel I've thought about our possibly messing around"; when the opportunity presents itself, the two exchange kisses and caresses until Soledad stops herself: "I contemplate also making a move, touching her breast, hers smaller and pointier than mine, but I can't, I'm too nervous. What if we ruin our friend-ship over this? What if I don't like it and I hurt her feelings? What if I really like it? I have to go pee, I say, pushing her away gently" (Cruz 117).

Though never explicitly stated by any of the characters, it is clearly implied that Soledad's extended absence from home is the catalyst of Olivia's catatonia. In a stream-of-consciousness passage, Olivia explains how she births and loses a nameless child: "*I have this one recurring dream where this faceless child climbs out of me from right between my legs. She's all grown, speaking in full sentences, with perfect hand-eye coordination*" (Cruz 46).[60] Here, Soledad is represented as a nameless child, but the remainder of the dream and Olivia's response to it clearly link her loss of Soledad to her depression. Olivia explains, "*And like a bird, she perches up on the fire escape and asks me to join her. . . . So I go to the fire escape and open my arms and try to lift myself into the sky but before I can fly away Victor grabs me and takes me inside. I promise this child that came through me that when I have the chance, I will try again*" (Cruz 47). The pos-sibility of losing Soledad sends Olivia into the catatonia, where she does not eat, move, or speak for weeks; a man in the neighborhood succinctly explains the nation's crisis, which is manifested in Olivia's depression: "You know, when I was your age, no maybe even younger than you, I knew I had to get out of that country. When Trujillo died, the whole country went mad. You never seen madness until you see people about to lose everything they got" (Cruz 167).[61] Olivia's madness started when she was duped into prostitution, continued when Manolo's domestic violence disillusioned her, and peaked when her daughter became estranged from her.

Soledad's grandmother believes that Olivia's crisis started when she rec-ognized her losses: "After Manolo died your mother thought she could just go back to D.R. and relive her *niñez*.[62] . . . And when she couldn't buy our old land in Juan Dolio, because the government owns it now and leased it to a bunch of Germans, Olivia cracked and her spirit spilled out from her" (Cruz 155).[63] The concept of return to the island is also fraught for Soledad but in an oppositional and ironic manner. In her discussion of allegory in US Latina/o literature, Di Iorio Sandín makes a critical point: "allegory is a trope that emphasizes division and fragmentation" (6). Citing Walter Benjamin's theorization of allegory, Di Iorio Sandín argues that "the most interesting aspect of this notion of allegory is, then, that the allegorist reassembles the fragments—of a past that can never really be accurately reproduced or pre-sented—into his own version" (7). In *Soledad*, everyone in Soledad's family allegorizes the motif of return. Di Iorio Sandín's analysis is superb for read-ing *Soledad*: "This challenge to the notion of the past as an unbroken series of events leading to the present is clearly relevant to US Latino/a Caribbean literature in which the recent dislocations from a Spanish Caribbean home of origin are constantly remembered, lived, reinvented" (7). Soledad's family engages in all three of these relationships with the past. Soledad, for example, remembers negative treatment as a gringa and fears returning to the Dominican Republic, a place where she could be trapped in poverty: "sometimes I have nightmares about it, where I somehow land in the Dominican Republic and I have no papers to get out of the country, no extra clothes to wear and I need to go to the bathroom but the toilets don't flush" (Cruz 127). Because this nightmare is a reverse image of how Olivia remembers the past, mother and daughter are like foils. Olivia, in contrast, recalls entering in the United States, with very credible falsified documents, new clothes, and in awe of the modernity and abundance of the water in the city (Cruz 66).

Soledad knows that for her mother and aunt, the memory of the Dominican Republic has kept them alive: it is their home, and she longs to connect to her mother, if only to understand her own origins. She recalls her mother's words: "In New York, they don't live, they work, until we go home. My mother always told me that home is a place of rest, a place to live" (Cruz 219). The immigration narrative Olivia and Gorda tell is a false story for Soledad and Flaca, one that does not help them reclaim their dominicanidad. Once the truth is revealed, Soledad and her mother must reclaim the past, even if it is fragmentary. Olivia's first attempt to reclaim the Dominican Republic may have failed because it was based on a falsely perceived social status. Her exilic nostalgia led her to desire returning to a higher social class than she was relegated to in the United States. Because her father sought to "marry her off," readers can surmise that her family was not affluent in the way Olivia's mother and sister choose to remember.

The novel's depiction of contrasting attitudes about the island is an effective illustration of what scholar Daisy De Filippis is advocating. *Soledad* implies that for the Dominicanas who survived the Trujillato, the United States is a place to work so that they can build a home on the island. For their children, the island is a foreign place with which they do not identify, much like the failures to identify with Puerto Rico by the adolescent protagonists of *The Latin Deli*. Angie Cruz articulated this about her own family in an interview with Nelly Rosario: "you know, they came here and they felt lucky to be in the U.S. and they worked really hard and tried not to create any problems and they tried to save as much as possible to go back, which they never will, not in the way that they imagined" (749). Set alternatively on the island and in the United States, the novel depicts what remains true for Dominican immigrants: a long, complicated visa process, relative newness as immigrants to the United States, and a sense of dispossession of their own country. Readers are introduced to anti-yanqui sentiment, silence about the Trujillato, and Dominicans' constant desire to return to the island. For the mothers in this novel and Yunior's mother in *Drown*, survival means several moves—the last of which is most likely, and unfortunately, not to the space they consider home.

Some of Olivia's final words capture Cruz's belief that Dominican women, in particular, can never really return home: "*I remember back to a time when I could walk on the beach without a pass from the hotel. When I was too young to fear getting raped, hurt, or lost*" (Cruz 221). Understanding these conditions may help readers understand that not everyone comes to the United States to shed their original national identity; many people come because the United States or other foreign nations have stripped their country of its sovereignty, and they hope they will return home to reclaim it. Francis makes a compelling point about the concept of home for the women in the novel: "They underscore that neither familial home, national homeland, nor immigrant nation functions as a safe space of belonging; and female characters therefore often dwell in liminal spaces of vulnerability" (53). Virtually all of the novel's action is set in the family's small apartments, including the containment and violence Manolo perpetuates against Olivia and Soledad. The novel rushes toward its dénouement when Olivia and Gorda's father dies. His illness echoes Manolo's, and his death causes a reconfiguration of the home. Soledad experiences posttraumatic stress recalling the moment when her own father died, in the same apartment.

Remembering his death also triggers Soledad's memory of her father's molestation of her. Cruz foreshadows Soledad's rape throughout the novel, illustrating silences the home space holds (30) and how urgently Soledad has worked to contain them (Cruz 184–89). Cruz also uses the metaphor of sleep to illustrate how Soledad dealt with this sexual abuse: "I try to choke my father but his image splits, blowing apart like a dead dandelion, leaving no trace of him. I want to fall asleep. My eyes burning, my ears ringing, I want to fall asleep forever" (Cruz 191). Sleep is no comfort for mother or daughter in this novel. Soledad begins to have nightmares, and Gorda decides that they must get rid of Manolo's spirit to help both Soledad and Olivia—to reclaim the space of the home for the three generations of women who occupy it.

Archiving Secrets

As they are cleaning out Olivia's things, Soledad finds mementos her mother had saved: Soledad's first passport, her baby hair, and some drawings she had made in preschool. Initially, these objects comfort her, but when Soledad opens the container with her mother's things, she is immediately distressed: "Inside it I find a sheer floral wrap, a postcard of la Virgen María, a matchbook from a restaurant called Puerto Plata Disco. Why would she save this? She's never said anything about Puerto Plata, or has she?" (Cruz 193). Soledad finds Olivia's list of clients. Not knowing what the names mean, she starts to read the names out and she and Gorda are horrified to see the ghosts of all the naked men appear, including Manolo. Soledad has found out her mother's secret—that Olivia's husband might not have been her father—and Gorda realizes what has rendered Olivia silent. Like Pandora, Soledad opened a box she ought not have and unleashed evil into her home. In a rare instance of metafiction in the novel, Gorda asserts, "When you write something down, it keeps it alive. There is a certain power to words, memories, ideas when one writes them down. You see the moment your mother made this list of all these men, she trapped a memory and therefore kept them alive. When someone writes something, its because they want to be found out in a way" (Cruz 196).

The idea of the archive—the textual construction of the indigenous by colonizing nations—resonates with Nelly Rosario's use of the erotic postcard to write against the archive of the native in *Song of the Water Saints*. In that novel and in *Soledad*, images are used to depict both the sexual arousal of the sex tourist and the sexual repulsion of the sex worker. Soledad is reliving her mother's disgust and is repulsed by the ghosts. Francis aptly notes, "Attention to how children fare in the aftermath of their mother's labor shows that bodies bear archival memories that cannot be erased by simple geographic relocation" (67). What bothers her most is their presumed ownership of the home space, which Soledad likens to a historic image: "Like an old painting of bathers at a bathhouse, they assemble peacefully; there's a sepia cast to them all" (Cruz 195). The images suggest the distancing needed to perform sex work: "that geographic and psychic distancing were central shows that work does impact Olivia's sense of self and that she has to steel herself from the various acts of sexual-economic transactions" (Francis 62). Francis notes, "Through Olivia's character, we explore what happens when one stuffs one's insides into the deepest corners, connecting one's labor choices to one's mental health and overall well-being" (57). Olivia's silence is caused by more than her labor; Cruz does not portray the labor of sex work as a choice and she ends the labor years before, by killing Manolo.

The novel's focus on secrets among mothers and daughters offers another example of the failure of the diasporic romance and the need for the narrative of reclamation. It reconfigures mother-daughter relations so that daughters have to work to identify with mothers they perceive do not love them.[64] Flaca, Gorda's daughter, has a strained relationship with her own mother and an unusually close relationship with Olivia.[65] This closeness drives Soledad to believe that her mother does not love her. Olivia's catatonia is amplified by her realizing how disconnected she is to her country and how that has affected her relationship with Soledad. Just before the family leaves for Santo Domingo, Olivia dreams of the unnamed child again: "*I know to follow her onto the fire escape. But this time I had to ask her, Who are you? Let me see your face. And the girl turns her face looking at me in disbelief. How come you don't know? Wasn't it you who gave me my name?*" (Cruz 212). The urgency of her condition is revealed in this dream variation. No longer physically tied to her homeland or to her daughter psychologically, Olivia's "rest" is interrupted by incidents of floating and dreams of flight, which are not seamless moments of magical realism. Olivia's movements are explained as near fatal exits through windows and off the fire escape.

Olivia's family turns to traditional healing methods, eschewing hospitalization. Soledad represents a second generation of immigrants who place blind faith in American institutions; she is similar to Fe in *So Far from God*. Initially, she distrusts her ethnic culture's ways: "What they need to understand is that maybe my mother might be critically ill, that they're wasting time, but of course they're not rational. . . . My grandmother is split between ideas, countries, her dreams and what's real" (Cruz 11). Soledad's view illustrates that "Cruz's novel alternatively allows for the possibility of reading magical realism as a potential avenue for depicting a specifically Latina/o historical baggage" (Dalleo and Machado Sáez 95). The naked men who haunt the family's apartment "represent a historical past that is still relevant to the Latina/o present" (Dalleo and Machado Sáez 95). Because Dominican women are still the objects of sex tourism exploitation not only on the island but now also in Puerto Rico and Spain, where they migrate for domestic work but are often forced into prostitution, Cruz's novel serves as a narrative of reclamation for women who cannot break their silence and may never be able to do so.

When all else fails, the family decides to bring Olivia to the island to perform a Santería ritual to save her.[66] They go to *Tres Bocas*, an existing area in the country, which Cruz is fictionalizing from the *Tres Ojos*, three connected pools of cave water on the outskirts of Santo Domingo. The word *boca* has numerous meanings, but in Dominican Spanish, it has a double entendre Cruz may be using. A boca can be an entrance to a natural space, the "mouth" of a cave as in the fictionalized *Tres Bocas*. A boca can also be the entrance to a woman's body, through her vaginal opening, popularly known as her *otra* *boca.*Through their travel and until the ritual's start, Soledad questions her culture's epistemology: "These are *cuentos campesinos*, just silly superstitions, how could this ritual tell us anything about our lives?" (Cruz 225).[67] In this questioning, she reifies her lack of dominicanidad: "Soledad as a *gringa* in the Dominican Republic is then a vulnerable one; she is in a sense trespassing in a space that is foreign to her and they may see her as a foreign presence as well" (Dalleo and Machado Sáez 98). Her trespass is a good example of how Santería can function in US Latina/o literature: "Latinos practice Santería or Dominican Vodún episodically, with ambivalence, through mediation, and with a degree of unfamiliarity, for they often come to the practices second or third hand" (Di Iorio Sandín 12).

The two most often recurring symbols in the novel—water and photographs—are united in the ritual to be performed. The ritual entails burning the list of Olivia's clients and placing the family members' photographs in the water. Cristina, Soledad's aunt, explains: "The photographs of those that need to be cleansed from all the trappings in life will dip and then float. When we see them float we will know they will be ok" (Cruz 223). All of the pictures float except Soledad's and Olivia's. In a climactic gesture, Soledad defies her Americanized sensibility, jumping in the water to retrieve the sinking photos. As she swims and becomes disoriented, her story risks becoming a narrative of loss: "Everything is becoming harder to understand. I don't know if I am dying, but if someone asked me what it feels like, I'd say it's more like surviving. As I swim, I'm surviving like I have never had to survive before" (Cruz 226). Dalleo and Machado Sáez assert, "Soledad seeks to posit the narrative force of her individual agency to contest that of the photograph as symbol of her fate" (98). Soledad does not want to become like the naked men, who are "an ancient photograph, an old memory" (Cruz 195). The combination of ritual and allegory—water as a space of cleansing and rebirth—culminate in Soledad's transcendence of the "splits" in her family's identity: "And when I surrender to the warmth of the water, I feel the past, present and future become one. My mother becomes the ocean and sky, wrapping herself around me. I can't remember where I am or where I'm going, but when my mother's photograph flips over I see this window into another world" (Cruz 227). Soledad's surrender to the ritual reconciles the novel's extended metaphor of blindness and vision as well.

The physically sighted, including Soledad and Olivia, are the most blind to realities around them, even though they have "seen" more of the world than their family members. Gorda and Flaca remain closer to Dominican culture by remaining in the neighborhood and maintaining Dominican rituals; thus, they are plagued by the vengeful spirits of Gorda's ex-husband, Raful, as well as Manolo. El Ciego, the Dominican incarnation of Tiresias, sees everything but is not often heeded. Finally, it is Richie, the character that is most secure in his dominicanidad, who sees Soledad's problems clearly. The allegory of the photo is used when Soledad comments on a picture of his mother. She notes the beauty of the frame, and Richie comments that he never notices frames. He tells Soledad, "No you didn't see the possibilities because you noticed the frame, where it all ends" (Cruz 98). Richie's comment is particularly apt; Soledad is always looking to the future and trying to avoid her past by containing her secrets to her home or her mouth.

The physical and metaphorical liberation occur as Olivia screams—she literally opens her mouth for the first time in months—when she realizes Soledad is drowning. The physical threat of losing her daughter prompts Olivia to pierce her silence and use her own voice to tell Soledad the story of both of their lives: "She tells me about the day I was born, how when she first looked down at me, so tiny and vulnerable, she named me Soledad. She said this would open people's hearts and make them listen. She thought with a name like Soledad I would never be alone" (Cruz 227). Marta Cutter makes a point about translation and it is quite applicable to *Soledad*: "Many of [ethnic writers] imply that the more languages, codes, or dialects one has in one's linguistic reservoir, the more effective an individual will be as a translator and storyteller, and more agency he or she will wield as a subject" (914). By shifting the name of the ritual space from three eyes (*tres ojos*) to three mouths (*tres bocas*), Angie Cruz implies that Dominican women's silence began on the island and can be ruptured only by a return to it. In an earlier metafictional moment in the novel, Caramel discusses how her mother "collected words," and Soledad was envious of their linguistic bond. With the silence between her and her daughter broken, Olivia shares the words Soledad has always wanted to collect.

The use of the word *bocas* instead of *ojos* resolves an unspoken yet audible central concern with which the novel began: the consumption and perceived "dirtying" of the Dominican woman's body. The ritual allows both Olivia and Soledad to use their voices to cleanse their bodies *through* the process of cleansing their spirits. The ritual is an embellished baptism; if read through Judeo-Christian ideology, Soledad's sins against her mother are washed away, and she emerges cleansed. Completed with Olivia's storytelling and Soledad's listening, the ritual is a collective enterprise. Olivia's narrative of reclamation is the beginning of her and Soledad's healing; it brings them back into relationship.

Toward *Narratives of Fracture*

Because *Soledad* ends in this ritual space, readers are left to wonder how this healing will manifest itself in the United States. The positive resolution implies that Soledad understands her mother more, and this understanding will help them both reclaim their dominicanidad. Both *So Far from God* and *Soledad* illustrate the urgency for women, particularly, to break the silences that structure their lives. Each book starts with questioning ideologies about lost identity, cultural practice, gender, and class that have long been accepted by the novel's communities. Both novels end with the characters' realization that what is lost at the border, or beneath the surface of the cave, must be reclaimed through collective voice. The books discussed in this chapter move beyond rumination on the loss to a proactive search for possibilities of reclamation. As in chapter 1, these novels were not united by the ethnonational origins of their authors. The convergences of *So Far from God* and *Soledad*, particularly within spiritual, feminist, and formal narrative discourses, suggest that they would elucidate the relationships between Chicana/o and Latina/o fiction as this book's subtitle of *The New Memory of Latinidad* indicates.

Judith Ortiz Cofer's hybrid text *The Latin Deli: Telling the Lives of Barrio Women* and Ernesto Quiñonez's novel *Bodega Dreams* develop similar narrative concerns but differ in form and scope. Though the authors share Puerto Rican ethnonationalism, they are linked because of their shared temporal context: the intersections of the American Dream and the civil rights movement. Both function as *narratives of fracture*: they illustrate how individuals undermine static notions of Puerto Rican identity and limiting conceptions of pan-Latino solidarity. Set in urban northeastern spaces with larger and more diverse groups of Latinas/os and other minority populations, the texts challenge continuously reinscribed definitions of *puertorriqueñidad*: the essence of one's Puerto Rican identity.

Chapter 3 aims to follow the process of chapters 1 and 2 in that while the primary texts are similarly set, the analysis of them pays attention to the books' differences. Between Ortiz Cofer and Quiñonez, those differences include but are not limited to the gendering of each text as a bildungsroman from the perspective of the narrator ("immigrant" or "native") and the formal elements comprising the text. The focus on Ortiz Cofer's book will be her exploration of concepts of Puerto Rican identity, institutionalized racism, and interethnic conflict. The discussion of *Bodega Dreams* focuses on Quiñonez's portrayal of geography, solidarity, and ethnonationalism; the novel depicts the rhetoric and the realities of social protest.

3

Narratives of Fracture

Defining Latinidades

> I was born a white girl in Puerto Rico but became a
> brown girl when I came to live in the United States.
> —Judith Ortiz Cofer, *The Latin Deli*

> As long as Latino kills Latino . . .
> we'll always be a little people.
> —Ernesto Quiñonez, *Bodega Dreams*

"Everyone is *independentista* on New Year's Eve." This adage reflects political pressures not to be associated with Puerto Rican nationalist movements. The island's complex "free associated state" status has yet to be resolved via protest or plebiscite.[1] In *From Bomba to Hip Hop: Puerto Rican Culture and Latino Identity* (2000), Puerto Rican studies scholar Juan Flores argued Puerto Ricans' "in-betweenness"—their identity as "citizens" but treatment as "immigrants"—fosters resistance to acculturation. He asserts, "Rather than embracing the hyphen . . . Puerto Ricans typically challenge the marker of collusion or compatibility and erase it as inappropriate to their social position and identity" (180). Puerto Ricans are becoming the major Latina/o population in Florida, expanding historic communities in urban New York, New Jersey, Pennsylvania, Connecticut, and Illinois.[2] Understanding their neocolonial subjectivity clarifies Puerto Ricans' relationships to other Latinas/os, including Puerto Ricans who remained on the island.

Puerto Ricans are not exiles, nor are they immigrants in the same manner of nineteenth- and twentieth-century European and Asian immigrants. Thus, the relationship of Puerto Ricans living in the United States to Puerto Ricans living on the island is one literature and literary scholarship often examine. Contemporary US Puerto Rican literature has two strains: a mid-twentieth-century immigrant perspective emphasizing the differences between

Puerto Rico as "home" and the United States as "here" and a late twentieth-century native perspective emphasizing a call for an equal distribution of rights. Kanellos notes, "the texts of most of the working-class writers who had migrated to the city during the twentieth century exhibit many of the classic patterns of Hispanic immigrant literature, including the emphasis on returning to the island" (20). These patterns are fraught for characters in Judith Ortiz Cofer's work because they were born on the island but did not come of age on it. They observe their parents' classic immigrant perspectives and conflict with them when they embrace a native perspective. As David J. Vázquez argues of Ortiz Cofer and Puerto Rican writers in general, "national belonging is thus produced in the dynamic between *aquí* and *allá* (here and there)" (119).

The processes through which younger Puerto Ricans in the United States distinguish themselves are central to both *The Latin Deli* and *Bodega Dreams*. Ernesto Quiñonez explores the lives of *Nuyorican*s in East Harlem, New York; this barrio is just across the Hudson and East Rivers from the Puerto Ricans living in Ortiz Cofer's setting of Paterson, New Jersey. The re-creation of identity and ethnonational belonging functions as a shield against urban renewal, and the end of gentrification is the quest the characters in *Bodega Dreams* undertake. The novel offers an interesting complement to *The Latin Deli* for several reasons. First, set a generation later, *Bodega Dreams* examines the legacy of the civil rights movement the characters of *The Latin Deli* glimpse but do not get experience. Second, the novel depicts the hostile external world of the city men still move in, while the women in *Bodega Dreams* have more mobility than do their predecessors in *The Latin Deli*. Finally, because a number of immigrant writers who were born in or relocated to the United States as children have been trained in creative writing programs, they have written and developed audiences outside the immigrant enclave (21).[3] This is true of Ernesto Quiñonez; the differences in his visibility as a writer and Ortiz Cofer's visibility partly explain the difference in the quantity and range of criticism on their work.[4]

The *narrative of fracture* situates US Puerto Rican literature as developing explicitly out of late nineteenth-century, anticolonial political and artistic expression as well as the literature's consistent engagement of modern and contemporary American literary aesthetics. This chapter focuses on the prose selections in *The Latin Deli* because they reveal the literary aesthetics Ortiz Cofer uses to present an alternative to the essentializing puertorriqueñidad she encounters. Not as much scholarship exists on *The Latin Deli* (1993) as does on her memoir *Silent Dancing* (1990) and her novel *The Line of the Sun*

(1991). The principle arguments made about Ortiz Cofer's work more generally include discussions of movement as a recurring trope (Bruce-Novoa 1991); her portrayal of sexism and the restrictions it places on women (Faymonville 2001); and her construction of identity as psychocultural and not physically bounded (Bruce-Novoa 1991; Vázquez 2011).

In examining the political and social issues depicted in these two examples of contemporary Puerto Rican literature, a point Sánchez González makes about literary figures being largely ignored when their work is critical of nationalist discourse or culture becomes clear. Of Arturo Schomburg and Luisa Capetillo, Sánchez González argues, "This elision is related to how both Schomburg and Capetillo struggled *within* the Puerto Rican and Cuban nationalist organizations of their time" (57; emphasis in original). While the two authors examined in this chapter are writing toward the end of the twentieth century, they, too, have been ignored by scholars for their critiques of Puerto Rican communities on both the mainland and the island.[5] Sánchez González calls for a "new frame of reference that helps historicize Boricua narrative experimentation in its unique moments and milieus" (56). The narrative of fracture is such a frame of reference: it situates US Puerto Rican literature as originating in late nineteenth- and early twentieth-century anticolonial political and artistic expression and further develops in the contemporary period as part of the Nuyorican aesthetic. The third of the four stories, the *narrative of fracture*, illustrates how Nuyorican literature that emerged in the 1960s was a response not only to the continuation of US neocolonialism but also to the practices of ethnonationalism and colorism *within* the Puerto Rican diaspora.[6]

Nourishing Story: Consumption and Creation in *The Latin Deli*

The contents of *The Latin Deli: Telling the Lives of Barrio Women* are as its subtitle indicates: tales of the lives of barrio women. The book is a literary smorgasbord of loosely related poems, stories, and essays. Many of the characters are something closer to the term Gustavo Pérez Firmat used to describe Cuban Americans, 1.5ers—immigrants or exiles who immigrated at such a young age that they lack cultural memories of their nations of origin.[7] In Rumbaut's words, "members of the 1.5 generation form a distinctive cohort in that in many ways they are marginal to both the old and the new worlds, and are fully part of neither of them" (Rumbaut qtd. in Pérez Firmat). *The Latin Deli* represents the first, 1.5, and second generations of Puerto Rican immigrants; thus, Pérez Firmat's conception of stages of immigrant literature is useful for Ortiz Cofer's work. The 1.5- and second-generation Puerto Ricans of *The Latin Deli* comprises the dominant speaking voice of the collection. The first generation of characters is generally spectral: parents and grandparents are referred to but speak infrequently. Unlike in African American and Asian American literatures, in Puerto Rican narratives, centuries-old ancestors do not often haunt contemporary protagonists. Rather, the younger characters understand the sense of loss and nostalgia their parents express but do not share it or seek a way to reclaim it. Thus, the young adult voices in this text primarily engage the narrative of fracture. The principal narrator, Elena, begins this process by abandoning the need for a physical home and beginning to articulate intellectual pursuits as emotional homes.

Judith Ortiz Cofer's hybrid text, *The Latin Deli*, opens with the metapoem "The Latin Deli: An Ars Poetica." The poem characterizes the multiple nationalities considered Latin and outlines a perspective on how each group does or does not acculturate. Puerto Ricans "complain / that it would be cheaper to fly to San Juan / than to buy a pound of Bustelo coffee here"; Cubans are "perfecting their speech" while they speak "of a 'glorious return' to Havana—"; and Mexicans speak "lyrically / of *dólares* to be made in El Norte—" (Ortiz Cofer 3), all illustrating a psychocultural migration. The poem and the book's selections of poetry, fiction, and creative nonfiction portray the differences between generations of Caribbean immigrants.[8] The poem's women "of no age" are older immigrants, those who long for a return to the island home; the younger generation of "Latin" women, who immigrated when very young (1.5-ers) or who were born in the United States (second generation), do not share this nostalgia. Ortiz Cofer illustrates the ways the younger generation of Puerto Ricans question the construction and measurements of "puertoricanness"—their puertorriqueñidad. She depicts the shift in self-perception from the older to the younger generation through the narrative of fracture.

Caribbean migration patterns disrupt the continuity of matrilineal lines in particular, and such relationships are infrequent in Puerto Rican, Dominican, and Cuban American literatures, so alternative homes become very important.[9] Chicana/o literature, in contrast, often depicts proximity to ancestral homes or regions and strong relationships between grandparents and grandchildren, as seen in . . . *And the Earth Did Not Devour Him* and *So Far from God*. In some novels, such as *Dreaming in Cuban* for example, the grandmother/granddaughter relationship is constructed through the perspective of the narrator, Pilar, but the two women actually interact very little. In *Soledad*, granddaughters and their grandmother live very close to one another, but the granddaughters do not cherish their grandmother. Soledad, in particular, sees her grandmother as being from another cultural reality, one she begins to reject in her teenage years. *The Latin Deli*'s opening story, "American History," flashes back to the death of the narrator's grandmother in Puerto Rico; this is the narrator's only mention of that generation. The death is significant because it crystallizes the speaker's cultural memory as outside the nation of origin and illustrates how cultural membership changes as extended families break down into immediate, more American, "nuclear" families.

Lessons in American History

The prose selections within *The Latin Deli* that function most clearly as narratives of fracture include the stories "American History" and "Not For Sale"; the essay "The Paterson Public Library"; and the creative nonfiction essay "The Myth of the Latin Woman: I Just Met a Girl Named María."[10] Each of these pieces showcases a speaker who uses the narrative of fracture as she attempts to define precisely what empowers her, where she belongs, and where she will ultimately make her home.[11] "American History" is the first prose selection of the text. Set in or around El Building, which has a unique location, it fictionalizes the intersections of popular culture and politics during the 1960s. The first line of the story challenges the geography imposed upon El Building's residents, foreshadowing a number of ideologies Ortiz Cofer will fracture as the text progresses: "I once read in a *Ripley's Believe It or Not* column that Paterson, New Jersey, is the place where the Straight and Narrow (streets) intersect. The Puerto Rican tenement known as El Building was one block up from Straight. It was, in fact, the corner of Straight and Market; not 'at' the corner, but *the* corner" (Ortiz Cofer 7).

The story continues with a description of the residents, echoing the distinctions of the generations of immigrants as "older" and "newer" in "An Ars Poetica." The narrator observes, "At almost any hour of the day, El Building was like a monstrous jukebox, blasting out salsas from the open windows as the residents, mostly new immigrants just up from the island, tried to drown out whatever they were currently enduring with loud music" (Ortiz Cofer 7). The lively rhythm of salsa is quieted immediately in a watershed moment of American history: "But the day President Kennedy was shot, there was a profound silence in El Building, even the abusive tongues of viragoes, the cursing of the unemployed, and the screeching of small children had been somehow muted" (Ortiz Cofer 7). The death of JFK signals a rupture in America's perception of itself.[12] The promise of civil rights offered by Kennedy's presidency was "deferred," and the persistent socioeconomic and racial problems in urban Paterson began to "fester."[13] What makes this opening story particularly interesting, though, is the way the narrator, Elena, distances herself from her family and neighbors: "President Kennedy was a saint to these people" (Ortiz Cofer 7). The narrator does not say "our," "us," or anything that would identify her as a member of El Building's Puerto Rican community.

As a Puerto Rican born on the island but raised in the United States, Elena rarely has access to her birthplace; subsequently, she has a different relationship to her ethnonational culture.[14] As a persona for Ortiz Cofer, the character Elena reflects the growing-up experience of many Puerto Ricans, Dominicans, and Cubans born or raised in the United States: she does not speak Spanish fluently. Just as the characters Yunior (*Drown*) and Soledad (*Soledad*) were, Elena is linguistically and culturally distanced from her ethnonational community. Additionally, her education challenges her parents' efforts to maintain their cultural practices. This, in turn, makes it difficult for Elena to feel rooted to Puerto Rican culture on the island or in urban New Jersey.

"American History" illustrates not only the narrator's painful shift from the expression of a native perspective to the realization of her immigrant status but also how institutional racism affects the opportunities Puerto Ricans have and the ways they attempt to circumvent educational disparity. Elena emphasizes that she is barred from honors classes because English is not her first language. She is keenly aware that the practice is discriminatory because she excels academically. Nonetheless, she comes to identify education as her way out of what she has called her parents' "fairy tales" (Ortiz Cofer 9). The residents of El Building, who as Elena notes are "mostly new immigrants just up from the island," are a constant reminder of the island. They renew and increase the nostalgia for what Elena's parents consider their true home but mark Elena's psychocultural distance from that home.

Elena outlines the difficulty of belonging within the city. Various ethnic groups—Latinas/os, African Americans, Anglo-Americans—are in a constant state of racial stratification as city planners began systematic movement and containment of minority populations through "urban renewal." Just as the characters of *Drown*, *Soledad*, and *Bodega Dreams* do, Elena and her school peers living in New Jersey in the 1960s through the 1980s navigate interracial strife on a daily basis. Even though she lives among mostly Puerto Rican families, the main institution structuring her life—public school—becomes a locus for her exclusion. Institutional racism perpetuated in the city public school system has a significant impact on the opportunities she has as well as her relationship to other students of color. The adult voice of Ortiz Cofer's persona connects this employment and educational competition among minorities to the fighting of schoolchildren in "The Patterson Public Library."

Throughout "American History," Elena is the victim of verbal and physical abuse from African American girls in school. Their taunting exceeds the usual childhood bullying and highlights the specific ethnic differences among various underrepresented ethnic groups, similar to Rafa's anti-Haitian slurs against his brother Yunior in *Drown* and Caramel's admonishment of Soledad's dating white boys in *Soledad*. Though Elena longs to be accepted by them, she is relegated to turning the rope as they invent racially inflected jump-rope rhymes: "'Didn't you eat your rice and beans and pork chops for breakfast today?' The other girls picked up the 'pork chop' and made it into a refrain: 'pork chop, pork chop, did you eat your pork chop'" (Ortiz Cofer 8). Moreover, Elena is not as voluptuous as some of the girls her age, which not surprisingly makes her less able to identify with girls her age in any ethnic group. She experiences this taunting daily and eventually becomes the target of physical violence for a particular African American classmate, Lorraine.

Despite the racism and exclusion she faces, Elena embraces the idea that education will be her path out of the barrio. Elena's parents are very strict; thus, her social interaction with her neighbors is limited to her school hours. She spends a good deal of time reading and trying to excel in her classes. Her solace is found in the library until Eugene, an Irish American boy from Georgia, moves in next door. Elena becomes infatuated with him because he is also a bookworm. Elena's father is largely absent, so she and her mother spend most of their time together rather than in social groups of their respective ages. When her mother realizes Elena is getting "moony" over Eugene, she warns her: "'You are forgetting who you are, *Niña*. . . . You are heading for humiliation and pain'" (Ortiz Cofer 13). Elena's mother clearly resists her daughter's socialization with Anglo-Americans because she expects her daughter to be rejected for her ethnicity.

Elena's belief that studying with Eugene is acceptable indicates that she sees herself as having unrestricted entrée into Anglo-American society. Her mother's warning implies that she is aware of Elena's sense of herself as native and Anglo-Americans' perception of her as immigrant. Her mother does not prohibit her from going to Eugene's; despite her mother's warning, Elena goes to the study date with Eugene only to be thwarted by his mother's racism. When his mother realizes that Elena lives in El Building, she says, "I don't know how you people do it"—implying that even though she lives next door, her family is superior to Elena's (Ortiz Cofer 14). Eugene's mother does not use overt racist statements, but what she does say is just as effective in making Elena feel as if she has no value to offer Eugene: "I am truly sorry if he told you you could come over. He cannot study with you. It's nothing personal. You understand?" (Ortiz Cofer 15). Unlike Eugene's mother, the African American girls allowed Elena some participation in their social circle. Though they taunted her, the greater shame she felt was due to her physical underdevelopment; her shame was more gendered than racialized. Eugene's mother would not even allow Elena in the house; her racism physically blocks Elena's movement over the threshold.

Elena is truly shocked, though she ought not to be, given the way some of the Anglo-American teachers address the students of color in school. When Mr. De Palma, the somewhat stereotypical gym teacher, addresses "the mostly black and Puerto Rican kids" about JFK's assassination and the children do not share his grief, he concludes, "I should have known that wouldn't mean anything to a bunch of losers like you kids" (Ortiz Cofer 11). The racial mixing within the city schools begins a movement that is not present within Elena and Eugene's parents' generation. Working-class adults were subject to each other's presence on the streets and minimally at work, but they interacted much less otherwise. In the increasingly diverse, desegregated public schools, children were subject to each other every day, all day, and they developed strategies for interacting in these public spaces. These larger social conditions and lost hope following JFK's death become catalysts for the narrator's personal experience of "American History."

Elena's parents' exposure to racial hostility and discrimination does not alter their dreams, but their inability to achieve those dreams becomes motivation for Elena to differentiate herself from other Puerto Ricans. The dreams of adult immigrants seem very distant to the adolescent Elena. Her parents articulate their dreams in Spanish; their generation retains linguistic and cultural ties to the island Elena and her friends never had: "I had learned to listen to my parents' dreams, which were spoken in Spanish, as fairly tales, like the stories about life on the island paradise of Puerto Rico before I was born" (Ortiz Cofer 10). Beyond the loss of a language that might connect her to the island, Elena has little cultural memory; she does not link the island to anyone or any memory that is positive.

The principal memory Elena has of Puerto Rico is from the visit when her grandmother dies, and that is fragmented at best: "All I remembered was wailing women in black, my mother becoming hysterical and being given a pill that made her sleep two days, and me feeling lost in a crowd of strangers all claiming to be my aunts, uncles, and cousins. I had actually been glad to return to the city" (Ortiz Cofer 10). The description of people as "all claiming" to be relatives suggests that whatever family connections Elena might have developed are so overwhelming that she rejects Puerto Rico as an extension of this familial estrangement. She simply does not feel like she belongs in Puerto Rico.[15]

Challenging the idea that immigrants born in Puerto Rico have an innate connection to it is significant. Elena shares this fracture with Pilar, the narrator of *Dreaming in Cuban*; Elena cannot belong "*more*" to a nation she has never really connected to by living in it or visiting it often.[16] She does not reject Puerto Rico, but she is honest about her lack of connection to the island. When Elena articulates a position of ambivalence toward Puerto Rico, Ortiz Cofer writes a narrative of fracture. Unlike the narrator of *When I Was Puerto Rican*, Elena does not struggle with retaining cultural authenticity, because she never identified with any culture outside of the United States. While this story seems much like an arrival text, Elena does not choose the United States, aquí, over Puerto Rico, allá; she lacks any identification with Puerto Rico and therefore cannot abandon it. Most importantly, Elena's recognition of her lack of memory does not inspire her to attempt to re-create the past; she cannot reclaim what she never had. Whereas the various "Latin" people described in "The Latin Deli: An Ars Poetica" and the characters in *So Far from God* and *Soledad* try to reclaim their individual past or a communal one, Elena never tells that story. She tells a narrative of fracture.

Though Ortiz Cofer does not claim a literary inheritance from the Nuyorican poets, Pedro Pietri's "Puerto Rican Obituary" (1969) immediately comes to mind when Elena describes her parents. They have lived in the country for over a decade, but they are unable to move out of El Building to buy a house. Ortiz Cofer describes how "every Sunday we drove out to the suburbs of Paterson, Clifton, and Passaic, out to where the people mowed grass on Sundays in the summer and where children made snowmen from pure white snow, not like the gray slush of Paterson" (Ortiz Cofer 10). She evokes Pedro Pietri's critique of suburban neighborhoods in his poem "Puerto Rican Obituary": "Dreaming about Queens / Clean-cut lily-white neighborhood / Puerto Ricanless scene" (Pietri st. 7, ll. 9–11). These weekend drives provide Elena the opportunity to see the distance between her parents' dreams and their reality. She hopes to break her parents' cycle of working and dreaming by taking a professional path. Her parents, who represent the Puerto Rican everyman and everywoman characters, "Juan / Miguel / Milagros / Olga / Manuel," of Pietri's "Puerto Rican Obituary," "talked constantly about buying a house on the beach someday, retiring on the island" (Ortiz Cofer 10). Elena makes it very clear that her sense of home is institutional, not geographic: "As for me, I was going to go to college and become a teacher" (Ortiz Cofer 11). This is not surprising given that school is the site where she continually loses any power she does try to obtain.[17]

Ortiz Cofer's home is initially her educational process, not the school itself, and thus, the home is not necessarily a physical space. In early, important scholarship on the author, Carmen Faymonville examined several of Ortiz Cofer's texts, distinguishing them from modern immigrant texts by Mary Antin and Anzia Yezeierska. She argues that Ortiz Cofer builds a home through writing: "Ortiz Cofer discovers a complex way to make sense of migrant identity by not exclusively rooting the 'self' in any one home or country" (Faymonville, "New Transnational Identities" 130).[18] Elena's desire to be a teacher is the first articulation of how she will depart from her parents' expression of Puerto Rico as their home. The significance of the notion that there is more than one way to be Puerto Rican should not be underestimated; as several of the essays in *Writing Off the Hyphen* illustrate, a nationalist paradigm has long dominated Puerto Rican literary and cultural production. Authors challenging essentialized understandings of puertorriqueñidad before, during, and after the Nuyorican movement have been sharply chastised, if not ignored.[19]

Through the 1990s, as identity politics were valorizing ethnic authenticity, Ortiz Cofer was already resisting it. Another premise of "New Transnational Identities" is that Ortiz Cofer's "stance can best be described as transnational, neither assimilationist nor necessarily oppositional" (Faymonville 131–32). As an author, Ortiz Cofer has been explicit about her lack of desire to represent a monolithic Puerto Rican experience: "There used to be a time when the Puerto Rican experience was the experience of the people on the island; then it became the experience of people in New York City. Now it is the experience of people like me, who started out in New Jersey, and now I am in Georgia and it is a different reality" (Ortiz Cofer, "Interview" 735). Though Ortiz Cofer develops characters that subscribe to a common notion that education is a way out of the barrio, she contrasts models of ethnic exceptionalism articulated by Mexican American writers such as political conservatives Richard Rodríguez and Linda Chávez. Ortiz Cofer makes it clear that she had left Latina/o America long before she left *el barrio*.

The final passages of the story culminate in a generic formalist pattern the whole story has developed: the use of color as symbol and personification. The color green is used several times to depict hope, especially in the references to the door of the house Eugene's family rents, which has been the home of various immigrants. Elena shows awareness of the process of immigration on a larger scale, positioning herself within the city's successive body of immigrants: "My guess was that the little houses had been there first, then the immigrants had come in droves, and the monstrosities had been raised for them—the Italians, the Irish, the Jews, and now us, the Puerto Ricans, and the blacks" (Ortiz Cofer 14). Her inclusion of African Americans as immigrants echoes the construction of their relocation from the rural South to northern cities in the 1940s as "a second great migration."[20] More importantly, Elena sees Eugene and his family as migrants, like everyone else in the city. As she approaches Eugene's house for the study date, she notes, "The door was painted a deep green: *verde*, the color of hope. I had heard my mother say it: *Verde-Esperanza*" (Ortiz Cofer 14). Moments later, Elena explains her shock when she experiences Eugene's mother's racist rebuff: "She seemed very angry, and I finally snapped out of my trance. I turned away from the green door and heard her close it gently" (Ortiz Cofer 15).[21]

When Elena goes to bed that night, she looks at the streetlight, which "had a pink halo around it" (Ortiz Cofer 15). The pink halo echoes the description of Eugene's mother, who "had a halo of red hair" when Elena first meets her (Ortiz Cofer 14). She describes the "white snow falling like a lace veil over [the light's] face" (Ortiz Cofer 15). Elena's personification of the light evokes the images of Jacqueline Kennedy's mourning veil, returning readers to the story's opening. The final color the story meditates upon is gray, which represents Elena's now complicated sense of herself: "I did not look down to see [the snow] turning gray as it touched the ground below" (Ortiz Cofer 15). When in the building or standing above the street, Elena has imagined herself as invisible, if not white; after this experience of racism, she was assigned a color undesirable to racists such as Eugene's mother: not white. Sadly, her infatuation with Eugene teaches her the most shamefully persistent aspect of American history: racism. The girl experiences what, drawing on W. E. B. Du Bois' concept of "double consciousness," Sollors and Kanellos have called the immigrants' "double gaze." The closing of the story, however, is a powerful example of the story as a narrative of fracture: Elena does not return to her earlier desire for the "pure white" suburban snow (Ortiz Cofer 10). While she knows that she has been the victim of racism in the outside world, her bildungsroman occurs when she chooses how she will see herself in her inside world. She refuses to become gray, the color of dirty city snow.

Feeling Not Brown

Though most of her characters are from her own ethnonational group, Puerto Ricans, Ortiz Cofer describes her writing as narrating universal human experience specified by time and place. In the story "Not for Sale," Elena comes to identify herself with Scheherazade, the famous storytelling survivalist of *A Thousand and One Nights*, and Anne Frank, the Holocaust victim whose diary would become a literary symbol of resistance to ethnic cleansing. Having been educated within the United States, Ortiz Cofer was exposed to a childhood literary curriculum that was decidedly Anglo-American and Western European. Despite the concurrent and quite close development of African American and Nuyorican writing, Elena's narrator has understandably come to identify with female storytellers who survive and achieve individual power despite containment. Ortiz Cofer has explained her literary influences in this way: "I did not grow up in Puerto Rico, I did not go through a Latino studies program, and I was exposed to the women writers of Spanish and Latin American traditions only after I became a writer. My degrees are in English literature. And so, in my studies of English literature, also male-dominated, I found a few models that I could adapt. Virginia Woolf opened my eyes" (Ortiz Cofer, "Interview" 732). Thus, Ortiz Cofer's narrative of fracture in the story "Not for Sale" foregrounds gender, rather than race, as a site of fracture. She is more concerned with undermining notions of femininity than puertorriqueñidad.

In an interview with Edna Acosta-Bélen, Ortiz Cofer explains that her writing draws on the oral tradition within matriarchal Puerto Rican culture. When describing lessons gleaned from her grandmother's stories, Ortiz Cofer notes, "So early on, I instinctively knew storytelling was a form of empowerment, that the women in my family were passing on power from one generation to another through fables and stories. They were teaching each other how to cope with life in a world where women led restricted lives" ("Interview with Acosta-Bélen" 86). Suzanne Bost offers a similar conclusion in her analysis of several Puerto Rican authors: "Both Levins Morales and Ortiz Cofer, from their locations on the mainland, remember Puerto Rico . . . through the stories of their mothers, grandmothers, or other female heroes and role models. . . . Culture is handed down from woman to woman through story-telling, so that it is laid on a foundation of networks that are woman-centered, woman-fabricated, and woman-organized" (202). The fleeting images of Puerto Rico and the bilingualism of "The Spanish Poems" within *The Latin Deli* make Bost's point about the authors' relationship to the islands especially clear: "Their contact with Puerto Rico is limited to childhood memories and fictionalized narratives" (202). In the essay "And Are You a Latina Writer?," Ortiz Cofer confirms that her mainland sensibility does not delude her sense of her Puerto Rican identity. She concludes with the assertion, "I am not lost in America. I am not searching for an identity. I know who and what I am. . . . I don't feel a need to have others authenticate my work as 'Puerto Rican' literature" (Ortiz Cofer, "And Are You a Latina Writer?" 159).

Ortiz Cofer's persona describes how reading saved her from the restrictions her father placed on her: "Since I was not allowed to linger at the drugstore with my high school classmates nor to go out socially—unless my father could be persuaded to let me after interrogations and arguments I had come to dread—I had turned to reading in seclusion. Books kept me from going mad" (Ortiz Cofer 17). In "Not for Sale," Ortiz Cofer depicts both the empowerment of stories and the potential oppressions they reveal for women. Elena's mother buys her an elaborate bedspread, the Scheherazade, from "El Árabe," a man who sells decorative linens door to door. The girl is taken by the depiction of the woman: "In each panel she sat slightly behind the action in the posture of wisdom" (Ortiz Cofer 17). As El Árabe finishes the tale, Elena feels uneasy: "It was always the same with these fairy tales: the plot was fascinating but the ending was unsatisfactory to me. 'Happily Ever After' was a loose knot tied on a valuable package" (Ortiz Cofer 18). Ortiz Cofer foreshadows what her father's confrontation with El Árabe reveals— the man wants Elena to marry his son—and he "was willing to bargain with my father over what I was worth in this transaction" (Ortiz Cofer 20). Even though she notes that El Árabe's Spanish is difficult for her to understand, Elena comprehends how women remain commodities in patriarchal cultures.

Her realization alerts readers to what Vázquez describes as "the difficulties of constituting opposition within the contexts of racism and sexism on the mainland" (124). The story's title is taken from her father's repetition that his daughter is "not for sale" as he forces the man out of their home. In this moment, however, Elena's father understands that his restrictions put his daughter at risk in the first place: she notes, "my father learned the word 'yes' in English and practiced saying it occasionally, though 'no' remained NO in both languages" (Ortiz Cofer 21). Martha Cutter, in her exhaustive study *Lost and Found in Translation*, discusses the relationship between translation and identity in multiethnic literature. Cutter's discussion of translation is especially resonant in "Not for Sale": "translation is often about the clash and conflict between worldviews—about cultural power and disempowerment" (18). Ortiz Cofer closes the story not embracing her Puerto Rican culture more but by her persona further identifying with the foreign storyteller: "On my bed Scheherazade kept telling her stories, which I came to understand would never end—as I once feared—since it was in my voice that she spoke to me, placing my dreams among hers, weaving them in" (Ortiz Cofer 21). The narrator's choice to live in translation—to combine her voice and dreams in Scheherazade's narratives—is a narrative of fracture. This choice for agency fractures the limitations placed on Elena's female body by the Puerto Rican cultural imaginary.

"The Paterson Public Library" is a work of creative nonfiction told from Ortiz Cofer's adult writer perspective. It shares the central themes of the stories "American History" and "Not for Sale": literacy, racism, containment, and the liberating power of narrative. "The Paterson Public Library" combines storytelling and reflection and might be read as a bildungsroman, though it functions more as a *kunstleroman*, a narrative of an artist's development, where Ortiz Cofer narrates her coming of age as a writer. The text illustrates the relationship between narratives of reclamation and fracture: because Ortiz Cofer does not have a "lost" Puerto Rican identity to reclaim, she needs to destroy limiting notions of puertorriqueñidad and create alternative spaces of identity and empowerment. The discussion of *Drown* in chapter 2 illustrated that Bhabha's conception of the "third space" illuminates how characters make choices to define themselves.[22] The young and adult voices in *The Latin Deli* are similarly in a process of becoming: Ortiz Cofer's "hypothetical 'third space' is a critical category that raises questions of subjectivity as much as physical location, positing quite different literary political questions from the traditional immigrant novel" (Faymonville, "New Transnational Identities" 145).

"The Paterson Public Library" clarifies the tensions between African American and Puerto Rican communities first raised in "American History." Elena is not safe in the school hallways, where her African American classmate Lorraine threatens her, nor is she safe walking to and from school, where Lorraine stalks her. Despite multiple requests for help, Elena's mother and the school principal fail to empower her. They dismiss Lorraine's violence as random, and Lorraine remains unpunished. The adult Ortiz Cofer suggests that even as a child, she knew why Lorraine victimized her: "Both Lorraine and I knew that the violence she harbored had found a target: me—the skinny Puerto Rican girl whose father was away with the Navy most of the time and whose mother did not speak English; I was the perfect choice" (Ortiz Cofer 131). Ortiz Cofer describes how she came to understand this violence as being emblematic of larger conflicts between adult African Americans and Puerto Ricans in Paterson: "It would be many years before I learned about the politics of race, before I internalized the awful reality of the struggle for territory that underscored the lives of blacks and Puerto Ricans in Paterson during my childhood. Each job given to a light-skinned Hispanic was one less job for a black man; every apartment leased to a Puerto Rican family was one less place available to blacks" (Ortiz Cofer 133). The mixture of racism and economics pitted underrepresented ethnic communities against one another, despite their cognizance of their mutual oppression by Anglo-Americans.

The library becomes a sanctuary from danger and restraint: from Lorraine's violence, from teachers who deemed her ignorant because of her ethnicity, and from her mother's constant surveillance because she has recently "become a señorita": she has started to menstruate (Ortiz Cofer 130). Once she is in the library, books offer Elena views of worlds and ideas she might never have had access to otherwise. Elena's school reading options were defined by a premulticulturalism literary canon. The library, however, offers her international perspectives outside mainstream America's narrowly defined Eurocentric literary canon: "I made my way first through the world's fairy tales. Here I discovered that there is a Cinderella in every culture, that she didn't necessarily have the white skin and rosy cheeks that Walt Disney had given her, and that the prince they all waited for could appear in any color, shape, or form. The prince didn't even have to be a man" (Ortiz Cofer 132). Elena's analysis of Cinderella's ethnic mutability undermines the racism and standards of beauty that she encounters on a daily basis and that persist today.[23] As an author, Ortiz Cofer makes yet another important critique about 1960s American culture: as the demographics of urban areas were rapidly browning, American film and television industries were depicting a virtually white America.

Elena's discovery contributes to her narrative of fracture because it serves as a model to undermine constructions of beauty and power both outside and *inside* her own culture. Ortiz Cofer explains how reading helped her resist internalizing racism; it developed a sense of self and pride in her culture as part of a world, not national, culture. Though Ortiz Cofer often refers to the verbal abuse she withstood for being thin and short, her intellectual activities help her see her mind as a source of power and beauty separate from her body. Within a Latina/o culture that is deeply concerned with the appropriate performance of gender and the possession of "good" hair and features, Ortiz

Cofer's ability to break apart these narrow standards of beauty and inscribe a new mode of puertorriqueñidad is significant.[24]

Reading becomes, then, Ortiz Cofer's psychological home. As Faymonville notes, "her imagination of 'home,' however, does not have to take the shape of a particular community rooted in a particular sort of place" (Faymonville, "New Transnational Identities" 134).[25] In the one hour a week she spends reading at the library, she develops not only self-esteem but also a sense of agency as a storyteller: "It was the way I absorbed fantasy in those days that gave me the sense of inner freedom, a feeling of power and the ability to fly that is the main reward of the writer. As I read those stories I became not only the characters but their creator" (Ortiz Cofer, *The Latin Deli* 132). This is where her home as a writer was built.[26] Just as Ortiz Cofer's persona Elena defined herself by what she would do—attend college to become a teacher—Ortiz Cofer has defined herself by her reading and writing practices. Reading allows her the flexibility and freedom to "travel"; this traveling, though, is not a form of tourism. As Vázquez observes, Ortiz Cofer's "identity is portable: it allows her to carry her home—including aspects of island and mainland life—with her" (123). Ortiz Cofer asserts how writing helps ameliorate the cultural and familial losses intrinsic to immigration: "I read to escape and also to connect: you can come back to a book as you cannot always come back to a person or place you miss" (Ortiz Cofer 133).

"The Myth of the Latin Woman: I Just Met a Girl Named María" illustrates that despite her ability to fracture binary concepts of Puerto Rican authenticity, Ortiz Cofer faces prescriptive roles for Puerto Rican women outside Puerto Rican culture as well. The process of fracture can be just as cyclical and fraught as the attempt to arrive because it requires a similar public recognition. In this piece of creative nonfiction, Ortiz Cofer asserts that her body can sometimes betray her attempts to maintain her intellectual home. The essay begins with describing a bus trip from London to Oxford, during which a drunk British man broke out into the song "María" from the 1961 film production of *West Side Story*. Ortiz Cofer laments that her socially constructed latinidad follows her. This episode is striking, not simply for illustrating the power of American cultural productions outside of the United States but also for its power to have Ortiz Cofer rearticulate her sense of self: "But María had followed me to London, reminding me of a prime fact of my life: you can leave the Island, master the English language, and travel as far as you can, but if you are a Latina, especially one like me who so obviously belongs to Rita Moreno's gene pool, the Island travels with you" (Ortiz Cofer 148). Moreno was one of the few leading Puerto Rican actresses in the

1960s; however, she was passed up for the lead role in the film adaptation of *West Side Story*. By today's social perceptions, Moreno is not a dark-skinned Latina.

Natalie Wood, a very fair, straight-haired Euro-American, was chosen instead. Despite this choice, as Negrón-Muntaner illustrates, three other production decisions inscribed the concept of Puerto Ricans as dark-skinned: "The use of 'brownface' for Bernardo, the always shifting, asinine accent deployed by most Puerto Rican characters, and the unnaturally blonde hair of the Jets. Without these three devices, most actors would simply look and sound like what they technically were: 'Americans'" ("Feeling Pretty" 91). Wood's casting is a perfect example of the way Hollywood constructed Puerto Ricans choosing acculturation as "white"—conflating race and class in a single mode of puertorriqueñidad.

Ortiz Cofer continues to discuss how one's ethnic appearance can determine how people interact with you: "In positive ways, such exoticism can grant you the attention you might not ordinarily receive. In more negative ways, it allows people to perpetuate the stereotypes they already possess about Puerto Ricans" (Ortiz Cofer, "The Myth of the Latin Woman" 148). Read in the context of the whole collection, this assertion emphasizes Ortiz Cofer's larger project: complicating internal and external conceptions of Puerto Rican identity. Such complication was newly possible only after the Young Lords' and other civil rights actions. As Faymonville suggests, "In that median position, negotiating between cultural nationalism and cultural intermixing, Ortiz Cofer has developed a defiant voice" (46). Indeed, there is "not just one reality to being a Puerto Rican writer" (Ortiz Cofer qtd. in Faymonville, "New Transnational Identities" 143).

Ortiz Cofer moves from this scene into a related discussion of its manifestation as a significant problem: the differences between what styles of dress signify in Puerto Rican and mainland culture. According to her, Puerto Rican girls are taught a different sense of femininity than Anglo-American girls are taught: "It was, and is, cultural, yet I often felt humiliated when I appeared at an American friend's party wearing a dress more suitable to a semi-formal than a playroom birthday celebration" (Ortiz Cofer 149). She also describes the career day in school where Puerto Rican girls stood out for their perceived excess: "The way our teachers and classmates looked at us that day in school was just a taste of the culture clash that awaited us in the real world, where prospective employers and men on the street would often misinterpret our tight skirts and jingling bracelets as a come-on" (Ortiz Cofer 150). This fashion problematic seems generational; many immigrants of

Elena's parents' generation and neighborhood were undereducated. In Puerto Rico, they might have had minimal education, and once they immigrated here, they garnered blue-collar employment that did not require dressing for a career (Ortiz Cofer 152). This difference in perception of what is appropriate in one's home culture and one's work or school culture is certainly not limited to Puerto Rican culture; yet the responses to it are consistent in Latina/o culture.

These stereotypes, for example, are focused on women: " . . . the Hispanic woman as the 'Hot Tamale' or sexual firebrand. It is a one-dimensional view that the media have found easy to promote. In their special vocabulary, advertisers have designated 'sizzling' and 'smoldering' as the adjectives of choice for describing not only the foods but also the women of Latin America" (Ortiz Cofer 150). Yet the semantics of sexual and racial stereotyping were prevalent at least a generation before the production of *West Side Story*. One need think only of Lupe Velez, an actress perhaps less famous than Carmen Miranda, but just as culpable for portrayals of the Hollywood creation of stereotypical Latina in the "Mexican Spitfire" series of movies. The first movie, *The Girl from Mexico* (1939), met with such success that subsequent movies, released at least one a year between 1939 and 1943, all bore a variation of the title *Mexican Spitfire*. Yet ethnic markers trump gender roles; in "The Myth of the Latin Woman," the British man singing on the bus continues with a vulgar song where "the lyrics were about a girl named María whose exploits all rhymed with her name and gonorrhea" (Ortiz Cofer 152). Ortiz Cofer believes that the man might have treated her differently if she was Anglo-American: "He would perhaps have checked his impulse by assuming that she could be somebody's wife or mother, or at least somebody who might take offense. But to him I was just an Evita or a María: merely a character in his cartoon-populated universe" (Ortiz Cofer 152). Such a perception locks women of color into the role of a specific kind of sex object, regardless of ethnicity—one many heterosexual men feel they have an inherent right to consume.

Ortiz Cofer's emphasis on "somebody" recalls Richard Rodriguez's primary arguments about how Mexican Americans should participate in mainstream American life: by developing a "public self." Ortiz Cofer clarifies what Rodriguez ignores: one can only develop a public self only if the "public" recognizes and affirms that "self."[27] Ortiz Cofer's assertions about her experiences of racism are tempered. She acknowledges the privilege education affords her and is in agreement with some Chicana writers, including theorists such as Cherríe Moraga and Gloria Anzaldúa, in that she articulates how privilege—in her case garnered through education—distinguished her experiences from those of other Latinas. She explains, "There are, however, thousands of Latinas without the privilege of an education or the entrée into society that I have. For them life is a struggle against the misconceptions perpetuated by the myth of the Latina as a whore, domestic, or criminal" (Ortiz Cofer 154). Where Ortiz Cofer departs from Chicana writers such as Anzaldúa and Moraga, though, is in her response to class oppression. She argues, "We cannot change this by legislating the way people look at us" (Ortiz Cofer 154). To suggest that people are unable to legislate the way others look at them is not self-defeating; it is less community-oriented than Chicana feminist responses, especially responses to the chauvinism of El Movimiento.

Ortiz Cofer suggests that as a public artist, she has the opportunity to change people's attitudes on a one-to-one level. Emphasis on the individual and his or her difference from a group characterizes the narrative of fracture. Chicana writers and Latina writers from the Hispanic Caribbean are often quite different in this regard. Whereas Chicana writers often lobby for the recognition and resolution of their community's racially based oppression, Ortiz Cofer, Puerto Rican writer Esmeralda Santiago, and Dominican American writer Julia Alvarez articulate more individualized responses to racism. They define themselves as writers first and foremost, whereas Anzaldúa and Moraga prioritize their queer, then their collective, subjectivity.[28] Some Latina/o writers prioritize their sexual identity, such as Puerto Rican Aurora Levins Morales, Puerto Rican–Cuban American Achy Abejas, and Puerto Rican–Dominican Erika Lopez.[29]

The difference between Chicana/o and Latina/o relationships to public memory explains the variation among the writers in each tradition. Caminero-Santangelo has argued that the construction of nostalgia in Cuban American literature has largely closed off the possibility of reading other Latina/o literatures as exilic: "memories are no guarantor of cultural authenticity; rather, they are just one more story we tell ourselves as a way of constructing the meaning of our ethnicity and, in certain cases, of granting ourselves a cultural authority" ("Contesting the Boundaries" 513). When responding to a question about language use and her cultural identity, Ortiz Cofer exemplifies Caminero-Santangelo's point: "Even if I cannot be geographically in the place where I was born, I consider myself a Puerto Rican the same way that anybody living on the Island is a Puerto Rican and if I could, I would write in Spanish" (Ortiz Cofer, "A MELUS Interview" 90). Many writers publishing since the 1980s are explicit about their sense of identity, and their characters do not always reflect a sense of self that prioritizes ethnic origins. Because Mexicans preceded Anglo-Americans in their settlement of the New World, Mexican Americans have attempted to recuperate their cultural past and turn it into public memory. This simply has not been the case for Latinas/os from the Hispanic Caribbean.

Ortiz Cofer ends "The Myth of the Latin Woman" by combining her personal commitments with her transformations of public perception: "My personal goal in my public life is to try to replace the old pervasive stereotypes and myths about Latinas with a much more interesting set of realities. Every time I give a reading, I hope the stories I tell, the dreams and fears I examine in my work, can achieve some universal truth which will get my audience past the particulars of my skin color, my accent, or my clothes" (Ortiz Cofer 154). Ortiz Cofer's writing projects have always illustrated a sense of the mutually constructing writer/reader relationship that empowers her by writing with her own passions in mind. Juan Bruce-Nova noted this about Ortiz Cofer's earliest work, her poetry: "her writing is her real home, simultaneously her origin, place of residence, and guest house for fellow travelers called readers" ("Rituals of Movement" 98). If her work convinces people to view Latinas in a different way also, then she will have managed to fracture the one-dimensional view of Latinas so pervasively replicated in neocolonialism's version of Puerto Rico's story.

Mapping Puertorriqueñidad: From Loisaida to East Harlem in *Bodega Dreams*

Bodega Dreams (2000) is about one man's—Willie Bodega's—vision of an empowered East Harlem. Set in the 1990s, the novel depicts Bodega's efforts to provide the neighborhood's residents quality housing, higher education, and small business development. The novel's flashbacks to the 1960s and 1970s portray Bodega as a Young Lord; he rallied for development of those services and access to other civil rights in the early 1970s. Ernesto Quiñonez, the novel's author, has vivid but ambivalent memories of the Young Lords: "I remember being about five years old, and being led by the hand across the street by some of them. They seemed so strong and good to me then" (Quiñonez, "Author Q&A"). Willie Bodega posits a similar but ultimately negative view of the movement: "And when the Young Lords got too high and mighty, they began to bicker among themselves. Later they even changed their agenda and became somethin' else" (Quiñonez, *Bodega Dreams* 33). Bodega's assertion that the movement failed because of internal difference troubles established conceptions of the Young Lords as well-intentioned activists undermined by municipal authorities.

The epigraph from *Bodega Dreams* at the beginning of this chapter revises a quotation from another text about internal strife, the film *Lawrence of Arabia*: "So long as the Arabs fight tribe against tribe, so long will they be a little people, a silly people" (1962). The quotation appears as the title of chapter 8 of *Bodega Dreams*, midpoint of the novel, foreshadowing ethnonationalism's threat to Latino empowerment. Here, as throughout *Bodega Dreams*, Quiñonez uses intertextuality to speak the unspeakable realities of hierarchy within Latina/o America generally, and within the Puerto Rican ethnonation more specifically.[30] Willie Bodega never states precisely what the "something else" the Young Lords became was; however, Quiñonez endeavors to articulate it. His central project in *Bodega Dreams* is to unravel the relationship between activism and aesthetic—to understand why the Young Lords and their closely associated Nuyorican literary artists are becoming spectral figures in el barrio.

Bodega Dreams makes an important contribution to Nuyorican literary aesthetics by conversing with germinal works of rites of passage such as Piri Thomas' memoir, *Down These Mean Streets* (1967; 1997).[31] Both texts explore the intimate and fraught relationships among geography, social mobility, and ethnonationalism. Each author explores these issues within Puerto Rican ethnonation; thus, they are rightfully situated as narratives of fracture. *Bodega Dreams* implies that the shift in ethnic composition of East Harlem's residents amplifies the challenges to East Harlem's empowerment the Young Lords faced a generation ago. Whereas *The Latin Deli* foregrounds competition among Puerto Ricans and African Americans in the early 1960s, *Down These Mean Streets* illustrates both interethnic competition among Latinos, Italians, and African Americans and intra-ethnic conflicts among Cubans and Puerto Ricans of the late 1960s and early 1970s. *Bodega Dreams* reexamines some of these challenges among Cubans and Puerto Ricans, in the 1970s, 1980s, and 1990s. *Down These Mean Streets* and *The Latin Deli* precede *Bodega Dreams*; however, all three books expose false conceptions of Puerto Ricans as being ideologically united. The splits and fractures within Puerto Rican discourses of race, language, and class not only pervade the texts but also link them in a continuum of urban, East Coast, and Puerto Rican narratives of fracture.

Bodega Dreams extends its analysis to the utter institutionalization of puertorriqueñidad through rites of passage. *Bodega Dreams* suggests that even if one earns his name as a youth through petty crime, as an adult, he must prove his loyalty to the neighborhood by doing "solids" for childhood friends, long after they have chosen different paths in life.[32] The serious manipulations and crimes required of the adult protagonists in *Bodega Dreams* become the rites needed to *pass* for Puerto Rican in East Harlem. Ernesto Quiñonez has been largely ignored for his critique of the limiting conception of puertorriqueñidad operative in Nuyorican East Harlem. Lisa Sánchez González makes a similar argument that authors are largely ignored when their work is critical of Puerto Rican nationalism. She uses the work of Luisa Capetillo as a case study in diasporic scholarship that recognizes Puerto Rican literature's "invisibility in a context of forced exile from *dual* identities and nationalities" (Sánchez González 5; emphasis in original). Perhaps more problematically, as ethnic literatures scholar Werner Sollors has suggested, the problem is related to the interpretation of literature. He argues that scholars, who do shape what and how people read, less often study "the innovative aspects of ethnic writing, the invention of ethnic traditions, the syncretism and modernism that characterizes so many of the forms of ethnic culture in America" (*Beyond Ethnicity* 240). Reading *Bodega Dreams* as a narrative of fracture allows readers to see the unison of ethnic tradition and modernist formal aesthetics.

The principal scholarship on *Bodega Dreams* has emphasized its revision of Fitzgerald's *The Great Gatsby* (Dwyer 2003); discussed it as an example of "ghetto literature" or "dirty realism" (Di Iorio Sandín 2004); and interpreted it as revision of the American Dream (Domínguez Miguela 2008). I prefer to listen to Quiñonez's story as a jazz riff on *The Latin Deli* and the works of his other predecessors—first-generation Nuyorican writers including Piri Thomas and Pedro Pietri. *Bodega Dreams* opens with a narrative of reclamation; it looks back to cultural history of Nuyoricans briefly, especially its civil rights activists, the Young Lords. The refrain is a narrative of loss engendered by US neocolonialism in the nineteenth century and gentrification in the twentieth century. The novel's melody varies the song, especially riffing on the dangers of ethnonationalism. *Bodega Dreams* is ultimately a narrative of fracture that examines puertorriqueñidades.

Bodega Dreams suggests that a current hindrance to an empowered Puerto Rican Harlem is the shift in Latino immigration occurring after *Down These Mean Streets* was published. Today, East Harlem is home to Latinas/os from the Hispanophone Caribbean Basin and the varying nations of Central America and South America.[33] The shift began in the 1960s when "new legislation opened the door to a host of other immigrant groups" (Sharman 62). The Hart-Cellar Immigration Act (1965) ended the restriction on Asian and Latin American immigration, resulting in their significant population developments in the United States. Subsequent legislation meant to deter the growth of Mexican immigration did not stop the flow of Mexican immigrants to areas such as East Harlem (Sharman 114). Between 1990 and 2000, for example, the number of Mexican immigrants in East Harlem rose to approximately 17 percent of its Latina/o population (Sharman 120). The continuous migration of its people into and out of the US mainland has shaped Puerto Rican literature since the Cuban-Spanish-American War (1896–1898).

Life between aquí and allá is becoming yet more complex; several positions on the current state of Nuyorican literature evidence the complexities. William Burgos sees this shift as having significant consequence to Nuyorican identity because "as other Latino groups are now displacing Puerto Ricans in New York neighborhoods they once dominated, and as *Nuyoricans* are increasingly moving to other places in the United States or moving to Puerto Rico, the centrality, indeed the hegemony of that New York–based culture may be ending or entering a new phase" (Burgos 126). Nuyorican culture is certainly experiencing a metamorphosis, if not migration.

In her germinal study of neoliberalism, *Culture Works: Space, Value, and Mobility across the Neoliberal Americas* (2012), anthropologist Arlene Dávila discusses this shift in a visual arts context. She foregrounds the work of artists such as Juan Sánchez, who moved from New York to Florida but identifies as a Nuyorican artist. Dávila asserts, "The key identification is neither geographic nor historical; a 'Nuyorican' tradition is thus conceived as the extension of the politicized and community interventions of Taller Boricua and the community of Nuyorican artists who broke artistic barriers in the 1970s alongside the Nuyorican movement to formulate work that was in intimate conversation with the empowerment of the Puerto Rican community both in the states and on the island" (*Culture Works* 121). Ernesto Quiñonez's depictions of these changes in Nuyorican culture are timely; however, because of their similar powerful critiques of the difference between these two Puerto Rican communities, neither *Bodega Dreams* nor his second novel, *Chango's Fire* (2004), has received critical attention comparable to either Thomas' autobiographical novel, *Down These Mean Streets*, or Ortiz Cofer's *The Line of the Sun*.[34]

The superb use of metafiction, intertextuality, and allusion in *Bodega Dreams* interrogates the concept of puertorriqueñidad at many levels, beginning with authorship. Quiñonez has said, "I didn't want to write a coming of age novel. I didn't want to exploit my poverty either. But I did want to write a book from the place I knew" (Quiñonez, "Author Q&A").[35] These two kinds of writing clearly refer to *Down These Mean Streets* and later Nuyorican cultural production contributing to the body of contemporary Latina/o literature.[36] His critique is readily visible in one of the chapter titles, "My Growing Up and All That Piri Thomas Kinda Crap," which the narrator says he will "spare you from" (Quiñonez, *Bodega Dreams* 86). Because he spends less time on the themes such as addiction, despair, and incarceration than Thomas does, critical analysis of Quiñonez's novel has foregrounded his work as a reengagement of Nuyorican social protest (Dalleo and Machado Sáez 2007) and an interrogation of neoliberalism's false promises of community revitalization (Dávila, *Culture Works*; Moiles, "The Politics of Gentrification").

The events of *Bodega Dreams* coincide with the height of systematized urban renewal, which Quiñonez further details in *Chango's Fire*.[37] Burned out of their homes, displaced Latinos had to move to the projects consuming the skyline starting from 96th street and moving north toward East Harlem's boundary at 125th Street.[38] Latinas/os from various neighborhoods and nations were now contained in the same projects, resulting in their further displacements.[39] Arlene Dávila draws explicit connections between Puerto Rican nationalism, gentrification, and the neoliberalization of housing and community spaces in *Bodega Dreams* in her precursor to *Culture Works*, the essay "Dreams of Place, Housing, Gentrification, and the Marketing of Space in El Barrio." She concludes that the neoliberal rhetoric of community revitalization and home ownership continues to "challenge Puerto Ricans' longing for a permanent place in El Barrio" (Dávila, "Dreams of Place" 131). Quiñonez's novel is simultaneously a prescient exploration of East Harlem's changing identity and a record of Nuyorican efforts to map puertorriqueñidad onto its streets permanently.[40] For Dávila, "*Bodega Dreams* represents the ultimate neoliberal novel. The context it speaks to is one where the purchase of place is presented as the only alternative for lasting power, even when the feasibility of such a dream is quickly fading" (Dávila, "Dreams of Place" 114). Though Quiñonez does not portray gentrification in this novel to the extent he does in *Chango's Fire*, he does craft *Bodega Dreams* as a bittersweet memorial to East Harlem's fight to remain Nuyorican. The following discussion illustrates how Quiñonez portrays two possible responses to neoliberalism's challenges in urban America: the development of pan-Latino solidarity or the further stratification of Latinos along geographic, class, and ethnonational lines.

¿Down Whose Mean Streets?

Thomas' autobiographical novel depicts East Harlem as a refuge within racially hostile New York City.[41] Quiñonez's *Bodega Dreams* extends Thomas' narrative, both spatially and chronologically, returning to East Harlem and blaming the current stagnancy of el barrio on ethnic hierarchies developing there since the late 1960s. *Down These Mean Streets* and *Bodega Dreams* foreground the protagonists' efforts to identify as Puerto Rican based on an understanding that Puerto Ricanness is a privileged identity facilitating greater social mobility than other Latino ethnonationalities allow. Piri Thomas' father is Cuban but first migrated to Puerto Rico to obtain the value of American citizenship (Thomas, "Interview with Hernandez"). Thomas explains that his father "went to Puerto Rico and stayed there for a year because he wanted to come to the United States and the Jones Act of 1917 had made Puerto Ricans citizens of the United States, whether they wanted to or not. He stayed there for a year, working and learning Puerto Rican mannerisms and ways of speaking because Cubans and Puerto Ricans speak a little bit differently" ("Interview with Hernandez"). In the memoir *Down These Mean Streets*, Thomas' father is portrayed as a Puerto Rican, but the following passage echoes Thomas' description of his father's experience as a Cuban. Piri explains why Poppa performs an über–Puerto Rican identity in his speech and mannerisms in America: "I saw the look of white people on me when I was a young man, when I walked into a place where a dark skin wasn't supposed to be. . . . I can remember the time when I made my accent heavier, to make me more of a Puerto Rican than the most Puerto Rican there ever was. I wanted a value on me, son" (Thomas 153). Chino, the narrator of *Bodega Dreams*, prioritizes his puertorriqueñidad though his father is Ecuadorian. Both Thomas' and Quiñonez's portrayals of their fathers point to a cultural reality: Latinas/os acknowledge and perpetuate hierarchies among themselves, including national, physiological, and linguistic hierarchies.

If *Bodega Dreams* illustrates that the streets are now mean because East Harlem's struggle with racial difference has been complicated by hierarchy among Latinos, what made the streets mean for Piri Thomas, a generation prior? *Down These Mean Streets* addresses Thomas' struggle for what he defined as respect: acknowledgment of his belonging to the Puerto Rican ethnonation by Latinos and non-Latinos alike.[42] Thomas was a dark-skinned Cuban/Puerto Rican, often assumed to be African American. When his family moves a few blocks within what he calls Spanish Harlem, Thomas asserts, "Even when the block belongs to your own people, you are still an outsider who has to prove himself a down stud with heart" (*Down These Mean Streets* 47). This means he must endure a jumping-in to be nicknamed and garner a reputation associated with a particular gang.[43] Reputation, Thomas argues, is what defines a man and earns him respect and loyalty. The importance of rep—one's reputation in el barrio—cannot be underestimated. It is more powerful than shared ethnicity: "They were Puerto Ricans just like we were, but this didn't mean shit, under our need to keep our reps" (Thomas 52). The novel spans decades and ends with Thomas' embrace of an Afro-Latino identity. Before that acceptance, though, Thomas struggled with racism from non-Latinos as well as from Latinos, including his own family members.[44]

Marta Caminero-Santangelo's essay "'Puerto Rican Negro': Defining Race in Piri Thomas' *Down These Mean Streets*" is especially useful in historicizing scientific and literary debates over race that shaped readings of Thomas' novel.[45] She illustrates a key paradigm of the first half of Thomas' narrative: to resist discrimination, Thomas attempts to deconstruct his racial identity, blackness, and claim his mother's ethnonational one, Puerto Ricanness. Thomas asserts his ethnonational cultural identity when he is the victim of racially motivated assaults, institutionalized racism in school, or job discrimination. Wholly eliding his father's Cuban national origin, he asserts his puertorriqueñidad: "I ain't no damn Negro and I ain't no paddy. I'm Puerto Rican" (Thomas 123). Caminero-Santangelo asserts Thomas' desire and struggle to be identified as Puerto Rican "is not nationalistic or ethnic pride but an assertion of privilege in a complicated racial hierarchy" ("'Puerto Rican Negro'" 210). Privilege, or Thomas' version of it, respect, offers more than belonging; it offers protection from physical violence.

Caminero-Santangelo describes the relationship between race hierarchy and physical violence in *Down These Mean Streets* thus: "Piri's insistence on a higher place within that hierarchy is, furthermore, clearly a self-protective denial of shared experience with African Americans; if he is not black, he assumes he need not fear being lynched" ("Puerto Rican Negro" 209). Quiñonez's narrator, Chino, asserts that this context remains, a generation later, in *Bodega Dreams*: "Some Italians from the old days of the fifties and sixties were still around. They lived on Pleasant Avenue off 116th Street, and if you were caught around there at night you'd better have been a light-skinned Latino so you could pass yourself off as Italian" (Quiñonez, *Bodega Dreams* 6). For Thomas, the need to pass is operational not only outside his turf but also inside his home. Colorism, as noted previously, can be the determining factor of one's place in social and familial hierarchies. Burton and colleagues observe, "Race scholars have long pointed to colorism as a source of internal differentiation and inequality among people of color" (Burton et al., "Critical Race Theories" 442).

Recalling Duany's findings on racial hierarchies discussed in the context of *Soledad*, it is important to note that colorism in Hispanic-descended communities is prevalent. Thomas' father practices colorism in his preference for his lighter-skinned children; this drives Piri to question the reality of racial origins in Puerto Rican identity (Thomas 87; 145). His family denies African ancestry in Puerto Rican and Cuban racial composition, denying Thomas' reality as a racially black and culturally Latino man (Thomas 135; 143). Through his friendship with Brew, an African American from the rural South, Piri realizes that it is his sensitivity to the harsh realities of racism, not his skin color, that makes him black. His acceptance of his blackness separates him from his family because they view his darkness as being *prieto* and refuse to view him as he does himself, as being *moyeto*: not dark but black (Thomas 145). The narrator of *Bodega Dreams*, Chino, is also of mixed Latino nationalities: part Puerto Rican and part Ecuadorian.[46] Mirroring Thomas' father, Chino claims puertorriqueñidad as his primary identity and as a means of belonging in East Harlem. Chino is well aware of his lower position in the Nuyorican hierarchy; he "felt compelled to tell Bodega" he was only "half Rican, my father was from Ecuador" (Quiñonez 36). Elsewhere in the novel, we see colorism in discussions of who is "Latin" or authentically "Spanish" in East Harlem.[47]

Perhaps because of these critical foci, Quiñonez's modernist author influences have been less often discussed: "There were two models for Willie Bodega, Jay Gatsby and Kurtz of *Heart of Darkness*" (Quiñonez, "Author Q&A"). The novel is saturated with literary references not only to the modernist authors of these works but also to Nuyorican and African American writers and leaders, and film and music, spanning the 1960s to the 1990s.[48] Raphael Dalleo and Elena Machado Sáez locate *Bodega Dreams* as an effort to simultaneously reinvigorate the social justice politics of the 1960s Latina/o canon and engage contemporary literary market aesthetics: "seeing this renewal requires developing new lenses that acknowledge the ways in which the relationship between literature and the public sphere is being redefined in light of post-Sixties' realities—the market's centrality in the creation, dissemination, and reception of virtually all contemporary cultural texts" (7).

Quiñonez said his impetus for writing the novel was his frustration with the fact that the negative aspects of his youth had not changed: "Why is that we keep failing the residents of inner city ghettos? Someone has to have a vision and try to change things. In *Bodega Dreams* it's up to ordinary people to bring change because politicians won't" (Quiñonez, "Author Q&A").[49] Because politicians have not changed East Harlem for the better, a generation later, Quiñonez is exploring a second strategy, pan-Latinism, to illustrate how the people of Harlem might accomplish what decades of public policy have not. Though Chino breaks his promise to spare the reader from "all that Piri Thomas Kinda Crap," he does offer readers a powerful critique of Nuyoricans' failure to engage pan-Latino activism (Quiñonez, *Bodega Dreams* 86). While Chino spends less time portraying his youth than Thomas does, he consistently digresses to memories of his identity formation by detailing urban poverty, institutional discrimination, and homosocial bonding.

Bodega Dreams examines the legacy of civil rights movements that characters glimpse but do not get to fully experience in *Down These Mean Streets* and *The Latin Deli*. Thomas' discussion of racial discourse in Harlem significantly shapes Quiñonez's novel.[50] In addition to Thomas' novel, Quiñonez uses parts of Pedro Pietri's epic Nuyorican poem "Puerto Rican Obituary" and Miguel Piñero's poem "La Bodega Sold Dreams" for epigraphs beginning each of the novel's three books.[51] The critical difference between the representation of puertorriqueñidad in *Down These Mean Streets* and *Bodega Dreams* is that *Bodega Dreams* implies that Harlem's "mean streets" are no longer the European American–dominated blocks confining Puerto Ricans physically, economically, and psychologically. Rather, Puerto Ricans are both perpetuator and victim of national, racial, and class hierarchies. June Dwyer suggests that these epigraphs are part of Quiñonez's project to celebrate Puerto Rican cultural writers and political figures (168). This assertion undermines the significance of and the challenge to the Nuyorican aesthetic Quiñonez reconciles in this novel. East Harlem's shifting demographic promotes cultural and political differences that Quiñonez implies prevent Latinos from achieving effective coalition. Quiñonez's portrayal of Bodega explicitly represents Nuyoricans' cultural pride as a weapon against neoliberalism's flattening of ethnic difference and façade of neighborhood revitalization. Piri Thomas' point about keeping one's reputation, even among "your own people," suggests what the novel *Bodega Dreams* illustrates powerfully: shared ethnicity does not guarantee ethnic solidarity or respect (52).

Several passages depict racism or ethnonational difference among Latinos more generally: Chino refers to his displacement because he is half Puerto Rican, half Ecuadorian at least three times (Quiñonez 8; 36; 177). Chino's aunt-in-law, Vera, is criticized for abandoning Puerto Rican Harlem for Cuban Miami (Quiñonez, *Bodega Dreams* 44). Chino draws on extreme religious conflict to denote the significant difference between the two Caribbean nations: "For a Rican to marry a Cuban he better be rich. . . . Cubans and Puerto Ricans never hit it off. The Arabs and Jews of the Caribbean" (Quiñonez 46). This anti-Cuban sentiment is repeated in Chino's mockery of Vera's husband: "I would never have guessed he was Latin. He was more American than Mickey Mouse and just as old" (Quiñonez 187). These differences are not rhetorical; readers see them manifested in very tangible ways, including in how Bodega and his associate, Edwin Nazario, practice ethnonational discrimination in their rhetoric and benevolence (Quiñonez 100; 147; 207).

Dreaming in Nuyorican

According to Chino, "Bodega took pride in helping someone who had just arrived from Puerto Rico or Nicaragua or Mexico or any other Latin America country"; however, "his buildings were run by good, hardworking men from Puerto Rico" (Quiñonez 100). The cultural, racial, and political competition between Latinos from the Caribbean is not new; it reflects the rhetoric of various colonizers and is reinscribed in the United States as immigrants compete for resources and social status.[52] The newest immigrants, regardless of national origin, are considered the "bottom dwellers" until they have attained some economic stability and social presence.[53] By the 1980s, however, when the United States experienced the first mass Central American migrations, from refugees of US-financed civil wars, and the second Caribbean mass migrations, this time from economic refugees from Cuba and the Dominican Republic, Puerto Ricans' position in the economic hierarchy shifted up, not down. As those immigrations continued and various groups occupied more and more of Harlem, their position shifted again, as they were dispersed among the five boroughs, as Dávila illustrates in *Barrio Dreams* (2004).

Readers see the remnants of Thomas' racial hierarchy and the trope of respect in Willie Bodega's first comments to Chino. Bodega complains about the ethnic identity options one has, each of which ignores the Puerto Rican's ethnonational uniqueness: "But when you go fill out a job application you get no respect. You see a box for Afro-American, Italian-American, Irish-American, but you don't see Puerto Rican–American, you see just one box, Hispanic" (Quiñonez 26). The equation of respect vis-à-vis ethnonational distinction reiterates the Young Lords' cultural pride platform; it appears early in the novel and is repeated throughout. Because of the demographic shifts occurring between the two novels' publications, the motif of respect takes on even greater significance in *Bodega Dreams* than it does in *Down These Mean Streets*.

Respect is so integral to Nuyorican identity that Quiñonez opens and closes the novel with it. Of his best friend, the narrator, Chino, notes: "I loved Sapo because he loved himself" (Quiñonez 3; 85). Close to the novel's end, Sapo suggests that Chino should "do one last R.I.P.," a memorial in graffiti form, with which Chino earned his respect in el barrio (Quiñonez 205). The trope of respect in the friendship between Chino and his best friend, Sapo, replicates that of Piri and Brew. Because of Sapo, Chino managed to survive the "mean streets": "Sapo had arrived at a time when I needed someone there, next to me, so I could feel valuable" (Quiñonez 11). Thanks to Sapo, Chino survives long enough to graduate from high school and obtain all that Bodega has been unable to acquire: political innocence, an institutional education to help him acquire social mobility, and the love of a "good" woman. Blanca represents a means to what Chino perceives Bodega has, unquestionable respect: "Like with Sapo while I was growing up, I needed Blanca with me so I could feel valuable" (Quiñonez 18). This echoes Piri Thomas' recollection of his father's confession of disguising his Cuban identity: "I made my accent heavier, to make me more of a Puerto Rican than the most Puerto Rican there ever was. I wanted a value on me, son" (Thomas, *Down These Mean Streets* 153).[54] Thus, Chino's emphasis on being valuable—metaphorically and semantically—is a direct intersection, if not a clear blues riff, on Thomas' novel.[55]

The portrayal of the younger generation of Nuyoricans in *Bodega Dreams* illustrates the persistence of racial and ethnonational hierarchy among them. Colorism permeates the relationships of the younger characters in the novel, just as it does in Angie Cruz's *Soledad* and Junot Díaz's *Drown*. Chino describes his best friend, Sapo, as if he had stereotyped African American features: "He was strong, squatty, with a huge mouth framed by fat lips, freaking *bembas* that could almost swallow you" (Quiñonez 3). Despite consistent racial discrimination, Sapo did not need external affirmation; Chino notes, "Sapo loved himself. He didn't need teachers or anyone else telling him this" (Quiñonez 4). Yet Sapo is critical of Chino; he accuses him of preferring white women and denies the puertorriqueñidad of Chino's wife, Blanca: "I mean, I know you like white girls. You always liked white girls. . . . Even though she might be Spanish, she's a white Spanish" (Quiñonez 153). The nicknaming of Blanca (Nancy) and her sister, Negra (Debra), reflects the simplistic, racist binaries common in Thomas' generation. To be a blanca is to be "culturally white" and enjoy social mobility by abandoning your cultural roots. To be a negra is to be "culturally black" and to be tied to Harlem without hope of mobility. Neither choice reflects the complexity of Puerto Rican racial, cultural, or class realities. Quiñonez re-inscribes a problematic gender system the Nuyoricans of Thomas' generation illustrated, and he is not successful in scripting a more realistic puertorriqueñidad for Puerto Rican women than Thomas had in his novel.

Chino's relationship with Blanca reveals another layer in the social stratification of Nuyoricans; the discourses of religion and gender intersect in

Chino's wife, Blanca.[56] Blanca is a devoted Pentecostal whose loyalty is to her church, not el barrio, or her Puerto Rican ethnonation (Quiñonez 153). She is subservient to the rules of the church; when Blanca marries Chino, who is non-Pentecostal, she loses privileges in the church, and she frequently asks Chino to join, not so that he can save his soul but so she can regain those privileges (Quiñonez 17). Blanca only expresses interest in "the street" when she needs something institutions, including her church, cannot provide; for example, when she wants to help an undocumented Colombian woman in her church get a green card, Chino explains that "getting someone a Green Card is tough. Especially since Blanca had cut herself off from the Street. There was no way she could ask around, put the word out on the street wire, because the street was never her playground" (Quiñonez 63). Since Blanca's primary allegiance is neither geographic to el barrio nor ethnonational to other Puerto Ricans, Chino's own comments undermine his wife's puertorriqueñidad.

Quiñonez structures his novel in three books, each chapter being one of twelve "rounds," reflecting the novel's metaphor as a boxing match from its start to its knockout finish. He opens book 1 of the novel with an epigraph from Pedro Pietri's 1969 poem "Puerto Rican Obituary," quoting a repeated line, "All died waiting dreaming and hating" (Pietri qtd. in Quiñonez, *Bodega Dreams* 2).[57] Quiñonez uses a stanza that encapsulates the negative portion of the poem, critiquing the Puerto Rican community as it turns its hatred inward and begins to self-destruct. Quiñonez uses another stanza of the poem to open book 2 of the novel: "These dreams / These empty dreams" (Pietri qtd. in Quiñonez, *Bodega Dreams* 84). Quiñonez is affirming Pietri's view that the Puerto Rican community is partly responsible for its inability to "pull itself up by the bootstraps."[58] Pietri suggests that Puerto Ricans must gaze inward to free themselves from oppression.[59] Quiñonez establishes this self-reflection early, aligning himself with Pietri and other Nuyorican writers: "Bodega would go down as a representation of all the ugliness in Spanish Harlem and also all the good it was capable of being. Bodega placed a mirror in front of the neighborhood and in front of himself" (Quiñonez 13–14). In this way, Quiñonez illustrates the initial response to the oppression Puerto Ricans faced in New York: the rejection of neocolonial subjectivity and the denial of Puerto Rican belonging, through the invention of the Nuyorican ethnicity.[60]

Bodega Dreams fractures the representation of Nuyorican activists as selflessly concerned with community empowerment. Unfortunately for East Harlem, Bodega's desire for respect can come *only* with an individual mobility that undermines communal uplift: "The things I do, they're just a means to get what I need, and when I'm done, I'm going to be respectable and send my kids to Harvard like Joe Kennedy" (Quiñonez 37). Though his skin color is not described, Bodega's "curly hair" (Quiñonez 23) suggests he is also a dark-skinned Puerto Rican, one who routinely experienced discrimination as did Thomas and Ortiz Cofer. His idealization of the Kennedys' ability to rise above their second-class ethnicity of the time—Irishness—suggests that Willie Bodega believes in the American Dream more than he realizes. The novel's pointed depiction of Bodega's selfishness is a narrative of fracture about social protest movements that simultaneously problematize and perpetuate the desire for the impossible dream, the American Dream.

As a narrative of fracture, Quiñonez's novel foregrounds identity discourses including the reliance on the "street" as a literary metaphor. Lyn Di Iorio Sandín identifies Nuyorican writers Piri Thomas, Miguel Piñero, and Pedro Pietri as key figures writing a "melancholia of the street" (105). She argues, "the old objects—Puerto Rico and Americanness—have been introjected, not mourned and then forgotten as the speaker [of Piñero's poem] would have us believe. However, having been removed as external objects and possibilities, they have been replaced by a new, accessible object, the street" (Di Iorio Sandín 107). When activism failed, Bodega did return to the "street," developing a methodical but criminal plan to renovate East Harlem. Antonia Domínguez Miguela similarly offers an optimistic reading of the novel in relation to the street and the American Dream: "Using the language of the 'masters' and in some ways disguised as ghetto literature, *Bodega Dreams* tropicalizes the American space of the *barrio* and builds a Puerto Rican sense of community as it transforms the American Dream into a Puerto Rican communal dream" (Domínguez Miguela 175). The street, however, ultimately fails to be an empowering space both for Bodega and for the current generation of activists he enlists, Sapo and Chino.

Bodega garners respect by defying gentrification; he renovates burned tenements and puts Puerto Rican families in them (Quiñonez 29–30). Yet when he talks about his actions, he does not discuss street loyalty, or even communal ownership of housing, which could give Puerto Ricans, in general, respect within the rhetoric of neoliberalism. June Dwyer claims that Bodega's "dream is not to become *someone* else but to make his neighborhood *somewhere* else" (170). Bodega wants to make his neighborhood some*thing* else. He does not move people out of it; rather, his real estate scheme is developed precisely to keep Puerto Ricans *within* East Harlem, not dispersed among the five boroughs of New York City. As Dávila observes, his dream is "to become the second largest slumlord in the city of New York" ("Barrio Dreams" 28). Because he wants to own East Harlem "the way the Kennedys own Boston," it is clear Bodega wants to live in East Harlem but become *someone* else (Quiñonez 37). Bodega wants to be recognized for having pulled himself up by his bootstraps; this is poignantly clear when Vera's husband insults him and Bodega yells, "I'm not a nobody," the infamous line spoken by Tony Montana, the Mariel Cuban refugee turned drug lord of the film *Scarface* (Quiñonez 191).

For Chino, Bodega has a mythic if not historical status, which reverses the migration trope of return: Chino imagines that Bodega "would free Vera from her mother, then free Puerto Rico and they would both sail back to America like conquistadors in reverse. They would arrive in New York Harbor and Latinos from all five boroughs would be there to greet them" (Quiñonez 125). Readers might consider the novel "a counter invasion, a reappropriation of a 'home' that has been historically denied to Puerto Ricans" (Domínguez Miguela 170). Chino's vision of Bodega and Vera, his lost love, liberating Puerto Rico depicts this counterinvasion in tragicomic mode. The novel's events are triggered by Vera's return to New York. Bodega was driven to achieve social status because his lack of it prevented him from winning Vera's heart. In this regard, Bodega is similar to Jay Gatsby of F. Scott Fitzgerald's novel *The Great Gatsby*: "Bodega seems to fit the model posed by Jay Gatsby, but his dream differs from Gatsby's in that it responds to his community's social and economic needs" (Domínguez Miguela 174). Domínguez Miguela's assertion that "social responsibility makes Ed Vega and Ernesto Quiñonez depart from the literary tradition of Piri Thomas and lead readers into a more critical and different depiction of the barrio" crystalizes the differences between Gatsby and Bodega. Their difference is further accounted for in her observations about the literary projects of Vega and Quiñonez (Domínguez Miguela 168).

That Quiñonez's text is a more critical literary project is evidenced in its consistent ambivalence. Readers are, from the start, subject to Chino's trajectory from seeing Bodega as a Fitzgeraldian "green light of hope" (Quiñonez 14) to "some drug lord" (Quiñonez 25) to a "lost relic" of activism (Quiñonez 31). At novel's end, he depicts Bodega as a tragic hero whose fall was caused by a woman: "in that transitory moment when at last the pearl was about to be handed to him, like Orpheus or Lot's wife, he had to look back to find Vera" (Quiñonez 213). The author describes his characterization thus: "I wanted to invoke some ambivalence in the figure of a street hero, a hero who isn't just a hero, a villain who isn't a villain, to look at both sides of the coin, in the figure of one particular street lord, a guy who's getting older and is seeing his dreams starting to tarnish" (Quiñonez, "Author Q&A"). Quiñonez depicts Bodega as a former idealist turned paternalistic crime boss who believes Puerto Ricans should be grateful to him: "But what it means is fourteen families that would riot for Bodega. Fourteen families that would take a bullet for Bodega. . . . In order for me to keep my slice, I also have to issue grants. But I take care of the community and the community will take care of me. They must, because their shelter depends on me" (Quiñonez 29–30). During this conversation, Chino challenges Bodega's social responsibility in comic irony. As they smoke pot, Chino condemns Bodega for selling drugs in el barrio; Bodega responds, "Any Puerto Rican or any of my Latin brothers who are stupid enough to buy that shit don't belong in my Great Society" (Quiñonez 31). Regardless of what Chino believes Bodega's dreams were or are, the former Young Lord's actions are now the means to his own ends.

The Importance of Being Named

Mirroring Piri Thomas' hierarchy, Bodega prioritizes geography in identity formation. He embraces those who share his geographic loyalties and class background, not necessarily excluding others due to their national background. When Chino explains he is half-Ecuadorian, Bodega retorts: "So what? You're Spanish, this is your neighborhood. . . . Just remember, no matter how much you learn, no matter how many books you read, how many degrees you get, you are from East Harlem" (Quiñonez 36). In "Getting There and Back: The Road, the Journey, and Home in Nuyorican Diaspora Literature," Solimar Otero argues, "That Julio is a 'halfsie' becomes a moot point when we begin to realize that a strict biological and national essentialism cannot operate in a cultural context that is based on the more open social epistemologies that are set in place in East Harlem" (Otero 280). Part of that social epistemology is another recurring trope in the novel: the importance of being named.

Julio's biculturalism does not matter to Bodega because of his geographic origins and loyalty, but there is great significance to names in the novel, including Julio's nickname "Chino," Enrique's nickname "Sapo," and the barrio names East Harlem and Loisaida. Of Chino's name, Otero notes, "We learn that Julio 'earns' the name Chino for being different from the 'other' Puerto Ricans at his school in Spanish Harlem. The name 'Chino' may be exoticizing, the name literally meaning 'Chinese' in Spanish" (Otero 281). Chino describes himself thus: "And since I was born with high, flat cheekbones, almond-shaped eyes, and straight black hair (courtesy of my father's Ecuadorian side of the family) and because kung fu movies were very popular at the time, when I was in the eighth grade, I was tagged Chino" (Quiñonez 8). Beyond this orientalism, Julio becomes Chino only because the "street" allows it. He uses the word *tagged*, which in graffiti culture refers to the symbol an artist or a gang uses to mark turf and claim ownership of specific geographic space. This language recalls Thomas' acquiescence to being named by the gang in his new neighborhood (48). By examining the other character and neighborhood names, readers can see how place and name still intersect and matter terribly for Nuyoricans.

Sapo gets named early—in the fourth grade, when "he threw a book at Lisa Rivera's face because she had started to make fun of his looks by calling out 'ribbit, ribbit'" (Quiñonez 3). Sapo has a range of meanings. First, it does remind readers of *el coquí*, the tree frog symbolic of Puerto Rico. Sapos, however, are not frogs; they are toads, as Chino confirms: "But in truth, Sapo did look like a toad" (Quiñonez 3). In a Central American context, to be *sapo* is to be either sly or cunning, or to be extremely angry.[61] These semantic connotations are more apt for characterizing for Enrique Guzman, because Sapo never articulates Puerto Rican nationalism and Chino directly links anger to Sapo's habit of biting: "it had been a gruesome display of hate and anger and Sapo, as only Sapo could, presented it with showmanship" (86). Finally, the use of given names versus street names signals one's belonging to the street. When detectives question Chino about "an Enrique Guzman," Chino exposes them as outsiders: "That right there told me that although they were Hispanic they weren't homegrown. They knew as much about East Harlem as Oscar Lewis. Only Blanca referred to Sapo as Enrique" (Quiñonez 174). Naming and the use of names establish how one is or is not allowed to belong in el barrio.[62]

Chino and Blanca embody the rhetoric of neoliberalism Dávila interrogates (*Dreams of Place* 124–26). They "enrolled in Hunter College because we knew we needed school if we were ever going to change ourselves" (Quiñonez 13). Chino relates to the Futurists, noting, "I wanted to reinvent myself too" (Quiñonez 13). Even though she wants to change, specifically to leave the crime-ridden neighborhood, Blanca criticizes people for changing their names. When she criticizes her aunt for Anglicizing her name—using Vera instead of her given name, Veronica—Blanca claims, "I'm not going to do that. I'm going to keep my name, Nancy Saldivia, and my friends can always call me Blanca" (Quiñonez 13). Her comments reveal a naïveté about race privilege that Thomas, Bodega, Chino, and Sapo cannot enjoy because of their dark skin or curly hair or gender. Blanca does not have to change her given name because it is already Anglicized; moreover, her "light tan skin, hazel eyes, and a beautiful mane of semibrown, semiblond, hair" allow her freedom of movement only she and one other character in the novel, Edwin Nazario, enjoy (Quiñonez 9). Blanca's physical representation twins the appearance and character of María, portrayed by Natalie Wood in *West Side Story*.

Negrón-Muntaner observes this of the majority of the cast of *West Side Story*: "Puerto Ricans are made of dark powder, bright-colored ruffled costumes (women), black and dark colors (men), accents, and unlimited movement" ("Feeling Pretty" 94). The same could be argued about the characters of *Bodega Dreams*. Most of the characters are described in sparse detail; Blanca and Nazario, however, are described in terms of their physical appearance and dress, both of which set them apart from the other characters. Negrón-Muntaner links the name, costuming, and character of María in *West Side Story*: "The single exception is María, who is dressed in white. María's name and white costume connotes her as a 'virgin,' but also as untouched by American culture and uncontaminated by racism. That the film's arguably 'perfect' character is thoroughly incoherent and otherworldly suggests that the narrative cannot resolve its rips at the seams" ("Feeling Pretty" 94). Chino notes how both Bodega and Vera had reinvented themselves, also suggesting that Vera's lack of loyalty could cause his demise: "But unlike William Carlos Irizarry, now Willie Bodega, Veronica Linda Saldivia didn't want to be considered Puerto Rican. Hence the name Vera" (Quiñonez 119).[63] Chino's assertion, "with that misleading last name she could fool anyone into thinking she was some middle-aged Anglo woman who had a taste for shopping on Fifth Avenue, threw dinner parties, and loved expensive jewelry," clearly implies that Vera's self-invention was problematic in both racial and class contexts. She Anglicizes her name because of her desire to shed its Nuyorican, and thus less respectable, class origins (Quiñonez 119).

Willie Bodega speaks infrequently in the novel, which makes his descriptions of Edwin Nazario especially compelling. Bodega represents their relationship as close; yet Quiñonez provides subtle hints contrasting that depiction. Readers see the differentiations Bodega makes between himself and Nazario; for example, Bodega identifies Nazario through his class, not his ethnicity: "He's a lawyer, but he hustled. He could hustle because he never forgot he is street" (Quiñonez 29). The two met after Bodega had left the Young Lords, while Nazario was finishing Brooklyn Law School. Bodega claims that Nazario was "hustlin'. In Loisaida and in East Harlem," suggesting that Nazario is from the Lower East Side, not East Harlem.[64] These and other distinctions illustrate how each man is the foil of the other in class, racial, and national contexts.

While biological essentialism seems inoperative in their relationship, Bodega's local and Nazario's national epistemologies are increasingly operational. The fact that Quiñonez does not use Miguel Piñero's well-known poem "A Lower East Side Poem" for any epigraphs indicates that beyond the geographic distance, there are socioeconomic and psychocultural distances between East Harlem and Loisaida. Trenton Hickman, in "The Political Left and the Development of Nuyorican Poetry," compellingly illustrates that Nuyorican poetry derives from several milieus, including "the early diasporic Puerto Rican *colonias* and their associated publications, to contact with U.S. prison culture in the 1960s and 1970s, and to the encouragement and sponsorship of various political and cultural organizations, from the Socialist and Communist parties to other avant-garde artistic movements in New York City" ("The Political Left" 143). In discussing the movement, Hickman states that it was Bimbo Rivas and Chino García who "famously rechristened the Lower East Side as 'Loisaida'" ("The Political Left" 149). Hickman describes García as having tried to "reclaim the broken-down buildings and other public and private spaces in the Lower East Side as part of an effort to reinvigorate that terrain for the Nuyoricans living there" ("The Political Left" 149). In *Short Eyes*, Miguel Piñero's germinal and award-winning drama, the character named "Julio 'Cupcakes' Mercado" is the youngest and most vulnerable of the community of inmates in a New York City prison. Cupcakes acts as a moral compass for the other inmates.[65] Clearly, it is no coincidence that Julio is nicknamed Chino.

Chino is being trained to fight in the war against gentrification. Bodega views him as a future Nazario, imagining their partnership: "Nazario the lawyer and his sidekick Julio College, both Ricans helping Ricans" (Quiñonez 36). Interestingly, here, Bodega uses Chino's given name, Julio, to refer to him in relationship to Nazario. Bodega links Chino's institutional education to his given name, Julio, marking differences in Chino's relationships with Bodega and Nazario. Even more compelling is the fact that Nazario, not Bodega, indicates that Loisaida has been lost to gentrification and that East Harlem may suffer the same demise: "All those white yuppies want to live in Manhattan, and they think Spanish Harlem is next for the taking" (Quiñonez 107). Neither the Lower East Side nor East Harlem enjoyed a decent standard of living in relation to other parts of Manhattan such as the Upper West Side or Mid-Town. The Lower East Side, however, after gentrification, grew in its racial and economic distance from "black Harlem's" massive projects, which bordered East Harlem. Though the Lower East Side would also become home to projects, East Harlem would be the first to do so.[66]

Bohemian in the 1960s and yuppified in the 1980s, Loisaida may have been perceived as better than East Harlem. Because one's barrio defines one's social belonging, Nazario and Bodega have *always* walked different streets. If Chino represents Nazario's past and Sapo represents Bodega's, the novel can be interpreted further through its dialogue with *West Side Story*, which exposes this ethnonational schism. Negrón-Muntaner notes, "In addition, one of the major criticisms of the 'America' sequence is that 'Puerto Ricans insult each other for being divided politically and ideologically between nationalists and assimilated'" ("Feeling Pretty" 93). In the context of gendered racial construction, Chino of *West Side Story* is incarcerated and later dies. He shares more of the experiences of Piri Thomas than does Chino of *Bodega Dreams*. Because Chino of *Bodega Dreams* escapes this fate, the novel has more in common with the pointed critique the "America" scene makes of the United States: "If anything, 'America' portrays an ambivalent picture of life in the United States, with all its oppression and promise" (Negrón-Muntaner 93).

Bodega's use of the name *East Harlem*, not *Spanish Harlem*, is equally significant. Nazario uses the term *Spanish Harlem*, illustrating the middle- and upper-class Latino assertions of Iberian origins. Chino goes back and forth between the two names, and Sapo just refers to the area as "the neighborhood." Thomas, Brew, Bodega, Sapo, and Chino all grew up in a narrowly defined turf defended through physical fights, graffiti, and petty crime. The combination of their names and their neighborhood is what affords their belonging. Solimar Otero explains the relationship between ethnicity and place for Chino's generation: "It is Chino's contribution to the neighborhood that 'counts' toward his 'Nuyorican' identity. . . . The public artwork of his R.I.P murals commemorating the dead of the barrio, and his own upbringing, make him part of East Harlem. That the community will recognize his belonging to the space of the barrio, regardless of how he performs his *latinidad* in terms of national origins, is the point" (Otero 281). Even though he claims that Nazario is "street," Bodega's omission of him in this early description is conspicuous: "B'cause men that made this country, men who built this country were men from the street. Men like me, men like you, men like Sapito" (Quiñonez 25). Bodega praises Chino and Sapo for earning their names through painting RIPs and fighting. While Nazario is his friend, because Nazario did not earn a nickname the way he, Sapo, and Chino earned theirs, Bodega does not consider Nazario a man of the street. Nazario's use of a formal name—he is the only character in the novel *without* a nickname—crystalizes his nonbelonging in East Harlem.[67]

When Bodega first meets Chino, Bodega claims, "Nazario is my brothuh. We share the same vision," which is this: "With Nazario, I intend to own this neighborhood and turn *El Barrio* into my sandbox" (Quiñonez 24; 25). The fact that Bodega wants to make el barrio his sandbox, not his and Nazario's, suggests that the two men are not equal partners, nor is their vision the same. Nazario refers to something different as Bodega's vision: "Willie Bodega plans on building a professional class, slated to become his movers and shakers of the future" (Quiñonez 106). Nazario also speaks infrequently in the novel, so the reader must pay close attention to these gaps in the two men's articulations of "the vision." Institutionally—not street—educated, Nazario speaks grammatically correct, nonaccented, standard American English. He wears alligator shoes and expensive Italian suits and walks the streets without fear of being mugged or arrested. After meeting him, Chino begins to understand the men's relationship: "Nazario with his clean-shaven face and the good looks of someone who never in his life has been in a street fight, went around spreading favors for Bodega" (Quiñonez 70). Nazario works in the public, garnering the respect Bodega urgently craves, but he is no less a criminal than Bodega. Nazario charms municipal clerks into losing, stealing, or modifying legal documents, among other crimes they commit (Quiñonez 99).

Chino realizes the consequences of how the two men functioned: "Nazario would lead, leaving Bodega to take all the hits, absorb the stigma, because of what he was" (Quiñonez 100). Quiñonez does not specify the "what," but Dávila's analysis of gentrification makes the "what" perfectly clear: ". . . Puerto Rican nationalist discourse, which saw urban New York life and the Nuyorican—the New York born/bred Puerto Rican from El Barrio—as evidence of polluted culture, in theory always opposed to the supposedly authentic culture of the island" (Dávila, *Barrio Dreams* 121). Nazario is linked to Puerto Rico through his relationship to the Salsa Museum, his references to Santería, and his alignment with the Puerto Rican Independence Movement. When Chino says that Nazario "was not some docile Latino you could push around," he definitively links Nazario with the work of the important Puerto Rican author René Marqués (Quiñonez 108).

Marqués' collection of essays *The Docile Puerto Rican* (1976) is an exemplar of Puerto Rican nationalism; it was supportive of the Independentista movement and threatening to US neocolonialism. Nazario's Puerto Rican nationalist, anticolonial rhetoric is evident when he tells Chino that after they take over Harlem, "we'll free our island without bloodshed" (Quiñonez, 101). He does not mean Manhattan, which is technically an island; he means Puerto Rico. In her discussion of the Young Lords, Oboler describes the political schism between Puerto Rican Nationalists and Nuyoricans thus: "Those who became more convinced of the need to focus on the independence of the island clashed with others who increasingly maintained that their struggle should be limited to their barrios in the United States" (58). Their marked difference in class and national allegiance—Bodega to being Nuyorican and Nazario to being Boricua—makes them strange bedfellows, if not potential adversaries.

Bodega articulates a Nuyorican perspective similar to that of Pedro Pietri and Miguel Piñero. The novel also engages linguistic difference as part of its narrative of fracture. Nuyorican literary aesthetics are reflected in the characters' speech patterns. The fracture between colonial Iberian language (Spanish) and neocolonial American language (English) are marked in each character. When with Nazario, Chino's narration of his own speech matches Nazario's; they both use grammatically correct, standard American English. When Nazario does speak Spanish, Chino translates it completely into English, not Spanglish. When with Sapo or Bodega, Chino narrates their speech as Spanglish. The novel never explicitly states where Bodega or Nazario was born; however, readers are given clues such as this assertion by Bodega: "They gave us citizenship and then sent us to the garment district" (Quiñonez, *Bodega Dreams* 78), which refers to Puerto Ricans on the island before their mass migrations starting in the 1930s. His comments suggest that Bodega might be a 1.5-generation Puerto Rican, the child of a family immigrating after 1917, when US citizenship was imposed on all Puerto Ricans. Nazario uses the rhetoric of Puerto Rican nationalism again when trying to calm the community after another building fire: "You have to tough it out. Help each other. We're *Boricuas*, we're Latinos!" (Quiñonez 147). He suggests that he spent his youth on the island: "I have an aunt in Mayagüez. She raised me" (Quiñonez 147). Their characterization and respective allegiances, Bodega to Nuyoricans and Nazario to Boricuas, suggest that Bodega is U.S-born and Nazario island-born. Even if Bodega was island-born, his commitment to a Nuyorican identity cannot be doubted when he asks Chino, "in a few years, why not a Nuyorican president?" (Quiñonez 37).

The challenge of coalition among Puerto Ricans is aptly described in Rafael Pérez-Torres' assertion that "ethnic identification plays into the ways Latinos engage with regimes of power, an engagement overwritten with racialized and/or nationalist identities" (Pérez-Torres, "Ethnicity, Ethics, and

Latino Aesthetics" 538). Quiñonez's portrayal of two Latino detectives who interrogate Chino fractures the idea that pan-Latinism is possible. Chino says, "If you want me to cooperate with you, answer my question. Out of common courtesy, one Latino to another" (Quiñonez 177). Detective DeJesus replies, "You and me having nothing in common. . . . I'm Cuban and you're Puerto Rican" (Quiñonez 177). DeJesus then antagonizes his partner, and Chino does not rise above the situation; he repeats popular, derisive comments about Cubans, especially those who arrived via the Mariel Boatlift: "You're from a monkey island yourself. At least Puerto Ricans leave of their own free will. Castro kicked your ass out!" (Quiñonez 177). The other detective, Ortiz, rationalizes his partner's ethnonationalism: "*Mira*, Mercado, I was raised in Jersey, but I'm originally from San Juan. I hope you understand. . . . DeJesus is my partner. I didn't like what he said about us. But, right or wrong, I have to back my partner" (Quiñonez 179). Because such identity politics take precedence over pan-Latino identity, coalition becomes increasingly unlikely.[68]

The reunion of Bodega and Vera reveals the most compelling evidence of the barriers to ethnonational solidarity. From Blanca, we understood that Vera was in love with "some street activist or something" when her mother made her marry a wealthy Cuban (Quiñonez 46). For Bodega the rejection was painful, not because the other lover was Cuban but because he was not a man of the Cuban street; he was an exile. Bodega asserts that the man "fled Cuba in 1958 . . . with a shitload of money they had siphoned off the people of Cuba," and that he tried to tell Vera "who this guy was, the reason why he was rich. I was telling her that he was not a friend of the people right up to the night of the wedding" (Quiñonez 78–79). Bodega laments that Vera rejected him for the personal quality of which he is most proud, being a man of the street: "She said she wouldn't mind being poor for a few years, but since I only had a vision for political stuff, I was going to be poor for the rest of my life" (Quiñonez 79). Trusting Bodega's version of his failed romance, Chino assumed and readers were led to believe that the street activist Vera jilted for the Cuban was Bodega.

In the novel's dénouement, Willie Bodega is murdered and chaos erupts. When Chino's sister-in-law, Negra, reveals that someone from Loisaida killed Bodega, readers learn that the "street activist" Vera loved was actually the young, idealistic Edwin Nazario. As Blanca snidely tells Chino, readers painfully realize that we, too, "have been played" (Quiñonez 200). Somewhere between his youth and his middle age, Nazario prioritized his national, class, and geographic origins over his cultural identity. Whether he orchestrated the betrayal or seized an opportunity, he chose to betray his friend for the wealth of Vera's husband and the power he could usurp from Bodega. Negrón-Muntaner's analysis of *West Side Story* offers an interesting corollary for this aspect of the novel: "In *West Side Story*, the ethnic community—be it in the form of all-male gangs (whites) or siblings (Puerto Ricans)—is more desirable than heterosexual marriage. In fact, heterosexual love is death: Bernardo dies defending Maria's honor, Riff dies defending Tony (who is sent by Maria to detain the rumble), and Chino will surely rot in jail to both avenge Bernardo and make sure Tony does not marry Maria" ("Feeling Pretty" 100). The love triangle in *Bodega Dreams* is an ethnonational antiromance: Vera's husband dies believing he is protecting Vera's honor; Bodega dies believing he is protecting Nuyorican honor; and Nazario will rot in jail for trying to prevent the empowering union of Nuyoricans and Boricuas.

Pérez-Torres' analysis of the novel form offers an additional mode of interpretation that similarly concludes that the failure of pan–Puerto Rican alliance depicted in the *Bodega Dreams* is rooted in ethnonationalism: "Within a Latino context, this disjuncture manifests itself along numerous lines of rupture having to do with ethnicity, identity, affirmation, and interrogation of tradition, the assertion of citizenship, an imposition of 'alienness' and the vagaries and delimitation of class identity, all negotiated through the creative self-destruction of the novel form" ("Ethnicity, Ethics, and Latino Aesthetics" 548). Willie Bodega's dreams are never realized because the geographic, class, and nationality differences between Lower and Upper East Side Puerto Ricans were played out between Nazario and Bodega, long before the bell rang signaling "Round One."

Readers must surmise that Ernesto Quiñonez has reserved his praise for another vision of East Harlem.[69] He opens the last section of the novel with a stanza of Miguel Piñero's poem "La Bodega Sold Dreams," linking Bodega, Chino, and East Harlem in the rhetoric of poetic vision he began with the epigraphs from "Puerto Rican Obituary." This last epigraph from Piñero, though, is positive in tone and shifts from Pietri's moribund view to rejuvenating poetics: "dreamt I was this *poeta* / words glitterin' brite & bold / in *las bodegas* / where our poets' words & songs are sung" (qtd. in Quiñonez, *Bodega Dreams* 202). These lines recall the symbolic conflation of a literal *bodega*, the neighborhood supermarket you went to when you needed something, and Willie Bodega, a man to whom you went when you needed something you dreamed about: a college education for your children; a small business; a decent place to live.

In Latina/o literature more generally, bodegas help immigrants survive cultural dislocation in hostile cities and rural towns. As Ortiz Cofer's poem "The Latin Deli: An Ars Poetica" suggests, bodegas are meeting places for nostalgia and for connecting to relatives through new immigrants. Then and today, even in areas with large Latina/o populations, most *mercados* simply lack foods bodegas carry: *pasta de guayaba, canepas, dulce de leche, salchichón,* and *queso blanco*. Thus, Piñero's poem "La Bodega Sold Dreams" is a reminder that bodegas hold vital cultural and economic spaces in Latina/o America. The epigraph also reminds readers that the Young Lords, present in Bodega's noble moments, have a rep: they own the turf that is the cultural and historical space known as East Harlem.[70]

June Dwyer suggests that similar to Nick Carraway of *The Great Gatsby* assuming Gatsby's role, Chino will take up Bodega's role: "Chino, in contrast, not only stays, but, as his surname *Mercado* suggests, will carry on Bodega's aspiration in a more evolved, more assimilated way" (171). She follows that assertion with this definition of a *bodega*, linking Bodega and Chino: "In name and in purpose, *bodega* (Spanish for those little grocery stores, often associated in the *barrio* with the selling of drugs) become *mercado* (a larger, more legitimate American market)" (Dwyer 171). While some stores—bodegas, *botánicas,* or any business in a neighborhood—could be fronts for drug sales, to assert that bodegas are de facto often associated with drugs is to ignore the cultural origins and significance of bodegas and to stereotype them. Kevane's description of the significance of bodegas is accurate and consistent with the function Willie Bodega plays in the novel: "A *bodega* is a little store with goods from Puerto Rico, Latin America, or the Caribbean in general, that sells items like plantains, black beans, rice, and all of the special condiments that are staples of the Latino diet. In addition, a *bodega* is where people gather to *chismear* and *conversar,* to gossip and chat, to share news of family members left behind on the island, or island politics, to dream of their return to Puerto Rico; of escaping the poverty of the barrio, of becoming successful" (132).

Dalleo and Machado Sáez offer this linguistic significance to bodegas: "Still the differences between *bodega* and *mercado* are hard to reduce to this formula; to begin with, to say that a *mercado* is an 'American market' obscures the fact of linguistic difference. Furthermore, the final scene in which Chino becomes confused with Bodega in the minds of the newcomers to the neighborhood suggests that the *mercado* has become 'bodega-fied' as the novel's protagonist has gone from an atomized individual looking to make it on his own to a politically conscious representative of the community"

(*The Latina/o Canon* 69). Regardless of Quiñonez's intent, his portrayal of Bodega renders any image of him as a selfless activist unstable if not moot. The respect Bodega seeks is based on illegally acquired wealth, not cultural or national pride. When others stopped caring about the people, his altruism became a means to his individual social mobility. His dreams may yet be realized because he has indeed "bodega-fied" East Harlem. While Bodega does sell drugs, his profit is respect.

Of el barrio, Chino predicts, "Tomorrow, Spanish Harlem would run faster, fly higher, stretch its arms out farther, and one day those dreams would carry its people to new beginnings" (Quiñonez 213). Quiñonez's use of Judeo-Christian allusion is exemplified in Chino's questioning of the efficacy of religion as ethnic minorities are sacrificed to neoliberalism and urban renewal nationwide.[71] Bodega sets up this context early in the novel, merging Old Testament and Mean Street aesthetics: "But when the spoils of the father are being divided, I better get some or I'll have to take the booty by force. East Harlem, East L.A., South Bronx, South Central, South Chicano, Overtown down in Miami, they're all the same bastard ghetto" (Quiñonez 26). Chino riffs on Bodega's sentiments with New Testament aesthetics: "They nailed his left hand to Spanish Harlem, his right to Watts, his feet to Overtown, Miami" (Quiñonez 139). Though Chino equates Christ with these oppressed ethnic enclaves, he denies Christ's presence: "His spirit was all over El Barrio, but I didn't see Him living among us. You wouldn't catch Christ, in the flesh, living in the projects" (Quiñonez 139).

Two moments of apotheosis occur toward the novel's close. Once, Bodega pretends not to be himself and tells Chino, "If you see God he won't seem all that powerful" (Quiñonez 139). A few pages later, Chino describes Nazario's Pentecostal appearance to the people of East Harlem: "Someone appeared. Someone who looked like he came out of the fire itself. Slowly like a mirage from a desert sandstorm, a figure emerged walking toward the people. A tall, elegant man came into focus with his arms outstretched and a face of pure empathy" (Quiñonez 145). As are most of Nazario's appearances, this one is more mirage than reality.[72] Readers may not view any character, especially Bodega, as a sacrificial lamb, but this variation in Chino's language obviously evokes Jesus Christ's crucifixion. East Harlem's outstretched arms resurrect it to "new beginnings," bringing the motif of Christian suffering to its pinnacle. The recurring trope of "newness" circles readers to the novel's start, where Chino confesses how changing schools fractured his sense of self and exposed him to modernist aesthetics: "I now left East Harlem every day and without my quite knowing it, the world became new" (Quiñonez

13). Quiñonez reminds readers that Chino has always been more interested in language and its potential to transform.[73]

RIP, Willie, aka Willy, aka William Bodega

The novel closes with a beautifully literary sequence in which Chino's engagements with modernist and Nuyorican aesthetics are united. Bodega's ghost appears to Chino in a dream, showing him the future: "You will use a new language. Words they might not teach you in that college. Words that aren't English or Spanish but at the same time are both" (Quiñonez 212). As Dalleo and Machado Sáez suggest, language is the future of East Harlem: "Community is still a work in progress, under construction by these individuals when the novel ends, expressed in the metaphor of Spanglish" (*The Latina/o Canon* 69). Because Quiñonez ends the novel with a dream sequence, not a *deus ex machina*, we understand that East Harlem will not change until Latinos enact what Spanglish enacts: a blending of Nuyorican and Boricua experiences and perspectives. The blending is critical: Chino suggests that code-switching, even when perfectly fluid, makes one suspect: "It was the first time I heard [Vera] speak Spanish. It sounded as natural as her English. Like she was two people" (Quiñonez 125). Vera and Nazario are the only two characters that do not speak Spanglish in the novel. Chino's comment implies that their betrayal manifests Bodega's early warning to Chino: Nazario and Vera forgot where they came from: they forgot that they will always be from the street.

It would be comforting to read the respect of Spanglish as a prophecy that Chino will realize Bodega's dreams, but the religious and cultural allusions in the final chapter, "Eulogy," suggest otherwise. Community empowerment, represented in Holy Communion, the consumption of the Eucharist, has disintegrated: "Bodega was gone and his dreams had dissolved like a wafer in the water; his buildings would be reclaimed by the city" (Quiñonez 205). The more feasible hope Nuyoricans have to avoid being a "little people" lies in Sapo, who believes that Bodega's "underground empire was still there for the taking" (Quiñonez 205). Initially drawn to a "green light of hope," Quiñonez suggests that Nuyoricans will fare better by rejecting neoliberalism's bait of social mobility and retaining their cultural practices: "It was a game of chicken, and after the smoke cleared, all the cocks would fight for Bodega's spoils" (Quiñonez 205).[74] Chino rallies the reader, though, by exclaiming, "My money was on Sapo. Because Sapo was different" (Quiñonez 205).

My money is on Sapo, too, for several reasons. Quiñonez opened the novel by discussing Sapo, not Bodega. Chino repeats that he loved Sapo because

Sapo loved himself within book 1 (Quiñonez 3; 4) and book 2 (Quiñonez 85; 92). Unlike Bodega, Sapo did not need others to make him feel he was respected, and unlike Chino, Sapo did not need others to feel valuable (Quiñonez 11; 18). Last but not least, unlike Chino and Nazario, who code-switch between English and Spanish depending upon their companions, Sapo "was the same around everybody, it didn't matter if it was the president of the United States or some junkie. Sapo was himself" (Quiñonez 8). Thus, while Blanca and most others think that Sapo is a street thug with no value, it is Sapo who articulates the broadest political vision: "I don't wanna be some manager of a few crack houses; I wanna be part of history" (Quiñonez 41). When Chino doubts him, Sapo foreshadows the novel's events: "Bodega is going to own the neighborhood. Legally. And I want to be part of it. Maybe someday, take it over when he's gone or somethin'. You too happy with your alleluia girl to understand" (Quiñonez 41). Sapo combines Bodega's desire for legal acquisition of the local neighborhood and Nazario's desire for nationalist recuperation that could get Puerto Rico, to use boxing taxonomy just once more, off US neocolonial ropes.

Bodega's street education and desire for social mobility rendered him vulnerable to betrayal by Nazario, whose sweeping vision was to redefine national boundaries, not local ones. Willie Bodega becomes Willy Loman, Arthur Miller's quintessential self-made salesman whose dreams for success and recognition of it brought about his death. In *Death of a Salesman*, Willy Loman could not survive the industrialization and youth culture obsession of postwar 1950s America. In *Bodega Dreams*, Quiñonez foreshadows Willie Bodega's fall, replacing Loman's happy delusions with Bodega's tragic memories: "Bodega's eyes . . . were pools of ghosts and sadness" (Quiñonez 98). Willie Bodega could not survive the newly mean streets of post–civil rights, 1990s East Harlem.

Once Nazario is arrested for Bodega's murder, Sapo might just be able to jump-start Harlem. Chino uses the same language to describe his RIPs at the novel's start: "I painted dozens of R.I.P.s for guys in El Barrio who felt small and needed something violent to jump-start their lives and at the same time end them" (Quiñonez 5). Chino notes this about the RIP: "It was guys like these who on any given day were looking to beat someone up, so it was up to me to either become like them or get the shit kicked out of me" (Quiñonez 6). I prefer to read Chino's portrayal of Bodega as an extensive RIP. In contrast to Bodega's expectations, ". . . No cars were overturned. No fires were set. No cops were conked. Nothing. The people of Spanish Harlem had to go to work" when he is killed (Quiñonez 203). At the funeral, however, the "entire barrio was there," and Quiñonez catalogs East Harlem's literary, cultural, and political greats (Quiñonez 206–8). This passage, if not the whole novel, ought also to be read as a RIP for the social activists of Piri Thomas' generation, the Young Lords. Quiñonez has masterfully united the literary, visual, and musical aesthetics of modernists and Nuyoricans. Because RIPs are respected and not usually painted over by rival graffiti artists, unlike tags, Quiñonez's writing of *Bodega Dreams* is an exquisite RIP, memorializing Nuyoricans' significance to East Harlem and ensuring their place in the community, no matter how high or how fast they will fly in the future.

Toward Narratives of New Memory

What will become of Chino, who is going to college not because he "knows what to do when you get that degree" but because he "likes books and all that stuff" (Quiñonez 15)? It is in these wonderful last pages that Chino states, for the third and most emphatic time, Willie Bodega's given name: "When I returned to Spanish Harlem, the sun had set. It had set for the first time on the remains of William Carlos Irizarry" (Quiñonez 210). From his fire escape ascending to Heaven, Willie tells Chino that Spanglish "is a poem." In this moment, Quiñonez transforms Willie Bodega into the important American poet William Carlos Williams, whose free verse brought a new language to poetry (Quiñonez 212). Those familiar with Williams' biography will especially appreciate this conflation, as Williams was also the product of two cultures: his father was British and his mother was Puerto Rican. For all three visionary men present in *Bodega Dreams*—Piri Thomas, William Carlos Irizarry, and Julio Mercado—the men's Puerto Rican identity derives matrilineally. The discourses on the oral traditions poetry and storytelling in Ortiz Cofer's *The Latin Deli* and in women's continuity of ritual in *So Far from God* thus resonate in *Bodega Dreams*.

This chapter has illustrated how the narrative of reclamation and the narrative of fracture relate; because reclamation is not always desirable or even possible, some contemporary Chicana/o and Latina/o writing questions fiercely maintained but false conceptions of Chicana/o and Latina/o identity. Ortiz Cofer and Quiñonez open narrative space for reconfigurations of identity by deconstructing those faulty conceptions. Chapter 4 is occupied by two exemplars of the narrative of new memory: *The Greatest Performance* by Elías Miguel Muñoz and *Mother Tongue* by Demetria Martínez. The chapter illustrates how these writers actively construct new memories and how these memories resist neocolonialism's silencing narratives.

4

Narratives of New Memory

Ending the Neocolonial Story

Everything else is remembering. Or dismembering. Either
way, I am ready to go back. To create a man out of blanks
that can never wound me.

—Demetria Martínez, *Mother Tongue*

After searching Heaven and Earth for a true love, for a
generous homeland, for a family who wouldn't abuse
us or condemn us, for a body that wouldn't betray our
truest secrets, we found each other: a refuge, a song, a
story to share.

—Elías Miguel Muñoz, *The Greatest Performance*

This chapter discusses the *narrative of new memory* in two novels: Demetria Martínez's *Mother Tongue* (1993) and Elías Miguel Muñoz's *The Greatest Performance* (1991). Martínez's novel depicts an intimate relationship between two displaced people: a US Chicana and a Salvadoran refugee for whom she provides sanctuary. Muñoz's novel portrays the friendship of two Cubans; one is considered an exile, and the other, a refugee. Both novels portray characters undertaking intense emotional journeys through memory. Throughout this study, books ostensibly quite different in form and content have been paired to illustrate the utility of the narratives of loss, reclamation, fracture, and now, new memory. Both novels discussed here are set in the 1980s but within different political contexts: *Mother Tongue* in the Central American Sanctuary Movement; *The Greatest Performance* in the post-Mariel migrations of Cuban refugees. The geographic settings are cross continental: *Mother Tongue* is set in New Mexico and El Salvador; *The Greatest Performance* is set in Cuba, Spain, Florida, New York, and California. Both novels offer readers the opportunity to witness how refugees of different nations engage in similar patterns of self-reconstruction. Martínez and Muñoz employ the narrative of new memory to portray characters' resistance to displacement and nonbelonging.

Mother Tongue and *The Greatest Performance* feature a vaguely defined type of exile of the 1980s: the refugee. In *Mother Tongue*, the character José Luis flees the genocide in El Salvador; he would have been considered a refugee, but the United States denied political asylum to most refugees of Central American civil wars. The narrators of *The Greatest Performance* are different kinds of Cuban exiles. Rosa emigrates as a child with her parents shortly after Castro takes over; these Cubans are considered political exiles by the US government and are often referred to as "émigrés" or the "Miami Cubans." Mario leaves Cuba via the Mariel Boatlift afterward. Because Mario leaves at a time of economic chaos, he is considered an economic migrant rather than a political exile. Despite their experiences of systematic surveillance and detention by Castro's regime, gay Mariels were not considered exiles needing asylum.

Mother Tongue and *The Greatest Performance* distinguish themselves from the preceding narratives of loss, reclamation, and fracture in their deliberate and self-conscious efforts to tell a different story for exiles and refugees. These novels tell a story that is based on but not limited to the characters' identities, especially their designated political status. Both texts draw on nonlinear, mimetic aesthetics to depict the changing experience of exile in the United States. As the protagonists incorporate voices in their narratives—storyteller, listener, and witness—they invite readers to consider their own ethnic, political, sexual, and intellectual community memberships. The narrative of new memory combines experience, imagination, and agency to tell a new story of one's identity, culture, or other community defining her or his belonging.

To contextualize the narrative of new memory operative in both *Mother Tongue* and *The Greatest Performance*, this chapter briefly returns to the start of this study by discussing Muñoz's novel *Brand New Memory*, which reflects a critical period in the Cuban exile imaginary. No longer exiles from communism, the first wave of Cubans has been in the United States for a generation, and their children and grandchildren have rarely, if ever, been to Cuba. *Brand New Memory* opens with what Cristina García describes as "the big B.C. and A.D." of Cuban Americans' lives: the focus on the revolution and anticommunism in exile families ("Interview with Ylce Irizarry" 178). The revolution itself and living under a communist government was not the only reason to flee Cuba, though that is the popular narrative most often told about Cuba, and it is the official story told by United States government.

Elisa Domingo had always wanted to flee Cuba; Benito, her husband, does so for her sake. Thus, as their daughter, Gina, searches for understanding of her parents' experience of Cuba, she creates a narrative of new memory. When the narrator dismembers the Cuba of her parents' false, or falsely told, story of Cuba, she eliminates Fidel Castro as the defining figure in the Cuban American imaginary. *Brand New Memory*, *The Greatest Performance*, and *Mother Tongue* foreground the collaborative and communal nature of new memory: the protagonists show that others are needed in the creation and telling of the story. Each novel combines elements of metanarrative and communal consciousness evoking discursive qualities of the human rights narrative form, testimonio.[1]

Much of the scholarship of Cuban American literature has focused on exile authors for practical reasons. The primary reason is that first-wave writers have simply been here longer; their self-conception as exiles creates a space for continued interrogation of their experiences of displacement. Moreover, authors of the first wave primarily were themselves or had parents who were well educated; when they immigrated to the United States, they had access to educational and economic opportunities facilitating more immediate artistic expression and dissemination. The Cubans of the second wave were received less positively than their predecessors by US citizens and their compatriots alike. Arriving via the Mariel Boatlift, with less education and no economic resources, writers leaving Cuba after 1980, as in the case of the Mariel generation, have taken longer to develop a significant body of cultural production.[2]

Muñoz arrived between these two watershed migrations, in May 1969. He left Cuba in October 1968 but spent the next eight months in Spain before immigrating to the United States. Ricardo Ortíz explains how the reunion of these different classes affected Cuban American life in the 1980s: "the significant collective shift from an 'exile' to an 'immigrant' mindset among inhabitants of the US-based Cuban diaspora . . . motivated many to accept the possible permanence of their settlement on US ground, and in turn motivated many of them to declare US citizenship, a move that fundamentally transformed political life in South Florida, but also everywhere else in Cuban America" (Ortíz, "Cuban-American Literature" 416). The different zeitgeists of *Brand New Memory* and *The Greatest Performance* reflect this difference in experience and reception of Cuban émigrés. *Brand New Memory* is set in 1981—a year after the Mariel Boatlift; *The Greatest Performance* is set a few years later, in the mid-1980s. The significant differences within the Domingo family's views on being Cuban and American and their disassociation with the Mariel population are examples of Ortíz's conclusion. The Mariel refugees experienced rejection by the émigrés: their fellow Cubans, especially in Florida, ostracized them. Muñoz's indictment of Miami Cubans, thus, is not surprising. His multiple migrations—from Cuba to Spain, from Spain to the United States, and within the United States—inform his fiction and distinguish his authorial perspective as one laboring for the acknowledgment of *cubanidades*.

Benito represents the exilic wave and its consistent nostalgia. His national allegiance to Cuba is suggested by the fact that as much as he loves living in the United States, he never attempts to be naturalized. As María Cristina García asserts, "In exile, the émigrés find Americans puzzling, their customs alien" (175). He wants to understand American culture, but he never says he wants to *be* American (Muñoz 12). Gina's grandmother, Abuela Estela, serves as the mediating voice in Muñoz's *new memory* of Cuba. Her stream of consciousness offers the novel's readers a view of Cuba inflected by its culture, not its communism. Abuela does not deny Cuba's struggles with communism, but she does not mourn Cuba as if it were a relic or a petrified rock, long dead.[3] Her main reason for coming to America was to connect her granddaughter Gina to Cuba by telling an oppositional narrative: "No, she wouldn't paint a sad picture of her life, of her country, for those plastic women. She wouldn't give Elisa that pleasure. Gina needed to hear a few good things, not just the misery. That, Estela realized now, was the main reason she had come to the North: to give history a balance and the past a fair chance" (Muñoz 151).

The storytelling of both Gina and her grandmother balances Cuba's past. Each uses the medium of their generation: Abuela Estela draws on the oral storytelling tradition, and Gina is equipped with the most current technology of the time, the video camera. Ready to film her Abuela, Gina has become writer and director: "Benito is pacing by the gate; Elisa is seated, reading poetry. I'm filming the whole scene (panning shot with lots of zoom-ins for close-ups, my favorite) while a hot salsa tune plays in my head. Sounds better than the Sixties original!" (Muñoz 101).[4] Abuela Estela's resistance to being videotaped because she feels "*duplicada*" makes Gina consider the function of recorded memory: "Abuela dislikes the camera and discourages Gina from filming her. She hates seeing herself *duplicada*, she says, viewing that image of someone who talks and looks just like her, a person who *is* Estela and yet who isn't" (Muñoz 117). Abel's fear of her doppleganger mimics the false story of Cuba: that there is one truth of the nation—that communism is effective governance for it.

Abuela Estela *is* Cuba in this regard: she wants to be perceived for the person she is, not a literally or figuratively projected version of herself. Her ability as a storyteller, however, thwarts Gina's efforts to document the Domingo family story: it is compelling enough to get Gina to stop video recording. The collaborative nature of Abuela's storytelling is provocative: "She spoke to Gina of these intimate imaginings and the girl shared visions of her own with Abuela. . . . So vivid were their memories, invented memories of a factual place, that they spoke of Varadero Beach as though they'd been there, together. As though they'd conquered time and space to meet on the Caribbean shore" (Muñoz 125). Rather than attempting to continuously assemble images in order to document a story she does not know, Gina absorbs her grandmother's stories and her father's memories. Gina reflects on practices necessary to keep hearing about Cuba: "Coffee was the building block of storytelling, guardian of conversations. . . . She'd partake in the ritual the way one takes a disgusting medication or eats a gross vegetable. Because it's good for you, because you need it to be strong and healthy. And, in this case, more Cuban" (Muñoz 171). This last sentence resonates with Pilar's final assessment of herself in *Dreaming in Cuban*: she belongs in New York "more than Cuba" (García 236). Muñoz seems to be trying to reverse the weight of the hyphen, which in some 1.5- and second-generation Cuban American books leans toward America.

As Estela's visit continues, grandmother and granddaughter exchange worlds: Gina absorbs Abuela's stories about Cuba, and Gina drags Abuela to gaudy theme parks and the pop-culture maze known as "the mall." With every adventure, Gina grows closer to this "lady from Cuba" she thought she might never love. She does so because Abuela Estela animates her son, Gina's father, as well as Gina. Gina was always closer to him than to her mother, but Abuela Estela allows Gina to create *new memory* of her father in Cuba: "The past, which has become an open book. These people—so alive, so three-dimensional—who weave for her an elaborate tapestry of yore, of a world which includes Estela as protagonist, and Nitín as the dwarf prince of childhood adventures" (Muñoz 157). The novel develops like a movie, if not a dream sequence in a movie. The author's use of metafiction functions as a voiceover, causing the reader to wonder if the narrative action is real or not, even in the fictive world of the novel/movie: "Gina longs to find the puzzle's missing piece, the gaps in her family's history. Answers. And her subconscious life could be traced like a map leading to some of the answers, like a blueprint of the character's self. A sort of fiction" (Muñoz 5). The fictions are visible in Gina's many sleepwalking nightmares.

Gina's alter ego, Taina, represents the indigenous ancestors of Cubans (Muñoz 138). Gina dreams Taina's memories and experiences a middle passage similar to the protagonist of Paule Marshall's *Praisesong for the Widow*

(1983). Gina connects Cuba's colonial past to its neocolonial present. With the exception of portrayals of cultural practices such as Santería or references to pre-Colombian African rituals, few authors have written books or undertaken multiple projects to reconstruct an indigenous or African collective memory.[5] Another story from the already referenced collection *Salsa Nocturna*, "Red Feather and Bone," evokes the pre-Colombian by depicting "the entrapped souls of the first ghosts of Ancient New Yorkers" (Older 69–75). The lack of anthropological material to connect Hispanic Caribbean people to original Taíno, Carib, and Arawak cultural practices has hindered literary efforts to represent these cultures. Thus, Gina's memories are a *sort* of fiction—they are figments of her imagination based in the real experiences of her ancestors. Gina's dreams raise more questions than they answer and represent the broader gap in her family's history: the origins of pre-Colombian Cuban culture. The academic discourse on colonialism is extensive; however, the literary discourse on it within Latina/o literature has used this as a motif to define the modern condition (2011).[6]

The construction of collective memory is quite visible in some Latina/o literature, though Latina/o literature has not produced as significant a body of texts invested in collective and/or public memory as those comprising Chicana/o, Native, and African American literatures. The specificity of ethnonational history explains this disparity; the construction of collective memory is pervasive in Chicana/o writers' attempts to re-create Aztlán, the mythic cultural space discussed in chapter 1. This imaginary dominated literary representations during El Movimiento, excluding women's voices and moving narratives of fracture toward narratives of reclamation, as discussed in chapter 2. In a reverse of much of Latina/o literature portraying first-generation immigrants, the American of *Brand New Memory* wants to become Cuban.[7] The novel ends with Gina's return to Cuba in a parallel to the economically successful but culturally exhausted Xavier Cuevas of Virgil Súarez's *Going Under*: "in the pursuit of the unattainable, Xavier Cuevas was swimming home" (155). Gina steps away from the camera to become part of the now imaginable new memory of Cuba.

Dismembering Memory:
Solidarity and Self in *Mother Tongue*

Demetria Martínez's *Mother Tongue* depicts a Chicana, María, who understandably does not experience either type of exile the narrators of *The Greatest Performance* and *Brand New Memory* live; she has always lived in the United

States with the ostensible benefits of US citizenship. The other protagonist, the war refugee José Luis, is older and quite fixed to his nation of origin, El Salvador. He has more in common with Cuban exiles because he views the United States as a temporary refuge, not a permanent home. María begins her story explaining that at nineteen, she had "no axis about which to spin" (Martínez 5). She tries to ground herself in a variety of cultural, spiritual, and religious practices, including Buddhism, Catholicism, Hinduism, and cultural paraphernalia representative of Mexican, Native American, Middle Eastern, Asian, and African heritages. When she falls in love with the refugee from El Salvador, José Luis, she recedes even farther from any axis that could ground her identity.[8]

The epigraph beginning this chapter appears early in *Mother Tongue*. Dismembering is a powerful visual metaphor with a dual function. First, as María articulates her readiness to face the past, she foreshadows taking it apart, piece by piece.[9] Secondly, the graphic nature of dismembering emphasizes the brutality the people of El Salvador suffered during its civil war (1979–1991). Tragically, El Salvador's experience is not unique.[10] Even though we have entered an age where it seems as if everything can be documented, testimonio, the telling of a communal story of oppression and empowerment, remains desperately important. As truth commissions have shown, memory is the only tool with which the disappeared[11] can fight history's erasure of them. Fiction written from the perspective of the first generation of refugees of Central American genocides, or their children, is increasingly visible. For example, Héctor Tobar's *The Tattooed Soldier* (2000) and Sylvia Sellers García's *When the Ground Turns in Its Sleep* (2007), which are set in Guatemala, and Daniel Alarcón's *War by Candlelight: Stories* (2009), which is set in Perú, are all narratives of loss. Each novel returns characters to the sites of their or their parents' trauma in search of answers the protagonists may never find or understand.

The Tattooed Soldier and *War by Candlelight* are set in different historical moments and geographic environments than *Mother Tongue*. Most of the content of *Mother Tongue* occurs at the start of El Salvador's civil war and takes place within the United States. The book fictionalizes some of the people opposing the war; Martínez opens the novel asserting its realistic context: "The characters in this novel are fictional but the context is not. More than 75,000 citizens of El Salvador died during a ten-year civil war, which officially ended in 1991. Most died at the hands of their own government" (prologue). The author clearly has a political aim in writing this novel: "The United States supported this effort with more than $6 billion in military aid. Declassified

State Department documents indicate that officials at the highest levels of the US government knew of El Salvador's policy of targeting civilians, including Archbishop Romero, who was assassinated in 1980. Those in power chose to look the other way" (prologue).[12]

Focusing on the violence and legacy of El Salvador's civil war, *Mother Tongue* is a Chicana novel that troubles the concept of transnational solidarity. The need for such solidarity, though, is urgent because of the genocide and obstacles to transnational sanctuary Salvadorans face. Criticism of the novel has focused on its discourse on solidarity. Marta Caminero-Santangelo argues, "The fundamental necessity of recognizing difference, as a prelude to the forging of 'solidarity' or of coalitions, is at the heart of Demetria Martínez's novel" (*On Latinidad* 196). Dalia Kandiyoti also points to the failure of solidarity in the novel, noting that the novel "is an example of the difficulties in representing the possibilities and the perils of forming transnational identities and solidarities" (424). Other scholars who have read the novel through its exploration of solidarity include Arturo Arias and Laura Lomas.

Mother Tongue is an early text contributing to the growing body of testimonial novels that assert the factual nature of their content or that foreground the wars in Central America through significantly voiced refugees.[13] While Martínez could tell a "true," nonfiction story, for legal and humanitarian reasons, she chose to tell a story about "the truth."[14] Of the civil war in Guatemala, Nobel Peace Prize recipient Rigoberta Menchú Tum has remarked, "To name names is to sentence people to death."[15] Despite the controversy surrounding the veracity of Menchú Tum's testimonio, the facts now evident are that the United States did indeed finance and provide military support for the civil wars in Chile, El Salvador, Guatemala, and Nicaragua. Martínez has already been compelled to tell "the truth": in 1987, she was indicted on the charges of "smuggling Central American refugees."[16] The prosecution could not "prove that she and Lutheran Minister Glen Remer-Thamert conspired to violate immigration laws by helping two pregnant Salvadoran women enter the United States" ("Interview with Karen Ikas" 114). Thus, in 1989, Demetria Martínez was acquitted based on her assertion of her right to freedom of speech, as a reporter gathering narrative from refugees.[17] Other authors writing testimonial novels or novels with testimonial elements include Isabel Allende (*The House of the Spirits*, 1985), Graciela Limón (*In Search of Bernabé*, 1993), and Julia Alvarez (*In the Time of the Butterflies*, 1994).

Mother Tongue draws more on the form of the testimonio than do the novels just mentioned. Throughout the text, María confesses her inability to remember events and conversations. She switches to a second-person voice, and readers assume she is telling someone the story. When she addresses the listener/reader, which readers may have presumed to be themselves, they understand she is writing her story by assembling the fragments of her past in a journal: "As I write this" (Martínez 31). Whether or not the reader is the intended "audience," the reader may feel as if he or she has entered María's private world and that María is a reliable narrator because she is trying to convey her own experience only. The voyeurism produced through this narrative form allows readers to consider her story relatively free of fictive autobiography.[18]

María's narrative of new memory begins with a return to her own differences: those between her interior and exterior psychological worlds. *Mother Tongue* takes place during specific years: 1982 and 2002. The novel dramatizes how stuck the narrator, Mary/María, has been in her past.[19] María is a Chicana who has spent the last twenty years storing the memories of her lover (the father of her son) in a shoebox. As the novel unfolds, the reader learns of the atrocities of the civil war in El Salvador and its bloody legacy. María simultaneously creates a new memory of her father's son. This memory is reflective and honest; it is new because her past memories have been shaped by her desire for her relationship with José Luis to be more romantically fulfilling than it was in actuality. She creates this new memory for her son because he has never met his father and has only his mother's disjointed memories upon which to rely. As the reader enters the narrative, he or she becomes a witness to María's self-invention, which hinges on dismembering her original fictionalization of José Luis.[20]

Mother Tongue demonstrates that in the narrative of new memory, the creative and destructive processes are inextricably linked: one must dismember to remember. The novel opens with a description of José Luis, the Salvadoran refugee María met and fell in love with at age 19. The physical action of the storytelling occurs as María sifts through her shoebox of memories and writes the story. The first document María discusses is a letter from her godmother, Soledad, who enlists María's help with the refugee's sanctuary. María entreats the reader with pathos: she does not remember everything (Martínez 26, 59, 60, 62, 101, 166). She has a truth to tell, "These and a few journal entries are all I have left to fasten my story to reality" (12), and a metafiction to confess: "You see, I am good at filling in blanks, at seeing meaning where there may have been none at all. In this way, I get very close to the truth. Or closer still to illusion" (Martínez 11). As María narrates how she fell in love with José Luis, her descriptions of his feelings are always tempered by confessions of uncertainty; however, her descriptions of her own feelings and actions are assertive, which lend a certain ethos and truthfulness to her narrative.

Telling the Truth, But Slant

María's vacillation between certainty and uncertainty humanizes her and compels one to keep reading, to get at the truth readers may desire, especially the truth of how it took twenty years to tell this story. The narrator pulls her reader deep into the narrative because she is honest and has been unraveling a story with danger, romance, and occasionally comedy: "Maybe I'm imagining things, maybe more time passed before we smiled back and forth. But everything happened so quickly, this is the amazing thing" (Martínez 15). María had been depressed since her mother's illness and death. Before meeting José Luis, she felt alone and unfocused in life. Unlike Gina of *Brand New Memory*, María is utterly alone: her parents, godmother, and the only man she has loved have all died or disappeared by the time she is writing her narrative. She foreshadows this: "During the years of my mother's illness, or maybe years before, I fled the world, went inside, ceased to feel. You could say I fell asleep" (Martínez 26). In a later reference to her depression, María uses *civil war* as a metonym for the causes of her abandonment: "My mother's cells had fought one another, a civil war that took her from me. When I was three, a woman lured my father from home" (Martínez 93). Her linkage of her mother's illness and her father's abandonment foreshadow some of the problems with her desire for José Luis.

María recollects how she tried to get him to love her so that her life would develop meaning: "From day one I looked for ways to graft a piece of myself onto him, to become indispensable" (Martínez 15). The recurring symbol of the mirror reveals the problem of her desire immediately: "Men were mirrors that allowed me to see myself at different angles" (Martínez 19). Caminero-Santangelo notes the problematic nature of this construction as well: "romantic fantasy regarding her natural connection to José Luis is accompanied, notably, by rhetoric invoking bridges, border crossings, and even borderlessness" (199). María first describes José Luis thus: "His was a face I'd seen in a dream. A face with no borders. Tibetan eyelids, Spanish hazel irises, Mayan cheekbones dovetailing delicately as matchsticks" (Martínez 3). The introduction and chapter 2 discuss scholars who have argued that borders matter; thus, readers may question why Martínez has chosen María's words to describe José Luis with the features of peoples subjected to violence and oppression precisely because of borders that matter.[21] Quickly, the narrator corrects herself: "I don't know why I had expected Olmec: African features and a warrior's helmet as in those sculpted basalt heads, big as boulders, strewn on their cheeks in Mesoamerican jungles. No, he had no warrior's face. Because the war was still inside him" (Martínez 4). This swift and powerful vacillation is the beginning of María's narrative of new memory, where she tells a different story than what she, or readers, might want to hear.

A series of documents are assembled to "tell" the story: María's own journals, letters to her, letters from her, poems, recipes, grocery lists, horoscopes, and political action bulletins. From a generic perspective, the text could be described as a hybrid text similar to *So Far from God*.[22] It also shares ekphrasis with *Soledad*; María not only includes verisimilar texts but also comments on them extensively. The documents assert more than María may ever be able to; they offer proof to her claims of mutual love and give her tangible objects with which to create a narrative of new memory. Perhaps more importantly, the widely varying importance of the documents piece together the story María tells slant: her years of depression.[23] The motifs associated with storytelling María uses include sleep, wakefulness, memory, invention, and change.

Even though the narrative of her depression will be interrupted, María begins her narrative of new memory in a tabula rasa, a "blank book" she buys to use as a journal not long after José Luis arrives: "I'm just sitting here listening to Gregorian chants and writing in this blank book I bought yesterday. It's like I'm going for longer and longer periods of time forgetting I'm depressed" (Martínez 22). The story she records is a tabula rasa because initially, she provides the reader very little description about her feelings. This may be because she does not remember them or because, as she notes, her depression was like being asleep: "They had words for women like me. Insane fell out of favor as did nervous breakdown. Clinically depressed was, I believe, in vogue. But ask any woman who has had times in her life when she was not all there. She will say she was asleep" (Martínez 27). Her explanation of how she coped with depression is metanarrative: depression is the lack of one's story of the self. The lack of one's story renders a person unable to live. Falling asleep is not the real problem; not understanding why one fell asleep is the problem: "And women who fall asleep and don't know why lack a plot line; this is the secret source of their shame. So I concocted a plot of my own, orchestrating what I could until characters began to say and do things I had never imagined, me included" (Martínez 27). The trope of sleep and its partner trope, "story," are the dominant oppositional sites of meaning in the novel.

María's awakening twenty years later after meeting José Luis evokes the classic American character sketch by Washington Irving, "Rip Van Winkle." Martínez's feminized and ethnicized discourse revises the story, however, to show how the protagonist changes, not the world to which she has awakened.[24] Martínez's female-gendered philosophy on sleep and awakening has significant consequence to the novel as a narrative of new memory. Part of María's solution to depression was invention; she created a plotline around José Luis where she had a role, but eventually she loses control of this plot. In contrast to the birth of the new nation, the United States, in "Rip Van Winkle," María's change is individual. María's "sleep" functions similarly to the sleep of the unidentified narrator of . . . And the Earth Did Not Devour Him and the catatonia of Olivia in Soledad: a significant loss of certainty in one's self (depression) requires the creation—not just a repair—of a new self. All three of the novels invoke Christian allegory of creation and rebirth. When María gives birth to their son, her depression returns and she shifts the center of her world to her son.

María simply does not remember everything she wants to: "Memory does not always serve me. It seeks images and feelings to hook on to, but at times encounters only voids" (Martínez 26). As in most of the works in this study, Mother Tongue personifies memory. Old memory, in particular, is not to be trusted: it is shadowy at its best and slow at its worst. For the unidentified narrator of . . . And the Earth Did Not Devour Him, memory is regained during "The Lost Year." For Soledad's mother, Olivia, returning to wakefulness takes months. For María of Mother Tongue, awakening takes twenty years. While it has taken María two decades to articulate her sleep and awakening, José Luis discovers her crisis within a month of their meeting. It is José's departure, ironically, that enables her to realize her lack of self-love, which is socially accepted if not encouraged: "To love a man more than one's self was a socially acceptable way for a woman to be insane" (Martínez 27).

To keep the story moving, María begins to articulate the situation in El Salvador in 1982 and the urgency with which activists were trying to save refugees' lives. The discourse on the war and the United States' refusal to provide sanctuary for the refugees of a war it was funding is a pointed critique. María constructs much of this discourse through José Luis or other characters' mouths; when she first met José Luis, she was ignorant and ambivalent about the situation; her assertions increasingly mix history, narrative, and theology. Martínez offers readers unfamiliar with the context definitions such as these: "But in those days, when a refugee told his or her story, it was not psychoanalysis, it was testimonio, story as prophecy, facts assembled to change not the self but the times" (32). This assertion, however, performs another task—it emphasizes the differences between María's story and the story of the refugees. María becomes aware of how the media contributes to the silence on El Salvador by presenting refugee testimony as untrustworthy: "I said, because your skin is brown, what you say will be followed by words like Romero claimed. Whereas if you were white, it would read, Romero said. That is how they disappear people here. Reporters aim cameras at you like Uzis. They insert notebooks and microphones between themselves and your history" (Martínez 33). María follows this recollection of her conversation with a copy of the news article on José Luis' press conference exposing the corruption and atrocities in El Salvador.

The insertion of this paratext is another example of the way María narrativizes the memories of her youth; she has moved from a simple love story to a sophisticated perspective on the racism of North American media. She questions herself rhetorically, "Did I really say all that about reporters?" (Martínez 36). Readers may begin to believe that María is making this story up and enhancing her self-portrait but not mind because of her frequent confessional, direct addresses. María follows the question about the reporters with one of her undated—only the month is given—journal entries. These entries are the most credible paratexts of her story; they achieve verisimilitude with the language and concerns of an American nineteen-year-old. The entries starkly contrast her reflective thirty-nine-year-old voice. Unmediated, they include quotations of José Luis' discussions of liberation theology and are juxtaposed with her horoscope clippings. This particular journal entry is followed by a dated (August 5, 1982) letter from her godmother Soledad, grocery lists, and some of her poems. María's journal entries are easier for readers to accept as truth because of the mundane artifacts of life surrounding them. Readers feel privy to the confessional María and are able to measure her present storytelling truthfulness against her previous unmediated reporting.

After this entry, the story continues for some pages without the interruption of a paratext, revealing María's growing understanding of the genocide in El Salvador. José Luis' emotional turmoil forces her to see the people she had never identified with in the past. Though I have referred to her as María, its important to remember that her given name is Mary and she is a mixed-race woman. She is Mexican and Anglo-American. She identifies herself as Chicana, but she may have assumed this identity without being fully aware of its signification. María's commitment to the refugees seems to answer a pointed question Chicana theorist Cherríe Moraga asked herself about the Nicaraguan Civil War: "I am a Latina, born and raised in the United States. I am a writer. What is my responsibility in this?" (Moraga 300).[25]

María's relationship with José Luis allows her to empathize with the refugees and to understand how their class status in El Salvador will repeat itself in the United States: "Unlike wealthy refugees who fled their pasts and bought homes in Santa Fe, people like José Luis lacked the money to reinvent themselves" (Martínez 56). Moreover, her description of them simultaneously alerts readers to their invisible but audible part of the immigrant labor machine: "So they became empty mirrors. A ghostly rustle of Spanish spoken in restaurants above the spit of grease on a grill" (Martínez 56). Ana Patricia Rodríguez's assessment of US Latina/o writing featuring refugees echoes María's reflections: "the refugee appears as a palimpsest—a trace of the violence of the New World Order, challenging public relations narratives of the global economy and revealing the United States not as the home of equal protection but the guarantor of unequal distribution in all its entailments" (Rodríguez 390). María's present-day meditations connect her realizations of others' suffering with a slow unraveling of her own losses and how distinct they were from the genocidal losses of Salvadorans.[26]

María's ability to discern these differences illustrates Rodríguez's important argument that the assumption of solidarity between Latinas/os in the United States and Latin Americans in South and Central America is problematic. Rodríguez contends, "This unifying strategy of solidarity, however, glosses over the histories, cultures, struggles, and resistance movements of Central American women, who deserve location-specific consideration of their own" (Rodríguez 391). As María describes the North Americans who provided sanctuary to the refugees, she realizes that the activists can play only a small part in God's larger plan. Well-intentioned groups and individuals cannot save El Salvador: "These were not isolated incidents but formed what became an involvement of sorts, of US citizens taking an 'option of the poor,' which liberation theologians said was God's way of acting in history. These conversions could be traced to the stories of Salvadorans, stories about torture, dismemberment, hunger, sickness" (Martínez 72). Every instance of María's affinity with José Luis and other refugees forms part of her political awakening. Kandiyoti notes that while "it is a novel of bridges, including those between Latinas and Latin Americans, US citizens and Salvadorans, the personal and the political, and carrying narrative modes, *Mother Tongue* is also a work that marks fractures and rifts in personal and collective identities and memories" (427). María's recollection and recognition of her incomplete memories and identity occur after José Luis has left; it is unlikely that she could come to these political and personal realizations with him there because she was so focused on healing his psychological wounds.[27]

Speaking in Tongues

Section 2 of the novel begins with José Luis' journal entries. For two decades, these have lain in a shoebox; only now María has begun to translate them. He left them for María, and one wonders how her life might have been different had she read them earlier. The first journal entry presents a strikingly different portrait of José than does María. He reveals himself the quintessential ordinary man in an extraordinary situation. His journals reveal a maturity and cognizance of the problematic nature of their relationship, dulling the luster with which the infatuated María had painted him. He has ambiguous feelings about María but lacks the personal strength to be honest with her: "I wish there was a way I could tell her. Say to María, you're inventing José Luis. And your invention may be very different from who I really am. She sees my scars and thinks I was brave for having survived. She doesn't understand that you don't always have to be brave to survive the most brutal injuries" (Martínez 81). His entries are confessional, revealing his confusion and complicity in the relationship.

José Luis needs her; she is a temporary solace for his posttraumatic stress disorder: "Sometimes the torment is so great that I turn to María for sleeping pills or sex or both. Sex to escape or at least to get me breathing again, to stop the cold shaking inside. And the next morning I have to live with my guilt at having used her. It wouldn't be bad if she just loved sex. But she loves me" (Martínez 84). His journal reveals his ideological distance from both María and North America. José Luis appreciates the efforts on his behalf, but his allegiance to his El Salvador is so strong that he does not align himself with the political history or agenda of Chicanos. US neocolonialism brought him to its borders: as Cherríe Moraga has written, "Every place the United States has been involved militarily has brought its offspring, its orphan, its homeless, and its casualties to this country" (32). He does not intend to become part of the surplus population US neocolonialism and its facilitators must integrate. While he acknowledges his selfishness, he fails to discuss it or make María aware of the inequity between them. Kandiyoti's assertion that "Reciprocity, *mutual* openness, and acknowledgement of difference between those engaged in solidarity are essential to the practices of solidarity and hospitality" glosses José Luis' failures in the development of solidarity with María (443).

José Luis believes that Americans have a fundamental misunderstanding about identity: "It is so American. The belief that people can be remade from scratch in the Promised Land, leave the old self behind" (Martínez 84). He makes it very clear to the reader that not everyone who migrates to the United States comes to shed his or her identity in the Puritanical tradition often called "the American way." This is evident in the novels discussed thus far, but José Luis' assertion is more poignant because he needs to live within a country financing a war in his home country. At this point, he is a traumatized refugee; it will take him months to adjust to the routine and normalcy of the United States. He is overwhelmed: "Any woman who talks that way a month into a relationship wants to be saved, from what, I don't know. If I knew, I could at least offer advice. But María doesn't want advice, she wants a whole new self" (Martínez 85–86). José Luis' emotional devastation allows him to see the complexity of María's scars and lament his inability to help her.

María interrupts reviewing his journals to continue her own narrative. She uses the discourse of human rights violations and genocide to describe her depression: "No, I haven't forgiven myself for being disappeared from myself any more than I have forgiven him" (Martínez 87). José Luis' journal is critical to her self-understanding; she uses Biblical allusions to illustrate his power of revelation for her: "Now, all these years later, my life has come to a halt because of words written long ago by a man whose name I didn't even know. One new testament is all it takes to warp time, to call into question the neatly bound volume of trivia and revelations you thought was your history" (Martínez 87). María's comparison of their losses, again, is undermined by her self-exposure: "All these years I have told myself that he returned to El Salvador, that the authorities found him and killed him. This was what happened to most Salvadorans who got deported. The truth is I don't know what happened to him" (Martínez 87). When she notes that six days have passed since she opened up the shoebox and began to tell her story, she evokes Genesis; she will create herself and perhaps rest on the seventh day.[28]

María confesses self-resentment and uses metafiction to suggest that the narrative is now out of her control, having assumed a persona unto itself: "because I tell you—whoever you are—I opened the wound. I told myself the part of the story I had hoped to keep from myself, the disappeared part. But the unspoken words were turning into hooks, they were caught in my throat. Once a story is begun the whole thing must be told or it kills" (Martínez 89). This personification echoes Gorda's warning about the danger of withholding story in *Soledad*: "When you write something down, it keeps it alive. There is a certain power to words, memories, ideas when one writes them down" (Cruz, *Soledad* 196). *When the Ground Turns in Its Sleep*, Sylvia Sellers-García's novel about postwar Guatemala, similarly unites spiritual narrative and violence; when the survivors of the genocide go to church, they uniformly confess to having an "illness." It takes months for the new priest to discern these confessions as strategic silences about the brutalities they witnessed and the complicity they felt in witnessing and surviving the genocide.

The last journal entries José Luis writes reveal that he is fighting his desire to stay with her. The murder of nuns in El Salvador triggers José's disappearance.[29] José Luis feels distanced from her; he knows that María is not at fault, but he hates the fact that her country is financing such brutality and its people are largely ambivalent about it. María understands that this act negates any sense of ethnopolitical affinity they had: "But after telling him of the nuns' deaths, I am transfigured. For a terrible, disfigured moment, I am a yanqui, a murderess, a whore" (Martínez 124). These lines parallel the representation of women as the Malinche within Mexican American culture.[30] The movement from the use of the word *transfigured*, which has the spiritual connotation of sublime transformation, to the word *disfigured* immediately shifts to a negative connotation of permanent disfigurement. Echoing the discourse of cultural miscegenation and genocide beginning with the Iberian conquest and continuing in US neocolonialism, María and her reader are compelled to examine the United States' role in the murders of human rights activists.[31] José Luis' response reaffirms the deep ideological gap between Chicanas/os and Central American refugees.[32]

The section ends with a poem José Luis had never shared with María. Titled "Lamentation," it was written by his wife in El Salvador. The prophetic poem evokes Christian imagery and the rhetoric of liberation theology. The poem speaks its own violence; one wonders for whom the lamentation is meant: "to take the war out of him, / she will make love to a man / and a monster / she will rise / from her bed, / grenades / ticking in her" (Martínez 135). María began the story by articulating sentiments about trying to take the war out of José Luis, so the poem is especially haunting for readers (Martínez 4). María notes that the poem was signed "Ana"; and the next time that name is said, María's world does explode.

María discusses her relationship with her son in the third and final section of the novel. For years, she has tried to make him love El Salvador for its language and culture; she is disappointed that during his summers at home, he types away on the computer and does not care about learning Spanish. Eventually, José Luis Jr. challenges his mother to enter the present and see him for who he is: "I don't wanna go there, I don't wanna major in Spanish. How come you never say anything about how good I'm doing in science? How come you never ask about my project for the science fair?" (Martínez

143). María's disappointment in her son's lack of interest in his father's mother tongue is ironic. Because of it, she ignored his interest in science and love of land similar to his father's. Caminero-Santangelo argues that José Luis Jr. "feels no natural or instinctive connection to the Spanish tongue or 'cause' of El Salvador" (*On Latinidad* 210). She identifies what she finds to be other problematic constructions of "primordial connectedness" (*On Latinidad* 210). Revising the description of José Luis Sr. she used to start the story, María laments that this "one terrible afternoon my baby grew up and became himself: Olmec with a warrior's helmet, raging against me and the powers that had laid waste to his earth" (Martínez 143). José Luis Jr.'s lack of cultural memory requires collaboration with his mother to create a narrative of new memory of his parents and his own existence.

José Luis Jr.'s knowledge of environmental biology aids María in understanding her utter individualism. He explains what happens in topsoil when pesticides ravage it, but the metaphor explains María to herself: "Chemicals that my son, the budding topsoil expert, says act on the earth like a cancer—cells that don't know what they are in relation to the whole" (Martínez 142). Before, María used civil war as a metonym for her sense of abandonment by her mother. Now, however, María can articulate her fundamental problem in the past, and what her new memory must accomplish. She did not understand the pieces of José Luis or José Luis Jr. in relation to herself. For twenty years, she attached herself to the memories of her son's father and, in turn, tried to attach them to her son. She did not realize that she was always part of that whole and that she did not need to subsume herself within someone else to have an identity.

José Luis Jr.'s narrative is very short and dramatically accelerates their narrative of new memory. María describes how she told her son about his conception. After a magical night of lovemaking, José Luis experiences a posttraumatic stress attack. María mentions the name of Ana—another person, not his former wife—and he is transported back to El Salvador and the soldiers who have just mutilated and killed his wife. He assaults María, and once he stops, reentering the present, they weep together for the violence they have all suffered. María's physical and emotional shock culminates in the release of her disappeared memory: "The room began to spin, sickness washed over my abdomen. Then, I remembered" (Martínez 164). At age seven, María was left in the care of a neighbor who molested her. Despite years of psychologists and medication, it took an experience of great violence for María to recall her dismembered innocence and happiness. Even in narrating her process of remembering, the trauma is so great that she asserts, "I cannot recall everything. I might never recall everything" (Martínez 166). What María does not say is more powerful. Her language shifts to a third-person voice as she describes what happens, describing herself as "she" or "the girl," in a linguistic pattern common in victims of abuse who abstract events to cope with them: "The girl opens her mouth to say something to her mother. But she has no words for what has happened, no words for evil" (Martínez 167). After the assault, both José Luis and María start therapy with a trauma counselor, and María writes in her journal that she feels "better already, just writing things down" (Martínez 166).

Writing New Covenants

María engages metafiction for an assumed reader not only throughout the novel but also near its end, where she inserts notes directly addressing José Luis Jr. These notes, in addition to the rest of the elements used to tell the narrative of new memory, are compiled and read by her son on their flight to El Salvador. The notes have a caution for the young man, one that implies not the danger but the healing of the narrative: "Every story has its medicine; you must figure out what you need most from this one and let go of the rest" (Martínez 162). José Luis Jr. recounts how he and his mother travel to El Salvador together, to see if they can find out what happened to his father. Their discovery makes them very happy: José Luis is still on the list of *desaparecidos*, which means he might still be alive. They find a picture of him and learn his real name: José Luis Alegría Cruz y Romero.[33] José Luis Jr. tries to ease his mother's pain by assuring her that "he told you his real name because he loved you, and he wanted to give you something real" (Martínez 183). On this trip, mother and son heal the distance that has lingered between them. María notes how writing this story has transformed them: "My baby, my son, beloved stranger, disappearing into a new language and landscape, leaving me to look inside myself for the magic I love in you. I am forty years old. I have melted down sadness and joy into a single blade with which to carve out a life. And I am just beginning to discern the shape that was there all along. Just beginning to become me" (Martínez 190). María's use of the word *beloved* is poignant, as it evokes God calling Jesus Christ his beloved son. This expression appears in several chapters of the New Testament: Matthew 3, 12, 17; Mark 1, 9; and Luke 9.[34]

The Christian allusions in character names, concepts, and numerology used in *Mother Tongue* reveal another aspect of the narrative of new memory. José and María, Joseph and Mary, conceive a child whose gift is forgiveness. María's age is not just the number associated with Americans' midlife crises;

the number forty appears in the Bible numerous times, in both the Old and New Testaments. Generally, it measures the time events took to complete and is evidence of a fulfillment of one of God's promises. The best-known incidents measured in forty days/nights/years include Noah's Ark being rained upon for forty days; Moses taking forty years to lead the Jews out of the desert; Jesus experiencing forty days of temptation in the wilderness; and Jesus ascending from earth after his resurrection after forty days. Finally, forty weeks is the full gestation period for human pregnancy, which illustrates that María is creating herself anew as she writes a narrative of new memory.

Mother Tongue uses the trope of new language in a manner reminiscent of the "new language" Bodega tells Chino he will use in *Bodega Dreams*. The language is new for her son, not because he is interested in his father's mother tongue, Spanish, but because the process of hearing his mother's story has created a new memory of his own life. Martha Cutter argues that "a transcoding of ethnicity and a transmigration of tongues can occur only when the protagonists of these texts become 'writerly' translators who actively participate with the source text, struggle to understand its complexities, and refuse to take a passive and literal approach to its meaning" (8). When María finally decides to translate José Luis' journals, she becomes the "writerly translator." In doing so, she does, as Cutter suggests of translators in general, "finally realize that it is precisely their divergent and often contradictory cultural/linguistic heritages that engender the ability to produce new meanings, new stories, translations that break down binary oppositions, enriching and finally re-creating both cultural terrains" (98).

The novel's epilogue offers an unusual happy conclusion: a letter arrives from Canada, from José Luis. He has learned that María and a young man were looking for him. He apologizes for having left but affirms that he needed to return to his country. José Luis has become the hero he always could have been, and María has become the self-aware person who awoke from a Van Winkle–esque slumber. *Mother Tongue* achieves what the other books in this study have glimpsed but not realized: it not only offers a recognition of the challenges difference poses to pan-Latinism but also suggests that these problems can be remediated through retelling neocolonialism's version of history.[35]

At last, María is a woman with a plot line: the narrative of new memory. The novel illustrates that pan-Latina/o solidarity cannot be achieved through romantic or real estate dreams, as *Bodega Dreams* also implies. *Mother Tongue* emphasizes that solidarity requires collaborative storytelling.[36] Telling stories together—not necessarily contemporaneously or simultaneously—undermines the tallest tale neocolonialism tells: that a master narrative of the world exists a priori, outside of human construction. The final discussion of this chapter shows how powerful collaborative storytelling can be in the revision of nationalist narratives and the creation of a narrative of new memory.

"Your Native Island Is *Lesbos*": Disidentification in *The Greatest Performance*

Long before Raúl Castro was named president of Cuba, several events defined Cuba as a nation in the consciousness of US Americans: the incipience of the Communist Revolution in 1959, the Bay of Pigs Invasion of 1961, the Cuban Missile Crisis of 1962, and the Mariel Boatlift of 1980. The last event significantly altered Cuba's relationship with the United States because it exposed the deep fissure in what had been incorrectly perceived as a politically unified, pre-Castro Cuba. When Fidel Castro opened the Port of Mariel on April 20, 1980, he reintroduced distinct classes of Cubans that had not been in contact with one another since the Communist Revolution. The Cuban elite who left when Castro took power, known as the Miami exiles, now faced what he and they considered to be undesirable elements in Cuban society: homosexuals, black Cubans, the unskilled, the mentally ill, and the abject poor.

The false narrative Cuba and the United States maintained is that Castro opened the jails in Cuba, releasing the nation's criminals. But who were these criminals? Political dissidents and homosexuals comprised the majority of those Castro imprisoned. According to García, "Under Cuba's *ley de peligrosidad* [law of dangerousness], Cubans could be incarcerated for such offenses as alcoholism, gambling, drug addiction, homosexuality, prostitution, 'extravagant behavior,' vagrancy, and dealing on the black market" (64). Less than 4 percent of the Mariel Cubans had been incarcerated for felony crimes such as theft or homicide.[37] Despite educational opportunities for some Cubans, Castro considered homosexuals and the mentally ill to be threats to Cuba's social progress. When Acts of Repudiation and forced labor camps failed to "cure" these "illnesses" and economic crisis devastated Cuba, he encouraged these individuals to leave.[38] Given the pejorative context in which the Cubans exiting via the Port of Mariel has been construed, these Cubans were not perceived to be equal to the first wave of exiles.[39] In fact, in March of 1980, the US Refugee Act shifted the definition of refugee; thus, "Mariel marked the first time since the Cold War began that the government denied refugee status to individuals emigrating from a communist state" (García 69). This shift in status had significant consequences: Mariel immigrants were not afforded the same financial, medical, and social assistance their exile predecessors had been given. Those refugees who entered the United States without family were subject to extensive detention and delays in processing that did not guarantee permanent resident status.[40] Popularly, the Mariels were considered economic immigrants and thus have been perceived similarly to poor Puerto Ricans immigrating in the 1950s.[41]

The Mariel Boatlift refugees exposed the nation's longstanding class and race conflicts.[42] These conflicts have been underrepresented in Cuban American literature written by authors who immigrated or whose parents immigrated prior to the Mariel Boatlift; however, the conflicts have become a primary motif in novels by authors who immigrated some years after the revolution or experienced the boatlift. The Mariel Boatlift enabled a number of writers, including Reinaldo Arenas, Antonio Benítez-Rojo, Mirta Ojito, and Virgil Suárez, to flee Cuba and write uncensored in the United States. Some authors continue to write in Spanish; others produce bilingual and monolingual English texts.[43]

Scholars have developed a number of terms relevant to the exilic phenomenology of Cubans through sociological, literary, and economic models. Scholars such as Silvia Spitta, Frances Aparicio, and Susana Chávez Silverman, among others, engage modernist concepts such as Fernando Ortiz's "transculturation." Historical and narratological comparison, the kind of scholarship this study has performed, aims to consider authors or texts that are less often discussed in the public sphere but equally important to texts that have significant bodies of criticism devoted to them. Nilo Cruz, for example, has written and produced several dramas departing from the Cuban exile experience more typically represented by earlier dramatists such as Dolores Prida.[44] Born in 1960, immigrating via a Freedom Flight in 1970, Cruz moved from Miami to New York and earned an MFA in creative writing in 1994. His different experiences of exile are reflected in the Pulitzer Prize–winning play *Anna of the Tropics* (2003). As Ortiz observes, "By setting his play in 1929 Tampa, Cruz also explores aspects of the Cuban-American experience that are not directly dominated by the politics of the Revolution/Exile dialectic, although *Anna's* themes do offer themselves to be elaborated in that context as well" ("Cuban-American Literature" 420).

The focus on nostalgia within exilic literature appears in the work of scholars such as Isabel Alvarez Borland, Gustavo Pérez Firmat, Iraida H. Lopez, and Pamela María Smorkaloff. More recent Cuban American novels meet between the exilic literature of Latin America and the arrival literature of the United States. María Cristina García's *Havana USA* is one of the few monographs that approaches the various strains of Cuban American literature and identifies writers distinct from the exile generation: "By the late 1980s, the exile creative community had expanded to include a new generation of writers, among them Roberto G. Fernández, Elías Miguel Muñoz, Ana María Simó, Iván Acosta, Dolores Prida, Gustavo Pérez-Firmat, Ricardo Pau-Llosa, and María Irene Fornés" (169). She also explores the work of lesser-known authors, including Elías Miguel Muñoz, among those who "constituted a distinct generation not so much because of this age—many were first-generation immigrants themselves—but because of their thematic concerns. Unlike the exile authors who considered themselves Cubans writing outside of Cuba, writers of this new generation saw themselves as both Cuban and American" (169–70). Both Muñoz's first novel, *Crazy Love* (1989), and his second, *The Greatest Performance* (1991), exemplify this kind of text because they use multiple narrative forms to represent the differences within the Cuban communities that were transported to the United States. *Crazy Love* shares the multigenre format of *So Far from God* and *Mother Tongue*; the novel incorporates the epistolary, stream-of-consciousness narration, dramaturgical dialogue, and third-person omniscient narration in a highly musical bildungsroman.

Both novels question the Cuban—not Cuban American—construction of masculinity. Of the earlier novel, *Crazy Love*, García asserts, "Elías Miguel Muñoz best articulates the demands made on men and intolerance of homosexuality within Cuban exile culture" (191). Julian, the protagonist of *Crazy Love*, demonstrates how the forceful homophobic rhetoric of Cuban masculinity catalyzes familial exile. Julian's narrative, much like Mario's in *The Greatest Performance*, reconstructs the acts of physical and verbal rape by male family members that characterize the social construction of Cuban masculinity. Julian chooses to embrace the artistic sensibilities his family rejects; their rejection leads him to exile, to consent to homosexual acts, and eventually to a permanent heterosexual coupling. Julian's true "queering" act is to alter the Cuban exile's migration. Rather than leaving Cuba and remaining in Miami, he moves from California to a self-imposed exile to Spain. He returns to support the family during his grandfather's illness but refuses to perform the role of a nonartistic, normative heterosexual son.[45]

Queering Cuba

The Greatest Performance references the tropes of all four narratives—loss, reclamation, fracture, and new memory—but its primary mode is new memory. Early within the novel, a sense of loss for the *Cuba de ayer*, before Castro assumed power, sets the tone for the psychological losses the protagonists, Mario and Rosa, experience through homophobia.[46] The novel enacts reclamation in flashbacks, as the characters recall staging childhood performances that allowed them to embody their sexuality without negative repercussions. Some narrative time is spent in fracturing exclusionary conceptions of cubanidad. In a manner similar to *Brand New Memory*, the protagonists of this novel are at pains to locate themselves in the culture of Cuba, not the culture of the United States. Read as a whole, the project the narrators undertake—rewriting their sexual biographies and their friendship—makes the novel an exemplary narrative of new memory.

The Greatest Performance illustrates that the Cuban exile community carried its homophobia and intolerance with it during migration. This novel, set first in Cuba, then in Spain, and mostly in California, illustrates how the Miami exiles used compulsory heterosexism and the notions of the ideal immigrant to distinguish themselves from the Mariel community in the eyes of Anglo-American world. As María Cristina García argues, "Public opinion turned against them when the press revealed that Castro had used the boatlift to rid the island of 'undesirables' and that among the new immigrants were hundreds, if not thousands, of criminals. Even the exile community turned against this new wave, afraid that their golden reputations as model immigrants would be tarnished by the criminal element. Unlike the earlier refugees, the *marielitos* encountered hostility and discrimination wherever they settled" (46).

The time span of twenty years in *Mother Tongue* is replicated in the twenty years of separation the "Exiles" and the "Mariels" experienced. Texts such as Virgil Suárez's *Havana Thursdays* (1988), Oscar Hijuelos' *Our House in the Last World* (1983), and Achy Obejas' *I Came All the Way from Cuba so You Could Dress Like This?* (1991) each explore the problems of exile, but these texts foreground generational differences between exiles and their children. *The Greatest Performance*, in contrast, foregrounds not only what the characters "perform" but also the specific ethnonational context in which they do so: Cuba or Cuban America. Rosa and Mario's questions form the basis of the novel's dialogue on what identity means for Cuban Americans when nationality and ethnicity cease to be their primary signifiers of identity.

An early portion of the novel contextualizes identity as existing outside the body. Mario's mother patrols the streets of Havana, demanding of every driver and passerby, "show me your identity" (Muñoz 19). If the people do not have identification, she nonetheless offers them the opportunity to identify themselves with "anything that would prove who you are" (Muñoz 19). The scene is riotously funny: a homemaker armed with a whistle stops people in the name of the National Defense Committee and actually expects them to obey her. The scene mocks the regimented society Castro has created. Day after day, the travelers respond to her request with juvenile gestures such as farting or burping or lewd gestures such as exposing their genitalia. The most humorous portion of the exchange is the demand itself: to contain and provide your identity in a single statement or act.[47] *The Greatest Performance* depicts characters that resist such absurd demands for performance of one's identity. The novel functions as an explicit treatment of sexual identity formation, power within familial relationships, and performances within sexual, cultural, and immigration discourses. Muñoz creates a narrative of new memory of queer *cubanidad*.

Queer cubanidad functions independently of public discourse on sexuality and its attending acts of homophobic violence, making the protagonists' memories of their selves *new*. The difference in the depicted immigration experiences challenges readers to see homosexual Mariel Cubans as refugees—displaced persons who are neither exclusively political exiles nor economic immigrants. The erasure of the sexual refugee, rendered largely invisible in other Chicana/o and Latina/o texts, is fruitfully illuminated by *The Greatest Performance*. As Greg Mullins asserts, the general understanding of the term *refugee* is anyone "seeking protection from danger by moving to a safe jurisdiction" (147). Quite problematically, though, "neither US nor international law defines 'refugee' so broadly" (Mullins 147). Thus, Cubans who are homosexual are doubly disenfranchised. Persecuted in Cuba and ostracized if entering the United States via the Mariel Boatlift, gay Cubans remain at the margins of several discursive spaces. By holding both themselves and their culture's beliefs accountable for the perpetuation of homophobia and classicism, the protagonists Mario and Rosa attempt to alter the divisive hierarchies and discrimination migrating with the Cuban diaspora.[48]

Little scholarship exists on this novel, reflecting a critical gap in scholarship on queer Chicana/o and Latina/o literature more generally. More specifically, the general lack of scholarship on the novel reflects the lack of focus on queer texts with both male and female queer protagonists and on books by less-prominent authors.[49] The novel reflects what Sandra Soto has remarked about queer Latino phenomenology: "Because heteronormativity necessarily includes norms that help produce racialization and national formations, many Latinos/as have been drawn to the queer commitment to exposing and contesting the disciplining function of heteronormativity" ("Queerness" 75). Early and already noted is Karen Christian's discussion of heteronormativity in *Show and Tell: Identity as Performance in U.S. Latina/o Fiction* (1997), which argues, "representations of gay and lesbian subjectivities in *The Greatest Performance* further undermine static essentialist standards of Cuban authenticity that work to regulate performance of gender and sexuality in the émigré community" (58). Greg A. Mullins' essay "Seeking Asylum: Literary Reflections on Sexuality, Ethnicity, and Human Rights" reads the novel through human rights discourse (2003).[50] Lázaro Lima's study *The Latino Body: Crisis Identities in American Literary and Cultural Memory* (2007) positions the text as "another absence from the realm of the National Symbolic, the haunting specter of AIDS on the Latino Body" (Lima 140). Studies and edited collections by Aparicio and Chávez-Silverman (*Tropicalizations*, 1997), Quiroga (*Tropics of Desire*, 2000), and Hames-García and Martínez (*Gay Latino Studies*, 2011) have offered important frameworks for filling in the theoretical gap.[51]

The structure of the novel is a dialogue between two friends who have had to closet themselves from their family and nation. As Rosa narrates her life, the photo becomes a trope once again. She reveals the truths behind each of her family photos, and in stark contrast to the use of photos as signifiers of loss and shame, as in *Drown*, Rosa changes some of the photos' significance to positive, empowering paratexts. By asserting there is a story the photo does not capture, she reminds readers that no document, textual or visual, can capture the entirety or even the truth of an event. Rosa's use of the photo album recalls Pilar's statement about the Mariel Boatlift in *Dreaming in Cuba*: "Nothing can record this: not words, not pictures" (García 241). Lima's reading of Rosa's narration parallels my argument about the collective nature of new memory: "This dialogue between Rosita and Marito makes her address not only a re-memory of Marito's life but also a virtual reconstruction of her own as she grafts his aprocryphal present onto her childhood history" (149). The whole novel is a conversation between two people without a shared past who create a shared present and future.

The Greatest Performance tells its story fairly equally through both narrative voices. Most of the other texts in this study do not do that—they either have a single, dominant narrator or are polyphonic and use multiple narrators.[52] Early in the novel, Rosa announces the convergence of her childhood friend and her current friend, Mario: "In my childhood story you have become that kid, Marito. Or rather, he has become you. And I can no longer remember his real name" (Muñoz 16). Rosa's inability to distinguish the stories of her childhood friend and her adult friend suggest the artifice and utility of narrative, especially autobiography, which is a genre the characters perform throughout the novel.[53] Lima argues that Mario's "fictive presence in [Rosa's] real photograph fashions history out of need" (149). The extent to which any of the objects, including the photographs, are real in the fictive world of the novel is less significant, though, than what the fictive presences accomplish: "The survival of the body as a historical and material entity is directly related to its genre, ethnicity, and class, and although it follows that almost every 'body' has a story to tell, not all bodies matter equally to everyone" (Lima 140). Mario's body, especially its history, matters terribly to Rosa because it is a kaleidoscope of her own body, reflecting her changing experience of it.

Readers are equally uncertain about the reliability of Mario as a narrator. Most of his childhood narratives are a combination of dream sequences and memories; similar to Gina of *Brand New Memory*, he changes voice often and quickly, using first-person stream-of-consciousness, second-person direct address, and limited third-person omniscience. Often it is clear that Mario, himself, is not sure whether he is remembering events or dreams or fantasy. By the novel's close, readers understand that Mario is HIV positive and in the last stage of AIDS; some of his recollections may be hallucinations. *The Greatest Performance* is not a magical realist text in any way. Mario's body performs the painful *mimesis* that La Loca's AIDS-ravaged body does in *So Far from God*.[54]

Muñoz is less concerned with violence between men and women than he is with the violence between women in lesbian and mother/daughter relationships and between men in homosexual and father/son relationships. The repercussions of domestic violence and pedophilia become the sites for the change in their story: Rosa and Mario's new memories of their sexuality. As Rosa's narration moves back and forth, her focus on the stories of people outside her immediate family illustrates Moraga's concept of "Making Familia from Scratch"; one's self-actualization happens outside the homophobic family, and other homosexuals and allies become "family." Rosa narrates Mario into her life story; they have met as adults in the United States, not as children in Cuba. She articulates the narrative voices of a child and adult, with the adult mediating the childhood memories she is simultaneously constructing: "From my sinful hideaway I listened (I imagine now that I listened) to your cries. Things were much worse for you, because you had been born a man.

Your crime deserved no forgiveness and no mercy" (Muñoz 18). Rosa's relationship with Mario is what enables her, as an adult, to embrace her sexual orientation and acknowledge its primacy in her self-identification.

José E. Muñoz's important monograph *Disidentifications: Queers of Color and the Performance of Politics* (1999) creates a theoretical framework for reading performances of identity. He asserts, "disidentification is meant to be descriptive of the survival strategies the minority subject practices in order to negotiate a phobic majoritarian public sphere that continuously elides or punishes the existence of subjects who do not conform to the phantasm of normative citizenship" (5). For Rosa and Mario the "majoritarian public sphere" is both the state and the family. Muñoz's conceptualization of "disidentification" is extremely useful in considering how these two protagonists navigate homophobia in public and private spheres. Muñoz's qualification of the term is very important: "disindentification is *not always* an adequate strategy of resistance or survival for minority subjects. At times, resistance needs to be pronounced and direct; on other occasions, queers of color and other minority subjects needs to follow a conformist path if they hope to survive a hostile public sphere" (*Disidentifications* 5). To survive the violence, first of their families and later of both the Cuban state and the American state, Rosa and Mario have to choose conformity or performance of false identities. Their disidentification, their refusal to choose either of these identities, is productive; it allows them to live, not perform. Their agency helps them tell their story, the new memory of queer cubanidad.

Rosa's comment about the distinct treatments of gays and lesbians begins a powerful critique against homophobia in Cuba, especially in the early years of Castro's regime. Though such conceptions may seem dated because of the developments in queer theory in the 1990s, Muñoz's prescient critique is especially important because it linked Cuban cultural and legal discourses about homosexuality prevalent then, and unfortunately today as well.[55] Rosa's reconstruction of Mario's life acknowledges the different responses to homosexuality in men and women in Cuban culture. Even though Rosa does not suffer physical violence because of her homosexuality, she is compelled to reject her family as home because they have made no space for her lesbian body within it. Rosa fantasizes performing as a heterosexual male, as "the hero," or as "the rogue." In those moments, she was choosing the conformist path José E. Muñoz discusses. When Rosa casts herself as a heterosexual male and normalizes her sexuality to fit into the rigid gender system of her family and Cuba, she *disidentifies* with lesbians but achieves a kind of agency she will not experience again until she meets Mario.[56]

Rosa presents her sexual awakening in a positive manner. She falls in love with a teenage friend, Maritza, who is a few years older than she is. Their intimacy is mutual and their relationship forms the basis of a positive sexual initiation. Her relationship with Maritza, though, is tied to her topographical sense of Cuba; Rosa is able to meet Maritza secretly in "the country" while working for the cause at La Cooperativa. One of Castro's many countryside labor camps, La Cooperativa is presented as an edenic and safe space for otherwise taboo sexuality. In the city, family and social structures criticize her tomboy nature and confine Rosa. Rural Cuba, in a simplistic binary, offers a contrasting freedom from such domination and offers validation for Rosa and Maritza's love. As Rosa experiences her first kiss with Maritza, a woman emerges from the dark singing about love: "And then I saw that from behind the tree appeared this woman, this woman, who sang, entranced, *We are sweethearts*, who whispered, *because we feel this love, sublime and profound.* She hummed, she sang, *This love that makes us proud.* She cried, *This love so weary of goodbyes.* She pleaded, *Come hear, come hear, my sweetheart's lullaby*" (Muñoz 25). This scene has several implications.

La Cooperativa has become a safe space for unsanctioned sexuality in an ironic joke on Fidel Castro. Initially, Rosa might have felt caught, but the woman's singing puts her at ease and she does not fear that she will be reported for her "illness," as homosexuality was defined in Fidel Castro's regime. What is striking, though, is that the woman's song quickly moves from a pleasant singing to a tearful speaking: "She cried, *This love so weary of goodbyes.* She pleaded, *Come hear, come hear, my sweetheart's lullaby*" (Muñoz 25). Thus, while the girls Rosa and Maritza have begun to awaken sexually, the song lyrics suggests that the love will be short lived.[57] When the nameless woman says, "This love so weary of goodbyes," she reinforces the idea that their relationship is defined by their spatial proximity. The girls will not be together again, as their relationship was possible only in this space outside of their homophobic family units.

Later, Rosa will contrast Cuba with two places. Her initial immigration to Spain is described as a closed and cold space, where she must fight the molestations of her uncle. Her second immigration, to the United States, is defined as too open a space, where roads and cars overwhelm her. Rosa's sexual identity is so closely linked to Cuban topography that the nation loses its ability to comfort her in exile, once her first lover enters a heterosexual marriage: "Seeing her name printed over a red heart, on that cheap cream-colored paper and next to the name of a man, MARITZA GARCIA & DAVID PÉREZ, I felt for the first time that Cuba was vanishing from my life" (Muñoz

16). Rosa's primary identity is defined by the sexual safety and freedom that she enjoyed in Cuba, not a sense of Cuban ethnonationalism.

The Greatest Performance's depiction of homophobia and the repression of homosexual identity in Cuba and the United States renders the idea that Castro's revolution freed all Cubans absurd. Castro exercised a systematic surveillance, arrest, and detention of homosexuals.[58] Homosexual men and women both faced such potential discrimination; however, as Rosa noted, it was much worse for men. The classification of a man as homosexual indicated that a man was depraved. Being queer had the potential to indicate—depending on his perceived role in the sex act—that a man's masculinity was further decreased. Just as in Díaz's story "Drown," men who perform anal penetration are not subject to the denigrating terms of *pato* or *maricón*.[59] These terms are used to describe the recipient of penetration and signal him as being pasivo, effeminate, and deviant. The novel questions this inequity and implies that the distinction between the giver and the receiver is artificial and hypocritical.

Rosa and Mario experience homophobia from the time they are children. While Mario's first sexual encounter, with a boy of his age, is positive, he spends greater narrative time unraveling the abuse he experienced because he was "obvious." Mario's sexual identity develops through his relationship with his father and a sequence of sexual abuse by other men. In Mario's narrations of his sexual development, his father and his father's friends are physical and sexual abusers. At one level, these men, including his father, represent the state. Mullins' assertion that "the pinching and poking, forms of sexualized violence, enforce on the boy the stark realities of Cuban patriarchal heteronormativity" is an apt gloss for the father's treatment of his son (154). Mario's abusers' recognition of the boy's femininity becomes a site for the boy's questioning, as a boy and man, whether his sexuality was natural or created by his father's lack of affection and sexual deviance and/or the rapes Mario experiences.

Mullins asserts, "The merest hint of effeminacy is treated as treachery to masculinity, and traitors are subjected to the kinds of violence suffered by women" (154). Mario never explicitly says that his father molested him, but the reader senses Mario cannot admit that to himself. Even if Pipo, his father, did not molest or rape him, Mario's bruised and scarred body clearly indicates his father's inability to differentiate abuse from discipline. In her narrative, Rosa asks Mario, "Was it because the ogre you had for a father punished you by making you take off all of your clothes and then you had to sit in the living room, stark naked? Was that the reason? Did you associate your nudity with punishment and pain?" (Muñoz 20). His response reveals one of many traumatic experiences: "Pipo insisted on both of us using the same shower stall, so he could scrub me hard, the way little boys needed to be scrubbed. Men with long things and boys with tiny ones would pass by and stare, pointing at the father-and-son shower spectacle" (Muñoz 31). The language Mario uses here, "spectacle," evokes images of Cuban citizens being subjected to "Acts of Repudiation": public demonstrations of punishment designed to elicit confession of crimes against the state. In the familial context, Pipo is punishing Mario for what he perceives as him failing to hide his "filth." In a queer theory context, Pipo is performing the conformity described in *Disidentifications*. He is acting as a heterosexual male disciplining his son's body. His conformity, though, is not without consequence to others; it imposes power over and pain onto his son.[60]

Pipo's abuse of Mario included his failure to protect him from Hernando, a "friend" of Pipo's who owned a black-market plantain business. After meeting Mario, Hernando stalks the boy, eventually lures him to a secluded location, and rapes him. While disgusted by Hernando, Mario blames his father for this rape: "But you were the one, Pipo, who took me to Hernando's farm. You asked me to go with you" (Muñoz 35). Before and after the physical rape, Hernando enacts a verbal rape of the boy, articulating common views on homosexuals in Cuba and Latin America in general. Mario recalls Hernando's stereotypical homophobic comments: "He knew I was a *pájaro*, a queer, from the very moment he laid eyes on me, the day I came to his farm with my father and I acted like a sissy, refusing to get my feet dirty with mud and complaining about the weight of the plantain bunches" (Muñoz 36). Hernando performs as activo but Mario undermines this by quoting Hernando's pleas for Mario's consensual sex. Hernando repeats, "I swear I'll do anything for you, Marito," three times (Muñoz 37).

Hernando initially presented himself as the dominant male, having identified Mario as the pato. Now, their roles seem reversed because Hernando is begging Mario to give him oral and anal sex, which makes the reader consider the complexity of performance. Though clearly Hernando rapes Mario sexually, this vacillation between moments of rhetorical dominance and submission constitute a verbal rape of the boy.[61] Marito refuses to return, saying, "I never want to see him again," and Hernando threatens him anew (Muñoz 37–38). By rejecting Hernando's blurring of active and pasivo sex roles, Mario also disidentifies with Cuban society's narrative of homosexual identity. As an adult, he performs both roles during sexual intercourse with men, just as Julian, the self-identified heterosexual protagonist of Muñoz's novel, *Crazy Love*, performs.

This is an example of a textual moment that illustrates that essentialist queer identity paradigms simply do not function. José E. Muñoz's position on such binaristic readings is useful here: "the use-value of any narrative of identity that reduces subjectivity to either a social constructivist model or what has been called an essentialist understanding of the self is especially exhausted" (5). Muñoz's assessment is particularly relevant to the homophobic violence Mario experiences in Cuba and the United States.

Expelling Cuba's Queer Body

Mario's narrative shifts to a critical point when his father applies for an exit visa. Pipo is forced to complete labor in the countryside. Mario is very concerned about his father's "safety" during his forty days of labor, which is reminiscent of Jesus Christ's temptation in the wilderness. Mario's concerns about his father's sexuality imply that his father had indeed molested him. Mario ponders whether or not Pipo himself would be "safe" at such a camp, where his homosexuality might be "obvious." Emphasizing the differences in treatment of children and adults within the Castro regime, Mario indicates that he will "have to do my share of labor when my school goes to the country for forty days" (Muñoz 43). Mario's imagined version of the labor camp starkly contrasts with Rosa's positive description. Children were sent to the camps for indoctrination and adults for re-education; Mario makes this distinction between himself and his father: "But what about Pipo? They took him to *Las Barracas*, where all the traitors are being taken to receive their punishment. Faggots are taken there too, because the Revolution says they are sick and need reforming, treatment" (Muñoz 42). Nonetheless, he views the labor camps as dangerous spaces for all: "Pipo may have to sleep next to a *pájaro*" (Muñoz 42). In an abrupt shift, he writes a new memory of his father to cope with the possibility of past violation by him. The next sentence illustrates Mario's uncertainty about his father's sexuality: "Pipo may be doing it to him. Could he? No. Pipo has no prick, nothing to do it with. The Pipo I love has no sex; like the blonde angel who stole my pacifier, he has nothing to put inside a boy's ass. So he's safe" (Muñoz 43). Mario's inability to distinguish his father's sexuality reiterates that homosexuals are not all obvious. The reader wonders if Mario's use of "safe" in this last sentence means that Pipo is safe from being caught for homosexuality or if he is safe in relation to other prisoners and little boys because he will not rape them. Either reading suggests that Muñoz's anti-essentialist position of queer latinidad is apt.

Mario then narrates his being thrown out of the house, his subsequent change into a *jinetero* who cruises in Cuba, and his years as a sex worker in the United States.[62] At exactly midnovel, Mario recalls a conversation among several gay men. One of them is a doctor who recounts his experiences in medical residency in San Francisco. The doctor describes how the "Gay Rap" men initially joke but ultimately are terrified by the lack of knowledge about AIDS: "'They say you get it from butt-fucking.' 'Get what?' 'The plague'" (Muñoz 75). In the present, one of the men gathered asks, "'What does the late-blooming doctor have to say about this so-called Gay Plague?'" and the doctor responds, "'We don't know enough about it yet . . . '" (Muñoz 76). The conversation places the events of the novel in the early 1980s, especially the last line quoted above, which was repeated in news conferences as more AIDS cases of prominent Americans, such as Rock Hudson, were revealed. At that time, the medical community had no definitive information about the origin or transmittal of the disease; however, the homosexual community had become synonymous with AIDS because gay men were increasingly testing HIV positive and then being rhetorically constructed as the source of the virus. As Lima notes, "That Marito's body is imbricated in this economic web of power relations signals the representational participation of an absent and strongly affected body in the public discourse about AIDS: the Latino body" (151). Placing this conversation midnovel centralizes one space—perhaps the only one—of sameness gay men have experienced if they lived in this era.

Mario will experience other displacements due to his lack of economic power; he will move from Miami, to New York, to California. His movements resonate with those of the Mexican American narrator in John Rechy's *City of Night*. In Rechy's text, the nameless protagonist moves from city to city as a sex worker, examining his inability to develop monogamous relationships. *City of Night* and *The Greatest Performance* share a critical invisibility. Rechy, in particular, was among writers that the Chicano nationalist movement excluded in their construction of Aztlán.[63] Scholars including Juan Bruce-Novoa, Ramón Gutiérrez, and David William Foster have made similar assertions since the 1990s.

Bruce-Novoa argues that "the implicit rejection of monological cultural unity in texts such as *Pocho* by José Antonio Villarreal or *City of Night* by John Rechy once were explained as an aberration produced by the author's cultural alienation" ("Dialogical Strategies" 241). According to Gutiérrez, "It was [Rechy's] name, his homosexuality, and the themes he explored in print that excluded him from the community young men defined as Chicano. Ironically, at the very time that he was being rejected by Chicanos, the Texas Hall of Fame inducted him into its ranks as a Chicano author, an identity Rechy has always proudly claimed" ("Community, Patriarchy and Individualism" 62). Foster notes that Rechy "was at first systematically ignored or shoved to the margins of Chicano cultural production" (*El Ambiente Nuestro* 15). Arturo Islas is another example of an author whose work was excluded from the ethnic canon and literary criticism because of its queer focus. In the last few years, however, these authors have been recovered in both spaces.[64] Scholars have suggested another reason Muñoz's work has been elided—its graphic nature. Francisco Soto suggests that "one could argue that an important feature of this novel is its bold and direct treatment of both gay and lesbian sexualities. Aware of the homophobia of his audience, yet not willing to make concessions—Muñoz treated Marito's homosexuality and Rosita's lesbianism honestly and graphically" (291). The American public may still not be ready for true engagement with queer sexuality. The mainstream success of sexually graphic novels such as *Fifty Shades of Grey* suggests that it is not the graphic nature of the sex but the queer nature of the sex that determines some readers' ability to engage a novel or other form of cultural production.

The Greatest Performance also parallels the *City of Night* in that both novels' homosexual male narrators provide explicit descriptions of other characters' race, skin color, and performance of ethnicity but deliberately avoid describing their own physical appearances. This suggests that while the speakers may categorize others through cultural or racial markers, they are trying to perform homosexual identities devoid of these same markers. In *The Greatest Performance*, Mario does not articulate a lack of monogamous relationships. His comments about "performing" suggest that Mario has had a limited number of monogamous relationships but that performance affected those relationships, and that ultimately he chose to stop performing. Lima suggests the exhaustion of performance: "If the 'performance' is tiring, the excess violence against the john's body politicizes the varieties of possible queer pleasure as well as its cost on the 'performer's' body" (150). This exhaustive violence is painfully inscribed on Mario's body in his acquisition of AIDS.

Mario's lack of self-description is a *disidentification* with a specifically ethnic, or Cuban, queerness. For Mario and Rosa, ethnicity is not valued as a primary signifier of identity. In Mario's case in particular, ethnopolitical ideology has the potential to prevent him from acceptance within the gay community. Mullins suggests that in Cuba, "ethnic cohesion is subsumed under Cuban nationalism, which during the 1960s and 1970s called for the creation of a new man: a virile, patriarchal dominant heterosexual man who would create a socialist nation through sexual reproduction and heteronormative family life" (158). This argument is relevant to both the national space of Cuba and the leftist members of the US homosexual community. Mario's initial fears about his relationship with Jimmy illustrate some of the conflicts among queer Latinos: "Does he really not mind the fact that I'm a Cuban worm, a traitor to the Revolution?" (Muñoz 99–100). This comment unites intersecting identity parameters: ethnicity and class. Jimmy is a teacher; he espouses Marxism and decries the conditions of Puerto Ricans in New York. Mario fears that his lack of politics will keep him from identifying with Jimmy sexually, not racially: "Does he not mind that I don't give a fuck about politics?" (Muñoz 99–100). Because Mario and other Cubans have been repeatedly violated by the state under communism's guise of social progress, political differences are significant, sometimes irreconcilable, ideological challenges to queer solidarity in the United States.[65]

Muñoz explores the tropes of arrival just as the other authors discussed in this study. He renders the economic success of some Cubans, such as the first-generation exiles, absurd in light of the poverty and lack of access to health care and education by other Cubans, such as the Mariel refugees living in Miami and Los Angeles. The novel critiques successful Cubans who are rapidly becoming a marketing target group. For example, Rosa mocks the idea that Cubans have arrived when considering her lover's enthused marketing strategies for Hispanics. These advertising ploys are marked by attempts to change the tastes of "Hispanics," literally of the food they eat: "Thirst-quenching and delightfully sweet Pop Cola, DRINK IT LATINO! CATCH THE NEW ONDA!" (Muñoz 115). The advertising has a secondary effect of shifting their cultural tastes using the rhetoric of multiculturalism: "INCORPORATE YOURSELF, LATINO! BE PART OF THE NEW GRINGO CONSTELLATION!" (Muñoz 115). Rosa reflects on the extent to which it reflects the position of Latinos in Los Angeles: "Spanish-language billboards have sprung up all over the city. What more proof do we need of our important contribution to this great and fertile land? We've made it. We have *arrived*" (Muñoz 115; emphasis in original). The use of the words *incorporate* and *constellation* reify the critique of arrival that is present in all of the narratives this study has discussed.[66] A powerful double entrendre, *incorporate* links the erasure of the brown body (corpus/corpse) semantically to neocolonialism's consumption of human resources (incorporation). In Cuba, national and queer identities are irreconcilable under the gaze of the communist state; in the United States, they are not.

Rosa proactively begins her narrative of new memory when she chooses to *disidentify* with this false binary. She perceives that she has sexual agency in the United States. Rosa can determine how those identities intersect: "I had said to myself, Niña, your native island is Lesbos, not Cuba. Now what are you gonna do about it?" (Muñoz 92). The novel succeeds in crafting a narrative of new memory in important ways. By examining the underlying beliefs that inscribe heteronormative values, the text enriches our understanding of the differences within Cuban America. In her analysis of Rosa's relationship with Joan and Rosa's closeting of that relationship to her family, Christian rightfully argues, "*The Greatest Performance* thus suggests that within the microcosm of the US Cuban community, the performative acts that perpetuate the illusion of authentic cubanidad cannot accommodate non-heteronormative sexualities" (66). This argument can be extended by returning to the premise that homophobia in the US Cuban community travels from Cuba to the United States. If the US Cuban community is read as a microcosm of Cuba, Rosa's decision to move out of her home and to prioritize *Lesbos* over *Cuba* suggests that conceptualizations of a singular authentic cubanidad can no longer be accommodated or ignored. Rosa has not rejected Cuba; she has disidentified with the essentializing cubanidad that erases her queer body.

Rosa offers readers a final sense of performance powerfully juxtaposed by Mario's inevitable death from AIDS. As Lima argues, "Rosita's narrative presence is the structuring point and axis of the text's dialogue with itself, the issue of writing as a contestatory and transgressive practice in the age of AIDS, and the forms of cultural amnesia it attempts to deconstruct" (141). Lima's emphasis on Rosa's narration reflects the importance of agency: "In her difficult re-membering, AIDS becomes the catalyst for her tapestry of care and compassion. If he could not act in life in his body, Marito will live re-membered as a body that mattered" (151). Outside of the narrative time of Rosa's new memory, Mario exercised agency. His own narration of his childhood abuses and complicating essentialist notions of ethnic and sexual identity made him a body that mattered to Rosa, to Jimmy, and to others whose voices we may not have heard as often in the novel.

Rosa redefines the beginning of their collaborative life as a *disidentifica-tion* with their biographies: "You have never gone hungry. When things got rough, you didn't put your body up for sale. You never hustled. And I, I never found myself alone and violated in a cold, dark Spain" (Muñoz 150). She erases the narratives that have tried to erase her and Marito's existence: "We never heard of Castro. (Not even Castro Street). Nobody hides, waving a dagger in the air, behind the mask of God. A plague hasn't broken out" (Muñoz 151). Rosa's narration removes individuality from their narrative of new memory: "There, on that solitary prairie overflowing with light, that's where we met. I was resting on the grass. You came close and said that you had lost your way. I offered you a warm place by my side, you held my hand. Then we whispered a song to each other, 'We are sweethearts . . .'" (Muñoz 151).

The novel's closing offers the most powerful example of it as a narrative of new memory. Rosa and Mario's friendship allows them to choose to perform not as expected but as one chooses or not at all. As emphasized in the readings of *So Far from God*, *Soledad*, and *Mother Tongue*, contemporary narratives addressing US neocolonialism and its legacies are increasingly communal. Even in primarily single-voiced novellas such as . . . *And the Earth Did Not Devour Him* and Judith Ortiz Cofer's prose narratives, multiple voices and multiple stories are woven together to visualize Chicana/o and Latina/o phenomenology. While I focused more on Ortiz Cofer's first-person narrations of her childhood persona, Elena, there are, as the subtitle indicates, stories of many women: *Telling the Lives of Barrio Women*.

The Greatest Performance is a disidentification with performance and individualism. Readers understand where Mario's life might have begun and see that his friendship with Rosa has created *new memory* of both of their lives. The novel's dialogic structure discourages reading it as advocating or illustrating performativity as individual enterprise. The novel's end alerts readers to the novel's fuller context: Rosa is telling Mario stories, old and new, as he dies of AIDS complications: "Yes, I will create this place where you can be who you've always wanted to be, Marito. Where You and I have become the same person. This moment of greatness, I will create it. When the performance ends. And life begins" (Muñoz 151). The narrative of new memory she creates for them will be the last story, the last language, he will ever hear: it is brand new and beautiful.

Cultural Memory and Belonging in Chicana/o and Latina/o Fiction

Chicana/o and Latina/o Fiction has concerned itself with writers publishing fiction between the 1970s through the first decade of the twenty-first century, each descended from one of four distinct ethnonations: Cuba, the Dominican Republic, Mexico, and Puerto Rico. In contrast to the majority of studies in Chicana/o and Latina/o literature, this book has illustrated that the concern with internal community oppression, rather than with acculturation to the Anglo-American mainstream, developed well before the 1980s "boom" in ethnic literature. Drawing on each work's specific poetics, I have offered illustrations of the consistent movements toward narratives of new memory visible in both contemporary Chicana/o and Latina/o literature.

The books discussed within this study suggest that literary projects have forsaken the construction of a larger public memory in favor of exploring personal collaborative memory because extended collective memory is inaccessible, insufficient, or false. Chapter 1 discusses narratives representing neocolonial subjectivity. In both the novella . . . *And the Earth Did Not Devour Him* and the short stories of *Drown*, characters illustrate how the narrative of loss helps them acknowledge the impossibility of arrival in America. Chapter 2 outlines how texts progress to the narrative of reclamation, where adult characters rewrite their present through an engagement with their family's and their culture's pasts. Both *So Far from God* and *Soledad* reveal that in the narrative of reclamation, narrators meld allegory and ritual to connect to their cultures and redefine them. Chapter 3 illustrates how seemingly homogenous communities—Puerto Ricans in urban New York and New Jersey—can be heterogeneous to the point of communal disintegration. *The Latin Deli* and

Bodega Dreams revisit the legacy of the era of civil rights suggesting that the Puerto Ricans of New Jersey and New York must reengage the problems and possibilities of pan-Latinism.

Beyond historical proximity and narrative tropes, what links the books discussed here? I have focused my readings on texts that offer the most immediate and clearest analytical comparisons. The usefulness of *Chicana/o and Latina/o Fiction: The New Memory of Latinidad* becomes evident when trying to read texts through common tropes of literatures about immigration experiences or immigrant communities. It might seem like a simplistic model for reading: ask some questions about the book's recurring themes, and you understand the text pretty well. Reading the narratives of loss, reclamation, fracture, and new memory animates readers to a more complex engagement of the books by inviting them to examine their ontology and epistemology about ethnic identity. As a pedagogical tool, it reintroduces the author and the readers as agents in collaborative architectures of meaning.

Chicana/o and Latina/o Fiction shows that no single paradigm is unilaterally appropriate to contextualize all works of literature. The absence of a Chicano novel developing the narrative of new memory attests to the framework's limits. In selecting texts for the study, it became apparent that Chicano novels had fewer instances of the narrative of new memory than Chicana or Latina/o novels. At least two explanations for this are evident. One, as I have suggested, is related to the ethnonational rhetoric of El Movimiento. A major premise of the movement was that Chicanos have always been here, and thus Anglos are the aliens within Aztlán. This model does not often function for Chicana writers because, as many have argued, they were the marginalized aliens within Aztlán as well. Postmovement Chicana literatures clearly depict the need for women to write narratives of fracture and new memory.

The more frequent development in the narrative of new memory in Cuban American literatures and literatures about or portraying Central American characters has everything to do with the specificity of difference among immigrants, exiles, and refugees. As explained in chapters 1 and 4, the portrayal of exiles and refugees can offer authors the space to write new memories of their relationships to their own nations of origin, to nations they have emigrated to, or to nations with which they may wish to develop solidarity. In the case of Elías Miguel Muñoz's novels *Brand New Memory* and *The Greatest Performance*, the desire to rewrite both the neocolonial and the communist narratives of Cuba is explicit. Demetria Martínez's first novel, *Mother Tongue*, illustrates the desire to develop solidarity with refugees of US neocolonialism. Martínez's most recent novel, *The Block Captain's Daughter* (2012), offers another example of the narrative of new memory, one quite different from *Mother Tongue*.

The Block Captain's Daughter is not a work of science fiction or fantasy, but it is set in the past, present, and future simultaneously. The novel is primarily epistolary and is a literal representation of the process of writing a narrative of new memory. Lupe, an undocumented woman from Mexico, barely survives crossing into the United States. A Christian group rescues her; they are members of what seems to be a second Sanctuary movement. Unlike *Mother Tongue* or recent work about Central American border crossings with more in common with new journalism texts such as Urrea's *Devil's Highway* (2004), Gaspar de Alba's *Desert Blood* (2005), or Nazario's *Enrique's Journey* (2006), *The Block Captain's Daughter* portrays Lupe's border crossing in minimal detail. Within a concise three pages, the narrator illustrates that she lacks a complete memory of her crossing, due to severe dehydration and near organ failure. The novel renders the usefulness of the past ambiguous; we learn very little about her family in Mexico, except that she has made the crossing to find work to support her mother.

The Block Captain's Daughter and *Mother Tongue* share tropes, references, ideologies, and literary techniques. The discourse on Christian faith, human rights, and US neocolonialism expressed in *The Block Captain's Daughter* is less poignant and more didactic than it is in *Mother Tongue*. For example, when explaining her name, Lupe unites the Virgin Mary of the Anglo-Catholic tradition with the Virgen de Guadalupe of Mexican-Catholic tradition: "Five hundred years ago Our Lady of Guadalupe appeared to a Nahuatl-speaking Indian. Two thousand years ago the angel Gabriel appeared to Mary. Visitations, annunciations. You understand such things all too well. Like Juan Diego and Mary, you had no choice but to say yes" (Martínez, *The Block Captain's Daughter* 5). The narrator interrupts these thoughts with conversation and flashbacks to the crossing, noting, "You fell asleep and dreamed of things you'd seen on your journey" (Martínez 5). Lupe describes her awakening to the terrible present for Mexicans who are compelled to attempt the crossing and become undocumented in the United States: "When you woke up the stars shone like coins. They shone like the stars over China where the factory you had worked for relocated, leaving you and hundreds of women with no way to earn a living" (Martínez 5).[1]

The novel announces its purpose: almost full term in her pregnancy, Lupe realizes, "I might forget my own story. So it is that I am writing you this letter, with more to come, *Si Dios quiere*. I have decided to say yes to posterity"

(Martínez 9). Thus, the novel begins and is throughout a narrative of new memory. Lupe has already decided her child's name, Destiny; she addresses letters to her unborn child, each letter telling stories of the time before the child's own birth. Between the letters, first-person narrations of Lupe's friends and the people who will become Destiny's godparents all remember their stories. They narrate how they met and how they have come to belong in their ethnic, sexual, and intellectual communities. These stories, too, offer swift metafictional markers of political and religious history; for example, Flor is writing her dissertation "about the faith-based Sanctuary Movement of the 1980s, when US citizens clandestinely aided refugees who'd fled US-backed dictatorships in Central America" (Martínez 24). Her partner, Maritza, is a journalist; she offers metanarrative about the first Gulf War, in 1991: "I'm doing everything in my power to change the story" (Martínez, *The Block Captain's Daughter* 29). All of the principal characters—Lupe, her husband Marcos, Flora and her lover Maritza, and Cory and her husband Pete—tell their stories in first-person narratives.

The novel closes in both a resonance and reversal of *Mother Tongue*, with a young woman reading a "fat envelope" of letters approximately twenty years later (Martínez 93). The young woman is Destiny, Lupe's daughter, a college student. Unlike the protagonist's son in *Mother Tongue*, José Luis Jr., Destiny is fully drawing on her mother's tongue and political ideology. She writes to her mother, "So here I am in Cambridge, Massachusetts of all places, *tu lengua preciosa, Español, mi pasaporte*: at the Latino Center I am making friends with people from all of the Spanish-speaking world, *palabra por palabra cruzando fronteras*, erecting bridges, bull-dozing walls" (Martínez 93). Destiny's words, "your precious language, Spanish, my passport" and "crossing borders word by word," offer a new memory of Anzaldúa's *New Mestiza*. Destiny will realize Anzaldúa's theorization of the border; she has already crossed ethnonational borders and bridged people separated by ideological walls.

Cambridge, Massachusetts, is the home to several colleges and universities, most notably Harvard University; it is reasonable to assume that Destiny is alluding to attending the Ivy League institution. In 2012, Harvard was the subject of pejorative headlines—the university administration had once again prohibited the development of a Latino center.[2] In 2013, the situation had not changed; at the time of drafting this book in 2014, I could find no evidence that such a center yet existed.[3] If Martínez is indeed referencing Harvard, then her novel serves as a narrative of new memory not because a first-generation Mexican American has entered the prestigious Ivy League school but because a Chicana has used new "tools to dismantle the master's house." In rewriting the school's false narratives of equality, belonging, and empowerment for people from "all of the Spanish-speaking world," Destiny has indeed created a new memory of Chicana empowerment (Martínez 93).

Returning to the novel that inspired this study, *Brand New Memory* (1998), I believe that the 1994 relaxation of travel restrictions to Cuba partially inspired Elías Miguel Muñoz to write it. The text's hope toward this new cultural memory has been somewhat realized. Over the last few years, the increase in the freedoms within Cuba and the freedom of artists and families to visit Cuba has prepared the way for the narrative of new memory. Despite the fact that President Obama has yet to close Guantánamo Bay, the two nations' relations are improving. The freedoms of Cuba's citizens are slowly increasing, and travel restrictions are relaxing so that Americans have the opportunity to see Cuba for themselves. I remain inspired by Muñoz's positive vision in this novel, published in 1998, the one-hundredth anniversary of the Cuban-Spanish-American War and the turn of a new century around the globe. While the number of states legalizing gay marriage in the United States is not likely to have a similar occurrence in Cuba's immediate future, I am inspired by the public discourse on the emerging civil rights of homosexuals and transgendered persons in Cuba.[4] Current shifts in the treatment of gay Cubans suggests that real people, portrayed by fictional characters such as Rosa and Mario, can hope for change. They will be able to end their performances and write their own narratives of new memory.

Notes

Introduction. Neocolonialism's Bounty: From *Arrival* to New Memory

1. This relative ease does not apply to all immigrants, nor does it diminish the severe hardships some immigrants, particularly those from Central America, undergo while traveling on foot, with smugglers, or through harsh terrain.

2. See Levitt, *Transnational Villagers*, for anthropological research on the maintenance of cultural allegiance.

3. A variety of terms have been used to describe people of Hispanic descent. In keeping with critical discussions and the authors' self-identification, I use *Chicana/o* to describe authors of Mexican American heritage with a specific political and literary aesthetic developing since their civil rights movement, *El Movimiento*. I use the term *Latina/o* very broadly, to describe Cubans, Dominicans, and Puerto Ricans living in the United States. The *a/o* represents the gender-inclusive politics that emerged in the postmovement literary and cultural theory. When describing the individual authors or the communities they depict, I use the appropriate specific national term: Cuban, Dominican, Mexican, or Puerto Rican American. The *a/o* ending of *Latina/o* and *Chicana/o* acknowledges the gender-inclusive form of each word, which is generally preferred by scholars. *Anglo* is a prefix and is not used as a gender-specific adjective or noun. See Marta Caminero-Santangelo's introduction to *On Latinidad* for rigorous interrogation of the terms. For a nonliterary reference of the terms, see Allatson, *Key Terms in Latina/o Studies*.

4. I do not to hyphenate *neocolonial* and *neocolonialism* to be consistent with the practices of my colleagues in the fields of postcolonialism, cultural studies, and literary studies.

5. Terms used to describe cultural adaptation of minorities include *integration*, *assimilation*, and *acculturation*. *Integration* connotes a process of the colonizer.

Assimilation and *acculturation* denote processes of the colonized. In the era of political correctness, *acculturation* replaced *assimilation*. From this point on, unless directly quoting, I will use the term *acculturation*.

6. Historians established that within the first decades after the Conquest, the indigenous populations of the Caribbean were decimated, catalyzing the slave trade and the Caribbean's violent entry into modernity through the plantation system.

7. Santería remains a viable cultural practice throughout the Hispanic and French Caribbean, as well as the United States.

8. This list is representative but by no mean exhaustive. By "successful," I mean books that have been commercially and critically visible from the time of their publication to the contemporary era.

9. For the full text of their review, see Delgado and Stefanicic in Burton et al., "Critical Race Theories" (442).

10. McLaren, in Goldberg, *Multiculturalism*.

11. Pérez's words are echoed in the title of a comprehensive, edited collection, *Presumed Incompetent: The Intersections of Race and Class for Women in Academia* (2012).

12. See Pérez, "Opposition and the Education of Chicana/os," and Sánchez, "Ethnicity, Ideology, and Academia" for further discussion of the challenges women of color face while pursuing graduate education within ethnic and cultural studies.

13. There is a current call for papers with the book title "White Washing American Education: The New Culture Wars in Ethnic Studies." See the book's website, http://newculturewarsethnicstudies.wordpress.com.

14. Throughout, I will use *Anglo-American* to be consistent with the terms in ethnic literary studies. This term, though, lacks recognition of the fact that the US mainstream is Euro-American. *Anglo* connotes British and excludes other colonial powers of the time, including the French and the Dutch.

15. Lisa Lowe, Asian American studies scholar, defines *heterogeneity* as "the existence of differences and differential relationships within a bounded category" (*Immigrant Acts* 67).

16. Esmeralda Santiago's second novel, *América's Dream*, and Oscar Hijuelos' most recent novel, *Empress of the Splendid Season*, are examples of this.

17. For a discussion of the detective genre, see Figueredo, "The Stuff Dreams Are Made Of: The Latino Detective Novel."

18. Autoethnography can be understood as an author's writing about his or her community.

19. If movie production is a measure of success, we can measure the impact of authors whose writing has been made into one or more films: Julia Alvarez, Rudolfo Anaya, Tómas Rivera, and Oscar Hijuelos.

20. Other scholars present similar readings of the relationship between ethnic American authors and multiculturalism. McCracken argues, "Interactions between cultural production by minorities and other events in the every day lives of readers,

along with ruptural elements within the texts themselves, work against their smooth absorption into the discourse of multiculturalism and begin to reassert the discourse of social antagonism" (*New Latina Narrative* 14).

21. For a discussions of narrative and its development as an object of study, see Wallace, *Recent Theories of Narrative*, or Rimmon-Kenan, *Narrative Fiction*.

22. *Latinidades* is a term Marta Caminero-Santangelo develops in her study *On Latinidad*.

23. A notable exception to this is Kathryn Hume's comprehensive study, *American Dream American Nightmare: Fiction since 1960* (2000), which gracefully unites nearly one hundred contemporary American novels in a topical study of issues such as transplantation, innocence, spirituality, democracy, and civilization.

24. See the special issue of *The Americas Review*, "Is there a Boom in Latino/a Literature?," for discussion of US Latina/o literature in comparison to the "Latin American Boom," synonymous with the work of Jorge Luis Borges, Julio Cortázar, Gabriel Cabrera Infante, Gabriel García Márquez, and Juan Rulfo, among others.

25. Martin provides a useful review of narratology from the formalists to the post-structuralists. See *Recent Theories of Narrative*, especially chapter 2.

26. For discussions of contemporary narrative theory, see Phelan's *Living to Tell about It* and Alber and Fludernik's edited volume *Postclassical Narratology*.

27. Bell, *The Afro-American Novel and Its Tradition*.

28. Ramón Saldívar suggests the novel is part of what he claims to be "an inauguration of a new stage in the history of the novel by twenty-first-century US ethnic writers" ("Historical Fantasy, Speculative Realism, and Postrace Aesthetics" 574). Saldívar further outlines the characteristics of post-race aesthetics in "The Second Elevation of the Novel" (4–6).

29. See Elias' preface for additional examples of texts she characterizes as metahistorical romance, including Morrison's *Beloved*, Reed's *Flight to Canada,* and Momaday's *House Made of Dawn*.

30. See David Vázquez, *Triangulations*, for a discussion of Chicana/o and Latina/o life-writing.

31. See the National Council on State Legislatures for detailed information about Arizona Proposition 300 and other proposals related to the DREAM Act (http://www.ncsl.org/).

32. The term *Gang of Eight* originally referred to a 2008 group of members of Congress with whom then-president George W. Bush conducted unconstitutional domestic espionage during the War on Terror.

33. For a review of the three-generation model of assimilation, see Werner Sollors, *Beyond Ethnicity*. Sollors traces the three-generation model from Puritan authors to early twentieth-century Jewish immigrant biographies and contemporary African American poetry and fiction.

34. One need only think of important nineteenth-century texts such as Howell's *The Rise of Silas Lapham*, Dreiser's *Sister Carrie*, or Wharton's *The House of Mirth*;

each of these depicts ethnic or lower-class men who are "self-made" and able to climb up the American social ladder.

35. St. Jean de Crèvecoeur, in his 1782 essay "What Is an American," writes: "Here individuals of all nations are melted into a new race of men whose labors and posterity will one day cause great changes in the world" (67).

36. On July 18, 2013, one of the lead stories about social media was the report that over twenty individuals tweeted racist comments when Marc Anthony sang the national anthem at the 2013 MLB All Star Game in New York City's Citi Field. The tweets voiced ignorant and ultimately incorrect assumptions about his ethnicity (he is Puerto Rican), his national citizenship (he is American because he was born in the United States and because he is Puerto Rican), and his linguistic ability (he is fully bilingual and sung the anthem in English). A similar incident occurred a month prior in June 2013, when a young Mexican American, Sebastien de la Cruz, sang the anthem (in English) wearing a traditional mariachi costume.

37. Because I am citing quotations from the English section of the 1987 bilingual edition of. . . And the Earth Did Not Devour Him, from this point on, I will use only the English title to refer to the text.

38. The ellipses in this text, which also appear in the title of the book, do not represent missing text.

39. Flores explains his terminology in the book's introduction: "I hope to expand upon the term 'social remittances' as developed by Peggy Levitt in her book *The Transnational Villagers* (2001). Scholars have long been saying that it not just money and financial capital that are transferred in the multiple cross-border transactions of today's society, but also values, beliefs, and a host of other features of social life. Levitt did the welcome service of injecting this insight into the used and abused concept of remittance and thereby provided a handy term for a range of transnational studies. However, I contend that her theoretical innovation fails to live up to its potential because of the methodological and philosophical limitations of her notion of the cultural" (*The Diaspora Strikes Back* 9).

40. See Suzanne Oboler's collection *Latinos and Citizenship*.

41. Puerto Ricans living on the island can vote in presidential primaries but not presidential elections, and their Congressional representatives do not have voting power on issues of Puerto Rican governance, including amending their own constitution.

42. Anzaldúa's *Borderlands/La Frontera* and Pérez Firmat's *Life on the Hyphen* are key theoretical texts of the period.

43. Muñoz is a prolific bilingual writer. His English-language novels include *Crazy Love, The Greatest Performance*, and *Brand New Memory*. His Spanish-language books include *Los Viajes de Orlando Cachumbambe* (Colección Caniqui); *Desde esta orilla: poesía cubana del exilio* (Colección Ensayo), and *En Estas Tierras*.

44. Sollors notes this: "Double consciousness characters may be attracted to mirrors, reflecting windows, or smooth surfaced ponds" ("Ethnicity and Literary Form" 249).

45. Elías Miguel Muñoz entered the United States in 1969, which locates him within the 1.5 generation. Later than the 1959 exiles but earlier than the 1980 Mariel refugees, Muñoz's immigration and relocation to California distinguishes his perspective from that of his contemporaries.

46. The novel shares the re-memory of Toni Morrison's *Beloved*. Cuba is created through a combination of recollection and revision.

47. In 1995, an excerpt of the novel appeared in *Bridges to Cuba*; the title was "The Moviemaker."

48. A physical return to Cuba is a common trope in Cuban American fiction, including *Our House in the Old World* by Oscar Hijuelos, *Singing to Cuba* by Margarita Engle, *Dreaming in Cuban* by Cristina García, and *Going Under* by Virgil Suárez.

49. Literally, "Cuba of yesterday." This expression is used to describe a nostalgic version of pre-Castro Cuba both by exiles and nonexiles mocking exiles' nostalgia.

50. *El Movimiento* was the civil rights movement associated with Mexican Americans, especially the Brown Berets; the Young Lords were a Puerto Rican activist group who modeled themselves on the Black Panthers, a group associated with the Black Power movement; MECHA or MEChA is the Movimiento Estudiantil Chicano de Aztlán.

51. Pérez Firmat's important monograph *Life on the Hyphen: The Cuban American Way* draws on sociologist Rubén Rumbaut's term, the "1.5" generation, in order to distinguish the experiences of Cuban Americans from their parents, the Cuban exiles of the early 1960s.

52. For recent discussion on *La Carreta Made a U-Turn*, see Villa, "Urban Spaces," or the expansive volume *The AmeRícan Poet: Essays on the Work of Tato Laviera*.

53. For work from this period, see Esteves' *Bluestown Mockingbird Mambo* and *Heartsongs: The Collected Poems of Nina Serrano* (1969–1979).

54. *Beautiful Señoritas* was first staged in 1979; it was published by Arte Público in 1991 with the other plays *Coser y Cantar, Pantallas*, and *Botánica*.

55. For a discussion of US neocolonialism from a historical perspective that considers various groups of Latinos separately, see Gonzalez, *Harvest of Empire*.

56. Chapter 1 discusses these terms in greater detail. See also Muñoz's discussion of the debates about internal colonialism and postcolonialism (*Youth, Identity, Power* 146–49; 153–54).

57. The *Oxford English Dictionary* cites the first appearance of this term in reference to the United States' relationship with the Hispanic Caribbean. See Johnson, "The Crisis in Central America."

58. The Clinton Administration declassified records illustrating the United States' financial role in several Central American civil wars, including those in El Salvador, Guatemala, and Nicaragua.

59. For a germinal text on US neocolonialism from a Latin American perspective, see Galeano, *The Open Veins of Latin America*.

60. Some consider the United States' actions in the Middle East a form of neocolonialism. See, for example, Little's *American Orientalism*.

61. Even if one wanted to apply the model of internal colonialism to Native Americans living within US territories, technically, reservations are sovereign nations with tribal governing structures, law enforcement, and educational systems. This sovereignty has been a consistent challenge to the Federal government's attempts to recuperate taxes from Native American tobacco sales and casino revenue.

62. For further discussion of postcolonialism, internal colonialism, and neocolonialism, see Lora Romero, "Nationalism and Internationalism"; see also Santiago Colás' "Of Creole Symptoms, Cuban Fantasies, and Other Latin American Postcolonial Ideologies" and E. San Juan Jr.'s "The Poverty of Postcolonialism." See Moreiras and Embry's special issue of *Dispositio/n*, "The Cultural Practice of Latin Americanism," for a discussion of postcolonialism and Latin American studies.

63. For detailed information on the United States' sterilization program in Puerto Rico, known as "La Operación," see Harriet B. Presser, *Sterilization and Fertility Decline in Puerto Rico* (1976), or view "La Operación," Dir. Ana María García (1982). See also Philip R. Reilly, "The Surgical Solution" (1991), and Laura Briggs, *Reproducing Empire* (2002).

64. For more information, see Driscoll, *The Tracks North*.

65. See Whalen, *The Puerto Rican Diaspora*, for an extended discussion of Puerto Rican migration before and after 1898.

66. Reading the literatures separately elides the significant convergences in the literatures' exploration of coalition and conflict among the groups: "In fact, it is certainly possible to make the case that, until very recently, what is called 'the US Latino literary canon' did very little to construct or reaffirm a notion of collective latinidad—other than by appearing in multiple anthologies with the word 'Latino' or 'Hispanic' in the title" (Caminero-Santangelo, *On Latinidad* 21).

67. For a discussion of critical trends at the start of the "ethnic boom," see Sollors, *The Invention of Ethnicity*.

68. I am thinking of Sandra Cisneros and Junot Díaz, who attended the Iowa Writers' Workshop; Ana Castillo, Rolando Hinojosa-Smith, and Elías Miguel Muñoz, who hold PhDs; and Judith Ortiz Cofer, Denise Chávez, Ernesto Quiñonez, and Daniel José Older, who hold MAs or MFAs in creative writing.

69. The concept of "internal colonialism" is distinct from my concept of neocolonialism. In Barrera's model of internal colonialism, "the dominant and subordinate populations are intermingled, so there is not geographically distinct metropolis separate from the colony" (Barrera, qtd. in *Youth, Identity, Power* 153). See also Muñoz's discussion of the debates about "internal colonialism" and "postcolonialism" (*Youth, Identity, Power* 146–49; 153–54).

70. This is true of other contemporary immigrant literatures, such as Asian American literatures.

71. See José David Saldívar, *Border Matters*.

72. See also Soccorro Tabuenca Córdoba "Viewing the Border: Perspectives from 'the Open Wound'" for a review of problematic deployments of border theory.

73. This study is significantly different from other theorizations of community membership, such as Suzanne Oboler's *Ethnic Labels, Latino Lives* and Renato Rosaldo's "cultural citizenship" in *Latina/o Cultural Citizenship*. Both monographs are emblematic of sociological analyses focusing on ethnic acculturation and community empowerment in relation to "the dominant national community," Anglo-Americans (Rosaldo and Flores 57).

74. Caminero-Santangelo describes Latin American migration similarly: "it is the history of US intervention in the various Latin American nations, as well as its current position within a global economy that (for example) exploits cheap labor abroad, which provides the 'weave' of common experience (although within the weave differences inevitably emerge, such as the degree of direct intervention or of economic dependency" (*On Latinidad* 19).

75. I am using the term ethnonationalism as discussed extensively by political scientist Walker Connor. See Connor, *Ethnonationalism: The Quest for Understanding*.

Chapter 1. Narratives of Loss: Tracing Migrations

1. "Sleep" is a recurring metaphor in two other novels in this study: in *Soledad*, one character's catatonia is described as sleep. In *Mother Tongue*, the narrator describes her depression as a sleep where she lacked "a plotline."

2. For additional discussion of the relationship between *Pocho* and . . . *And the Earth Did Not Devour Him*, see Lima, *The Latino Body*.

3. For the full text of the Monroe Doctrine, see Yale Law School's Avalon Project. The sentences preceding the one I have excerpted illustrate the doctrine's distinction of the United States from European powers based on geopolitical difference: "In the war between those new Governments and Spain we declared our neutrality at the time of their recognition, and to this we have adhered, and shall continue to adhere, provided no change shall occur which, in the judgment of the competent authorities of this Government, shall make a corresponding change on the part of the United States indispensable to their security" (http://avalon.law.yale.edu/19th_century/monroe.asp).

4. In 1854, the Gadsden Purchase extended the territorial boundaries of the United States, adding land to what is present-day southern New Mexico and Arizona. For the full text of the Gadsden Purchase, see Yale Law School's Avalon Project (http://avalon.law.yale.edu/19th_century/mx1853.asp).

5. Beginning in the nineteenth century, some Mexican American authors self-identified with a region, calling themselves Tejanos or Nuevo Mexicanos if they were from Texas or New Mexico, respectively. Contemporary authors such as Denise Chávez and Rolando Hinojosa-Smith retain such designations: Hinojosa-Smith describes himself as Tejano and Chávez describes herself as Nuevo Mexicana.

6. Saldívar uses the term "Spanish-American-Cuban-Philippine War of 1898" ("Looking Awry at 1898" 388), but I retain Cuban-Spanish-American War for concision.

7. The United States did not officially declare war on Spain until April 25, 1898, after the US Congress voted to do so. This followed years of political tension between the two nations and Spain's refusal to acquiesce to the United States' demand for Cuban independence (April 20, 1898). An early and important work of scholarship tracing the evolution of Chicano self-perception is Chávez's *The Lost Land*, which connects the loss of land after the Mexican-American War to the development of Chicano identity during El Movimiento.

8. See Paredes, "Early Mexican-American Literature," for a discussion of colonial Mexican folklore, drama, and other narrative forms.

9. This is a point Arteaga makes as well: "The Chicano derives being not only from the Spanish colonial intervention but also from Anglo-American colonialism" (*Chicano Poetics* 27).

10. For readings on additional nineteenth-century texts, see Lima, *The Latino Body*.

11. For a recent, comprehensive review of Chicana/o and Latina/o literary traditions, see *The Routledge Companion to Latino/a Literature*.

12. For a detailed discussion of Valdez's role within the Chicano movement, see Xavier, "Politics and Chicano Culture: Luis Valdez and 'El Teatro Campesino.'"

13. Rivera's text was made into a movie in 1995 (Dir. Severo Pérez; American Playhouse); in 2012, the film production of Anaya's text *Bless Me, Ultima* was released (Dir. Carl Franklin; Gran Via Productions).

14. Ilan Stavans began the project in 1997; Norton anticipated publishing the volume in 2002; the anthology was not published until 2011.

15. See Suárez, "Is There a Boom in Latina/o Literature?"

16. See Sollors, "Ethnicity and Literary Form," for a critique of this approach.

17. Human rights advocates have consistently challenged the poor investigation of the assaults. For an extensive study of the crimes, see Monárrez Fragoso and Socorro Tabuenca Córdoba: *Bordeando la Violencia Contra las Mujeres en la Frontera Norte de México*. For a discussion of cultural production about the crimes, see Volk and Schlotterbeck, who argue, "Because the state has failed so abjectly in stopping these murders . . . 'fictional' narratives have become both the site where victims are mourned and the means by which justice can be restored," in "Gender, Order, and Femicide." Alicia Gaspar de Alba's novel *Desert Blood: The Juárez Murders* was published in 2005. At least one movie, *Border Town*, portrays the murders.

18. Luis Alberto Urrea's work of narrative journalism, *The Devil's Highway* (2004), is an account based on the true story of twenty-six male migrants who attempted to make the border crossing. The work provides explicit and sometimes excruciating detail about the effects of dehydration, heat stroke, and deaths of fourteen of the men.

19. See Amy J. Elias, *Sublime Desire*, for a useful distinction of modes of postmodernity: epistemological, sociocultural, and aesthetic. While Elias includes some notable writers of color as examples of the aesthetic postmodern, including Ishmael Reed, Maxine Hong Kingston, and Gerald Vizenor, the absence of Chicano authors is notable and consistent with my reading of Rivera, in particular, as drawing on Mexican and Iberian cultural forms, not postmodern literary aesthetics.

20. For a thorough discussion of genres from oral epics to the present, see Martin, *Recent Theories of Narrative*.

21. For more detail on *actos*, see Paredes, "Early Mexican-American Literature."

22. The science fiction novel *Lunar Braceros 2125–2148* illustrates this pattern continuing into the future, despite technological advances. Mexican Americans, indigenous people, domestic minorities, and poor white populations are restricted to reservations if they cannot obtain a job. Those who are employed often work as contract labor on the moon. Hierarchy exists there as well; lesser-skilled workers are literally expendable and are killed after their contract period is completed.

23. In the contents, of the twenty-seven chapters or vignettes, thirteen are not titled. The untitled sections are set apart from the titled ones by using the first line of the story as the title.

24. It is also possible that the narrator's translation of Rivera's term *mojadito* to "wetback" is based on the literal meaning of the adjective *mojado*, which means "wet" or "soaked." In the contemporary period, some Anglo-Americans and Mexican Americans refer to the undocumented as *mojado*, regardless of when, how, or where the person entered the country.

25. The meaning of the term *mojados* is complicated through its transcultural history. For further discussion, see Marta E. Sanchéz, "'I May Say Wetback but I Really Mean Mojado': Migration and Translation in Ramón 'Tianguis' Pérez's *Diary of an Undocumented Immigrant*." Sanchez asserts, "It can also be used by the migrants themselves with tinges of self-affirmation ('Me vine de mojado'/'I crossed as a mojado'; 'Soy un mojado'/'I am a mojado'). This redefinition of the term resembles the historical linguistic process in which words formerly derogatory (like 'queer', 'pocho', or 'Chicano') are revalued, their illocutionary effects semantically ameliorated" (8). This connotation is especially fitting for the narrator's changed sense of self in relation to the "wetback."

26. Avalos cites Ecclesiastes 2:18–21 to illustrate the parallels between the texts. The echo of Ecclesiastes 2:18 in Rivera's text is especially compelling: "I hated all my toil in which I had tolled under the sun, seeing that I must leave it to those who come after me—and who knows whether they will be wise or foolish?"

27. Avalos makes an interesting observation: "The earth swallowing people up may ultimately derive from Mesoamerican ideas about the earth as a cosmic jaw though the motif occurs in the *Bible* as well (Num.16:32)" (163).

28. For a discussion of how the relationship between Martí's work and Chicana/o and Latina/o Studies has been reassessed, see Belnap and Fernández, *José Martí's Our America*.

29. See Belnap and Fernández, *José Martí's Our America*.

30. For a detailed discussion of American plantation colonies in Cuba after the war, see Deere, "Here Come the Yankees."

31. This is excerpted from Vest's December 12, 1898, speech in the US Senate. For the full text of this and other speeches, see Fallows, Huntington, and Reed, *Splendid Deeds of American Heroes on Sea and Land*. For an analysis of the anti-imperial

movement, see Beisner, *Twelve against Empire*. For a discussion of the debate about taking the Philippines, see Bradford, *Crucible of Empire*.

32. Subsequent to the war, the United States annexed Guam and Hawaii.

33. See Archibold, "Cuban Leader Proposes Reforms as Sign of New Era," for a detailed discussion of the reforms Raúl Castro announced in 2011.

34. For an early discussion of the relationship between the rates of sterilization of Puerto Rican women and rates of unemployment in Puerto Rico, see Angela Davis, *Women, Race, and Class* (219–21). For a more recent discussion, see Briggs, *Reproducing Empire*.

35. In 2015, the bond debt of Puerto Rico reached a staggering $72 billion dollars. For information on the restructuring of the debt, see Brown, "Key Puerto Rican debt holders circle wagons as restructuring talks take shape."

36. A third significant migration, known as the Freedom Flotilla, carried over 35,000 Cubans to US shores in 1994. Since President Obama's normalization of relations with Cuba, refugee arrivals have surged almost 15 percent in 2015. See Piven, "Cuban Migration to US Rises amid Historic Thaw in Relations."

37. Cyrus Veeser's book, *A World Safe for Capitalism*, outlines US financial intervention in the Dominican Republic, which crippled this nation's economy and led to its financial dependence on the United States.

38. For a useful discussion of the problems inherent in studying Chicana/o and Latina/o cultural production separately, see Angie Chambram-Dernersesian, "Chicana! Rican? No, Chicana Riqueña!"

39. First used by Alice Walker in the essay "If the Present Looks Like the Past, What Does the Future Look Like?" in her book *In Search of Our Mother's Gardens*. Walker defined *colorism* as "prejudicial or preferential treatment of same-race people based solely on their color" (290).

40. See Rebolledo, "The Politics of Poetics," for a discussion of Western European theory within Chicana literature.

41. See Bruce-Novoa, "Dialogical Strategies, Monological Goals," for discussion of mestizaje.

42. Burton, Bonilla-Silva, et al., note, "Researchers in the area of Whiteness studies demonstrated that Whiteness, like any other 'race,' is a historically constructed social category characterized by substantial power and privilege for some Whites, but not for all" ("Critical Race Theories" 446).

43. Pérez-Torres originates this discussion in the 1999 essay "Whither Aztlán?"

44. On November 7, 2002, at a special news conference following the Republican sweep of Congress and the House of Representatives, President George W. Bush affirmed the political asylum granted to Cubans. He also indicated that Haitians would be afforded the same immigration opportunities as other immigrants, despite the fact that just days before the conference, the US Coast Guard had interdicted a group of Haitians, causing some to drown and others to return to Haiti.

45. Please refer to the introduction for a review of the term *Latina/o*.

46. Following Julia Alvarez's novel *In the Time of the Butterflies*, the government began a series of revisions of public memorials about the era. These included the repainting of Trujillo's Obelisk, issuing currency with the Mirabal Sisters' image, and the rededication of the Mirabal Sisters' Museum. For a discussion of the impact of *In the Time of the Butterflies*, see Ylce Irizarry, "When Art Remembers."

47. *Dominicanidad* refers to one's Dominican-ness or Dominican identity.

48. See reviews such as Ochwat's: "The collection serves up more of Díaz's energetic, hip-hop style—primarily revolving around one character, a stubborn, sci-fi loving, New Jersey Dominican named Yunior" (*Chicago Sun Times*). See also Tobar, who argues, "The Pulitzer winner's new collection once more showcases his talent in generating great heat and great literature" (*Los Angeles Times*).

49. While Dominicans, particularly women, have begun to migrate to Spain and Puerto Rico in larger numbers, these migrations also serve as a stepping-stone to the United States, with the final desired migration being the return to the Dominican Republic. See Duany, "Transnational Migration from the Dominican Republic," for demographic information and cultural analysis of these immigration patterns.

50. For a comprehensive study of Spanish Caribbean immigration and community establishment, see Daniel D. Arreola, *Hispanic Spaces, Latino Places*.

51. This chapter includes a revised version of the article "Making It Home: The Ethics of Dominican Migration" in *Hispanic Caribbean Literatures of Migration*.

52. See Bhabha, *The Location of Culture*.

53. This is a principal theme in Santiago's memoir, *When I Was Puerto Rican*. Díaz discusses this in interviews. For Díaz's comments, see Céspedes and Torres-Saillant. Also, this is Oscar Wao's principle trauma—the loss of his dominicanidad, which is recuperated only with a physical return to the island.

54. I find this to be true of other writers, including Puerto Rican authors Judith Ortiz Cofer and Ernesto Quiñonez and Cuban authors Elías Miguel Muñoz and Dolores Prida, among others.

55. Drawing on Margot Canaday's monograph, *The Straight State*, Stringer applies Canaday's larger conclusion to *Drown*: "Díaz's work suggests that, although the invitation to pass for straight is ostensibly race-neutral, it actually reinforces spatial and psychological limits on his Dominican characters' citizenship" (Stringer 113).

56. Méndez reads Díaz similarly in that we both view him as rejecting the modernist modes of narrative privileging acculturation (*Narratives of Migration and Displacement*).

57. Méndez considers the generation of Díaz's characters to be second, not 1.5: "the usual second-generation nostalgia for a premigration idyll has been jettisoned" (*Narratives of Migration and Displacement* 121).

58. See Bridget A. Kevane, *Latino Literature in America*, for a discussion of the stories' relationships to one another in the collection *Drown*.

59. A similar narrative pattern develops in Ortiz Cofer's novel *The Line of the Sun* and Santiago's novel *When I Was Puerto Rican*, both of which depict one family's cyclical movement between the city and the country. The former novel ends in the United States, where another cycle of migrations begins.

60. For analysis of Dominican/Haitian relations, see Wucker, *Why the Cocks Fight*, or Howard, *Development, Racism, and Discrimination*. In fiction, see Danticat, *The Farming of Bones*, or Vargas Llosa, *Fiesta del Chivo*, or Rosario, *Song of the Water Saints*.

61. See Planas, "Junot Díaz Speaks Out after Insults to His Dominican-ness." José Santana, Executive Director for the Dominican Presidency's International Commission on Science and Technology, called Díaz a "fake and overrated pseudo-intellectual" who "should learn better to speak Spanish before coming to this country to talk nonsense."

62. Significant differences in the immigration patterns and degrees of acculturation exist among Puerto Ricans, Cubans, and Dominicans. These differences are attributable to Puerto Rico's status as a "free associated state" (1952) and the immediate political asylum afforded to Cubans since the Cuban Adjustment Act (1966–2017). Dominicans, unlike both groups, have no special entrance to the United States; their visa process is long and complicated by their civil laws, making it very difficult to emigrate.

63. The voices of those lost at sea is a relatively unrepresented group. Mayra Santos Febres explores those voices in *Boat People*, a collection of poetry.

64. See Duany on Dominican migration to Puerto Rico, "Caribbean Migration to Puerto Rico." See also Angie Cruz's second novel, *Let It Rain Coffee*, whose female protagonist illustrates this stepping-stone migration.

65. Ramon's surname, de Las Casas, roughly translates to "of the houses"; it may be a play on the father's movement between the two families.

66. Méndez notes, "The uncanniness of return comes, in part, from the disparity between the image of return, which is mythically that of the moment of healing and wholeness, of 'reconciliation,' and the actuality, which is a simulacrum of repression" (*Narratives of Migration and Displacement* 121).

67. *Pato* is a derogatory term for a homosexual; *pinga* is a word for penis.

68. David William Foster presents a similar Material Queer reading of nerddom in his analysis of John Leguizamo's *Freak!* He notes, "Being a nerd, then, becomes also a queer form of gender identity because it too detracts form the proper construction of a full masculinity as defined by the macho" ("Performing the Freak" 175).

69. See Haggerty, *The Dominican Republic*, for statistical information on the religious practices of Dominicans.

70. For a discussion of male homosexuality specific to Latin American culture, see Almagüer, "Chicano Men." See also Manrique, "Resemantizing Maricón," for a discussion of the semantic variations of terms used to denote the performance of homosexual acts, especially the incongruity between the performance of those acts and the personas associated with gay men.

71. Stringer argues, "The word pato, an ordinary obscenity that ironically names Beto's most important betrayal. The friends are estranged because Beto performed sexual acts on the narrator" ("Passing and the State" 120).

72. Stringer applies the arguments of Parikh's monograph *An Ethics of Betrayal* to *Drown*. This is especially problematic because while Parikh claims to "read betrayals as performances of social difference in the context of Asian American and Latina/o racial formation and literary and cultural production," the study offers readings of two Chicano authors and the case of Cuban exile Elián González (1). The text does not include Dominican or Puerto Rican literatures in the study; the term *Dominican* does not appear in the index, and no works by Junot Díaz or any other Dominican authors appear in the bibliography or index.

73. The trope of leaving the community as a form of betrayal is common in US ethnic literatures dating to nineteenth-century African American passing narratives.

74. This trope is particularly recurrent in contemporary Puerto Rican and Cuban American fiction.

75. Alvarez's novel *In the Time of the Butterflies* does an excellent job of representing how Trujillo encouraged this political and spiritual nexus based on Catholicism's patriarchy and his dictatorship.

76. It was not until the publication of Julia Alvarez's novel *In the Time of the Butterflies* that the government began sponsoring public memorials about the era. In May 2012, on the fiftieth anniversary of Trujillo's assassination, the first museum dedicated to the resistance to the dictator's regime, *El Museo de la Resistencia*, opened in Santo Domingo's Zona Colonial. This marks the first effort of the Dominican government to address the legacy of Trujillo's brutal dictatorship.

77. For an extensive cultural studies discussion of racial identity in the Dominican Republic, see Candelario, *Black behind the Ears*.

78. Racial categories were developed in response to the expulsion of the Moors and Jews in fifteenth-century Spain. See Gutiérrez, *When Jesus Came*, for a description of colonial record keeping and racial identification.

79. Torres-Saillant makes a similar conclusion about the reality of racism on the island: "No matter how much ingenuity Afro-Dominicans may exhibit in negotiating inimical intellectual legacies, the fact remains that negrophobia has endured in the country and can still manifest itself in ways that interfere with the well-being of dark-skinned people" ("The Tribulations of Blackness" 140).

80. See Céspedes and Torres-Saillant, "Fiction Is the Poor Man's Cinema," for Díaz's comments that he remains outside of the Dominican elite due to his class origins.

81. For additional discussion of photographs and haunting in immigrant literature, see Maya Socolovsky, "The Homelessness of Immigrant American Ghosts."

82. "White Spanish" is the denigrating way a character in another novel, *Bodega Dreams*, describes his friend's acculturated wife.

Chapter 2 . Narratives of Reclamation: Embodying Ritual and Allegory

1. The present time of Cruz's novel *Soledad* is not explicitly stated; given the ages of the characters and some of the cultural references, it could be the late 1980s or early 1990s.

2. Despite the February 2014 capture of El Chapo, head of the Sinaloa Drug Cartel, many think the problems of the Mexican drug cartels will remain the same.

3. See the section "Native Hispanic Literature" in Kanellos' "Overview of Hispanic Literatures of the United States" for additional discussion of the distinction between native and immigrant literatures.

4. For an extended discussion of the development of the concept of La Raza Cósmica and the Aztlánists, see Staten, "Ethnic Authenticity, Class, and Autobiography."

5. These groups included the United Farm Workers, the Brown Berets, Movimiento Estudiantil Chicano de Aztlán (MECHA), the Chicano Youth Liberation Conference, the League of United Latin American Citizens (LULAC), and others.

6. For a discussion of Luis Valdez's *Teatro Campesino* and criticism of his later "apolitical" writing, see Xavier, "Politics and Chicano Culture."

7. See Gutiérrez, who in "Community, Patriarchy, and Individualism" argues, "The themes of marginality, or fractured identities, of suspension betwixt worlds, were themes [Rechy] first articulated, but which would not emerge again until 1987" (62).

8. In 1994, Bruce-Novoa asserted, "The intra-ethnic tension existed from the start of contemporary Chicano literature criticism, although both Chicanos and others preferred—and still prefer—not to focus on it" ("Dialogical Strategies, Monological Goals" 241).

9. For a historical and thematic overview of Chicana writing, see Rebolledo and Rivero, *Infinite Divisions*.

10. For an excellent review of the literary and political texts critiquing the sexism in the Chicano movement, see Gutiérrez, "Community, Patriarchy and Individualism."

11. For examples of critique related to mestizo consciousness, class, and linguistics, see Rivera, "Richard Rodriguez's *Hunger of Memory* as Humanistic Antithesis," and Alarcón, "Tropology of Hunger." For a close reading of *Hunger of Memory* and the main strains of criticism on the text, see Staten. He asserts, "Rodríguez describes his family as working class . . . but his parents never identified with the laboring underclass of Mexico" (Staten, "Ethnic Authenticity, Class, and Autobiography" 113).

12. See Lora Romero, "When Something Goes Queer," for a discussion of ethnic intellectuals and community isolation specific to Cherríe Moraga and Richard Rodriguez.

13. For a discussion of regional perspectives, see Kanellos, "Overview," 13–15.

14. For a discussion of the detective novel in Chicana/o literature, see Ralph E. Rodriguez, *Brown Gumshoes*.

15. See Rebolledo, *Women Singing in the Snow*, for a discussion of hybrid texts written by nineteenth-century Mexican American women. See also Rebolledo and Rivero's introduction to *Infinite Divisions*.

16. See Smith, "Racism and Women's Studies."

17. See Moraga's essay "A Long Line of Vendidas," for example, which discusses her gendered, bicultural experience. Moraga explains, "My sex was white. My brother's, brown" (*Loving in the War Years* 90).

18. See Rebolledo and Rivero, *Infinite Divisions*, for a discussion of Chicana writing and generic experimentation.

19. See Yarbro-Bejarano, "Chicana Literature from a Chicana Feminist Perspective"; Ortega and Saporta Sternbach, "At the Threshold of the Unnamed"; Chabram-Dernersesian, "And, Yes . . . The Earth Did Part."

20. Yarbro-Bejarano's "Gloria Anzaldúa's *Borderlands/La Frontera*" offers an excellent refutation of the "generalizing moves that deracinate" the text (8); the critiques "of the representation of the indigenous in the text that has evoked the most critical response from Chicana/o and non-Chicana/o readers alike" (12); and other lines of argument that challenge Anzaldúa's appropriation of "privileged sites for the construction of border consciousness" (14).

21. See works cited for several publications by Keating, including collaborative works with Anzaldúa.

22. Aranda mentions several texts that use some form of the word *border* in their titles (*When We Arrive*, "Introduction").

23. I am thinking particularly of Castillo's epistolary novel, *The Mixquiahuala Letters*, and *Sapogonia: An Anti-Romance in 3/8 Meter*.

24. For a discussion of mimicry and allegory in US Latina/o literature, see Di Iorio Sandín, *Killing Spanish*.

25. This novel, like many Chicana and Latina texts, has been described as magical realism. The debate about magical realism in literature is extensive so I will not review it here. My own reading of the novel situates Castillo with Alejo Carpentier, whose work tries to reconcile the unbelievable political realities of Latin America. Castillo, similarly, combines myth, the fantastic, and other elements one might consider magical for the purpose of highlighting the disparity between the promises of those in power with the realities of those oppressed.

26. Caminero-Santangelo offers a comprehensive engagement of the criticism locating *So Far from God* within a magical realist tradition; see also Manriquez, "Ana Castillo's *So Far from God*"; Faris, "Scheherezade's Children"; and Heide, "The Postmodern We."

27. According to Avalos' interpretation of Greek etymology, Sofi represents wisdom (73) and her daughters' names are "Cardinal Virtues" within the Catholic faith (78).

28. See Alistair Fowler, *Kinds of Genres*, for a discussion of novel kinds, subgenres, and modes in literature. Though Fowler uses British literature as his primary context for this study, the model fits Castillo's use of genres considered Western.

29. *Telenovelas* are Latin American soap operas. They differ from North American or European soap operas in that they have a finite length, usually several weeks. They are überdramatic, to the point of self-parody.

30. As Sonia Saldívar-Hull argues, Chicana feminism "exists in a borderland not limited to geographic space, a feminism that resides in a space not acknowledged by hegemonic culture" ("Feminism on the Border" 19).

31. For a discussion of Castillo's novel and others in the context of the "boom" of Latina/o literature, see Christian, "Performing Magical Realism."

32. Code-switching is a practice where writers change language to reflect a political or cultural nuance not conveyable in the primary language of the text.

33. See Rebolledo, "The Politics of Poetics," and Moraga, "Art in América con Acento," for discussions of intellectual and social responsibility.

34. For a discussion of education as trope in Chicana writing, see Heide's "The Postmodern 'We.'"

35. See sections especially that deal with Esperanza (Castillo, *So Far from God* 29–42; 239–41).

36. See the section about Caridad's attack and Esperanza's choice to leave Tome and cover the Gulf War (Castillo, *So Far from God* 29–42).

37. This discussion focuses on the themes given the most textual time. The narrative of Caridad's lesbianism suggests that questions of sexuality are less important to Castillo than the issues of environmentalism, educational equity, and cultural losses, as stated above.

38. For focused discussion on the use of religion as a response to the hegemonic influence of the Catholic Church, see Caminero-Santangelo, "'The Pleas of the Desperate.'"

39. Caminero-Santangelo makes this point through an examination of the lives of Caridad and La Loca. See especially pages 85–89 of "'The Pleas of the Desperate.'"

40. See the corresponding chapters of *Revelation* for these themes: Revelation 2, 6, 8, and 16.

41. Theresa Delgadillo notes the significance of the number four revealed in the four daughters and La Loca's "four part journey": "The number four is particularly important in many Native American cosmologies because it represents the earth's directions and air currents. It is symbolic of a balance of elements, including both the material and spiritual, as well as the links between them" (892–93).

42. In Christian ideology, the number three is particularly important. The Holy Trinity includes the Father, Son, and Holy Spirit. There are many places in the *New Testament* where three is invoked; the assertion that Peter denied Christ three times is being invoked, as well as the description of Jesus falling three times while carrying the cross.

43. Theresa Delgadillo asserts this point about the procession: "Its hybridity expresses this life experience—not the genetic makeup—of subordinated groups, and in so doing it challenges the corruption, exploitation, and environmental destruction of the strictly rational center from its previously silenced margins" ("Forms of Chicana Feminist Resistance" (890–91).

44. Caminero-Santangelo reads the procession differently than does Delgadillo, suggesting that it is another proof for rejection of the novel as a magical realist text: "the connections of the Holy Friday procession to Fe are much more striking since many of the scene's concerns directly echo the causes of Fe's 'realist' death' ("The Pleas of the Desperate'" 89).

45. For a discussion of the theorization of homosexuality in Chicana/o studies, see Yarbro-Bejarano, "Sexuality and Chicana/o Studies."

46. See especially chapter 9 of *Massacre of the Dreamers* (Castillo 130–49).

47. See Avalos for a discussion of the legend of the ninth-century "Pope" Joan, a woman stoned to death after an examination of her sex organs revealed that she was in fact, a woman, and therefore, ineligible to be Pope.

48. Established by Dedéa Mirabal in 1965, the museum is the home the sisters lived in within Ojo de Agua. In 2000, on the fortieth anniversary of their murder, the museum was expanded and rededicated, and the remains of the sisters and of Minerva's husband, Manolo Justo Tavarez, were moved to the site. In 1997, the obelisk Trujillo commissioned in his own honor in 1936 was repainted with images of the sisters. In 1999, the day the sisters were murdered, November 25, was named "International Day for the Elimination of Violence against Women" by the United Nations.

49. In 2001, actress Salma Hayek produced and starred in *In the Time of the Butterflies*. In 2010, actress Michelle Rodriguez produced *Trópico de Sangre*, a movie focusing on Minerva Mirabal. In 2007, a new denomination of Dominican currency was printed: the 200 pesos with the image of the Mirabal sisters.

50. For a discussion of the Trujillato in Dominican American literature, see Hickman, "The *Trujillato* as Desideratum in Dominican-American Fiction."

51. For a detailed analysis of the Dominican sex tourism industry, see Francis, "Novel Insights."

52. This is nearly the same percentage as Cubans, but is significantly higher than Mexicans (41 percent) and staggeringly higher than Puerto Ricans (0.8 percent). See the 2004 report "We the People: Hispanics in the United States," http://www.census.gov/prod/2004pubs/censr-18.pdf.

53. Francis seems to undermine her own point when she asserts, "She unwittingly enters the sex trade when a Swedish agent comes to their small town and tells her that she can work as a model" (60).

54. Francis makes this point regarding race in the novel: "But within an intracultural marriage, racial signs do not visibly mark otherness" ("Novel Insights" 64). The opposite, however, is true; Manolo desires Olivia precisely because she is a light-skinned mulatta, as Francis notes earlier (60).

55. *Moreno* literally means "brown" or "dark," but in a colorist view of Dominican racial composition, it is not as dark as *black*, which would be termed *negro*.

56. Duany observes, "light skinned Dominican mulattos have better prospects for social acceptance in Puerto Rico than in the United States" ("Dominican Migration to Puerto Rico" 161–62).

57. Francis' reading does not foreground this racism within Dominican culture.

58. Miscegenation and paternity are recurring tropes in Caribbean literature. See Irizarry, "Doubly Troubling Narratives," for a discussion of the tropes in *The Agüero Sisters* and *The House on the Lagoon*.

59. Cherríe Moraga discusses the relationship between skin color and betrayal in "La Güera."

60. All of Olivia's stream-of-consciousness passages are italicized in the novel, so I retain that format.

61. *Ciego* means "blind" in Spanish; this man is Tiresias, who "sees" and comments on everything in the neighborhood.

62. *Niñez* refers to childhood, or the time between birth and adulthood.

63. For decades, there was no public acknowledgement of Trujillo's human rights violations. Unlike the Mirabal Sisters' museum, El Museo Memorial de la Resistencia reveals a significant government investment. It is part of the "International Coalition of Historic Site Museums of Conscience."

64. This is also true in the depiction of Lola and her mother, Belicia, in Díaz's novel *The Brief Wondrous Life of Oscar Wao*.

65. Olivia did not breast-feed Soledad but secretly breast-fed Flaca, her niece. When her sister discovers Olivia feeding Flaca, the sisters' relationship is strained.

66. It is not stated if the ritual is based on Santería or Vodún.

67. This is another metafictional moment: *cuentos campesinos* are "country people's stories," something akin to old wives' tales.

Chapter 3. Narratives of Fracture: Defining *Latinidades*

1. The Senate and House of Representative of Puerto Rico ruled the most recent plebiscite, conducted by the Obama Administration on November 6, 2012, "inconclusive." Nearly 500,000 ballots were left empty, which prompted the Obama Administration to charge the committees with another plebiscite. See the *Congressional Record* for the referenda and voting results: May 17, 2013, 113th Congress, 1st Session Issue: Vol. 159, No. 70.

2. See Baribeau for a discussion of the shifting Latina/o population in Florida. One statistic Baribeau reports: "Florida Puerto Ricans, moving from the island and other mainland enclaves, grew 50.7 percent statewide from 2000 to 2009 to 726,637, or 4.5 percent of the total, the census community data show, while Cubans rose 30.7 percent to 1,088,747, or 5.9 percent" ("Puerto Ricans in Central Florida's Tourism Hub"). See also Jorge Duany, "Mickey Ricans? The Recent Puerto Rican Diaspora to Florida."

3. Kanellos usefully describes authors including Cristina García, Virgil Súarez, Junot Díaz, and Judith Ortiz Cofer as "acculturated in the United States from youth and preferring to write in English for a broad general public; these authors assume many of the stances of the native writers, but their predominant theme and their double gaze are distinctly immigrant in nature" ("Overview" 21). See also Heredia, introduction, in *Transnational Latina Narratives*.

4. Quiñonez returned for an MA in creative writing after he published his first book. Another emergent writer, Daniel José Older, returned to school for an MFA after his collection of short stories was published. He explained, "Without an MFA, you can't teach" (personal interview).

5. Cofer's novel *The Line of the Sun* and her memoir *Silent Dancing* have received substantial critical examination, while *The Latin Deli*, a hybrid text of poems, essays, and fiction, has received scant attention.

6. The 2008 edited volume *Writing off the Hyphen* offers readers sixteen essays that reflect changes in the direction of Puerto Rican studies. Four essays especially relevant to this chapter revisit the construction of puertorriqueñidad: Lisa Sánchez González's "For the Sake of Love: Luisa Capetillo, Anarchy, and Boricua Literary History," José L. Torres-Padilla's "When 'I' Became Ethnic: Ethnogenesis and Three Early Puerto Rican Diaspora Writers," Antonio Domínguez-Miguela's "Literary Tropicalization of El Barrio," and Solimar Otero's "Getting There and Back: The Road, the Journey, and Home in Nuyorican Diaspora Literature."

7. Chapter 4 offers a more detailed analysis of this model and its relevance to Cuban American fiction. Pérez Firmat applies Rubén Rumbaut's term, the "1.5 generation," to distinguish the experiences of Cuban Americans from their parents, the Cuban exiles of the early 1960s (Rumbaut qtd. in Pérez Firmat 4).

8. Caminero-Santangelo discusses the early comparative nature of the poem "The Latin Deli" (1991), noting, "it was a relative rarity at the time for its literary vision of US Latinos/as of different ethnicities actually gathering and interacting in a shared space" ("Latinidad" 18).

9. See *Triangulations* by Vázquez for a discussion of movement specific to Ortiz Cofer's novel *The Line of the Sun.*

10. I choose to analyze them as fiction because Ortiz Cofer makes this distinction herself: "By calling them creative nonfiction, by introducing the word 'creative,' I am admitting, so that there is no confusion, that what I am trying to do is nonfiction in intent, that these events actually happened, but that the way I am transmitting them to the readers may be a recreation" (Ortiz Cofer qtd. in Ocasio 735).

11. Carmen Faymonville discusses a similar narrative function in Ortiz Cofer's novel *The Line of the Sun* but concludes that all of Ortiz Cofer's work "thematizes experiences riddled with the tension of belonging to no place and an existential doubt about belonging" ("New Transnational Identities" 130).

12. Omi notes, "In the post–Civil Rights era, some racial minority groups have carved out a degree of power in select urban areas—particularly with respect to administering social services and distributing economic resources. This has led, in cities like Oakland and Miami, to conflicts between Blacks and Hispanics over educational programs, minority business opportunities, and political power" (Omi, "The Changing Meaning of Race" 253).

13. I'm thinking of these lines: "What happens to a dream deferred? / Does it . . . fester like a sore— / and then run?" from Langston Hughes's "Harlem" (*Montage of a Dream Deferred*).

14. Ortiz Cofer's text is semi-autobiographical; thus, her characters are often younger personas of herself and reflect her lived experiences and reflections about them.

15. Faymonville further links this physical separation to concepts of the construction of ethnicity developed by Walter Benjamin, asserting, "this separation of soil from the political and psychological space is nowadays necessary since community always has to be imagined" ("New Transnational Identities" 150).

16. In *Dreaming in Cuban*, Pilar concludes of New York: "I know now it's where I belong—not *instead* of here but *more* than here" (García 236).

17. When discussing the centrality of the "emotional home" within literature of the Puerto Rican diaspora and of other Latino literatures, Domínguez-Miguela defines these other forms of home as "a physical, social, and psychic space where the individual feels at ease and 'at home'" ("Literary Tropicalizations of El Barrio" 170–71).

18. Similarly, of Ortiz Cofer's work in general, Vázquez concludes, "Ortiz Cofer disrupts discourses that tie the nation to a specific geographical or cultural space" (*Triangulations* 133).

19. See Torres-Padilla's introduction for an extended discussion of nationalist paradigms of literature and identity (*Writing Off the Hyphen*).

20. See Trotter, *The Great Migration*.

21. I am not sure if Ortiz Cofer is drawing on the motif used by Fitzgerald in *The Great Gatsby*, who refers to the "green light of hope," or to a broader collective consciousness of green as representative of new life and thus hope. Quiñonez, in *Bodega Dreams*, very deliberately invokes Fitzgerald's phrase.

22. See Bhabha, *The Location of Culture*.

23. In 2012, the Walt Disney Corporation introduced its first "Latina" princess, Princess Sophia. The cartoon character did not seem Latina in any way to most US Latinas/os: she was very pale and had green eyes and straight hair. Moreover, her mother was "Spanish," and Sophia becomes a princess when a Scandanavian King marries her mother. Public criticism has not prevented Disney from producing and marketing Sophia's telelevision show and DVD-only releases.

24. Faymonville notes that the desire for Euro-American femininity often "brings with it intense cultural alienation and the loss of psychological and philosophical homes" ("New Transnational Identities" 133).

25. Faymonville contrasts Ortiz Cofer's work to modernist literatures, asserting, "whereas modernist theories of nation conceptualize nations as a particular community rooted in a specific place, geography or setting, Ortiz Cofer contends that the physical setting and the geography themselves are not a given but have to be imagined along with the more abstract 'home' or 'community'" ("New Transnational Identities" 134).

26. Bost argues, "Cofer's identity stretches across a continuum, rather than inhabiting a single, essential locus. Her world is fragmented, and of these pieces she constructs her own archipelago, with no pretense toward any solid mainland" ("Transgressing Borders" 203).

27. Here I refer to the discussion and citation of articles by Norma Alarcón and Henry Staten in chapter 1.

28. For an example, see Ana Castillo, *Massacre of the Dreamers*.

29. For a discussion on one's sexuality as epistemology, see Gloria Anzaldúa, "To(o) Queer the Writer."

30. As noted in the introduction, I am drawing on "ethnonationalism" as discussed extensively by political scientist Walker Connor. For scholarship particular to Puerto Rican ethnonationalism, see Negrón-Muntaner and Grosfoguel, *Puerto Rican Jam*.

31. My project in this chapter is not to perform a close comparison of the two novels; rather, I wish to illustrate what I believe to be Quiñonez's larger project in relation to Nuyorican literary aesthetics. For extended discussions of Thomas' novel, see Marta Caminero-Santangelo, "'Puerto Rican Negro,'" and Marta E. Sánchez, *Shakin' Up Race and Gender*.

32. In the movie *West Side Story*, the character who becomes allegorical of the Puerto Rican young man as criminal is Chino. He is incarcerated and later, presumably, dies, suggesting the inevitable end of those Puerto Ricans rejecting the assimilation that Natalie Wood's character, María, embraces. For further analysis of *West Side Story*, see Negrón-Muntaner, "Feeling Pretty."

33. See Arreola, *Hispanic Places, Latino Spaces*, for a discussion of the shifting Latina/o populations in New York and other major urban areas.

34. *Bodega Dreams* has suffered a lack of critical attention akin to Edward Rivera's *Family Installments: Memories of Growing Up Hispanic*. In a posthumous special journal issue devoted to the author, Lyn Di Iorio Sandín asserts, "This type of repression among Latinos leads to a rejection of solidarity among ourselves" ("Introduction" 109). Di Iorio Sandín's connection of these ethnonational politics is helpful in understanding the challenge Quiñonez faces: "Such insidiously varied fetishization goes a long way toward explaining why this wonderful book has been overlooked by Nuyorican and Puerto Rican writers and critics for such a long time" ("Introduction" 109).

35. The "Author Q&A" that I cite, http://knopfdoubleday.com/book/136934/bodega-dreams/, is no longer active, but the content now appears at http://www.random house.com/highschool/catalog/display.pperl?isbn=9780375705892&view=qa.

36. For a review and comparison of US Latino and Caribbean Hispanic writers of Thomas' time, including Pietri and Mohr, see Luis, *Dance between Two Cultures*.

37. *Chango's Fire* (2004), Quiñonez's second novel, examines gentrification and forcefully indicts Puerto Ricans for losing Thomas' hard-won turf. This novel never went into a second paperback printing, but it is now available as an e-book.

38. I retain the geographic and taxonomic distinction of "East Harlem" to be consistent with Bodega. See Sharman, *The Tenants of East Harlem*, who delineates East

Harlem's boundaries as 5th Avenue to the west, 125th Street to the north, the East River to the east, and 96th Street to the south.

39. For recent discussions of urban renewal specific to East Harlem, see Dávila, "Dreams of Place." See also chapter 8 of Sharman, *The Tenants of East Harlem*.

40. The term *puertorriqueñidad* refers to one's "authentic" Puerto Ricanness.

41. Thomas referred to *Down These Mean Streets* as an "autobiographical novel"; critics including William Luis, Lisa Sánchez-González, Marta E. Sánchez, and David Vázquez generally consider it autobiographical fiction. See Thomas' website: http://www.cheverote.com.

42. See Raúl Homero Villa for a discussion of barrio literature in the 1960s and 1970s: "While the barrio was subordinate in the urban social order, it was also a place of belonging for its residents. This quality gained tactical urgency for Chicano and Puerto Rican activists in this period, determined to use their aggrieved urban milieu as the locus of an empowered ethnic consciousness and political mobilization" ("Urban Spaces" 48).

43. Jumping-in is the process where established gang members beat up a prospective gang member.

44. Burton and colleagues note, "These racial hierarchies constitute the basis for racism, discrimination, and the perpetuation of inequality in a society and within families" ("Critical Race Theories" 445).

45. Because I focus on a shift in hierarchy in Quiñonez's text, I will not repeat a review of race theory on Thomas' *Down These Mean Streets*. See Caminero-Santangelo, "'Puerto Rican Negro,'" and Sánchez, *Shakin' Up Race and Gender*, for extensive critical discussions of race in Thomas.

46. Colorism remains an underexplored area of certain disciplines, including sociology: "Most importantly, there was also a lack of attention to colorism and how it shapes within race/ethnic socialization practices of families, specifically immigrants from countries of origin with racialized and color-conscious hierarchies" (Burton et al., "Critical Race Theories" 453).

47. This is a project Daniel José Older takes up in *Salsa Nocturna: Stories*. The story "Phantom Overload" is a wonderful example of critique of intra-Latina/o racism and ethnonationalism.

48. For a discussion of the relationship between *The Great Gatsby* and *Bodega Dreams* see Dwyer, "When Willie Met Gatsby."

49. "Author Interview," http://www.randomhouse.com/vintage/quinonez.html; this link is inactive.

50. Dalleo and Machado Sáez rightly argue, "Quiñonez explicitly invokes three major Nuyorian literary works of the Civil Rights generation that engage the legacies of the American dream and its anticolonial critique" (*The Latina/o Canon* 60).

51. See Dalleo and Machado Sáez, *The Latina/o Canon*, for a detailed analysis of the poems' roles in the novel.

52. See Torres-Saillant for a discussion of US neocolonialism and Caribbean racial stratification.

53. Kevane makes an important point about the novel: "Puerto Ricans on the mainland have been negatively affected by tremendous economic and social forces, racism, poverty, and violence, all of which have taken a toll on them and have stereotyped them as the bottom dwellers of the Latino immigrant hierarchy" (*Latino Literature in America* 131).

54. The word *value* appears frequently in contemporary Puerto Rican literature. *Down These Mean Streets* and *Bodega Dreams* use the term. Ortiz Cofer uses it as well in these comments from "Not for Sale": "happily ever after was a big bow loosely tied on a valuable package" (18) and "the old salesman was willing to bargain with my father over what my value was in this transaction" (20).

55. Music plays a significant role in the novel. Bodega's cousin, Nene, is often singing fragments of hit songs. Nene functions as a Greek chorus, often revealing information to the reader that Chino cannot determine.

56. *Bodega Dreams* draws surprisingly little on Santería. When Sapo, Chino, and Nene go to a Santera, Doña Ramonita, Chino describes her as having "strong African roots from Puerto Rico's Loiza Aldea" (Quiñonez 51). She shares her vision of Vera as "coming with a lot of trouble" (Quiñonez 53). Bodega's refusal to heed her warning is symbolic rejection of Puerto Rico.

57. Pedro Pietri (d. 2004) was an important Nuyorican poet and cofounder of the Nuyorican Poet's Café. His work is widely anthologized for its value as protest poetry, bilingual expression, and stylistic innovation. The volume *Selected Poems of Pedro Pietri* is forthcoming.

58. "Operation Bootstrap" was the name of an initiative began during the administration of Governor Luis Muñoz Marín. It altered the economic and cultural nature of the island, resulting in mass migrations that increased the Puerto Rican presence in Harlem after 1952, when the island officially became a "free associated state" of the United States.

59. The trope of the "ethnic gaze" Sollors articulates resonates clearly in this novel. Drawing on W. E. B. Du Bois' concept of "double consciousness"; Sollors asserts, "double consciousness characters may be attracted to mirrors, reflecting windows, or smooth surfaced ponds" (*The Invention of Ethnicity* 249).

60. For further discussion of the novel's structure as a boxing match, see Kevane, *Latino Literature in America*, especially pages 131–36.

61. Because Quiñonez is half Ecuadorian, it is possible he intended this Central American nuance to the name Sapo.

62. Oscar Lewis is the author of *La Vida*, a text widely considered to be racist and responsible for the image of the Nuyorican as inferior to the island-born and -raised Puerto Rican.

63. This is the first of three mentions of Bodega's full, given name; given Chino's discourse on the Futurists, Bodega's given name is likely a variation on the name of modernist poet William Carlos Williams.

64. The place name *Loisaida* is derived from the Spanglish pronunciation of *Lower East Side* or someone from the neighborhood: a *Lower East Sider*. The Puerto Rican

coastal city Loizaida is associated with African cultural expression and resistance to US neocolonialism; the neighborhood name may have developed from it. For further discussion, see Hickman, "The Political Left and the Development of Puerto Rican Poetry."

65. For a discussion of Puerto Rican homosexuality and masculinity depicted in the germinal works of Nuyorican poets Pedro Pietri, Miguel Piñero, Piri Thomas, and Miguel Algarín, see Arnaldo Cruz-Malvé, "What a Tangled Web!"

66. For an extensive discussion of gentrification in East Harlem, see Dávila, *Barrio Dreams*.

67. Chino describes RIPs as graffiti memorials to men killed because of criminal activity. For a discussion of RIPs see Sharman, *The Tenants of East Harlem*.

68. Achy Obejas's novel *Memory Mambo* is another narrative of fracture in this regard; it portrays the cultural and political differences between Cubans and Puerto Ricans.

69. This section title is drawn from Langston Hughes' terrifically important poem "Dream Deferred." The poem was originally titled "Harlem 2" in *Montage of a Dream Deferred*; in the *Selected Poems of Langston Hughes,* the title was changed to "Dream Deferred."

70. See Rhina Espaillat's poem "Bodega" for another example.

71. See Susan C. Mendez, "The Fire between Them," and Sean Moiles, "The Politics of Gentrification," for discussions of religion specific to Quiñonez's novels.

72. This trope is powerfully reversed in Quiñonez's second novel, *Chango's Fire*, when the local Santero, Papelito, sacrifices himself to a building fire after saving others from it.

73. For a discussion of religion in Latina/o literature, see Kevane, *Sacred and Profane*.

74. Quiñonez is referring to the illegal but common sport of fighting roosters (cocks) typical to Caribbean culture.

Chapter 4. Narratives of New Memory: Ending the Neocolonial Story

1. For a discussion of the relationships between US Latina fiction and testimonio, see Irizarry, "The Ethics of Writing the Caribbean."

2. For additional examples of nonexilic Cuban American literature, see Villa, "Urban Spaces."

3. Cristina García's novel about Fidel Castro, *The King of Cuba*, has been garnering positive reviews.

4. Readers should note the repetition of songs in *Crazy Love, The Greatest Performance*, and *Brand New Memory*. Most of the songs are from the 1950s and 1960s and enhance the motif of storytelling within both novels. Popular music of this period was characterized by narration; that is, the songs were more like a ballad or story than poetic lyrics.

5. Santería remains a viable cultural practice throughout the Hispanic and French Caribbean, as well as the United States.

6. For a discussion of texts depicting Iberian colonialism and US neocolonialism at the turn of the twentieth century, see Irizarry, "Doubly Troubling Narratives."

7. According to Villa, "Virgil Suárez figures it with more troubling effect in *Going Under* (1996). The novel's yuppie Cuban-American protagonist suffers a mental breakdown that compels him to explore and reflect upon the city's diffuse Cubanness, but he ultimately fails to satisfy his longing for a sustaining ethnic identity. The suburban spaces of a Cuban-American bourgeois dream are also figured in recent literature, ranging from mockery to affection" ("Urban Spaces" 52).

8. The protagonist's parents are both dead at the novel's start, and it is unclear if her mother had been an immigrant or was born within the United States.

9. Martínez is clearly in dialogue with Toni Morrison's idea of re-memory.

10. For reflections on testimonio about Guatemala's Civil War, see Arias, *The Rigoberta Menchú Controversy.*

11. I use the term *disappearance* as it defines the kidnapping, torture, and murder of political dissidents, their families, or anyone abducted for political reasons.

12. In September 2014, Pope Francis nominated the martyred Archbishop Oscar Romero for canonization—sainthood—in the Holy Roman Catholic Church. In 2013, Romero was honored by the creation of a commemorative mural in Los Angeles' MacArthur Park. This park is a central gathering space for the population of Salvadoran refugees who fled El Salvador during the Civil War. See http://www.huffingtonpost.com/2013/06/22/oscar-romero-macarthur-park-_n_3484205.html.

13. See the special issue of *Antípodas: Trujillo, Trauma, Testimony*, edited by Caminero-Santangelo and Osegueda.

14. For a discussion of the problems of "veracity" in testimonio, see Irizarry, "The Ethics of Writing the Caribbean."

15. Human rights advocates such as Menchú Tum argue that dissidents are at risk as long as the involvement of other nations remains uninvestigated.

16. Martínez's involvement with the Sanctuary movement, which was based in liberation theology, a religious movement linked to social justice, is not clear. She was arrested while interviewing refugees aided by the Sanctuary movement.

17. The story was covered in national and religious news media. For additional discussion of her case, see Valle, "Poet or Smuggler?"; Juffer, "Sanctuary Crackdown Nabs Reporter" and "An Ominous Indictment"; and Harbart, "Found Innocent" and "Aiding or Reporting on the Sanctuary Movement?"

18. This analysis departs from what David Vázquez describes as "Life Writing": "in fact, many Latina/o authors of the late twentieth century employ similar narrative strategies in their first-person personal narratives—a continuum of literary forms that includes memoir, autobiography, testimonio, a autobiographical fiction, and other forms of life writing" (Vázquez, *Triangulations* 2). His focus is on first-person narratives; not all of the books discussed in this study are narrated in the first person.

19. The novel begins with the protagonist using Mary as her name; when she meets José Luis, he calls her María, and she begins to identify herself in this way through the present time of the main narrative.

20. Dalia Kandiyoti provides a stimulating reading of the novel through the conception of "hospitality" in "Host and Guest in the Latino Contact Zone." Kandiyoti offers readings of the characters' failure to achieve solidarity through their misconstruction of one another and their failures to perform the appropriate roles of guest and host.

21. Caminero-Santangelo notes, "Mary's understanding of her romance utterly obscures the very real difference in experience created by distinct cultures and histories" (*On Latinidad* 200).

22. Jean Franco has articulated the form of such texts succinctly: "In the constant quest for meaning and identity, the Latina draws on a wide repertoire, experimenting with language, bilingual poetry, writing in Spanish and English, mixing poetry with prose, crossing gender and genre boundaries but also at times reviving older forms" (*In Other Words* xix).

23. I am drawing on Dickinson's construction of depression as "a certain slant of light" in the poem "There's a certain Slant of Light."

24. "Rip Van Winkle" can be read as a political allegory for the generation of colonists preceding the American Revolution. When he awakes, a nation has been born, and the changes associated with it are too overwhelming for him to do anything but remain who he always has been: a lazy, unappreciative man.

25. Cherríe Moraga, "Art in América con Acento."

26. The protagonist and narrator of Sylvia Sellers García's novel *When the Ground Turns in Its Sleep* comes to a similar acceptance of his lack of full knowledge of the war in his native Guatemala.

27. For a reading specific to the war and language, see Laura Lomas, "'The War Cut Out My Tongue.'"

28. In an interview, Cristina García first described her novel *The Lady Matador's Hotel* in this way: "it takes place over seven days and is a sort of a creation story" ("Interview" 187). Thus, I considered reading it as a narrative of new memory because one could argue that each character's creation is revealed and that some of them are able to re-create themselves in a manner very similar to María of *Mother Tongue*. The novel, however, is not collaborative or consistent in its depiction of new memory, so I consider it a narrative of loss.

29. Martínez changes the facts about the nuns' murders. In December 1980, three nuns, Maura Clarke, Jean Donovan, and Ita Ford, and a missionary affiliated with their order, Dorothy Kazel, were abducted, raped, and murdered. In 1998, the soldiers convicted for their murders admitted that they had been "ordered" to do so, but they were charged for committing civil crimes, not war crimes. See http://news.bbc.co.uk/2/hi/americas/107365.stm.

30. There is an extensive amount of literary criticism on the figure of La Malinche as a linguistic and cultural traitor and her reconfiguration in Chicana literature. One

of the most important analyses is Norma Alarcón's 1989 article "Traddutora, Traditora: A Paradigmatic Figure of Chicana Feminism."

31. My arguments may resonate with Barbara Harlow's readings of refugee narratives that compel readers to hold the United States accountable for its covert acts of neocolonialism that resulted in the displacement of thousands of people. See Harlow, "Sites of Struggle: Immigration, Deportation, Prison and Exile."

32. As Rodríguez argues, "Latino literature increasingly features Central Americans; their experiences reveal the deep dissonance between their ideology and that of well-intentioned Latinos" ("Refugees of the South" 83).

33. Martínez offers the careful reader more Christian allegory: in Spanish, *alegría* means "joy" and *cruz* means "cross." Romero is the surname of the Archbishop Oscar Romero, a key figure of resistance to El Salvador's civil war, who was assassinated in 1980 and to whom Martínez refers in the prologue.

34. Caminero-Santangelo finds that "the religious underpinnings of the [Sanctuary] movement are seriously downplayed" (*On Latinidad* 204). I see Martínez spending considerable but indeed subtle time on religious ideology, reference, and allegory that underpins the movement, as illustrated in the preceding analysis.

35. Caminero-Santangelo asserts, "*Mother Tongue* allows us to think in terms of multiple *latinidades*, organized around various points of interest, rather than of a singular, fixed, Hispanic identity with predefined borders of inclusion and exclusion" (*On Latinidad* 212).

36. Caminero-Santangelo suggests that the reader becomes part of "an act of collective remembering" (*On Latinidad* 202).

37. See María Cristina García, especially the chapter "The Mariel Boatlift," for a lengthy review of the context under which the Mariels were constructed as dangerous felons by the Cuban and American governments. See Aguirre, Fernandez, Hufker, and Martinez, "Race, Gender, and Class in the Persistence of the Mariel Stigma," for the racial, economic, and criminal statistics of the Cuban immigrants that arrived via the Mariel Boatlift.

38. For detailed information on Castro's treatment of homosexuals, see Quiroga and Peña.

39. For an analysis of the novel foregrounding questions of refuge and asylum based on sexual orientation, see Mullins, "Seeking Asylum."

40. The Refugee Act was modified in October of the same year to provide Cubans educational assistance. For more detail, see García, *Havana USA*.

41. The term *Marielitos* is a diminutive noun used to describe this wave of Cubans. Its diminutive tone immediately signals this group as a less productive, if not less important, part of Cuban society.

42. See Alberts, "Changes in Ethnic Solidarity in Miami," Portes, "The Enclave and the Entrants," and Skop, "Race and Place in the Adaptation of Mariel Exiles," for discussions of the 1959 exile and 1980 refugee communities.

43. For recent work on Cuban and Cuban American writers, see Borland and Bosch, *Cuban-American Literature and Art*.

44. Prida's play *Botánica/The Herb Shop* is a narrative of loss about acculturation to the US mainstream.

45. To date, few scholars have devoted significant time to Muñoz's work; Lima and Christian are among those. Several chapter sections treating queer Cuban literature offer brief (a few paragraphs) discussions of *Crazy Love* and/or *The Greatest Performance*. For examples of these short discussions, see Deaver, "The Prodigal Son in the Structure of *Raining Backwards, Crazy Love,* and *Latin Jazz*"; Alvarez Borland's discussion of *Crazy Love* and *The Greatest Performance* in *Cuban-American Literature of Exile*; and Emilio Bejels' reading of *Crazy Love* in *Gay Cuban Nation*.

46. Alternative names are used to refer to the male protagonist: Mario and its diminutive, Marito. Unless directly quoting the text or a critical discussion of it, I will use Mario to refer to the protagonist. Similarly, the female protagonist and dominant narrator, Rosaura, is sometimes referred to as Rosa or Rosita. Unless directly quoting, I will refer to her as Rosa.

47. Toward the end of the novel, the narrator Mario echoes this question when a doctor tells him, "Don't tell me your name, just who you are" (Muñoz, *The Greatest Performance* 129).

48. For a reading of a similar intervention within US pop culture, see José Esteban Muñoz's essay "Pedro Zamora's Real World of Counter-publicity." Zamora was a Mariel refugee; his presence as an HIV-positive gay man had well-documented, positive effects on viewer attitudes toward homosexuality.

49. As Sandra Soto notes, "There are many authors and scholars of Latino/a queer literature that I was not able to mention here but who have helped to shape what we think of as Latino/a queerness" ("Queerness" 83).

50. Mullins asserts, "representations of immigrant and refugee experience rendered in these literary accounts speak powerfully to human rights issues that US law overlooks and that INS practice ignores" ("Seeking Asylum" 146).

51. The lack of critical engagement of homosexuality-focused literature has been noted. See Sandra Soto, who argues, "In contrast to the significant visibility of Latina lesbians such as Cherríe Moraga, Gloria Anzaldúa, Carla Trujillo, Achy Obejas, and others, gay Latino authors and activists receive far less attention A recent intervention, *Gay Latino Studies: A Critical Reader* (Hames-García and Martínez 2011), sheds light on the culture of invisibility and deviance associated with Latino gay cultures and re-inserts questions of sexuality into Latinos/as' struggles for equality" ("Queerness" 68).

52. For a review of the sectional structure of *The Greatest Performance*, see Lima.

53. For a reading of Rosa's narrative of Mario's life as representing the problematics of heteronormative desire, see Lima.

54. The novel resonates with Reinado Arenas' memoir *Before Night Falls*. Arenas contracted HIV and subsequently died of AIDS.

55. Two other texts concerned with the ontology of homosexuality are Achy Obejas' *Memory Mambo* and Erika Lopez's *Flaming Iguanas*.

56. For an analysis of cultural production and performance as strategy for Latino sexuality, see José Esteban Muñoz, *Disidentifications*.

57. The lyrics to this song are repeated in the next section of the text as Mario reminisces about another boy he finds attractive. Mario is rejected by the boy, however (42).

58. For detailed discussions of the treatment of homosexuals, see Aguirre, "Cuban Mass Migration," and Peña, "Obvious Gays and the State Gaze."

59. See Almaguer, also referenced in chapter 1, who distinguishes European American and Latin American constructs of sexuality. Almaguer draws on the Freudian term *sexual aim* to illustrate that Latin American masculinity is determined by "the act one wants to perform with the person toward whom sexual activity is directed" (76). *Pato* literally means "duck" in Spanish, but it is derogatory slang for a gay man who receives sexual penetration. *Maricón* is another derogatory term for a gay man, but it is also applied to women ("maricona") and is suggestive of sexual deviance.

60. David William Foster identifies this pattern of abuse in the work of Chicano and Latino authors. In his discussion of Michael Nava's work, Foster asserts that abuse of the gay child's body is intrinsic to homophobic parents: "This discourse, among its many workings, obliges parents to be vigilantes of their children's sexuality, and to, quite literally, beat them into submissive conformity with the hegemonic compulsive heterosexist standard" (*El Ambiente Nuestro* 76).

61. Lima suggests that Mario's agency occurs through Rosa in his narration of revenge against Hernando (*The Latino Body* 143).

62. The term *jinetero* generally refers to anyone who tries to get foreign currency from tourists, through theft, sex work, or some form of deception.

63. Later in the 1990s, *City of Night* began to garner attention in queer studies, though Rechy looked at his work as intrinsically Mexican. See David William Foster's discussion of this in *Ambiente Nuestro*, especially in the introduction.

64. See the following critical analyses of Islas: Aldama, *Dancing with Ghosts*; Ortiz, "Sexuality Degree Zero"; Cutler, "Prosthesis, Surrogation, and Relation in Arturo Islas's the Rain God"; Nelson, *Critical Essays*; Sánchez, "Arturo Islas' *The Rain God*"; Rosaldo, "Race and Other Inequalities"; and Minich, "Enabling Aztlán."

65. Ricardo Ortiz suggests that Muñoz's geographical distance from Miami shapes his writing: "Muñoz, who was raised in Southern California, used his work in part to provide an alternative to the stereotype that all Cubans in the United States lived in Miami, and were exclusively driven by hardline, conservative, anti-Castro politics" ("Cuban American Literature" 416).

66. For a discussion of the construction of Hispanic ethnicity and commodification in the novel, see Caminero-Santangelo, *On Latinidad*, especially 174–77.

Conclusion. Belonging in Chicana/o and Latina/o Fiction

1. This a critique of NAFTA.

2. See Trejo, "Harvard's Latino Problem," April 18, 2012. Trejo notes, "Earlier attempts to establish a Center in 1971, 1979, 1993, 2001, and 2005 were all rebuffed by Harvard administration" (par. 5).

3. The school paper invokes the MIT/Harvard rivalry: "a little further down the river, techy MIT offers majors in Latin American and Latino Studies. See Ramirez, "¿A dónde Vamos?"

4. For an announcement of Raúl Castro's 2013 antidiscrimination employment law for homosexuals, see "Cuban Labor Code to Protect LGBT Rights," *Havana Times*, 23 December 2013. In May 2014 his daughter Mariela Castro hosted the first ever LGBT conference in Cuba. See Lavers, "Cuba to Host International LGBT Conference," *Washington Blade*, 2 May 2014. See also "LGBT Conference in Cuba Surrounded by Expectations and Controversy," *Global Voices Online*, 3 May 2014; and "Castro Continues to Fight for LGBT Rights in Cuba," *Out Magazine*, 15 May 2014.

Works Cited

Aguirre, B. E. "Cuban Mass Migration and the Social Construction of Deviants." *Bulletin of Latin American Research* 13.2 (1994): 155–83. Print.

Alarcón, Daniel. *War by Candlelight: Stories*. New York: Harper Collins, 2005. Print.

Alarcón, Norma. "Anzaldúa's *Frontera*: Inscribing Gynetics." *Displacement, Diaspora, and Geographies of Identity*. Ed. Lavie Smadar and Ted Swedenburg. Durham: Duke University Press, 1996. 41–53. Print.

———. "*Traddutora, Traditora*: A Paradigmatic Figure of Chicana Feminism." *Cultural Critique* 13 (Fall 1989): 57–87. Print.

———. "Tropology of Hunger: The 'Miseducation' of Richard Rodriguez." In Palumbo-Liu 140–52. Print.

Alber, Jan, and Monika Fludernik. *Postclassical Narratology: Approaches and Analyses*. Theory and Interpretation of Narrative. Athens: Ohio University Press, 2010. Print.

Alberts, Heike C. "Changes in Ethnic Solidarity in Cuban Miami." *Geographical Review* 95.2 (2005): 231–48. Print.

Alcoff, Linda Martín. "Latinos and the Categories of Race." *Visible Identities: Race, Gender, and the Self*. Oxford: Oxford University Press, 2006. 227–46. Print.

Aldama, Frederick Luis. *Dancing with Ghosts: A Critical Biography of Arturo Islas*. Berkeley: University of California Press, 2005. Print.

Alexie, Sherman. *Indian Killer*. New York: Grove Press, 2008. Print.

———. *Reservation Blues*. New York: Grove Press, 1995. Print.

Allatson, Paul. *Key Terms in Latino/a Cultural and Literary Studies*. Malden: Blackwell and Oxford, 2007. Print.

Allende, Isabel. *The House of the Spirits*. New York: Random House, 1985. Print.

Almaguer, Tomás. "Chicano Men: A Cartography of Homosexual Identity and Behavior." *Differences* 3.2 (1991): 75–100. Print.

Alvarez, Julia. *How the García Girls Lost Their Accents*. Chapel Hill: Algonquin Books of Chapel Hill, 1991. Print.

———. *In the Name of Salomé*. Chapel Hill: Algonquin Books, 2000. Print.

———. *In the Time of the Butterflies*. Chapel Hill: Algonquin Books of Chapel Hill, 1994. Print.

———. *Something to Declare: Essays*. Chapel Hill: Algonquin Books of Chapel Hill, 1998. Print.

Alvarez-Borland, Isabel. *Cuban-American Literature of Exile: From Person to Persona*. Charlottesville: University of Virginia Press, 1998. Print.

Alvarez-Borland, Isabel, and Lynette M. F. Bosch, eds. *Cuban-American Literature and Art: Negotiating Identities*. Latin American and Iberian Thought and Culture. Binghamton: State University of New York Press, 2009. Print.

Anaya, Rudolfo. *Bless Me, Ultima*. New York: Warner Books, 1972. Print.

. . . *And the Earth Did Not Swallow Him*. Dir. Severo Pérez. American Playhouse. 1995. Film.

Anzaldúa, Gloria. *Borderlands/La Frontera: The New Mestiza*. San Francisco: Aunt Lute Books, 1987. Print.

———. "To(o) Queer the Writer: *Loca, Escritora y Chicana*." *Inversions: Writing by Dykes, Queers, and Lesbians*. Ed. Betsy Warland. Vancouver: Press Gang Publishers, 1991. 249–63. Print.

Anzaldúa, Gloria, and Ana Louise Keating, eds. *The Gloria Anzaldúa Reader (Latin America Otherwise)*. Durham: Duke University Press, 2009. Print.

———. *This Bridge We Call Home: Radical Visions for Transformation*. New York: Routledge, 2002. Print.

Aparicio, Frances R., and Susana Chávez-Silverman, eds. *Tropicalizations: Transcultural Representations of Latinidad*. Reencounters with Colonialism: New Perspectives on the Americas. Hanover: University Press of New England for Dartmouth College, 1997. Print.

Aranda, José F., Jr. *When We Arrive: A New Literary History of Mexican America*. Tucson: University of Arizona Press, 2003. Print.

Archibold, Randal C. "Cuban Leader Proposes Reforms as Sign of New Era." *New York Times* 16 April 2011: Americas Section. Print.

Arreola, Daniel D., ed. *Hispanic Spaces, Latino Places: Community and Cultural Diversity in Contemporary America*. Austin: University Press of Texas, 2004. Print.

Arteaga, Alfred. *Chicano Poetics: Heterotexts and Hybridities*. Cambridge: Cambridge University Press, 1997. Print.

Avalos, Hector. *Strangers in Our Own Land: Religion in Contemporary U.S. Latina/o Literature*. Nashville: Abingdon Press, 2005. Print.

Bacho, Peter. *Dark Blue Suit: And Other Stories*. Seattle: University of Washington Press, 1997. Print.

Back, Les, and John Solomos, eds. *Theories of Race and Racism: A Reader*. New York: Routledge, 2000.

Baribeau, Simone. "Puerto Ricans in Central Florida's Tourism Hub Are Driving Hispanic Growth." *Bloomburg News* 18 Mar 2011. Print.

Beisner, Robert L. *Twelve against the Empire: The Anti-Imperialists, 1898–1900*. New York: McGraw-Hill, 1968. Print.

Bejel, Emilio. *Gay Cuban Nation*. Chicago: University of Chicago Press, 2001. Print.

Belknap, Jeffrey, and Rául Fernanández. *Jose Martí's Our America: From National to Hemispheric Cultural Studies*. Durham: Duke University Press, 1998. Print.

Benítez Rojo, Antonio. *El mar de las lentejas*. La Habana: Letra Cubanas, 1979. Print.

Bhabha, Homi K. *The Location of Culture*. Durham: Duke University Press, 1994. Print.

Bless Me, Ultima. Dir. Carl Franklin. Gran Via Productions, 2012. Film.

Bost, Suzanne. "Transgressing Borders: Puerto Rican and Latina *Mestizaje*." *MELUS: Journal of the Society for the Study of the Multi-Ethnic Literature of the United States* 25.2 (2000): 187–211. Print.

Bost, Suzanne, and Frances R. Aparicio. *The Routledge Companion to Latino/a Literature*. New York: Routledge, 2013. Print.

Bradford, James C. *Crucible of Empire: The Spanish-American War and Its Aftermath*. Annapolis: Naval Institute Press. 1993. Print.

Bradley, David. *The Chaneysville Incident*. New York: Harper & Row, 1981. Print.

Briggs, Laura. *Reproducing Empire: Race, Sex, Science, and US Imperialism in Puerto Rico*. American Crossroads 11. Oakland: University of California Press, 2002. Print.

Brooks, Cleanth. *The Well Wrought Urn: Studies in the Structure of Poetry [with a Portrait]*. New York: Reynal & Hitchcock, 1947. Print.

Brown, Nick. "Key Puerto Rican Debt Holders Circle Wagons as Restricting Talks Take Shape." *Reuters* 25 September 2015. Web.

Bruce-Novoa, Juan. "Dialogical Strategies, Monological Goals, Chicano Literature." Ed. Alfred Arteaga. *An Other Tongue: Nation and Ethnicity in the Linguistic Borderlands*. Durham: Duke University Press, 1994. 225–45. Print.

———. "Judith Ortiz Cofer's Rituals of Movement." *The Americas Review: A Review of Hispanic Literature and Art of the USA* 19.3–4 (1991): 88–89. Print.

Burton, Linda M., et al. "Critical Race Theories, Colorism, and the Decade's Research on Families of Color." *Journal of Marriage and Family* 72.3 (2010): 440–59. Print.

Butler, Alban. *The Lives of the Fathers, Martyrs, and Other Principal Saints*. New York: D. and J. Sadlier, 1846. Print.

Cabeza de Baca Gilbert, Fabiola. *We Fed Them Cactus*. Albuquerque: University of New Mexico Press, 1954. Print.

Calderón, Hector, and José David Saldívar, eds. *Criticism in the Borderlands: Studies in Chicano Literature, Culture, and Ideology*. Durham: Duke University Press, 1991. Print.

Caminero-Santangelo, Marta. "Contesting the Boundaries of 'Exile' Latino/a Literature." *World Literature Today: A Literary Quarterly of the University of Oklahoma* 74.3 (2000): 507–17. Print.

———. "Latinidad." Bost and Aparicio 13–24. Print.

―――. "The Lost Ones: Post-Gatekeeper Border Fictions and the Construction of Cultural Trauma." *Latino Studies* 8.3 (2010): 304–27. Print.

―――. *On Latinidad: U.S. Latino Literature and the Construction of Ethnicity*. Gainesville: University Press of Florida, 2007. Print.

―――. "'The Pleas of the Desperate': Collective Agency versus Magical Realism in Ana Castillo's *So Far from God*." *Tulsa Studies in Women's Literature* 24.1 (2005): 81–103. Print.

―――. "'Puerto Rican Negro': Defining Race in Piri Thomas's *Down These Mean Streets*." *MELUS: The Journal of the Society for the Study of the Multi-Ethnic Literature of the United States* 29.2 (2004): 205–26. Print.

Canaday, Margot. *The Straight State: Sexuality and Citizenship in Twentieth-Century America*. Princeton: Princeton University Press, 2009. Print.

Candelario, Ginetta E. B. *Black behind the Ears: Dominican Racial Identity from Museums to Beauty Shops*. Durham: Duke University Press, 2007. Print.

Canedy, Dana. "Bush Remark Gives Advocates Hope for Release of Haitians." *New York Times* 8 November 2002, late ed.: A14. Print.

Castillo, Ana. *Massacre of the Dreamers: Essays on Xicanisma*. Albuquerque: University of New Mexico Press, 1994.

―――. *The Mixquiahuala Letters*. Binghamton: Bilingual Press, 1992. Print.

―――. *Sapogonia: An Anti-Romance in 3/8 Meter*. New York: Anchor Books, 1994. Print.

―――. *So Far from God: A Novel*. New York: W. W. Norton, 1993. Print.

Castronovo, Russ. *Necro Citizenship: Death, Eroticism, and the Public Sphere in the Nineteenth-Century United States*. Durham: Duke University Press, 2001. Print

Céspedes, Diógenes, and Silvio Torres-Saillant. "Fiction Is the Poor Man's Cinema: An Interview with Junot Díaz." *Dominican Republic Literature and Culture*. Spec. issue of *Callaloo* 23.3 (2000): 892–907. Print.

Chabram-Dernersesian, Angie. "And, Yes . . . The Earth Did Part: On the Splitting of Chicana/o Subjectivity." *Building with Our Hands: New Directions in Chicana Studies*. Ed. Adela de la Torre. Berkeley: University of California Press, 1993. Print.

―――. "Chicana! Rican? No, Chicana-Riqueña! Refashioning the Transnational Connection." Goldberg 269–95. Print.

―――. "Introduction." *Chicana/o Latina/o Cultural Studies: Transnational and Transdisciplinary Movements*. Spec. issue of *Cultural Studies* 13.2 (1999): 173–94. Print.

Chávez, Denise. *Face of an Angel*. New York: Farrar, Straus and Giroux, 1994. Print.

―――. *The Last of the Menu Girls*. Houston: Arte Público Press, 1986. Print.

Chávez, Linda. *Out of the Barrio: Toward a New Politics of Hispanic Assimilation*. New York: Basic Books, 1992. Print.

Christian, Karen. "Performing Magical Realism: The 'Boom' in US Latina/o Fiction." *The Americas Review: A Review of Hispanic Literature and Art of the USA* 24.3–4 (1996): 166–78. Print.

————. *Show and Tell: Identity as Performance in US Latina/o Fiction*. Albuquerque: University of New Mexico Press, 1997. Print.

Cisneros, Sandra. "Ghosts and Voices." *The Americas Review: A Review of Hispanic Literature and Art of the USA* 15.1 (1987): 72–73. Print.

————. *The House on Mango Street*. New York: Vintage, 1984. Print.

Colás, Santiago. "Of Creole Symptoms, Cuban Fantasies, and Other Latin American Postcolonial Ideologies." *PMLA: Publications of the Modern Language Association of America* 110.3 (1995): 382–96. Print.

Córdoba, María Socorro Tabuenca. "Viewing the Border: Perspectives from the 'Open Wound.'" *Discourse* 18.1/2 (1995): 146–68. Print.

Corpi, Lucha. *Eulogy for a Brown Angel*. Houston: Arte Público, 1992. Print.

Cota-Cárdenas, Margarita. *Puppet*. Austin: Relámpago Press, 1985. Print.

Crenshaw, Kimberly, Neil Gotanda, and Gary Peller, eds. *Critical Race Theory: The Key Writings That Formed the Movement*. New York: The New Press, 1995. Print.

Crossed Genres Press. "*Long Hidden*: It's Here!" 2014. 1 December 2014. http://crossedgenres.com/. Web.

Cruz, Angie. "Angie Cruz in Conversation with Nelly Rosario." *Callaloo* 30.3 (2007): 743–53. Print.

————. *Let It Rain Coffee: A Novel*. New York: Simon and Schuster, 2006. Print.

————. *Soledad*. New York: Simon and Schuster, 2001.

Crucet, Jennine Capó. *How to Leave Hialeah*. Iowa City: University of Iowa Press, 2009. Print.

Cruz, Nilo. *Anna in the Tropics*. New York: Dramatists Play Service, 2003. Print.

Cruz-Malavé, Arnaldo. "'What a Tangled Web!': Masculinity, Abjection, and the Foundations of Puerto Rican Literature in the United States." *Differences: A Journal of Feminist Cultural Studies* 8.1 (1996): 132–51. Print.

Cutler, John Alba. "Prosthesis, Surrogation, and Relation in Arturo Islas's *The Rain God*." *Aztlán: A Journal of Chicano Studies* 33.1 (2008): 7–32. Print.

Cutter, Martha J. *Lost and Found in Translation: Contemporary Ethnic American Writing and the Politics of Language Diversity*. Chapel Hill: University of North Carolina Press, 2005. Print.

Dalleo, Raphael, and Elena Machado Sáez. *The Latina/o Canon and the Emergence of Post-sixties Literature*. New York: Palgrave, 2007. Print.

Danticat, Edwidge. *The Farming of Bones*. New York: Soho Press, 1998. Print.

Dávila, Arlene M. *Barrio Dreams: Puerto Ricans, Latinos, and the Neoliberal City*. Berkeley: University of California Press, 2004. Print.

————. *Culture Works: Space, Value, and Mobility across the Neoliberal Americas*. New York: New York University Press, 2012. Print.

————. "Dreams of Place: Housing, Gentrification, and the Marketing of Space in El Barrio." *Centro Journal* 15.1 (2003): 112–137. Print.

Davis, Angela. *Women, Race, and Class*. New York: Vintage, 1981. Print.

Deaver, William O., Jr. "The Prodigal Son in the Structure of *Raining Backwards, Crazy Love,* and *Latin Jazz.*" *The Americas Review: A Review of Hispanic Literature and Art of the USA* 24.3–4 (1996): 179–90. Print.

de Crèvecoeur, St. Jean. "What Is an American?" *American Visions: Multicultural Literature for Writers.* Ed. Dolores LaGuardia and Hans Paul Guth. Houston: Mayfield, 1995. Print.

Deere, Carmen Diana. "Here Come the Yankees! The Rise and Decline of United States' Colonies in Cuba, 1898–1930." *Hispanic American Historical Review* 78.4 (1998): 729–65. Print.

Delgadillo, Theresa. "Forms of Chicana Feminist Resistance: Hybrid Spirituality in Ana Castillo's *So Far from God.*" *Modern Fiction Studies* 44.4 (1998): 888–916. Print.

———. *Spiritual Mestizaje: Religion, Gender, Race, and Nation in Contemporary Chicana Narrative.* Durham: Duke University Press, 2011. Print.

Delgado, A. J. "Outrage against Marc Anthony Shows Racism against Latinos Is Alive and Well." *Fox News Latino* 18 July 2013. Web.

Díaz, Junot. *The Brief Wondrous Life of Oscar Wao.* Riverhead: Riverhead Books, 2007. Print.

———. "Diaspora and Redemption: Creating Progressive Imaginaries." Interview with Katherine Miranda. *Sargasso II* (2008–9): 23–40. Print.

———. *Drown.* New York: Riverhead Books, 1996. Print.

———. *This Is How You Lose Her.* New York: Riverhead Books, 2012. Print.

Dickinson, Emily. "There's a Certain Slant of Light." *The Poems of Emily Dickinson,* Vol. 1. Harvard University Press, 1998. 338. Print.

Di Iorio Sandín, Lyn. "The 'Culture-Conscious' Scribe and Introduction." Special Issue. *CENTRO: Journal of the Center for Puerto Rican Studies* 14.1 (2002): 107–9.

———. *Killing Spanish: Literary Essays on Ambivalent U.S. Latino/a Identity.* New York: Palgrave Macmillan, 2009. Print.

Driscoll, Barbara A. *The Tracks North: The Railroad Bracero Program of World War II.* Austin: University of Texas Press, 1999. Print.

Duany, Jorge. *Blurred Borders: Transnational Migration between the Hispanic Caribbean and the United States.* Chapel Hill: University of North Carolina Press, 2011. Print.

———. "Dominican Migration to Puerto Rico: A Transnational Perspective." *Centro Journal* 17.1 (2005): 243–68. Print.

———. "Mickey Ricans? The Recent Puerto Rican Diaspora to Florida." Florida's Hispanic Heritage Conference. Institute for the Study of Latin America and the Caribbean, University of South Florida, Tampa. 13 October 2012. Print.

———. "Reconstructing Racial Identity: Ethnicity, Color, and Class among Dominicans in the United States and Puerto Rico." *Latin American Perspectives* 25.3 (1998): 147–72. Print.

———. "Transnational Migration from the Dominican Republic: The Cultural Redefinition of Racial Identity." *Caribbean Studies* 29.2 (1996): 253–82. Print.

Dwyer, June. "When Willie Met Gatsby: The Critical Implications of Ernesto Quiñonez's *Bodega Dreams*." *LIT: Literature Interpretation Theory* 14.2 (2003): 165–78. Print.

Elias, Amy J. *Sublime Desire: History and Post-1960s Fiction*. Parallax: Re-Visions
of Culture and Society. Baltimore: Johns Hopkins University Press, 2001. Print.

Engle, Margarita. *Singing to Cuba*. Houston: Arte Público Press, 1993. Print.

Erdrich, Louise. *The Last Report on the Miracles at Little No Horse: A Novel*. New
York: Taylor and Francis, 2001. Print.

———. *Love Medicine*. New York: Bantam Books, 1984. Print.

Espaillat, Rhina. "Bodega." R. Fernández 88. Print.

Esteves, Sandra Maria. *Bluestown Mockingbird Mambo*. Houston: Arte Público Press,
1990. Print.

Fallows, Samuel, Ellery C. Huntington, and Elizabeth Armstrong Reed, eds. *Splendid
Deeds of American Heroes on Sea and Land: Embracing a Comprehensive Summary
of the Glorious Naval and Military Events from Washington to Dewey*. Washington,
D.C.: Library of Congress, 1900. Print.

Faris, Wendy B. "Scheherazade's Children: Magical Realism and Postmodern Fiction." *Magical Realism: Theory, History, Community*. Ed. Lois Parkinson Zamora
and Wendy B. Faris. Durham: Duke University Press, 1995. 63–90. Print.

Faymonville, Carmen. "New Transnational Identities in Judith Ortiz Cofer's Autobiographical Fiction." *MELUS: The Journal of the Society for the Study of the Multi-
Ethnic Literature of the United States* 26.2 (2001): 129–58. Print.

Febres, Mayra Santos. *Boat People*. San Juan: Ediciones Callejón. 2005. Print.

Fernandez, Gaston A. "Race, Gender, and Class in the Persistence of the Mariel
Stigma Twenty Years after the Exodus from Cuba." *International Migration Review*
41.3 (2007): 602–22. Print.

Fernández, Roberta, ed. *In Other Words: Literature by Latinas of the United States*.
Houston: Arte Público Press, 1994. Print.

Figueredo, Danilo H. "The Stuff Dreams Are Made Of: The Latino Detective Novel."
Multicultural Review 8.3 (1999): 22–29. Print.

Fitzgerald, F. Scott. 1995 [1925]. *The Great Gatsby*. Ed. Matthew J. Bruccoli. New
York: Scribner.

Flores, Juan. *The Diaspora Strikes Back: Reflections on Cultural Remittances*. New
York: Routledge, 2009. Print.

———. *From Bomba to Hip-hop: Puerto Rican Culture and Latino Identity*. New York:
Columbia University Press, 2000. Print.

———. "Puerto Rican Literature in the United States: Stages and Perspectives." *ADE
Bulletin* 91 (1988): 39–44. Print.

Foster, David William. *El Ambiente Nuestro: Chicano/Latino Homoerotic Writing*.
Tempe: Bilingual Press/Editorial Bilingüe, 2006. Print.

Foster, Sesshu. *Atomik Aztex*. San Francisco: City Lights Publishers, 2005. Print.

Fowler, Alastair. *Kinds of Literature: An Introduction to the Theory of Genres and
Modes*. Cambridge: Harvard University Press, 1982. Print.

Fox, Claire F. "The Portable Border: Site-Specificity, Art, and the U.S.-Mexico Frontier." *Social Text* 41 (Winter 1994): 61–82.

Francis, Donette. "Novel Insights: Sex Work, Secrets, and Depression in Angie Cruz's *Soledad." Sex and the Citizen: Interrogating the Caribbean*. Ed. Faith Smith. Charlottesville: University of Virginia Press, 2011. Print.

Franco, Jean. "Foreword." Roberta Fernandez xiv–xx. Print.

Frye, Northrop. *Anatomy of Criticism*. Princeton: Princeton University Press, 1957. Print.

Galarza, Ernesto. *Barrio Boy*. Notre Dame: University of Notre Dame Press, 1971. Print.

Galeano, Eduardo. *Open Veins of Latin America: Five Centuries of the Pillage of a Continent*. New York: New York University Press, 1997. Print.

García, Cristina. *The Agüero Sisters*. New York: Random House, 1997. Print.

———. "'. . . And There Is Only My Imagination Where Our History Should Be': An Interview with Cristina García." By Iraida H. López. *Bridges to Cuba / Puentes a Cuba*. Ed. Ruth Behar. Ann Arbor: University of Michigan Press. 1995. 605–17. Print.

———. *Dreaming in Cuban*. New York: Alfred A. Knopf, 1993. Print.

———. *A Handbook to Luck*. New York: Alfred A. Knopf, 2007. Print.

———. "An Interview with Cristina Garcia." By Ylce Irizarry. *Contemporary Literature* 48.2 (2007): 175–94. Print.

———. *King of Cuba*. New York: Scribner, 2013. Print.

———. *The Lady Matador's Hotel: A Novel*. New York: Simon and Schuster, 2010. Print.

———. *Monkey Hunting*. New York: Alfred A. Knopf, 2003. Print.

García, María Cristina. *Havana USA: Cuban Exiles and Cuban Americans in South Florida, 1959–1994*. Berkeley: University of California Press, 1996. Print.

Gaspar de Alba, Alicia. *Calligraphy of the Witch*. Houston: Arte Público Press, 2012. Print.

———. *Desert Blood: The Juárez Murders*. Houston: Arte Público Press, 2005. Print.

Gaston, Bachelard. *The Poetics of Space*. Boston: Beacon Press, 1994. Print.

The Girl from Mexico. Dir. Leslie Goodwin. RKO Radio Pictures. 1939. Film.

Goldberg, David Theo, ed. *Multiculturalism: A Critical Reader*. Cambridge: Blackwell, 1994. Print.

González, José Luis. *El país de cuatro pisos y otros ensayos*. San Juan: Ediciones Huracán, 1981. Print.

Gonzalez, Juan. *Harvest of Empire: A History of Latinos in America*. New York: Penguin, 2011. Print.

Gregory, James N. *The Southern Diaspora: How the Great Migrations of Black and White Southerners Transformed America*. Chapel Hill: University of North Carolina Press, 2005. Print.

Gutiérrez, Ramon A. "Community, Patriarchy and Individualism: The Politics of Chicano History and the Dream of Equality." *American Quarterly* 45.1 (1993): 44–72. Print.

———. "Hispanic Diaspora and Chicano Identity in the United States." *South Atlantic Quarterly* 98.1/2 (1999): 203–15. Print.

———. *When Jesus Came, the Corn Mothers Went Away: Marriage, Sexuality, and Power in New Mexico, 1500–1846*. Stanford: Stanford University Press, 1991. Print.

Haggerty, Richard A., ed. *The Dominican Republic: A Country Study*. Washington, D.C.: GPO for Library of Congress. 1989. Print.

Hall, Stuart. "Cultural Identity and Diaspora." *Contemporary Postcolonial Theory: A Reader*. Ed. Padmini Mongia. London: Arnold, 1996. 110–21. Print.

———. "Culture, Community, Nation." *Cultural Studies* 7.3 (1993): 349–63. Print.

———. "The Emergence of Cultural studies and the Crisis of the Humanities." *The Humanities as Social Technology*. Spec. issue of *October* 53 (Summer 1990): 11–23. Print.

———. "Ethnicity: Identity and Difference." *Radical America* 23.4 (1991): 9–20. Print.

Hames-García, Michael. *Identity Complex: Making the Case for Multiplicity*. Minneapolis: University of Minnesota Press, 2011. Print.

Hames-García, Michael, and Ernesto Javier Martínez, eds. *Gay Latino Studies: A Critical Reader*. Durham: Duke University Press. 2011. Print.

Harbert, Nancy. "Aiding or Reporting on the Sanctuary Movement." *Christian Century* 6 July 1988. Print.

———. "Found Innocent." *Christian Century* 17 August 1988. Print.

Harlow, Barbara. "Sites of Struggle: Immigration, Deportation, Prison, and Exile." Calderón and Saldívar 149–63. Print.

Heide, Marcus. "The Postmodern 'We': Academia and Community in Ana Castillo's *So Far from God* and Denise Chavez's *Face of an Angel*." *U.S. Latino Literatures and Cultures: Transnational Perspectives*. Ed. Francisco Lomelí and Karin Ikas. Heidelberg: Universitätsverlag, 2000. 171–80. Print.

Heredia, Juanita. "The Dominican Diaspora Strikes Back: Cultural Archive and Race in Junot Diaz's *The Brief Wondrous Life of Oscar Wao*." Pérez Rosario 207–21. Print.

———. *Transnational Latina Narratives in the Twenty-first Century*. New York: Palgrave Macmillan, 2009. Print.

Hickman, Trenton. "The Political Left and the Development of Nuyorican Poetry." Torres-Padilla and Rivera 143–61. Print.

———. "The Trujillato as Desideratum in Dominican-American Fiction." *Trujillo, Trauma, Testimony: Mario Vargas Llosa, Julia Alvarez, Edwidge Danticat, Junot Díaz, and Other Writers on Hispaniola*. Ed. Roy Boland and Marta Caminero-Santangelo. Spec. issue of *Antípodas: Journal of Hispanic and Galician Studies* 20 (2009): 157–71. Print.

Hijuelos, Oscar. *The Mambo Kings Play Songs of Love*. New York: Farrar, Straus and Giroux, 1990. Print.

———. *Our House in the Last World: A Novel*. New York: Persea Books, 1983. Print.

Hinojosa-Smith, Rolando. *Ask a Policeman*. Houston: Arte Público Press, 1998.

————. *Estampas del Valle y otras obras.* Berkeley: Quinto Sol, 1973. Print.

————. *Klail City y sus Alrededores.* Havana: Casa de las Américas, 1976. Print.

Horno Delgado, Asunción, ed. *Breaking Boundaries: Latina Writing and Critical Readings.* Amherst: University of Massachusetts Press, 1989. Print.

Hosseini, Khaled. *The Kite Runner.* New York: Penguin, 2004. Print.

Howard, David. *Coloring the Nation: Race and Ethnicity in the Dominican Republic.* Oxford: Signal Books, 2001. Print.

Hufker, Brian, and Gray Cavender. "From Freedom Flotilla to America's Burden: The Social Construction of the Mariel Immigrants." *Sociological Quarterly* 31.2 (1990): 321–35. Print.

Hughes, Langston. "Dream Deferred." *The Collected Poems of Langston Hughes.* Ed. Arnold Rampersad and David Roessel. New York, Vintage: 1994, 426. Print.

————. "Harlem 2." In *Montage of a Dream Deferred.* New York: Holt, 1951.

Hume, Kathryn. *American Dream, American Nightmare: Fiction since 1960.* Urbana: University of Illinois Press, 2000. Print.

Ikas, Karin. *Chicana Ways: Conversations with Ten Chicana Writers.* Reno: University of Nevada Press, 2002. Print.

Irizarry, Ylce. "Doubly Troubling Narratives: Writing 'the Oppression of Possibility' in Puerto Rico and Cuba." *Comparative American Studies* 4.2 (2006): 197–217. Print.

————. "The Ethics of Writing the Caribbean: Latina Narrative as Testimonio." *Literature Interpretation Theory* 16.3 (2005): 263–84. Print.

————. "Making It Home: A New Ethics of Immigration in Dominican Literature." Pérez Rosario 89–103. Print.

————. "When Art Remembers: Museum Exhibits as Testimonio de Trujillato." *Trujillo, Trauma, Testimony: Mario Vargas Llosa, Julia Alvarez, Edwidge Danticat, Junot Díaz, and Other Writers on Hispaniola.* Ed. Roy Boland and Marta Caminero-Santangelo. Spec. issue of *Antípodas: Journal of Hispanic and Galician Studies* 20 (2009): 235–52. Print.

Irving, Washington. "Rip Van Winkle: A Posthumous Writing of Diedrich Knickerbocker." *The Heath Anthology of American Literature: Concise Edition.* Eds. Paul Lauter, Richard Yarborough, and Jackson R. Bryer. New York: Wadsworth, 2004. Print.

Islas, Arturo. *The Rain God.* New York: Harper Collins, 1991. Print.

James, E. L. *Fifty Shades of Grey.* London: Arrow, 2012. Print.

Johnson, Charles. *Middle Passage.* New York: Scribner, 1990. Print.

Juffer, Jane. "An Ominous Indictment." *Columbia Journalism Review* May/June (1988). Print.

————. "Sanctuary Crackdown Nabs Reporter." *Progressive* 52.5 (1988). Print.

Kandiyoti, Dalia. "Host and Guest in the 'Latino Contact Zone': Narrating Solidarity and Hospitality in *Mother Tongue.*" *Comparative American Studies* 2.4 (2004): 421–46. Print.

Kanellos, Nicolás. "Overview." *Herencia: The Anthology of Hispanic Literature of the United States.* Recovering the U.S. Hispanic Literary Heritage. Ed. Nicolás Kanellos. New York: Oxford University Press, 2003. 1–32. Print.

Keating, Ana Louise. *Entre Mundos / Among Worlds: New Perspectives on Gloria Anzaldúa*. New York: Palgrave MacMillan, 2008. Print.

Keating, Ana Louise, and Gloria González-López. *Bridging: How Gloria Anzaldúa's Life and Work Transformed Our Own*. Austin: University of Texas Press, 2012. Print.

Kermode, Frank. *The Sense of an Ending: Studies in the Theory of Fiction*. 1967. New York: Oxford University Press, 2000. Print.

Kevane, Bridget A. *Latino Literature in America*. Literature as Windows to World Cultures. Westport: Greenwood, 2003. Print.

———. *Profane and Sacred: Latino/a American Writers Reveal the Interplay of the Secular and the Religious*. New York: Rowman and Littlefield, 2008. Print.

Kingston, Maxine Hong. *The Woman Warrior: A Girlhood among Ghosts*. New York: Alfred Knopf, 1976. Print.

Kwame, Nkrumah. *Neo-Colonialism: The Last Stage of Imperialism*. London: Thomas Nelson and Sons, 1965. Print.

Lahiri, Jhumpa. *Interpreter of Maladies*. Boston: Houghton Mifflin Harcourt, 2000. Print.

Laviera, Tato. *La Carreta Made a U-Turn*. Houston: Arte Público Press, 1979. Print.

Lawrence of Arabia. Dir. David Lean. Columbia Pictures. 1962. Film.

Levitt, Peggy. *The Transnational Villagers*. Berkeley: University of California Press, 2001. Print.

Lima, Lázaro. *The Latino Body: Crisis Identities in American Literary and Cultural Memory*. New York: New York University Press, 2007. Print.

Limón, Graciela. *In Search of Bernabé*. Houston: Arte Público Press, 1993. Print.

Little, Douglas. *American Orientalism: The United States and the Middle East since 1945*. Durham: University of North Carolina Press, 2008. Print.

Lomas, Laura. "'The War Cut Out My Tongue': Domestic Violence, Foreign Wars, and Translation in Demetria Martínez." *American Literature* 78.2 (2006): 357–87. Print.

Longauez y Vasquez, Enriqueta. "The Women of La Raza." Valdez and Steiner 272–78. Print.

Lopez, Erika. *Flaming Iguanas: An Illustrated All-Girl Road Novel Thing*. New York: Simon and Schuster, 1998. Print.

Lowe, Lisa. *Immigrant Acts: On Asian American Cultural Politics*. Durham: Duke University Press, 1996. Print.

Luis, William. *Dance between Two Cultures: Latino Caribbean Literature Written in the United States*. Nashville: Vanderbilt University Press, 1997. Print.

Machado Sáez, Elena. "Dictating Desire, Dictating Diaspora: Junot Díaz's *The Brief Wondrous Life of Oscar Wao* as Foundational Romance." *Contemporary Literature* 52.3 (2011): 522–55. Print.

Manríquez, B. J. "Ana Castillo's *So Far from God*: Intimations of the Absurd." *College Literature* 29.2 (2002): 37–49. Print.

Marqués, René. *The Docile Puerto Rican: Essays*. Philadelphia: Temple University Press, 1976. Print.

———. *La carreta: Drama en tres actos*. San Juan: Editorial Cultural, 1968. Print.

Marshall, Paule. *Praisesong for the Widow*. New York: Plume, 1984. Print.

Martin, Wallace. *Recent Theories of Narrative*. Ithaca: Cornell University Press, 1986. Print.

Martínez, Demetria. *The Block Captain's Daughter*. Chicana and Chicano Visions of the Américas. Norman: University of Oklahoma Press, 2012. Print.

———. *Mother Tongue*. New York: Ballantine Books, 1993. Print.

Martínez, Ramiro. "Homicide among the 1980 Mariel Refugees in Miami: Victims and Offenders." *Hispanic Journal of Behavioral Sciences* 19.2 (1997): 107–22. Print.

Martín-Rodríguez, Manuel M. "'A Net Made of Holes': Toward a Cultural History of Chicano Literature." *Modern Language Quarterly: A Journal of Literary History* 62.1 (2001): 1–18. Print.

McCarthy, Cameron, and Warren Crichlow, eds. *Race, Identity, and Representation in Education*. New York: Routledge, 1993. Print.

McCracken, Ellen Marie. *New Latina Narrative: The Feminine Space of Postmodern Ethnicity*. Tucson: University of Arizona Press, 1999. Print.

Mena, María Cristina. *The Collected Stories of María Cristina Mena*. Houston: Arte Público Press, 1997. Print.

Menchú, Rigoberta. *I, Rigoberta Menchú*. Ed. Elisabeth Burgos-Debray. Trans. Ann Wright. London: Verso, 1983. Print.

Méndez, Danny. *Narratives of Migration and Displacement in Dominican Literature*. New York: Routledge, 2012. Print.

Méndez, Susan C. "The Fire between Them: Religion and Gentrification in Ernesto Quiñonez's *Chango's Fire*." *Centro Journal* 23.1 (2011): 177–95. Print.

Menéndez, Ana. *Loving Che*. New York: Grove Press, 2004. Print.

Metzger, Bruce Manning, and Roland Edmund Murphy, eds. *The New Oxford Annotated Bible with the Apocryphal/Deuterocanonical Books: New Revised Standard Version*. New York: Oxford University Press, 1991. Print.

Miguela, Antonia Domínguez. "Literary Tropicalizations of the Barrio: Ernesto Quinonez's *Bodega Dreams* and Ed Vega's *Mendoza's Dreams*." Torres-Padilla and Rivera 165–83. Print.

Miller, Arthur. *Death of a Salesman: Certain Private Conversations in Two Acts and a Requiem*. New York: Viking, 1949. Print.

Modern Times. Dir. Charles Chaplin. Charles Chaplin Productions. 1936. Film.

Mohr, Nicholasa. Interview. *Puerto Rican Voices in English: Interviews with Writers*. Carmen Dolores Hernández. Westport: Praeger, 1997. 65–94. Print.

———. "Puerto Rican Writers in the U.S., Puerto Rican Writers in Puerto Rico: A Separation beyond Language." Horno-Delgado 111–16. Print.

Moiles, Sean. "The Politics of Gentrification in Ernesto Quiñonez's Novels." *Critique: Studies in Contemporary Fiction* 52.1 (2010): 114–33. Print.

Momaday, N. Scott. *House Made of Dawn*. New York: Harper Perennial, 1999. Print.

Moraga, Cherríe. "Art in América con Acento." *The Last Generation: Prose and Poetry*. Boston: South End Press, 1993. Print.

———. *Loving in the War Years: lo que nunca pasó por sus labios*. Boston: South End Press, 1983. Print.

Moraga, Cherríe, and Anzaldúa Gloria. *This Bridge Called My Back: Writings by Radical Women of Color.* New York: Kitchen Table, 1981. Print.

Morales, Alejandro. *The Rag Doll Plagues.* Houston: Arte Público Press, 1992.

Moreiras, Alberto, and Marcus Embry, eds. "Introduction: From Locational Thinking to Dirty Atopianism." *The Cultural Practice of Latin Americanism.* Spec. issue of *Dispositio/n* 22 (1997–98): 49–50. Print.

Moreno, Marisel. "Debunking Myths, Destabilizing Identities: A Reading of Junot Díaz's 'How to Date a Browngirl, Blackgirl, Whitegirl, or Halfie.'" *Afro-Hispanic Review* (2007): 103–117.

Morrison, Toni. *Beloved.* New York: Plume, 1988. Print.

———. *The Bluest Eye.* New York: Random House, 1970.

———. *A Mercy.* New York: Alrfred Knopf, 2008. Print.

Mukherjee, Bharati. *Jasmine.* New York: Grove Press, 1999. Print.

Mullins, Greg A. "Seeking Asylum: Literary Reflections on Sexuality, Ethnicity, and Human Rights." *MELUS: Journal of the Society for the Study of Multiethnic Literatures in the United States* 28.1 (2003): 145–71. Print.

Muñoz, Carlos. *Youth, Identity, Power: The Chicano Movement.* New York: Verso, 1989. Print.

Muñoz, Elías Miguel. *Brand New Memory.* Houston: Arte Público Press, 1998. Print.

———. *Crazy Love.* Houston: Arte Público Press, 1989. Print.

———. *The Greatest Performance.* Houston: Arte Público Press, 1991. Print.

Muñoz, José Esteban. *Disidentifications: Queers of Color and the Performance of Politics.* Minneapolis: University of Minnesota Press, 1999. Print.

———. "Pedro Zamora's Real World of Counterpublicity: Performing an Ethics of the Self." *Hispanisms and Homosexualities.* Ed. Sylvia Molloy and Robert McKee Irwin. Durham: Duke University Press, 1998. 175–96. Print.

Naylor, Gloria. *Mama Day.* New York: Vintage, 1989. Print.

Nazario, Sonia. *Enrique's Journey.* New York: Random House, 2007. Print.

Negrón-Muntaner, Frances. "Bridging Islands: Gloria Anzaldúa and the Caribbean." *PMLA: Publication of the Modern Lnaguage Association* 121.1 (2006): 272–78. Print.

———. "Feeling Pretty: *West Side Story* and Puerto Rican Identity Discourses." *Social Text* 18.2 (2000): 83–106. Print.

Negrón-Muntaner, Frances, and Ramón Grosfoguel, eds. *Puerto Rican Jam: Rethinking Colonialism and Nationalism.* Essays on Culture and Politics. Minneapolis: University of Minnesota Press, 1997. Print.

Obejas, Achy. *Memory Mambo: A Novel.* Pittsburgh: Cleis Press, 1996. Print.

———. *We Came All the Way from Cuba So You Could Dress Like This? Stories.* Pittsburgh: Cleis Press, 1994. Print.

Oboler, Suzanne. *Ethnic Labels, Latino Lives: Identity and the Politics of Representation in the United States.* Minneapolis: University of Minnesota Press, 1995. Print.

———. *Latinos and Citizenship: The Dilemma of Belonging.* New York: Palgrave Macmillan, 2006. Print.

Ocasio, Rafael, and Judith Ortiz Cofer. "Puerto Rican Literature in Georgia? An Interview with Judith Ortiz Cofer." *Kenyon Review* 14.4 (1992): 43–50. Print.

Ochwat, Dan. "Junot Díaz on Fire Again in *This Is How You Lose Her*." Rev. of *This Is How You Lose Her*, by Junot Díaz. *Chicago Sun Times* 9 September 2012. Web.

Older, Daniel José. *Salsa Nocturna: Stories*. Framingham: Crossed Genres Press, 2012. Print.

Omi, Michael A. "The Changing Meaning of Race." *America Becoming: Racial Trends and Their Consequences*. Ed. Neil J. Smelser, William Julius Wilson, and Faith Mitchell. Washington, D.C.: National Academy Press, 2001. 243–63. Print.

Omi, Michael A., and Howard Winant. "The Theoretical Status of the Concept of Race." Back and Solomos 3–10. Print.

Ortega, Eliana, and Nancy Saporta Sternbach. "At the Threshold of the Unnamed." Horno Delgado 2–23. Print.

Ortíz, Ricardo L. "Cuban American Literature." Bost and Aparicio 413–22. Print.

Ortiz Cofer, Judith. "And Are You a Latina Writer?" *Is There a Boom in Latina/o Literature?* Spec. issue of *The Americas Review: A Review of Hispanic Literature and Art of the USA* 24.3–4 (1996): 155–61. Print.

———. "The Infinite Variety of the Puerto Rican Reality: An Interview with Judith Ortiz Cofer." By Rafael Ocasio. *Callaloo: A Journal of African American and African Arts and Letters* 17.3 (1994): 730–42. Print.

———. Interview. *Puerto Rican Voices in English: Interviews with Writers*. By Carmen D. Hernandez. Westport: Praeger, 1997. 65–94. Print.

———. "The Latin Deli: An Ars Poetica." *The Latin Deli: Telling the Lives of Barrio Women* 1–2. Print.

———. *The Latin Deli: Telling the Lives of Barrio Women*. New York: W.W. Norton, 1993. Print.

———. *The Line of the Sun*. Athens: University of Georgia Press, 1989. Print.

———. "A MELUS Interview: Judith Ortiz Cofer." By Edna Acosta-Bélen. *MELUS: The Journal of the Society for the Study of the Multi-Ethnic Literature of the United States* 18.3 (1993): 83–97. Print.

———. "Puerto Rican Literature in Georgia? Interview with Judith Ortiz Cofer." By Rafael Ocasio. *Kenyon Review* 14.4 (1992): 43–50. Print.

———. *Silent Dancing: A Partial Remembrance of a Puerto Rican Childhood*. Houston: Arte Público Press, 1990. Print.

Otero, S. "Getting There and Back: The Road, the Journey and Home in Nuyorican Diaspora Literature." Torres-Padilla and Rivera 274–92. Print.

Palumbo-Liu, David, ed. *The Ethnic Canon: Histories, Institutions, and Interventions*. Minneapolis: University of Minnesota Press, 1995. Print.

Paredes, Raymund A. "Contemporary Mexican-American Literature, 1960–Present." *A Literary History of the American West*. Ed. Western Literature Association. Fort Worth: Texas Christian University Press, 1987. 1101–17. Print.

———. "Early Mexican-American Literature." *A Literary History of the American West*. Ed. Western Literature Association. Fort Worth: Texas Christian University Press, 1987. 1079–1100. Print.

Peña, Susana. "'Obvious Gays' and the State Gaze: Cuban Gay Visibility and U.S. Immigration Policy during the 1980 Mariel Boatlift." *Journal of the History of Sexuality* 16.3 (2007): 482–514. Print.

Pérez, Laura Elisa. "Opposition and the Education of Chicana/os." McCarthy and Crichlow 268–79. Print.

Pérez, Loida Maritza. *Geographies of Home*. New York: Penguin, 2000. Print.

Pérez Firmat, Gustavo. *Life on the Hyphen: The Cuban-American Way*. Austin: University of Texas Press, 1995. Print.

Pérez-Torres, Rafael. "Chicano Studies at the Millennium." *Contemporary Literature* 39.4 (1998): 675–86. Print.

———. "Ethics, Ethnicity, and Latino Aesthetics." *American Literary History* 12.3 (2000): 534–56. Print.

———. "Mestizaje." Bost and Aparicio 25–33. Print.

———. *Mestizaje: Critical Uses of Race in Chicano Culture*. Minneapolis: University of Minnesota Press, 2006. Print.

———. "Whither Aztlán? Considering a Millennial Chicana/o Studies." *Genre: Forms of Discourse and Culture* 32.1–2 (1999): 99–114. Print.

Phelan, James. *Living to Tell About It: A Rhetoric and Ethics of Character Narration*. Ithaca: Cornell University Press, 2005. Print.

Pietri, Pedro. "Puerto Rican Obituary." *Puerto Rican Obituary*. New York: Monthly Review Press, 1973. 1–11. Print.

Piñero, Miguel. "La Bodega Sold Dreams." *La Bodega Sold Dreams*. Houston: Arte Público, 1980. 5. Print.

Piven, Ben. "Cuban Migration to US rises amid Historic Thaw in Relations. *Al Jazeera* 14 August 2015. Web.

Portes, Alejandro, and Leif Jensen. "The Enclave and the Entrants: Patterns of Ethnic Enterprise in Miami before and after Mariel." *American Sociological Review* 54.6 (1989): 929–49. Print.

Portes, Alejandro, and Alex Stepick. "Unwelcome Immigrants: The Labor Market Experiences of 1980 (Mariel) Cuban and Haitian Refugees in South Florida." *American Sociological Review* 50.4 (1985): 493–514. Print.

Presser, Harriet B. *Sterilization and Fertility Decline in Puerto Rico*. Westport: Greenwood, 1976. Print.

Prida, Dolores. *Beautiful Señoritas and Other Plays*. Houston: Arte Público Press, 1991

Quiñonez, Ernesto. Author Q&A: Interview with Ernesto Quiñonez. 18 January 2012. Web. http://www.randomhouse.com/highschool/catalog/display.pperl?isbn=9780375705892&view=qa.

———. *Bodega Dreams*. New York: Vintage, 2000. Print.

———. *Chango's Fire*. New York: Rayo/Harper Collins, 2004. Print.

Quiñonez, Naomi H. "Re(Riting) the Chicana Postcolonial: From Traitor to Twenty-First Century Interpreter." *Decolonial Voices: Chicana and Chicano Cultural Studies in the Twenty-first Century*. Ed. Arturo J. Aldama and Naomi H. Quiñonez. Bloomington: Indiana University Press, 2002. 129–51. Print.

Quintana, Alvina E. *Reading U.S. Latina Writers: Remapping American Literature*. New York: Palgrave Macmillan, 2003. Print.

Quiroga, José. *Tropics of Desire: Interventions from Queer Latino America*. New York: New York University Press. 2000. Print.

Ramirez, Enrique. "¿A dónde vamos?" *Harvard Crimson* 9 September 2013. Web.

Rebolledo, Tey Diana. "The Politics of Poetics: Or, What Am I, a Critic, Doing in This Text Anyhow?" *The Americas Review: A Review of Hispanic Literature and Art of the U.S.A* 15.3–4 (1987): 129–38. Print.

Rebolledo, Tey Diana, and Eliana S. Rivero, eds. *Infinite Divisions: An Anthology of Chicana Literature*. Tucson: University of Arizona Press, 1993. Print.

Rechy, John. *City of Night*. New York: Grove Press, 1963. Print.

Reed, Ishmael. *Flight to Canada*. 1976. New York: Atheneum (1989). Print.

———. *Mumbo Jumbo*. New York: Scribner, 1972. Print.

Reilly, Philip R. *The Surgical Solution: A History of Involuntary Sterilization in the United States*. Baltimore: Johns Hopkins University Press, 1991. Print.

Rimmon-Kenan, Shlomith. *Narrative Fiction: Contemporary Poetics*. 2nd ed. London: Routledge, 2002. Print.

Rivera, Tomás. "Richard Rodriguez' *Hunger of Memory* as Humanistic Antithesis." *MELUS: The Journal of the Society for the Study of the Multi-Ethnic Literature of the United States* 11.4 (1984): 5–13. Print.

———. *. . . y no se lo tragó la tierra / . . . And the Earth Did Not Devour Him*. Houston: Arte Público Press, 1987. Print.

Rodríguez, Alfonso. "Time As a Structural Device in Tomás Rivera's *. . . y no se lo tragó la tierra*." *Contemporary Chicano Fiction: A Critical Survey*. Ed. Vernon E. Lattin. Tempe: Bilingual Press / Editorial Bilingüe, 1986. 126–30. Print.

Rodríguez, Ana Patricia. "Refugees of the South: Central Americans in the U.S. Latino Imaginary." *American Literature: A Journal of Literary History, Criticism, and Bibliography*. 73.2 (2001): 387–412. Print.

Rodriguez, Ralph E. *Brown Gumshoes: Detective Fiction and the Search for Chicana/o Identity*. Austin: University of Texas Press, 2009. Print.

Rodriguez, Richard. *Hunger of Memory: The Education of Richard Rodriguez*. New York: David R. Godine, 1982. Print.

Rodríguez Aranda, Pilar E. "On the Solitary Fate of Being Mexican, Female, Wicked and Thirty-Three: An Interview with Sandra Cisneros." *The Americas Review: A Review of Hispanic Literature and Art of the USA* 18.1 (1990): 65–80. Print.

Romero, Lora. "Nationalism and Internationalism: Domestic Differences in a Postcolonial World." *American Literature: A Journal of Literary History, Criticism, and Bibliography* 67.4 (1995): 795–800. Print.

———. "'When Something Goes Queer': Familiarity, Formalism, and Minority Intellectuals in the 1980s." *Yale Journal of Criticism: Interpretation in the Humanities* 6.1 (1993): 121–42. Print.

Rosaldo, Renato. "Cultural Citizenship, Inequality, and Multiculturalism." *Latino Cultural Citizenship: Claiming Identity, Space, and Rights.* Eds. William V. Flores and Rina Benmayor. Boston: Beacon Press, 1997. 27–59. Print.

Rosario, Nelly. *Song of the Water Saints.* New York: Vintage, 2002. Print.

Ruiz De Burton, María Amparo. 1885. *The Squatter and the Don.* Houston: Arte Público Press, 1997. Print.

Rumbaut, Rubén G. "The Agony of Exile: A Study of the Migration and Adaptation of Indochinese Refugee Adults and Children." *Refugee Children: Theory, Research, and Services.* Ed. Frederick L Ahearn and Jean L Athey. The Johns Hopkins Series in Contemporary Medicine and Public Health, 16. Baltimore: Johns Hopkins University. 1991. 53–91. Print.

Rumbaut, Rubén G, and Kenji Ima. "The Adaptation of Southeast Asian Refugee Youth: A Comparative Study." Final Report to the Office of Resettlement. Washington D.C.: Office of Health and Human Services, Family Support and Administration, Office of Refugee Resettlement, 1988. Print.

Saldívar, José David. "Looking Awry at 1898: Roosevelt, Montejo, Paredes, and Mariscal." *American Literary History* 12.3 (2000): 386–406. Print.

———. *Border Matters: Remapping American Cultural Studies.* Berkeley: University of California Press, 1997.

Saldívar, Ramón. "Historical Fantasy, Speculative Realism, and Postrace Aesthetics in Contemporary American Fiction." *American Literary History* 23.3 (2011): 574–99. Print.

———. "The Second Elevation of the Novel: Race, Form, and the Postrace Aesthetic in Contemporary Narrative." *Narrative* 21.1 (2013): 1–18. Print.

Saldívar-Hull, Sonia. "Feminism on the Border: From Gender Politics to Geopolitics." Calderón and Saldívar 203–20. Print.

Sánchez, Luis Rafael. "La Guagua Área." *La Guagua Área.* 2nd ed., San Juan: Editorial Cultural, 1994. Print.

Sánchez, Marta E. "Arturo Islas' *The Rain God*: An Alternative Tradition." *American Literature* 62.2 (1990): 284–304. Print.

———. "La Malinche at the Intersection: Race and Gender in *Down These Mean Streets.*" *Ethnicity.* Spec. issue of *PMLA: Publications of the Modern Language Association* 113.1 (1998): 117–28.

———. *"Shakin' Up" Race and Gender: Intercultural Connections in Puerto Rican, African American, and Chicano Narratives and Culture (1965-1995).* Austin: University of Texas Press, 2005. Print.

Sánchez, Rosaura. "Ethnicity, Ideology and Academia." *Cultural Studies* 4.3 (1990): 294–302. Print.

Sánchez, Rosaura, Beatrice Pita, and Mario A Chacón. *Lunar Braceros: 2125-2148.* Oak Park: Calaca Press, 2009. Print.

Sánchez González, Lisa. "For the Sake of Love: Luisa Capetillo, Anarchy, and Boricua Literary History." Torres-Padilla and Rivera 52–80. Print.

San Juan, E., Jr. "The Poverty of Postcolonialism." *Pretexts: Literary and Cultural Studies* 11.1 (2002): 57–74. Print.

Santiago, Esmeralda. *América's Dream.* New York: Harper Collins, 1996. Print.

———. *Conquistadora.* New York: Random House, 2012. Print.

———. *When I Was Puerto Rican.* New York: Vintage, 1997. Print.

Scarface. Dir. Brian de Palma. Universal Pictures. 1983. Film.

Sellers-García, Sylvia. *When the Ground Turns in Its Sleep.* New York: Penguin, 2007. Print.

Serrano, Nina. *Heart Songs: The Collected Poems of Nina Serrano (1969–1979).* Editorial Pocho-Che. San Francisco: Estuary Press, 1980. Print.

Sharman, Russell Leigh. *The Tenants of East Harlem.* Berkeley: University of California Press, 2006. Print.

Silko, Leslie Marmon. *Ceremony.* New York: Penguin, 1977. Print.

Skop, Emily H. "Race and Place in the Adaptation of Mariel Exiles." *International Migration Review* 35.2 (2001): 449–71. Print.

Socolovsky, Maya. "The Homelessness of Immigrant American Ghosts: Hauntings and Photographic Narrative in Oscar Hijuelos's *The Fourteen Sisters of Emilio Montez O'Brien.*" *PMLA: Publications of the Modern Language Association of America* 117.2 (2002): 252–64. Print.

Sollors, Werner. *Beyond Ethnicity: Consent and Descent in American Culture.* New York: Oxford University Press, 1986. Print.

———. *The Invention of Ethnicity.* New York: Oxford University Press, 1989. Print.

Soto, Sandra. "Queerness." Bost and Aparicio 75–83. Print.

Spitta, Silvia. *Between Two Waters: Narratives of Transculturation in Latin America.* Houston: Rice University Press, 1995. Print.

Staten, Henry. "Ethnic Authenticity, Class, and Autobiography: The Case of Hunger of Memory." *PMLA: Publications of the Modern Language Association of America* 113.1 (1998): 103–16. Print.

Stringer, Dorothy. "Passing and the State in Junot Díaz's *Drown.*" *MELUS: Journal of the Society for the Study of Multi-Ethnic Literature of the United States* 38.2 (2013): 111–26. Print.

Súarez, Virgil. *Going Under: A Novel.* Houston: Arte Público Press, 1996. Print.

———. *Havana Thursdays: A Novel.* Houston: Arte Público Press, 1995. Print.

———. *Latin Jazz.* Baton Rouge: Louisiana State University Press, 1989. Print.

———, ed. *Is There a Boom in Latina/o Literature?* Spec. issue of *The Americas Review: A Review of Hispanic Literature and Art of the USA* 24.3–4 (1996). Print.

Tan, Amy. *The Joy Luck Club.* New York: Random House, 1990. Print.

Thomas, Piri. 1997. *Down These Mean Streets.* New York: Vintage/Random House, 1967. Print.

Tobar, Héctor. "Junot Díaz on Fire Again in *This Is How You Lose Her.*" Rev. of *This Is How You Lose Her,* by Junot Díaz. *Los Angeles Times* 9 September 2012. Print.

———. *The Tattooed Soldier*. Harrison: Delphinium Books, 1998. Print.

Torres, Hector A. "The Ethnographic Component in Chicano/a Literary Discourse." *Aztlán: A Journal of Chicano Studies* 25.1 (2000): 151–66. Print.

Torres-Padilla, José L., and Carmen H. Rivera, eds. *Writing Off the Hyphen: New Critical Perspectives on the Literature of the Puerto Rican Diaspora*. American Ethnic and Cultural Studies. Seattle: University of Washington Press, 2008. Print.

Torres-Saillant, Silvio. "The Tribulations of Blackness: Stages in Dominican Racial Identity." *Latin American Perspectives* 25.3 (1998): 126–46. Print.

Trejo, Michael J. "Harvard's Latino Problem." *Harvard Crimson* 18 April 2012. Web.

Trópico de Sangre. Dir. Juan Delancer. Maya Entertainment, 2010. Film.

Trotter, Joe William. *The Great Migration in Historical Perspective: New Dimensions of Race, Class, and Gender*. Blacks in the Diaspora. Bloomington: Indiana University Press, 1991. Print.

Trujillo, Carla. *Chicana Lesbians: The Girls Our Mothers Warned Us About*. Berkeley: Third Woman Press: 1991. Print.

Urrea, Luis Alberto. *The Devil's Highway: A True Story*. New York: Little, Brown, and Company, 2008. Print.

Valdez, Luis, and Stan Steiner. *Aztlán: An Anthology of Mexican American Literature*. New York: Random House, 1972. Print.

Valle, Victor. "Poet or Smuggler? Demetria Martinez Says She Was Writing an Article; U.S. Attorney Says She Aided Illegals." *Los Angeles Times* 26 May 1988, sec. Reporters. Print.

Vargas Llosa, Mario. *Fiesta del Chivo*. New York: Farrar, Straus, and Giroux, 2001. Print.

Vázquez, David J. *Triangulations: Narrative Strategies for Navigating Latino Identity*. Minneapolis: University of Minnesota Press, 2011. Print.

Veeser, Cyrus. *A World Safe for Capitalism: Dollar Diplomacy and America's Rise to Global Power*. New York: Columbia University Press, 2002. Print.

Velasco, Juan. "The 'X' in Race and Gender: Rethinking Chicano/a Cultural Production through the Paradigms of *Xicanisma* and Me(x)icanness." *The Americas Review: A Review of Hispanic Literature and Art of the USA* 24.3–4 (1996): 218–30. Print.

Vigil, Ariana. "Transnational Community in Demetria Martínez's *Mother Tongue*." *Meridians* 10.1 (2009): 54–76. Print.

Villa, Raúl Homero. "Urban Spaces." Bost and Aparicio 46–54. Print.

Villareal, José Antonio. *Pocho*. New York: Anchor Books, 1959. Print.

Volk, Steven S., and Marian E. Schlotterbeck. "Gender, Order, and Femicide: Reading the Popular Culture of Murder in Ciudad Juárez." *Aztlán: A Journal of Chicano Studies* 32.1 (2007): 53–86. Print.

Walker, Alice. *The Color Purple*. New York: Pocket, 1985. Print.

Welch, James. *Fools Crow*. New York, Penguin, 1987. Print.

West, Cornel. "Foreword." Crenshaw, Gotanda, and Peller xi–xii. Print.

West Side Story. Dir. Jerome Robbins and Robert Wise. United Artists, 1961. Film.

Whalen, Carmen Teresa. "Colonialism, Citizenship, and the Making of the Puerto Rican Diaspora: An Introduction." *The Puerto Rican Diaspora: Historical Perspectives*. Eds. Carmen Teresa Whalen and Víctor Vázquez-Hernández. Philadelphia: Temple University Press, 2005. 1–42. Print.

Winant, Howard. "Race and Race Theory." *Annual Review of Sociology* 26 (2000): 169–85. Print.

Wucker, Michele. *Why the Cocks Fight: Dominicans, Haitians, and the Struggle for Hispaniola*. New York: Hill and Wang, 1999. Print.

Xavier, Roy Eric. "Politics and Chicano Culture: Luis Valdez and *El Teatro Campesino*, 1964–1990." *Chicano Politics and Society in the Late Twentieth Century*. Ed. David Montejano. Austin: University of Texas Press, 1999. 175–200. Print.

Yamashita, Karen Tei. *Circle K Cycles*. Minneapolis: Coffee House Press, 2001. Print.

———. *Tropic of Orange: A Novel*. Minneapolis: Coffee House Press, 1997. Print.

Yarbro-Bejarano, Yvonne. "Chicana Literature from a Chicana Feminist Perspective." *The Americas Review: A Review of Hispanic Literature and Art of the USA* 15.3–4 (1987): 139–45. Print.

———. "Gloria Anzaldúa's *Borderlands/La Frontera*: Cultural Studies, 'Difference,' and the Non-Unitary Subject." *Cultural Critique* 28 (1994): 5–28. Print.

———. "Sexuality and Chicana/o Studies: Toward a Theoretical Paradigm for the Twenty-First Century." *Chicana/o Latina/o Cultural Studies: Transnational and Transdisciplinary Movements*. Spec. issue of *Cultural Studies* 13.2 (1999): 335–45. Print.

Index

essentialism, 29, 144, 147

estampa, 42

ethnicity, 13, 26–27, 31, 177; authorship and, 17, 26; construction of, 141–42, 150, 152, 191, 220n15; gender and, 63, 65, 128; geography and, 148, 204n36; nationality and, 181; queerness and, 184, 191–92; race and, 55, 58; shared, 135, 138; as source of rejection, 117, 125

ethnic solidarity, 80, 138, 227n42

ethnonationalism, 22; Cuban, 187; limits to, 132, 151–52; Puerto Rican, 110, 113, 221n30; social mobility and, 131

Eulogy for a Brown Angel (Corpi), 13

exceptionalism, 79, 120

exile community: Cuban, 181; Dominican, 104; literature of, 17, 179–80; and nostalgia, 17, 34, 62

exploitation: economic, 12, 15, 24, 36, 92, 216n43; of sex workers, 98, 107

fairy tales, 116, 123, 125

fantastic, the, 83, 215n25. *See also* magical realism

fantasy, 8, 11, 12, 13, 22, 27, 58; historical, 11, 12, 25; within literature, 126, 167, 184

Faymonville, Carmen, 120, 127

feminism: Chicana, 85, 216n30; discourse on, 102, 110, 129; poetics of, 21, 78, 81, 82

flashback, 63, 76, 98, 130, 181

Flight to Canada (Reed), 10, 203n29

Flores, Juan, 30–32; on cultural remittance, 16, 204n39; Puerto Rican immigration, 48, 111

foodways, 2, 90, 101

foreign policy, 23, 24, 36

formalism, 9, 88, 121

Fornés, María Irene, 180

forty (biblical measurement), 57, 77, 189

Foster, David William, 65, 190, 212n68, 229n60

Foster, Sesshu, 10

Fowler, Alistair, 215n28

Fox, Claire, 29

fracture, narrative of. *See* narrative of fracture

Francis, Donette, 97, 217n51

"free associated state" status, of Puerto Rico, 53, 111, 212n62, 223n58

Freudian analysis, 64, 229n59

Frye, Northrop, 9

gangs, 135, 145, 152, 222n43

García, Chino, 147

García, Cristina, 3; as canonical author, 7–8, 218n3; on Cuban revolution, 159

García, María Cristina: on Cuban exile writers, 21, 161, 227n37

García Márquez, Gabriel, 84, 203n24

Gaspar de Alba, Alicia: writing on Juarez murders, 197, 208n17s

Geha, Joseph, 5

gender, 4, 7, 12, 30, 33; construction, 27; difference, 33, 79; intersecting race or class, 86, 96, 110, 140; performance of, 125, 128, 183, 212n68

generic experimentation, 12, 28, 42, 121, 168, 215n18

genocide, 2, 96, 159, 165, 170, 173–74

gentrification, 112, 132, 221n37, 224n66, 224n71; and neoliberalism, 134, 142, 147–49

geography, 13, 110, 131, 144

ghetto literature, 132, 142

Girl from Mexico, The (film), 128

Goldberg, David Theo, 1–2, 5–6, 202n10

Gomez-Peña, Guillermo, 57

Gonzales, Rudolfo "Corky," 39

González, José Luis, 32

Good Friday, 87, 91, 95

Good Neighbor Policy, 25

graffiti, 139, 145, 148, 157, 224n67; RIPs, 156–57; tags within, 157

Great Depression, 49, 88

Greatest Performance, The (Muñoz), 34; AIDS discourse, 184; critical neglect, 190–191, critique of homophobia, 157–59, 163, 178, 180–81; depiction of Mariel refugees, 160; disidentification, 194; rejection of compulsory heterosexism, 182; as narrative of new memory, 196; sexual refugees, 181–82; structure, 183

Great Gatsby (Fitzgerald), 132

Grosfoguel, Ramon, 221n30

Guatemala, 21, 164–65, 173, 205n58, 226n26

Gutiérrez, Ramón A.: on Chicano movement homophobia, 190, 213, 214n7; on Chicano movement sexism, 78–79; on racial identification, 52, 213n78

Haiti, 23, 25, 96, 270n44; and racial self-construction, 71

Hall, Stuart, 5, 22, 58

La Raza, 77, 179, 214n4

Latin America, 23, 26, 47, 53, 205n59; and homosexuality, 188; and magical realism, 83, 180, 215n25

Latina/o America, 10, 28, 32, 53, 55; vs. Anglo America, 8, 10, 20, 56; and belonging, 14, 22, 59, 71–72, 101, 120, 131; and internal difference, 14, 22

Latina/o studies, 28, 51, 52, 122, 209n28, 230n3

Latin Deli, The (Ortiz Cofer), 13, 33, 104; as narrative of fracture, 110, 112–15, 131–32

latinidad, 51, 126, 148, 189, 206n66

latinidades, 8, 33, 52, 203n22, 227n35; queer, 189; and solidarity, 192

La Vida (Lewis), 223n62

Laviera, Tato, 20

Lawrence of Arabia (film), 131

left-liberal multiculturalism, 3, 6, 26, 86. *See also* multiculturalism

Lesbos, as "native island," 178, 193

letters: embedded, 17–19, 22, 62, 168, 198; as narrative form, 22, 180, 197, 215n23

Levins Morales, Aurora, 122, 129

Levitt, Peggy, 16

Lewis, Oscar, 223n62

liberation theology, 92, 170, 174, 225n16

Lima, Lázaro, 8; on . . . *And the Earth Did Not Devour Him*, 41–42; on *Greatest Performance*, 183–84, 190–91, 193, 228n4

Limón, Graciela, 165

Line of the Sun, The (Ortiz Cofer), critical neglect of, 112, 133, 219n5

literary canon, 26, 40, 125, 206n66

Lives of the Saints, The (Butler), 86

Llorona, La, 89

Loisaida, 144, 147–48, 151, 223n64

Lomas, Laura, 165, 226n27

Longauez y Vasquez, Enriqueta, 78–79

Lopez, Erika, 129

Lopez, Iraida H., 179

Lorde, Audrey, 86

loss, narrative of. *See* narrative of loss

losses: cultural, 2–3, 36, 38–39, 85, 216n37; economic, 20, 35, 38; familial, 36, 39, 73, 126; linguistic, 29, 71, 73; of identity, 73; of memory, 73, 173, 181; of power, 14, 59; spiritual, 35, 73, 85; territorial, 36, 38–39, 73, 85; of self-respect, 71, 73, 103; tangible, 73, 75

Loving in the War Years: lo que nunca pasó por sus labios (Moraga), 13

Lower East Side, 147–48, 223n64

"Lower East Side Poem, A" (Piñero), 147

loyalty, 132, 135, 141–42, 144, 146

Luis, William, 32

Lunar Braceros 2125–2148 (Pita and Sánchez), 11–12

MacArthur Awards, recipients of, 40

Machado Sáez, Elena: on cultural baggage in *Soledad*, 97, 102, 107–08; on Latina/o studies, 28, 31; on masculinity in *The Brief Wondrous Life of Oscar Wao*, 65; on Nuyorican aesthetic in *Bodega Dreams*, 134, 137, 153, 155, 222nn50–51

magical realism, 83–84, 89, 107, 215n25

mainstream. *See* American mainstream

Malinche, 174, 226n30

Mariel Port: boatlift, 50, 151, 159–60, 178–79, 182–83; refugees, 161, 192, 227n37, 205n45

Marqués, René, 149

Marshall, Paule, 162

Martí, José, 46–47, 209n28

Martin, Trayvon, 4

Martin, Wallace, 11

Martínez, Demetria: as canonical author, 28, 33; and narrative of new memory, 157–58, 163; solidarity with Salvadoran refugees, 165, 196

Martínez, Javier, 183, 228n51

Martín-Rodríguez, Manuel, 38

Marxism, 8, 91

masculinity: Cuban, 180; Dominican, 58, 64–68; Latin American, 187, 212n68, 229n59; Puerto Rican, 226n65

matriarchy, 33, 76, 88, 122

McCracken, Ellen, 31, 202n20

McLaren, Peter, 2, 6, 202n10

"mean streets," as trope, 138, 140, 156

MECHA, 20, 205n50, 214n5

memoir, 13, 79, 135, 225n18

memories: ambivalent, 130; created, 19, 66, 157, 162, 166, 182, 184, 196; cultural, 32, 70, 96, 101, 113, 162–63, 184; haunting, 97, 156, 162–63; and identity formation, 130, 138; incomplete, 170–71, 184; new, 18–19, 157, 182, 184, 196; suppressed, 166. *See also* public memory; re-memory

novels, detective, 8, 80
Nuyoricans, 21, 53, 71, 133–34, 139; aesthetic
of, 138, 141–42, 150, 155, 221n31, 224n65;
as artists, 133; and literature, 113, 120,
122, 131–32, 138; and poetry, 20, 119, 138,
147, 160–61, 172, 180–81, 192, 196, 211n49,
223n57

Obama, Barack H., 19, 199, 218n1
Oboler, Suzanne, 77, 79, 150
Older, Daniel José, 206n68, 219n4, 222n42
Omi, Michael, 219n12
Operation Bootstrap, 223n58
Ortiz, Fernando, 179
Ortiz, Ricardo, 160, 229n64–65
Ortiz Cofer, Judith, 13; as canonical Latina
author, 28; and feminism, 33, 123, 126, 129;
and interrogation of *puertorriqueñidad*,
114, 120, 123–24; literary influences on,
122, 124–25, 206n68, narrative aesthetics
of, 112, 122, 124–26, 128, 219n10; and nar-
rative of fracture, 115, 119, 120, 157; public
role of, 129, 194; and resistance of stereotypes, 126–28, 130
Osorio, Pepón, 57
Otero, Solimar, 144

pájaro, 188–89
Panama, 23, 49, 75
pan-Latinism, 47, 137, 151, 177, 196
paratexts, 81, 170, 188
Paredes, Raymund, 36, 38–39, 42–43
pasivo, 67, 187–88
passing, 68, 72, 213n73
pato, 64–68, 187–88, 212n67, 213n71, 229n59
patriarchy, 70, 78, 213n75
Pérez Firmat, Gustavo, 113–14, 179; as creative writer, 180; use of Rumbaut's term
"1.5," 113, 205n51, 219n7
Pérez-Torres, Rafael, 51–53, 150, 152
performance, 57, 188, 191, 193–94, 199; of
ethnicity, 191; of gender, 125, 183; of sexuality, 67–68, 180–81
photographs, 17, 19, 34, 71, 108, 184, 213n81
Pietri, Pedro, 20, 120
Piñero, Miguel, 142
Plan Spiritual de Aztlán, El, 77–78
Pocho (Villareal), 36, 39, 190, 207n2
poetics, 21, 86, 152, 195
political asylum, 53, 159, 210n44, 212n62
polyphonic texts, 9, 12, 17, 80, 87, 183
postclassical narratology, 9, 203n26

postcolonialism, 23–25, 52–53, 57, 205n56,
206n62, 206n69. *See also* US neocolonialism
postmodernism, 31, 41–42, 83, 86, 88,
208n19
posttraumatic stress, 105, 172, 175
poverty, 55, 58, 62, 91, 133; global, 98; linguistic, 71; rural, 60–61, 104; urban, 60, 71,
100, 138, 153, 198
pre-Columbian era, 2, 82, 85, 89
Prida, Dolores, 13; as Cuban exile, 179–80;
and narrative of fracture, 21; works neglected, 21, 211n54
privilege, 52, 71, 128, 129, 136, 146
projects, 54, 60, 134, 148
public memory, 129, 130, 163, 195
"Puerto Rican Obituary" (Pietri), 20, 119–
20, 138, 141, 152
Puerto Rico, "free associated state" status of,
53, 111, 212n62, 223n58
puertorriqueñidad, 33, 114, 120, 122, 124–27;
assertion of, 135–37; defined, 110, 220n40;
limiting, 112, 131–32, 219n6; and interrogation, 133–34, 138, 140–41
Pulitzer Prize, 40, 55, 56, 179, 211n48

queer: as concept, 65, 183, 209n25; cubanidad, 182, 185, 228n45; desire, 65, 191; identity, 129, 187, 189, 192; studies, 5, 8, 65, 82,
185, 188, 191, 228n48
Quiñonez, Ernesto, 28; aesthetics, 131, 141,
155; authorship, 133, 206n68, 219n4; critical neglect, 112, 132, 137, 211n54, 221n34;
critique of ethnic hierarchy, 138–41, 144;
departure from *Great Gatsby*, 143; gender
constructs, 140; and narrative of fracture,
112, 157; neoliberalism, 133–34, 141; Nuyorican aesthetic, 138, 141, 147, 157; portrayal of pan-Latinism, 137–38; portrayal
of the Young Lords, 130–31; Puerto Rican
nationalism, 149
Quiroga, José, 18, 227n38

race: intersection with class, 7, 51, 87, 99, 102,
127; post-, 11, 25
racism, 36, 66, 121–24, 128, 137; discourse of,
86, 170; internalized, 59, 70, 72, 73, 125;
institutional, 3, 14, 59, 69, 70–73, 102, 110,
116–17, 125, 136; interethnic, 95, 138; intra-
ethnic, 51, 72, 73; state-sanctioned, 61, 71;
within family, 136
Rain God, The (Islas), 13, 229n64

Raza, La, 77, 179, 214n4
Rebolledo, Tey Diana, 81, 82, 210n40, 214n9, 215n15, 216n33
Rechy, John, 13, 190, 191, 214n6, 229n63
recipes, 81, 87, 89–90, 168
reclamantes, 38, 75
reclamation, narrative of. *See* narrative of reclamation
refugees, 159, 181, 196; Cuban economic, 50, 158, 161, 179, 192, 205n45; Cuban sexual, 72, 159, 182; Salvadoran, 165, 169–71, 225n12, 225n16; solidarity of, 196, 198; war, 23, 34, 139, 164, 174
remedies, 87–88, 90
re-memory, 183, 205n46, 225n9
remittance: cultural, 16, 204n39; economic, 16
repudiation, acts of, 178, 188
reputation, 135, 138
respect, 135–36, 139–40; desired, 141, 154; earned, 142, 149; for ethnicity, 138; for self, 71, 92
resurrection, 89, 92, 177
retentions: allegiance, 1; colonial influence, 2; cultural practices, 55, 58, 71
Revolutionary War, US, 48, 49
riff, 132, 140
Rimmon-Kenan, Shlomith, 9, 203n21
Rip Van Winkle, 169, 226n24
ritual, 87–89, 91, 157; effectiveness of, 33, 108; as trope, 82, 108–10, 162, 195
Rivas, Bimbo, 147
Rivera, Tomás, 15; as canonical Chicano author, 28; Junot Díaz compared to, 57; on *Hunger of Memory*, 80, 214n11; and narrative elements, 42, 208n19; and narrative of loss, 41–42, 73; sleep as central trope of, 36
Rivero, Eliana S., 82, 214n9, 215n18
Rodríguez, Alfonso, 42
Rodríguez, Ana Patricia, 171, 227n32
Rodríguez, Richard, 79, 120, 128, 214nn11–12
Romero, Lora, 24–25, 206n62, 214n12
Romero, Oscar, 165, 215n22, 225n12, 227n33
Roosevelt, Franklin D., 25
Rosario, Nelly, 95–96, 104, 106, 212n60
Ruiz de Burton, María Amparo, 39

sainthood, 88–89, 94, 225n12
Saldívar, José David, 29, 38

Saldívar, Ramon, 11, 203n28
Saldívar-Hull, Sonia, 216n30
Salsa Nocturna: Stories (Older), 8, 12, 163
Sánchez, Marta E., 44
Sánchez González, Lisa, 113
Sanctuary Movement, 158, 197–98, 225nn16–17, 227n34
Santería, 2, 107, 163, 202n7, 218n66, 223n56, 225n5
Santiago, Esmeralda, 7, 129, 202n16, 211n53, 212n59
Sapogonia: An Anti-Romance in 3/8 Meter (Castillo), 215n23
Scarface (film), 143, 221n32
Scheherazade, 122–24
Schomburg, Arturo, 113
science fiction, 7, 11–13, 197, 209n22
Sellers-García, Sylvia, 164, 173, 226n26
sexism, 51, 64, 78–79 , 87, 123; in Chicano movement, 87; critique of, 86, 113, 214n10
sex tourism, 97–98, 107, 217n51
Short Eyes (Piñero), 147
silence: on civil wars, 170; Dominican, 70, 95, 105; as trope, 97, 99, 100, 106–07, 109
Silko, Leslie Marmon, 3, 10, 40
skin color, 100, 137, 142, 191, 218n59
sleep, as trope, 35, 105, 168–69, 207n1
social mobility, 39, 43, 55, 64, 131; and assimilation, 14, 55, 74, 140; as desired, 154, 156, 135; false promises of, 155
Social Security Act, 41
Socolovsky, Maya, 213n81
So Far from God (Castillo), 13, 75–76, 83–90, 91–95, 101, 110, 114
Soledad, 13, 33, 109–10; allegory in, 84, 103; betrayal in, 102, 117; colorism in, 99–100, 117, 136, 140; critical neglect of, 97; domestic violence in, 96; and *dominicanidad*, 97 119, 196; immigration in, 50, 114–15; narrative elements in, 76, 168, 173; as narrative of reclamation, 73, 75–76, 82, 96–97; molestation in, 105; ritual as trope in, 110; sex tourism in, 106; sleep as trope in, 169; silence as trope in, 110
solidarity: challenges, 165, 192, 221n34, 226n20; ethnic, 80, 138, 151; ideological, 34; literary, 110, 165; pan-Latino, 46–47, 110, 134, 171, 177; transnational, 165, 196
Sollors, Werner, 8, 26–27, 121, 132
Something to Declare: Essays (Alvarez), 18